The Process of Research in
PSYCHOLOGY

To my family: Jeff, Halley, Zelda, and Daphne.

The Process of Research in
PSYCHOLOGY

Dawn M. McBride
Illinois State University

Los Angeles | London | New Delhi
Singapore | Washington DC

For information:

 SAGE Publications, Inc.
2455 Teller Road
Thousand Oaks, California 91320
E-mail: order@sagepub.com

SAGE Publications Ltd.
1 Oliver's Yard
55 City Road
London EC1Y 1SP
United Kingdom

SAGE Publications India Pvt. Ltd.
B 1/I 1 Mohan Cooperative Industrial Area
Mathura Road, New Delhi 110 044
India

SAGE Publications Asia-Pacific Pte. Ltd.
33 Pekin Street #02-01
Far East Square
Singapore 048763

Printed in the United States of America

Library of Congress Cataloging-in-Publication Data

McBride, Dawn M.
The process of research in psychology/Dawn M. McBride.
    p. cm.
Includes bibliographical references and index.
ISBN 978-1-4129-6078-6 (pbk.)
    1. Psychology—Research—Methodology. 2. Psychology, Experimental. I. Title.

BF76.5.M376 2010
150.72—dc22   2009021457

This book is printed on acid-free paper.

10   11   12   13   10   9   8   7   6   5   4   3   2

Acquisitions Editor:	Christine Cardone
Editorial Assistant:	Sarita Sarak
Production Editor:	Brittany Bauhaus
Copy Editor:	QuADS Prepress (P) Ltd.
Typesetter:	C&M Digitals (P) Ltd.
Proofreader:	Caryne Brown
Cover Designer:	Gail Buschman
Marketing Manager:	Stephanie Adams

Brief Contents

Detailed Contents

Preface

My goal in writing this text is to provide a clearly written, student-friendly introduction to doing research in psychology. In teaching psychological research methods courses over the past 10 years, I have found that many methods texts are written as a collection of chapters covering a myriad of concepts related to research. In this text, I cover topics in an appropriate order to help students understand the full process of developing, conducting, and presenting a research study (such as including ethics and sampling as early chapters in the text). In addition, concepts and skills relevant to more than one stage of the research process are covered in multiple contexts. Thus, important and difficult concepts are repeated in different scenarios to aid students' learning with spaced repetition so that knowledge and skills are truly gained. Using my expertise in memory research, I present material in ways that will optimize student learning. Most research in memory shows that spaced repetition of information leads to better long-term memory. In this text, I use this approach with different research design types such as in experiments and correlational studies. These designs are covered briefly in an early chapter of the text, as well as in separate chapters near the end of the text to allow instructors flexibility in amount of coverage and timing of coverage for each design type.

Further, I have included numerous examples and activities in each chapter that come from a wide range of psychological settings, giving students a useful overview of real research. Plus, end-of-chapter quizzes allow students to assess their progress.

This book mirrors the steps in the research process and creates logical scaffolding upon which students can build their knowledge. I trust students will find this text to be a readable and practical guide to conducting psychological research.

With J. Cooper Cutting, I have also written *Lab Manual for Psychological Research, Second Edition* that can serve as a perfect supplement by providing students with additional practice in conducting their own research project.

Acknowledgments

I'd like to acknowledge a number of important people who helped in many ways in the writing of this text and helped improve it from its initial drafts. First is Jeff Wagman, who read every chapter, offered feedback, and provided essential support during the project. In addition, my family, friends, and colleagues provided support and helpful feedback during the writing process. In particular, Cooper Cutting, Jennifer Coane, Nicole Gage, Derek Herrmann, Jef Kahn, John Williams, and Corinne Zimmerman provided useful feedback on individual chapters. Several reviewers also provided valuable suggestions that greatly improved the quality of the text. Lauren Saternus, Bruce Stoffel, Jackie Cavallo, and Geoff Anthony all contributed their time or expertise to the project. The helpful folks at Sage provided much-appreciated support during the project: Erik Evans, Sarita Sarak, Lindsay Dutro, Lara Grambling, and Cheri Dellelo. I would also like to thank Illinois State University College of Arts and Sciences and Psychology Department for providing a sabbatical leave during which much of the writing of this text took place, and the students at Illinois State University who have taken my PSY 231 course and influenced my teaching of this material. Finally, I wish to thank Jim Nairne, who encouraged me to begin this project and connected me with the folks at Sage, and Barbara Dosher, who mentored me as I learned how to put the material in this text into practice in my own research. All the individuals named here contributed in important ways to the production of this text and have my sincere thanks and gratitude.

The author and SAGE gratefully acknowledge the contributions of the following reviewers:

Elizabeth Arnott-Hill, *Chicago State University*

Deborah Baldwin, *University of Tennessee*

Tamara Bond, *Bradley Hospital, Chronobiology and Sleep Research Lab*

Birgit Bryant, *Le Moyne College*

Marcie Desrochers, *State University of New York, Brockport*

Kimberley Duff, *Cerritos College*

Carrie E. Hall, *Miami University of Ohio*

Heather Hill, *University of Texas, San Antonio*

Erika Hoff, *Florida Atlantic University*

Stephanie Keller, *University of Texas, San Antonio*

Katharine Kelly, *Carleton University*

Brenda Kirby, *Le Moyne College*

Sarah Kulkofsky, *Texas Tech University*

Kathryn LaFontana, *Sacred Heart University*

Sharolyn Lane, *North Carolina State University*

Charlotte Markey, *Rutgers University*

Stuart McKelvie, *Bishop's University*

Joe Morrissey, *State University of New York, Binghamton*

Carlotta Ocampo, *Trinity University*

Scott Peterson, *Southwest Minnesota State University*

Michael Rader, *Northern Arizona University*

Bob Ryan, *Kutztown University*

Royce Simpson, *Spring Hill College*

Harold Stanislaw, *California State University, Stanislaus*

Pamela Trotter, *Virginia State University*

John Wallace, *Ball State University*

Shannon Whitten, *University of Central Florida*

PART I

Overview of the Research Process From Start to Finish

Psychological Research

The Whys and Hows of the Scientific Method

CONSIDER THE FOLLOWING QUESTIONS AS YOU READ CHAPTER 1

- Why do psychologists use the scientific method?
- How do psychologists use the scientific method?
- What are the canons of the scientific method?
- What is the difference between basic and applied research?
- How do basic and applied research interact to increase our knowledge about behavior?

As an instructor of an introductory psychology course for psychology majors, I ask my first-semester freshman students the question "What is a psychologist?" At the beginning of the semester, students typically say that a psychologist listens to other people's problems to help them live happier lives. By the end of the semester and their first college course in psychology, these same students will respond that a psychologist studies behavior through research. These students have learned that psychology is a science that investigates behavior, mental processes, and their causes. That is what this book is about: how psychologists use the scientific method to observe and understand behavior and mental processes.

The goal of this text is to give you a step-by-step approach to designing research in psychology, from the purpose of research (discussed in this chapter) and the types of questions psychologists ask about behavior, to the methods psychologists use to observe and understand behavior and describe their findings to others in the field.

WHY PSYCHOLOGISTS CONDUCT RESEARCH

Think about how you know the things you know. How do you know the earth is round? How do you know it is September? How do you know that there is a poverty crisis in some parts of Africa? There are probably many ways that you know these things. In some cases, you may know things because you used your *intuition* or previous knowledge to *deduce* these facts. For example, you may know from past experience that where you live, in the month of September, days tend to still be warm but start to get cooler, especially at night. Remembering that this is the weather you have been experiencing and you are still living in the same location as past years, you can deduce that the month is September from your knowledge base. You may have first learned that the earth is round from an authority figure like your parents, teachers, or text authors. You may have also *observed* that the earth is round by viewing photographs taken from space of the earth. You may know there is a poverty crisis in some parts of Africa from *authority figures* as well (e.g., magazine and newspaper reporters, Bono). These are the primary ways that we learn new facts: **intuition**, **deduction**, **authority**, and **observation**.

Intuition: relying on common sense as a means of knowing about the world

Deduction: using logical reasoning and current knowledge as a means of knowing about the world

Authority: relying on a knowledgeable person or group as a means of knowing about the world

Observation: relying on what one observes as a means of knowing about the world

Suppose something occurred that caused you to suspect that the authority figures you have learned these facts from are not reliable sources of information. Perhaps they have been caught lying about other facts. You might also consider a situation where you do not have enough previous experience with a topic to use your intuition to determine the information for yourself. In these situations, what is the best way to find the facts for yourself? The answer is *observation*. If you had reason to believe, for example, that the poverty crisis in some parts of Africa is not being represented accurately, you could go there yourself and *observe* what is going on to find out if people are representing the true state of things. (In the case of poverty in some parts of Africa, you would probably find out that they are being accurately represented.)

This is why psychologists conduct behavioral research: It is the best way to make sure that the information they have about behavior is accurate. By conducting careful and systematic observations, they can be sure that they are getting the most accurate knowledge they can about behavior. This does not mean that every study conducted will yield accurate results. There are many cases where the observations different researchers collect conflict, but this is an important part of the process. Different ways of observing a behavior may yield different observations and these different observations help us better understand how behaviors occur. See Table 1.1 for some examples of different ways of knowing.

TABLE 1.1	Examples of Ways of Knowing
Way of Knowing	**Example**
Intuition	I suddenly recognize the solution to a crossword puzzle.
Deduction	The sun is setting to my right, so if I turn right, I will be headed west.
Authority	I know that a high white blood cell count indicates an infection because that is what my high school biology teacher said.
Observation	The results of a survey indicate that most Americans get an average of 6 to 8 hours of sleep per night (Moore, 2004).

Using Science to Understand and Explain Behavior

Observation is really what sets scientific fields apart from other fields of study. Someone who wants to know about the political situation during the Civil War may read historical documents and use his or her intuition to describe the situation from these documents. He or she might also read books by experts (authority figures) on the Civil War period or important figures who lived during that time. However, historians typically cannot observe the historical event they are studying. Psychologists have an advantage in that the behavior they want to learn about is happening in humans and other animals in the world around them. The best way to learn about it is to just observe it.

Some behaviors, such as mental processes, cannot be directly observed (e.g., thoughts or memories). Thus, psychologists have developed techniques for inferring information about mental processes through observation of specific behaviors that are affected by the mental processes. Psychologists then attempt to understand mental processes through these behaviors and may investigate the factors that influence those behaviors. That is what this book (and the course you are taking) is all about—understanding the methods psychologists use to observe, measure, and study behavior and mental processes (Figure 1.1).

Figure 1.1   Psychologists May Study Communication Differences Between Men and Women by Observing Their Behavior While They Talk to Each Other

SOURCE: Copyright by Cartoon Stock, www.cartoonstock.com.

Research is the foundation of the field of psychology. Many people think of helping professions when they think about what kinds of things psychologists do. This is because most people with a graduate degree in psychology work in these (or related) professions (American Psychological Association, 2003). However, to do their jobs well, helping professionals such as clinicians and counselors need to understand the findings from research about behavior so that they know what types of treatments and therapies will best help their clients. The research studies conducted in psychology also help clinicians and counselors understand what constitutes "normal" behavior and what behaviors might be considered "abnormal."

Thinking about the field of biology may help you understand how influential research is in the field of psychology. In the biological field, there are researchers who investigate the way our bodies react physically to the world around us (e.g., after being exposed to a virus). This knowledge helps other researchers determine which drugs may be effective in helping us improve these physical reactions (e.g., reduce our symptoms as we fight the virus). Finally, the knowledge gained in biological research helps doctors correctly diagnose and treat their patients (e.g., what symptoms indicate presence of a particular virus and which drugs are most effective in treating these symptoms). The field of psychology works a lot like the field of biology (although the term *psychologist* applies to both scientists and practitioners in psychology, sometimes causing confusion). Some researchers investigate what causes certain types of behaviors (e.g., distraction in people with attention deficit hyperactivity disorder, or ADHD). Other researchers may investigate what treatments are effective in reducing these behaviors (e.g., rewarding someone for staying on task). Finally, some psychologists work with clients to help them deal with problem behaviors. For example, school psychologists may work with teachers and parents to develop a reward system for students with ADHD who have difficulty completing work in class because he or she becomes distracted easily. The research that investigated the behaviors associated with ADHD and the factors that can reduce those behaviors was necessary for the school psychologist to be able to develop an effective treatment plan for the client.

HOW PSYCHOLOGISTS USE THE SCIENTIFIC METHOD

Empiricism: gaining knowledge through systematic observation of the world

Determinism: the assumption that phenomena have identifiable causes

Parsimony: the assumption that the simplest explanation of a phenomenon is most likely to be correct

Testability: the assumption that explanations of behavior can be tested and falsified through observation

Our starting place for conducting research studies in psychology is an understanding of the assumptions that come along with the methods of science. We need to keep some concepts in mind when we use the scientific method to understand behavior. As discussed earlier, scientific study requires observations. It is the primary aspect of the scientific method. However, there are actually four primary facets or *canons* (i.e., rules or principles that guide a field of study) that define the scientific method. They are **empiricism, determinism, parsimony,** and **testability**.

Empiricism

The first canon is empiricism, and this is just what we have been discussing already—that the scientific method relies on observations. We have several important people to thank for the empirical nature of science. Galileo, for example, was an influential scientist who used observations to understand the world (Sharratt, 1996). Much of the learning up to Galileo's time (1564–1642) had relied on authority figures, such as Aristotle and Plato, and their ideas about the world to understand how the world worked. However, Galileo (Figure 1.2) and his contemporaries (e.g., Copernicus, Newton) claimed that to learn how the world works, one should observe it. When Galileo wanted to understand how our solar system worked, he *observed* the movement of the planets around the sun through a telescope, instead of simply accepting the authoritative position held by Aristotle that the earth was the center of the solar system and everything revolved around it. He made careful, systematic observations of the phenomena of interest to better understand those phenomena. What we do in psychology is not very different from what Galileo did. If developmental psychologists want to know about bullying behaviors in elementary school children, they go out and carefully observe specific playground behaviors among these children or systematically observe the behaviors of children who have been identified as bullies.

Figure 1.2   Galileo

SOURCE: Copyright by Jupiter Unlimited, www.jupiter unlimited.com.

Why do psychologists observe behavior? Observing behavior gives researchers a more accurate understanding of the causes of behaviors than other methods of gaining knowledge. Relying on an authority to learn about behavior, for example, would greatly limit our understanding of behaviors across large groups of individuals, because not all authority figures are equally reliable and some may have faulty information.

How do we use empiricism to learn about behavior? There are many different ways to do this. We can simply observe people in their normal environment (e.g., children on a playground at recess). We can ask them to complete a survey (e.g., have them respond to items that help us measure their mood). We can ask them to come into a lab and complete a task on a computer (e.g., test their memory for different types of information). Each of these methods allows us to gather empirical measurements of behavior (observation techniques will be discussed further in Chapter 3).

Determinism

Another important aspect of the scientific method is the adherence to determinism. This is the concept that phenomena in the world (and human behaviors) occur naturally and have identifiable causes (in extreme cases, determinism can indicate a denial of free will). In other words, by conducting studies to observe behavior, we can understand the factors that *cause* those behaviors to occur. One goal of psychological research is to be able to explain behavior by understanding the causes of different types of behavior. For example, why do people get depressed? What causes false memories? Does sleeplessness cause anxiety? Does anxiety cause sleeplessness? The assumption of determinism in psychological research is that each of these behaviors (depression, false memories, anxiety, sleeplessness) has a specific cause or set of causes and we can understand these causes through observation of behavior in different circumstances. For many behaviors studied by psychologists, multiple causes may affect the behaviors.

How is determinism used in psychological research? Because the goal of research is typically to gain a better understanding of behavior and its causes, researchers begin with a prediction (often based on predictions tested in and results from past studies) about what causes behavior and look for behaviors they can observe in their study that are consistent or inconsistent with that prediction. The specifics of how causes of behavior are studied are discussed in Chapter 3.

Parsimony

In the 1997 film *Contact,* Jodie Foster's character, Dr. Ellie Arroway, attempts to explain what she believes in as a scientist to Matthew McConaughey's character, Palmer Joss. She tells him that simpler explanations of the world are preferred over more complex explanations, particularly if there is no scientific evidence that a complex explanation is correct. She calls this concept "Occam's Razor" (after the Franciscan friar who suggested it as an important part of the scientific method). Parsimony is what Arroway is speaking of when she talks about the preference for more simple explanations. In psychological research, we develop explanations of behavior starting with the simplest descriptions and expanding those descriptions only when it becomes clear that the behavior is more complex than our original description of it. In other words, simple explanations are preferred. It is assumed that the simpler explanation is more likely to be correct. More complex explanations should be developed only after more simple explanations have failed to be supported by research studies.

Why is parsimony useful in psychological research? Parsimony helps scientists test their ideas more easily, because it is easier to develop a study that might falsify a simple explanation than to develop a study that might falsify a more complex explanation. Falsification is an important part of the research process. This idea is relevant to the concept of testability as well and will be discussed further in the next section.

Testability

The fourth canon of science is testability. The scientific method can only be used to examine ideas that can be tested through observation. The only explanations of behavior that can be tested with the scientific method are those that can be contradicted with observations of behavior. *Why* is falsifiability important? It is important because a test of an explanation of a behavior that allows that explanation to be falsified provides a stronger test of that explanation. If we look only for evidence to support our explanations of behavior, we are likely to find that evidence and hold on to those explanations longer even if they are wrong. If, instead, we design research studies that can show us behaviors inconsistent with our explanations, we are more likely to find evidence against them, if such evidence exists. It takes only a few studies with results inconsistent with an explanation of behavior to falsify it. However, it takes many studies conducted in many different contexts that produce results consistent with an explanation of behavior to support it.

Testability is one of the reasons that many of Sigmund Freud's ideas have not had more influence in current clinical and personality psychology theories—they are difficult to test using the scientific method. For example, Freud proposed that many of our personality traits are a product of a struggle between constructs of our minds (id, ego, and superego) that we do not have full conscious access to (Nairne, 2006). It is difficult to test this theory, because the constructs Freud proposed are difficult to connect to observable behaviors. Thus, it is difficult to systematically observe behaviors in a research study that would contradict the theory. We can, however, answer questions about other types of mental processes that are indicated by observable behaviors. For example, we can test the idea that anxiety will cause sleeplessness. We can observe behaviors of sleeplessness in situations where people are placed in anxiety-provoking situations with anxiety verified by self-report. If anxious people are sleeping well, this will contradict our explanation of sleeplessness (i.e., anxiety) and provide us with a good test of our explanation (although this particular result is one that is unlikely to be found). As psychologists using the scientific method, it is important that we ask questions and test explanations about behavior that can be falsified by observations of those behaviors.

Why is falsifiability so important in psychological science? As indicated above, falsification of explanations of behavior advances psychological science much more than supporting explanations (Platt, 1964). Whenever researchers can show that an accepted explanation is not supported, it changes the direction of investigation in an area of research and moves psychological science forward in gaining new knowledge about behavior.

The canons of science provide a general "how to" guide for psychologists designing research studies, because they help us conduct good tests of our explanations of the causes of behaviors and further our understanding of why certain behaviors occur. The rest of this text describes more of the details of how psychologists apply these canons in designing and conducting research and will step you through the process of developing research studies of your own.

BASIC AND APPLIED RESEARCH

As you begin to consider the types of questions that can be answered in psychological research studies (a topic that will be covered more in Chapter 2), it is important to keep in mind the goals of two major categories of research: **basic research** and **applied research**.

The goal of basic research is to understand the most fundamental processes of behavior and how they operate. Research questions in basic research are typically about how a behavior works. How much information can we store in short-term memory? Who exhibits more symptoms of depression: men or women? Do we have implicit stereotypes that affect our social behavior?

— ✃ —

Basic Research: research conducted with the goal of understanding fundamental processes of phenomena

Applied Research: research conducted with the goal of solving everyday problems

Applied research is generally focused on answering questions related to solving real-world problems. What type of automated teller machine (ATM) is the easiest to use? Which treatments are best in helping people who are depressed? What type of work environment increases productivity of employees?

Typically, basic research provides fundamental knowledge of how behaviors operate that is useful to researchers conducting applied studies. For example, suppose that a researcher finds that people who report having insomnia also report symptoms of anxiety (a similar result was recently reported by Morphy, Dunn, Lewis, Boardman, & Croft, 2007). A conclusion from this study might be that anxiety and sleeplessness are related in some way (note that this does not mean that anxiety *causes* sleeplessness, only that they are related). This conclusion represents basic knowledge about the connection between emotional state and sleeplessness or insomnia. Researchers interested in the more applied question of how we help people with sleep problems may use this basic knowledge to test treatments for sleeplessness that focus on reducing anxiety to determine whether the relationship found in the above study is causal or not. The basic research in this case is vital for the development of applied studies that address a real-world problem (i.e., insomnia). Table 1.2 provides some additional examples of basic and applied research studies.

TABLE 1.2   Basic and Applied Research Studies

Basic research

- Researchers investigated participants' awareness of the effects of handheld objects on their ability to pass through an opening (such as a doorway). Participants held objects while viewing an opening and reported whether they could pass through the opening holding the objects (Wagman & Taylor, 2005).
- To investigate possible spatial-ability differences in male and female infants, 5-month-olds completed a task to determine if they recognized objects that had been rotated from their original orientation (Moore & Johnson, 2008).
- Participants were randomly assigned to mixed-race groups, while their brain activity was recorded to investigate brain areas involved in in-group biases (Van Bavel, Packer, & Cunningham, 2008).

Applied research

- Researchers investigated how to increase volunteers for charitable organizations by presenting participants with information about the organizations to determine what type of information affects whether someone will volunteer (Boezeman & Ellemers, 2008).
- Two experiments were conducted to determine which emotional states contribute to people being willing to accept advice from others (Gino & Schweitzer, 2008).
- From self, peer, and supervisor ratings, researchers determined if managers with better work-life balances were less likely to advance in their careers (Lyness & Judiesch, 2008).

Because applied research investigates realistic problems, applied researchers are often concerned with the **external validity** of their studies. This means that they attempt to observe behaviors that can be applied to real-life situations. This is important because these researchers want to be able to apply their results to a problem that applies to individuals who are not participants in their study (as well as to those individuals who were observed in the study). External validity is also a consideration in basic research but in some cases can be less important than it is in applied research.

External Validity: the degree to which the results of a study apply to individuals and realistic behaviors outside the study

Knowledge gained in applied studies can also feed back to basic researchers to help them refine their theories about how behavior works. Suppose in the example above regarding anxiety and insomnia, the applied studies showed that treatments reducing anxiety did not cure the symptoms of insomnia (similar results were reported by Morin, Belanger, & Fortier-Brochu, 2006). In this case, the basic researchers may use this knowledge to hypothesize that the link between anxiety and insomnia may not be a simple causal relationship and conduct further studies to better understand the causes of insomnia and how it is related to anxiety. In this way, the two types of research, basic and applied, interact with each other, showing that both types of research are critical to the field of psychology.

As you encounter descriptions of psychological research, you may find that not all research fits neatly into basic or applied categories. Some research can both answer fundamental questions about behavior and help solve a realistic problem. It may be better to think about research as primarily basic or applied. In other words, basic and applied descriptors may be end points in a continuum of types of research studies with each research study falling somewhere between these end points.

CHAPTER SUMMARY

Reconsider the questions from the beginning of the chapter:

- Why do psychologists use the scientific method? Psychologists use the scientific method because it provides the best way to gain new knowledge about behavior.
- How do psychologists use the scientific method? Psychologists use the scientific method to observe behaviors as they occur in everyday life and in situations researchers are interested in learning about.
- What are the canons of the scientific method? The canons are empiricism, determinism, parsimony, and testability.
- What is the difference between basic and applied research? Basic research is designed to answer fundamental questions about behavior. Applied research is designed to gain solutions to everyday problems.
- How do basic and applied research interact to increase our knowledge about behavior? Basic research advances our understanding of the causes of behavior. In applied research, these explanations are tested in everyday situations to inform researchers about the best solutions for everyday problems. Knowledge gained

about these problems in applied research then informs basic researchers about how explanations of behavior may need to be revised to explain behaviors that occur in everyday life.

THINKING ABOUT RESEARCH

A summary of a research study in psychology is given below. As you read the summary, think about the following questions:

1. What behaviors are the researchers observing?
2. How are the observations being recorded by the researchers?
3. Were the researchers able to identify a cause of behavior from this study?
4. Were the researchers able to answer their research question with the observations they collected? How?
5. What results would have falsified the explanation of behavior the authors were testing?
6. Do you think this study qualifies as primarily basic or applied research? Why?

Study Reference

Olson, K. R., Banaji, M. R., Dweck, C. S., & Spelke, E. S. (2006). Children's biased evaluations of lucky versus unlucky people and their social groups. *Psychological Science, 17*, 845–846.

Purpose of the Study. The researchers were interested in how we develop views of other people in terms of how lucky they are. Do people view lucky individuals more positively than unlucky individuals, or do they prefer unlucky individuals because they feel bad for them? Olson, Banaji, Dweck, and Spelke (2006) examined this way of thinking by measuring children's preference for individuals portrayed as lucky or unlucky.

Method of the Study. Children between 5 and 7 years old participated in the study. A group of study participants listened to stories about other children. In these stories, the children either performed an intentional action that was positive (i.e., helpful) or negative (i.e., harmful) or were involved in an uncontrollable event that was either positive (i.e., something good happened to the child that he or she had no control over—the child was "lucky") or negative (i.e., something bad happened to the child that he or she had no control over—the child was "unlucky"). After hearing the stories, the participants were asked to rate how much they liked the child in the story by choosing one of six different facial expressions (e.g., smiling face, frowning face) that matched how they felt about the child they heard about.

Results of the Study. Study participants preferred children who experienced positive events. This result was shown for both intentional actions (i.e., children who were intentionally good were preferred over children who were intentionally bad) and for uncontrolled events (i.e., "lucky" children were preferred to "unlucky" children). Participants also preferred children who experienced uncontrolled negative events (i.e., "unlucky" children) as compared to children who performed an intentional negative action. However, the difference in preference for intentional positive actions and uncontrolled positive events (i.e., "lucky" children) was less clear.

Conclusions of the Study. The authors concluded that children prefer lucky individuals as compared with unlucky individuals. This preference was present in children as young as 5 to 7 years old. According to the researchers, these results may help explain negative attitudes that are sometimes present for disadvantaged individuals.

COMMON PITFALLS AND HOW TO AVOID THEM

Problem: Assuming that psychology equals practice in a "helping profession": ignoring or dismissing the scientific aspect of psychology

Solution: Understand that science and practice are both important aspects of the field of psychology. In addition, although there is debate about this issue, many psychologists find it important that practitioners of psychology stay abreast of current research findings to ensure that the most effective treatments are used.

Problem: Positive test bias—designing studies that provide supportive evidence of an explanation of behavior without including the possibility for contradictory evidence

Solution: Carefully design studies to allow collection of data that can support or contradict explanations of behavior.

Problem: Misinterpretation of causation—study of cause and effect relationships requires manipulation (e.g., randomly assigning participants to different situations), but many people confuse reports of relationships with evidence of causation. For example, misinterpretation of causation: confusing evidence of relationships with evidence of causation.

Solution: Do not assume a reported relationship between factors is evidence that one factor causes another unless the study has been designed in such a way that other noncausal relationships can be ruled out.

Problem: Dismissing basic research—some people dismiss basic research as unimportant because it is not designed to solve a real-world problem.

Solution: View the "big picture" of knowledge in psychology to see how basic research informs applied research by providing fundamental knowledge of behavior that guides research questions and interpretation of results in applied studies.

TEST YOURSELF

Match each canon of science below with its correct definition.

1. Determinism
   (a) The scientific method can be used to test descriptions and explanations of the world that can be contradicted by observations.

2. Empiricism
   (b) The scientific method is used to examine phenomena that have an identifiable cause.

3. Testability   (c) An assumption of science is that simpler explanations are more likely than complex explanations to be correct.

4. Parsimony   (d) Knowledge is gained in science by systematically observing the phenomenon being studied.

5. Freud hypothesized that many of our personality traits are controlled by an unconscious conflict between the id, ego, and superego aspects of our selves that we do not have conscious awareness of (Nairne, 2006). Using what you know about the scientific method, explain why this hypothesis is difficult to support with observations of behavior.

6. Explain how parsimony is helpful in psychological studies.

7. For each reference listed below, decide whether the study is primarily basic or applied.

(a) Drews, F., Pasupathu, M., & Strayer, D. (2008). Passenger and cell phone conversations in simulated driving. *Journal of Experimental Psychology: Applied, 14,* 392–400.

(b) Roediger, H. L., III, & Geraci, L. (2007). Aging and the misinformation effect: A neuropsychological analysis. *Journal of Experimental Psychology: Learning, Memory, and Cognition, 33,* 321–334.

(c) Bratcher, N. A., Farmer-Dougan, V., Dougan, J. D., Heidenreich, B. A., & Garris, P. A. (2005). The role of dopamine in reinforcement: Changes in reinforcement sensitivity induced by D-sub-1-type, D-sub-2-type, and nonselective dopamine receptor agonists. *Journal of the Experimental Analysis of Behavior, 84,* 371–399.

(d) Declercq, F., Vanheule, S., Markey, S., & Willemsen, J. (2007). Posttraumatic distress in security guards and the various effects of social support. *Journal of Clinical Psychology, 63,* 1239–1246.

(e) West, R. (2007). The influence of strategic monitoring on the neural correlates of prospective memory. *Memory & Cognition, 35,* 1034–1046.

Answers: 1. b, 2. d, 3. a, 4. c, 5. If we do not have conscious awareness of the conflict (if it is unconscious), then it would be difficult to support the existence of this conflict through direct observations of behavior. In other words, it is difficult to falsify this theory by directly observing behavior. (6) Parsimony (assuming that simple explanations are more likely to be correct) is useful in psychological studies because this assumption makes it easier to test explanations of behavior. It is easier to devise a study that can falsify a simple explanation than to devise a study to falsify a more complex explanation. 7a. applied, 7b. basic, 7c. basic, 7d. applied, 7e. basic.

CHAPTER 2

Hypothesis Development

Where Research Questions Come From

CONSIDER THE FOLLOWING QUESTIONS AS YOU READ CHAPTER 2

- How do researchers develop a research question?
- How do researchers conduct a literature review?
- What are some useful resources for a literature review?
- What will you find in a literature review?
- What are the different types of research articles, and how are they organized?
- How do we use a literature review to make hypotheses?
- What are the different types of hypotheses that a researcher can make?

A few years ago, I was playing the game Catchphrase with some friends. In this game, a handheld device displays a target phrase (e.g., a name or object) while ticking down a timer. The players with the device must provide clues to the target phrase (without saying it) to get their teammates to say the target phrase. Meanwhile, the timer ticks faster and faster until it runs out and buzzes. The players who end up with the device when the time runs out lose a point for their team. The game moves swiftly, with teammates constantly calling out phrases to guess the target phrase.

After the game ended, we discussed the sequence of guessing of a particularly difficult phrase. Two players, Joel and Renée, claimed to have guessed the phrase, but only one had actually done so. Everyone agreed that Renée had actually guessed the phrase, but Joel claimed to have a clear memory of guessing it. It was determined that although Joel believed that he had guessed the correct phrase, he actually had an inaccurate memory for the events of the game. He had a false memory in remembering who had actually guessed correctly. Perplexed by his error, Joel suggested that "someone should study this phenomenon." As a memory researcher, I became interested in this phenomenon and conducted experiments to investigate false memories like the one that Joel had during the game (e.g., Coane & McBride, 2006). This story illustrates how everyday events such as these can spark psychological research questions (e.g., Why do false memories occur?).

DEVELOPING A RESEARCH QUESTION

Choosing a research question is the first step in the research process (see Figure 2.1). Answering a research question is the researcher's primary motivation for designing and conducting a study. These questions come from many sources. Primarily, they come from

Figure 2.1   Steps in the Research Process: Choosing a Research Question

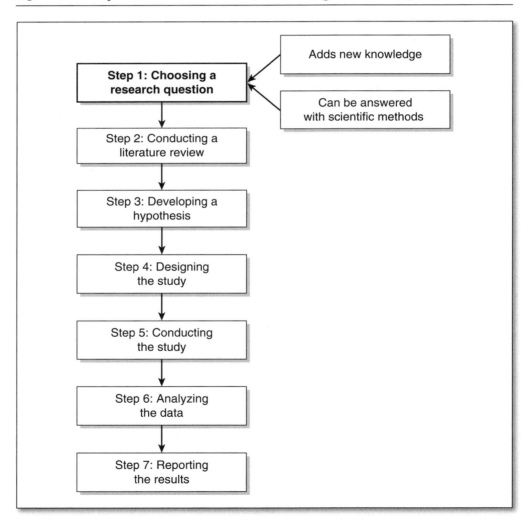

what the researcher is interested in learning about. Think about what topics in psychology interest you most. Can you think of questions about behavior in this area that you would like to have answered? Have you ever asked yourself a "What if . . ." question about a behavior? That is often where research questions begin: from the questions a researcher is interested in. In the situation described above, a research question was sparked by an everyday event (e.g., Why do false memories occur?). In other cases, research questions are developed to solve a real-world problem (e.g., How does the use of a cellular phone affect driving behavior?). Finally, explanations of behavior that need to be tested, called theories, can guide research questions (e.g., Do negative thoughts cause depression?).

Research questions can be **descriptive**, such as whether a specific behavior occurs (Are college students anxious?), what the nature of the behavior is (How does anxiety manifest itself in college students?), or whether behaviors occur together (Do college students who smoke also tend to be anxious?). Questions can also be **causal**—about causes of behavior (What types of events cause college students to be anxious?). Many causal research questions are also designed to test a **theory** about the cause of a behavior (Is anxiety in college students caused by a lack of confidence in their abilities?) or to compare theories about behavior to see which theory has more support (Is anxiety in college students caused by a lack of confidence in their abilities or a lack of social support?). As described in Chapter 1, research questions can answer fundamental questions about behavior (What are the causes of anxiety among college students?) or questions about how to solve a real-world problem (What kinds of student-oriented programs can a college initiate that will reduce anxiety in college students?). This is the difference between basic research questions and applied research questions. The type of question a researcher pursues is based on whether the researcher is interested in basic questions about a behavior or applications of the behavior in daily life. However, even though researcher interest is often a starting place for choosing a question to study, researchers should consider how appropriate their question is for both scientific methods and the specific field of study before moving on to designing a study.

Descriptive Research Question: a research question that asks about the presence of behavior, how frequently it is exhibited, or whether there is a relationship between different behaviors

Causal Research Question: a research question that asks what causes specific behaviors to occur

Theory: an explanation of behavior that can be tested through research studies

One important issue in choosing a research question is whether the question can be answered with the scientific methods described in Chapter 1. Can observations of behavior provide an answer to the question? If specific observations of behavior can be made to help answer the question, then it might be an appropriate question for psychological research. Table 2.1 provides some examples of research questions that have been examined in different areas of psychological research to give you some examples of questions that can be answered by observing behavior. In addition, Chapter 3 describes some specific types of observations that can be made and how they help answer a research question. Some questions that would be difficult to test with scientific methods are "Does God exist?" and "Was the Iraq War a moral war?"

TABLE 2.1   Examples of Research Questions in Different Areas of Psychology

Area of Psychological Research	Examples of Research Questions
Social psychology	How does an authority figure influence behavior? (Milgram, 1963)
	What types of faces are considered attractive? (Corneille, Monin, & Pleyers, 2005)
Cognitive psychology	What types of memory decline as people age? (Lipman & Caplan, 1992)
	How does our knowledge of the world influence our perception? (Ban, Lee, & Yang, 2004)
Industrial-organizational psychology	How does work environment affect job stress? (Pal & Saksvik, 2008)
	How does perception of power in the workplace affect perceptions of sexual harassment? (DeSouza & Fansler, 2003)
Clinical psychology	What types of people benefit most from cognitive behavioral therapy? (Green, Hadjistavropoulos, & Sharpe, 2008)
	What are the causes of schizophrenia? (Compton, Goulding, & Walker, 2007)
Biological psychology	What are the effects of amphetamine on the brain? (Heidenreich, 1993)
	What are the neurological causes of Parkinson's disease? (Olzmann, 2007)

Another important consideration in choosing a research question is how much is already known about the question. In other words, what has been learned from previous studies about the question? To investigate what is known about a research question from previous studies, a thorough **literature review** should be conducted. A literature review involves searching research databases or other sources to find relevant research that has been done in an area of the field. In reading about what other researchers have done, the literature review will help a researcher to determine what is already known about a research question, determine what methods have been used to investigate the question, and find information that can help them make a prediction about what the answer to the research question will be. (Making predictions will be discussed in detail later.) Conducting a literature review will ensure that a new study will add to the knowledge in an area without duplicating what is already known. However, it can take many studies with the same research question before the answer to that research question is supported by enough evidence. Thus, replication of results is an important part of the scientific process. Just because a study had been done before on a specific research question does not mean more studies are not needed to fully answer the question. A research question does not need to be wholly original to contribute to psychological science (Figure 2.2).

Literature Review: a process of searching for and reviewing previous studies related to a study being developed to add to the knowledge in an area and make appropriate predictions about the data

Figure 2.2   A Literature Review Can Help a Researcher Determine What Is Already Known About a Topic

SOURCE: Copyright by S. Harris, www.sciencecartoonsplus.com/scimags.html.

HOW TO CONDUCT A LITERATURE REVIEW

There are many sources researchers use to conduct a literature review. Searching through databases will help identify relevant studies to a research question. Databases may also hold references to helpful reviews of research in an area. If you want to learn about the most recent studies in an area, though, databases may not be the best source, because these databases typically reference published works, and the publication process can take a year or more from the time an article or a book chapter is written to when it is published and cataloged in the database. Therefore, to conduct the most up-to-date literature review, it can be helpful to attend a psychological conference in an area, where researchers often present studies that have not yet been published. More information about each of these sources for a literature review is provided in what follows (Figure 2.3).

Figure 2.3   Steps in the Research Process: Conducting a Literature Review

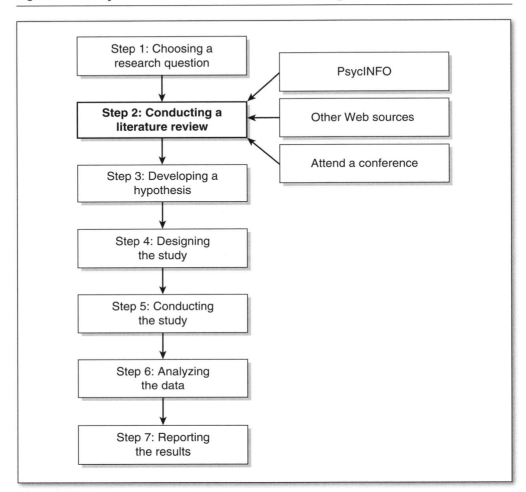

PsycINFO

A very useful database for a literature review of psychological research is PsycINFO. PsycINFO is a searchable database that contains records of articles, books, and book chapters written by researchers about research studies in an area of psychology. Although each version may have a different appearance, all versions of PsycINFO can be searched by topic words, words that appear in the citation information for the article (this includes the title, authors, abstract, and topic words), author names, journal in which the article was published, and so on. In other words, there are many ways to find articles and book chapters about a research question using PsycINFO. Searching by topic words (called key words in PsycINFO) is a good way to start a search for a literature review.

There are two primary ways to search for articles and chapters by key words. One is to map the term to a subject heading. The American Psychological Association (APA) has designated specific subject headings as general topics of study in psychology. Each article or chapter has been coded by the subject headings that best describe the topic of the article. In PsycINFO, you can click a box or a button to turn the mapping to subject headings on, and various subject headings will appear that correspond to the key words you have typed in (you do not have to know the exact subject heading—PsycINFO will search for subject headings similar to what you type in). You can choose to focus on a specific heading or "auto explode" the search to include all the subheadings that might be contained in the more general heading. You can also choose to search just the key words you entered, which will allow PsycINFO to search for articles and chapters that contain those words in the title or abstract. You can also combine searches that focus on different key words.

An example will help explain how this works (you can follow along by trying this out in PsycINFO). Suppose that you are interested in conducting a literature search for the relationship between depression and bullying behaviors in children. A good place to start is a key word search in PsycINFO. You can start by typing in "depression" into the key word window and mapping it onto the subject headings if such an option is shown. A window such as the one shown in Table 2.2 may appear where you will see several different forms of depression as well as the general heading of "depression." Different versions of PsycINFO have different appearances, so your version may not show the window shown in Table 2.2, or it may display different subject terms. Continue to execute a search of articles that have depression anywhere in the full reference of the article (e.g., title, abstract, topic words). You should find that PsycINFO has yielded a large number of records that fit these key words. Depending on which subject terms you choose, different sets of articles will be found. Obviously, there are far too many for us to search through one by one, so we need to narrow the search further and include the bullying portion of our topic.

TABLE 2.2	An Example of Key Word Search in PsycINFO for "Depression": Each Version of PsycINFO May Have a Different Appearance		
Select	**Subject Heading**	**Auto Explode**	**Focus**
○	Anaclitic depression	○	○
○	Atypical depression	○	○
○	Beck Depression Inventory	○	○
○	"Depression (emotion)"	○	○
○	Endogenous depression	○	○
○	Major depression	○	○
	⋮		
○	depression.mp search as keyword		

We can conduct a second key word search for "bullying" using the same procedure described above for "depression." This search should find a large number of records as well but fewer records than the search for "depression" as there have been fewer studies conducted on the topic of "bullying." Finally, to narrow our search to the specific topic we started with (depression and bullying), we can combine our two searches. Your version of PsycINFO may have a Combine function for this purpose. If not, you may be able to type "1 and 2" into the search window and PsycINFO will combine the searches for you. If you combine your searches, you should find a more reasonable number of records to look at (when I conducted this search in April, 2008, I found 149 records, but you may find more if your search terms included more choices or if additional articles have been published on these topics since that time).

Before we look at what the search has gotten us, consider a possible outcome of our bullying search. Suppose that bullying had not been the proper term, and we found no subject headings that were relevant. One thing we can do to be sure that we get the right subject headings is to use a shorter form of our term and search for truncations. We can do this by shortening our term to "bully" and adding a "*" or "$" to the end of it in the search window. This will search for all words that begin with bully and find any variation that might get us closer to the term we are looking for. Be sure to use the truncation symbol if you are not certain that you have the right term or if you do not find appropriate subject headings with a search term.

What will the PsycINFO search give you? If you view the results of the search we conducted above, you will see a list of articles (probably the most recently published articles first) that indicates the names of the authors, the title of the article, what type of article it is (journal article, book chapter, dissertation, etc.), where the article was published, and when it was published. For each article, you can choose to view the *abstract* of the article. The abstract is a short paragraph that summarizes the content of the article (abstracts are discussed in detail later when the structure of journal articles is presented). You can then read through the abstracts of articles that might be relevant to your topic. You may also see a link to the article available online in PDF format or a link to search your library for the journal or book in which the article was published, so that you can locate any articles you find relevant to your literature review. Finally, the reference section of the articles you find may also lead you to other relevant articles on your topic.

Suppose that you find an article that is especially relevant to your topic and that you would like to know if the same author(s) published other articles relevant to your topic. You can find articles by a particular author by conducting an author search in PsycINFO. Simply type the author's last name and first initial into PsycINFO, and you will see choices that match what you typed in alphabetical order. You can choose any that seem relevant (sometimes the same author will be listed in a few different ways—with or without middle initial) and PsycINFO will list the publications by that author. You can also limit key word and author searches by year if you are just interested in the most recent articles that have been published. Finally, articles in a particular psychology journal can be searched in PsycINFO (see below for a description of psychology journals). For more information on PsycINFO searches go to http://www.apa.org/databases/training/searchguides.html for APA guides on how to use PsycINFO.

PubMed and ERIC

Although most articles published in psychological journals can be found in PsycINFO, some journals publish articles in other topic areas that overlap with psychology, and you will find them only in other databases. For example, journals that publish research in biological and medical areas can be found by searching the PubMed database. If you are interested in conducting a literature review on topics in biological psychology or about psychological disorders or specific conditions such as autism, you may want to search PubMed in addition to PsycINFO to complete a thorough literature review. Articles in areas related to education can be found in the ERIC (Education Resources Information Center) database. Thus, if you are conducting a literature review on topics such as standardized testing, you may also want to search for articles in ERIC. Like PsycINFO, PubMed and ERIC can be searched by topic, author, and journal with advanced search capabilities that can include year of publication, language of publication, and so on. The search screen will have a different layout, depending on the version of the database that you are viewing, but many versions of both PubMed and ERIC have drop-down menus for choosing a search by these features of an article. A more general topic database, called Web of Science, is also available for searching for journal articles in different areas of research.

Other Sources

In addition to PsycINFO, there are search engines that can be searched to obtain articles relevant to your topic. The first is a sub-engine of Google called Google Scholar. You can access Google Scholar at http://scholar.google.com/. Google Scholar will search the Web for academic journals and books to find articles relevant to a topic or written by a specific author. As with PsycINFO, you may not always find links to copies of the articles on Google Scholar, but you may find articles that were not found in a search of PsycINFO. With search engines, you are also more likely to come across articles that have not been peer reviewed (see below for more discussion of peer review). Articles that have not been peer reviewed are typically less reliable sources of information because they have not been reviewed by experts in the field who verify the quality of the study.

Other search engines may yield information on a topic, but the veracity of that information may vary. Whereas PsycINFO and Google Scholar will yield peer-reviewed articles on a topic, most search engines will yield other types of information, such as popular press articles that may or may not report research findings accurately. Thus, a search of a database such as PsycINFO or Google Scholar is a necessary step in any literature review.

Finally, psychological conferences can provide a way to get the most up-to-date information about research conducted in an area (often so new that it has not been published yet). If you are unable to attend such a conference yourself, you can often search the program of these conferences online to view titles, authors, and abstracts or research studies that will be or have been presented at the conference. Some of the larger conferences that cover many areas of psychology are the American Psychological Association (APA) Convention (typically held in August each year) and the Association for Psychological Science Convention (typically held in May each year). In addition, there are many area-wide psychological association conferences for all areas of psychology (the Midwestern

Psychological Association, the Southeastern Psychological Association, the Western Psychological Association, etc.) that can be found on the APA Web page under Conferences. Many areas of psychology also hold annual conventions (a quick Web search will yield some of these meetings and sites).

WHAT YOU FIND IN A LITERATURE REVIEW

As described above, a PsycINFO search (or search of one of the other sources) will provide you with a list of journal articles and/or book chapters that are relevant to your topic. How will these sources help you as you attempt to make a prediction about your research question? As you read the articles, you may find important information for your literature review in different sections of the articles. Being familiar with the structure of different types of articles and what type of information you can expect to get from the different sections before you complete your literature review will help you complete your literature review more easily. Thus, we discuss here the structure of some of the different article types. We begin by describing journal articles.

What Is a Journal Article?

An empirical journal article is written by a researcher (or researchers in many cases) to describe a research study to others who might be interested in knowing about what the researcher did (someone like you if you are conducting a literature review on the researcher's topic). The researcher's article may describe a single study (e.g., one experiment) or it may describe multiple studies, all of which relate to the same research question. After the researcher has written the article, the researcher submits it to a psychological journal to attempt to get it published. If the article is published, it will be cataloged in PsycINFO or another database if the journal topic is outside of psychology.

The article is typically sent out to several reviewers who are experts on the general topic of the article (i.e., they are other researchers who have done studies on the topic in the past). This is a process known as **peer review**. These reviewers make recommendations about revisions that should be made to the article to improve it and whether or not it should be published in the journal it was submitted to. The editor of the journal uses these reviews to decide if the

Peer Review: a process that takes place prior to publication of an article in many journals where experts make suggestions for improving an article and make a recommendation about whether an article should be published in the journal

article can be published in the journal and which revisions are most important. The author(s) of the article then revise the article or may attempt to submit it to a different journal (if the editor has decided not to publish the article in that particular journal). If the revised article is submitted to the same journal, it may then be reviewed again, or it may be accepted by the editor for publication. The review process can be lengthy (sometimes taking many months or even a year), but it is important in verifying the quality of the study before it is published. Thus, articles that are not peer reviewed may describe studies of lower quality. After the article is accepted for publication, it can then take a few more months before the article appears in the journal. Thus, articles are rarely published very soon after they are written, which means that research is already a year or more old before it is published.

Empirical journal articles are considered primary sources for research information, because they are written by the researchers who conducted the research and details of the study are provided. Journal articles differ from popular magazine articles. Popular magazine articles often contain short summaries of the study written by another author from the primary source (i.e., they are secondary sources) and may not provide an accurate account of the study in all cases. Thus, popular magazine articles are considered secondary sources. An accurate and thorough literature review requires review of primary sources (i.e., journal articles).

Many areas of psychology have journals devoted to research on a particular topic, but there are also journals that publish research in all areas of psychology. Table 2.3 provides a list of

---

TABLE 2.3   A List of Psychological Journals by Type of Article Published

General psychology journals—these journals publish studies from various areas of psychology

Psychological Science

Journal of Experimental Psychology: General

Journal of Experimental Psychology: Applied

American Psychologist

Canadian Journal of Experimental Psychology

Experimental Psychology

Personality and social psychology

Journal of Personality and Social Psychology

Journal of Experimental Social Psychology

Personality and Social Psychology Bulletin

Personality and Individual Differences

Journal of Research in Personality

Cognitive psychology

Journal of Experimental Psychology: Learning, Memory, and Cognition

Journal of Experimental Psychology: Human Perception and Performance

Cognition

Journal of Memory and Language

Memory and Cognition

Applied Cognitive Psychology

(Continued)

TABLE 2.3 (Continued)

Developmental psychology

Journal of Experimental Child Psychology

Child Development

Psychology and Aging

Developmental Psychology

British Journal of Developmental Psychology

Biological psychology

Neuropsychology

Neuropsychologia

Applied Neuropsychology

Review and theoretical journals—these journals publish review articles and/or articles describing new or revised theories about behavior (some of these journals publish empirical studies as well)

Psychological Review

Psychological Bulletin

Psychonomic Bulletin & Review

Developmental Review

Best Practices in School Psychology

Behavioral and Brain Sciences

some general psychology journals, as well as journals in a particular area. In most cases, you can figure out what types of studies are published in the journal from the title of the journal.

Structure of an Empirical Journal Article

Journal articles are organized into sections. Each section provides specific information about a study. Each major section of a journal article is described below.

———— ❧ ————

Abstract: a summary of an article that appears at the beginning of the article and in searchable databases of journal articles

Abstract. As described above, an **Abstract** is a short summary of the study that allows readers to decide if the article is relevant to their literature review without their reading the entire article. Abstracts of articles are cataloged in PsycINFO. They are typically 120 to 150 words long (strict APA style allows a maximum of 120 words—see Chapter 8 for more information about APA style) and include a sentence or two summarizing each of the major sections of the article. Thus, the abstract usually includes (a) the general topic of the study, (b) a brief description of the methodology, (c) the major results of the study, and (d) what was learned from the study.

Introduction. As the title implies, the **Introduction** section of the article introduces the topic, research question and other relevant information for the study. If an Introduction is written well, it should contain the following information:

- Introduction to the general topic of the study (e.g., the bystander effect)
- General problem that the study addresses (e.g., factors that affect the bystander effect)
- Discussion of relevant background studies that inform the researchers about what is known about the problem and how these studies are related to the present study the researchers are describing in their article (e.g., studies that were found in a literature review of factors that affect the bystander effect)
- Justification of the present study (i.e., what aspect of the research question the present study will answer that has not been determined from past studies)
- Brief description of how the current study will address the relevant aspect of the research question (may include variables that are being studied and a short outline of the method of the study)
- Predictions (i.e., hypotheses) that the researchers made about the outcome of the present study

Introduction: a section of an APA-style article that introduces the topic of the study, reviews relevant background studies, and presents predictions for the data

The Introduction should essentially make an argument about what the present study will contribute to knowledge in the area of psychology it addresses and why the researchers made the hypotheses they did. If you can identify the points of support for the authors' argument, then you probably have a reasonable understanding of the important information in the Introduction.

Method. The purpose of the **Method** section is to provide enough information about how a study was conducted so that others can evaluate and (if they wish) reproduce the study to see if the results replicate. There are four subsections of the Method: Participants (also called "subjects" in non-APA-style journals or if animal subjects are used), Design, Materials, and Procedure. The Participants subsection describes who the participants in the study were (How many were there? Were they college students? How many males and females participated? If they were animal subjects, what species were they?). How the participants for the study are obtained is also described (Did they volunteer from a participant pool? Were they recruited on a Web site? If they were animal subjects, were they bred by the researcher?). The Design subsection describes the design

Method: section of an APA-style article that describes the participants, design, stimuli, apparatus, and procedure used in the study of the study (What were the variables studied? How were they studied?). The Materials subsection describes the various materials and/or apparatus that were used in the study (If there were stimuli shown to the participants, what were the stimuli? If a survey was used, what kinds of items did it include?). The Procedure subsection provides a chronological description of what the participants did in the study (What were their tasks? What instructions were they given? How many trials did the participants complete?). Sometimes authors will combine some of these subsections (e.g., Design and Materials) as the information in these sections can overlap. In very short empirical articles (e.g., *Psychological Science* short reports), the sections will all be combined into one large Method section.

---------------- ✂ ----------------

Results: section of an APA-style article that presents a summary of the results and the statistical tests of the predictions

Results. The **Results** section provides a summary of the data (often in tables or figures) and information about the statistical tests that were performed to analyze the data. The findings are described in the text with statistical values given as support for the findings described. The specific types of values given depend on the type of tests the researchers conducted. Thus, if the tests themselves are not familiar to you, focus on the description the authors provide of the findings. Were there group differences? Was there a relationship between the behaviors measured? Look back at what the authors expected to find and see if you can match their findings to their predictions.

---------------- ✂ ----------------

Discussion: section of an APA-style article that compares the results of a study to the predictions and the results of previous studies

Discussion. The last section of the article is the **Discussion** section. The authors will go back to their predictions and discuss the findings that either support or do not support their predictions. If the findings support their predictions, the authors will indicate what they learned about the research question and perhaps where researchers should go next in this area. If the findings do not support their predictions, they should describe some possible explanations for why they did not support the predictions. A discussion of the results in the context of previous findings will also be included. Finally, a summary of what was learned from the study should be included in the Discussion section, including possible limitations of these conclusions based on strengths and weaknesses of the study conducted. Researchers may also suggest a direction for future research in that area.

Multiple Experiment/Study Articles. Many articles that are published include more than one study that addresses the same research question. In this case, the article will include one Introduction that provides the background and motivation for all the studies. It may also include short introductions to each study/experiment to describe the motivation for each study separately. The article will also include separate Method and Results sections for each study. The Results section for each study may also include a short Discussion section for that study, but a General Discussion section will conclude the article that ties all the studies together for the article.

Review Articles and Book Chapters

Most of the articles you will come across in a literature review will be empirical journal articles as described above. However, a smaller set of articles may be found that fit into the categories of review article or book chapter. The purpose of these articles is to organize and summarize research in a particular area of psychology to give researchers a review of the research to date. Thus, these sorts of articles can be very useful in a literature review, because they allow a researcher to find a lot of information about a topic in a single article. These reviews also provide a list of references that can be helpful in searching for empirical articles about specific studies that may be important for developing a prediction for the researcher's study. The main difference between review articles and book chapters is where they are published. Some psychological journals are devoted entirely to review articles (see Table 2.3 for some examples). There are also journals that reserve a small portion of space for review articles (e.g., *Psychonomic Bulletin & Review*). Review articles go through the same rigorous review process as that for empirical journal articles (described above). Book chapters are typically published in a book that is either entirely written by a set of authors (i.e., every chapter is written by the authors) or in an edited book where editors compile chapters on a similar topic from multiple authors. The review process for book chapters is variable and may not be as rigorous as that for journal articles.

USING THE LITERATURE TO MAKE HYPOTHESES

The primary goals of a literature review are to (a) determine what research has been done on a research question to avoid duplicating previous research and (b) review previous findings and theories to allow a **hypothesis** to be made about the outcome of a study. A hypothesis is the prediction for the findings of the study. For example, a researcher may hypothesize that a relationship exists between two measures of behavior. For a different type of study, a researcher may predict that one group of participants will have higher scores on average than another group. There are two primary types of information that researchers use to make hypotheses from a literature review: theories and previous results. These types of information result in **theory-driven hypotheses** and **data-driven hypotheses**. However, regardless of the types of hypotheses that are developed, hypotheses should be stated as specifically as possible in terms of how behaviors and conditions are related (Figure 2.4).

Hypothesis: prediction regarding the results of a research study

Theory-Driven Hypothesis: hypothesis for a study that is based on a theory about the behavior of interest

Data-Driven Hypothesis: hypothesis for a study that is based on the results of previous, related studies

---

Figure 2.4   Steps in the Research Process: Developing a Hypothesis

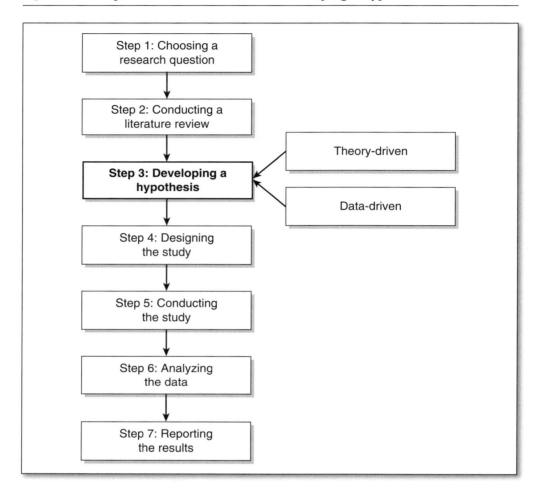

Theory-Driven Hypotheses

Theory-driven hypotheses are made from the predictions of a theory. These are typically made for studies designed to test a theory (i.e., look for data that support or falsify a theory—see testability in Chapter 1). For example, suppose a theory has been proposed that anxiety causes insomnia. A researcher conducting a study to test this theory may then predict that if two groups of participants are compared, one that is put in an anxiety-provoking situation and one that is put in a relaxing situation, the anxious group will report more problems sleeping than the relaxed group. In other words, they might predict that the anxious group, on average, will report fewer hours of sleep per night than the relaxed group.

Deductive Reasoning: using general information to make a specific prediction

This hypothesis would be consistent with the theory that anxiety causes insomnia and is therefore a theory-driven hypothesis. A theory-driven hypothesis involves **deductive reasoning** in that a researcher is taking a general statement about behavior (the theory) and making a specific prediction (the hypothesis) about the study from this general statement.

Another example of a theory-driven hypothesis can be seen in a recent study of short-term memory (memory for information that was encountered recently). Matsukura, Luck, and Vecera (2007) tested a theory that visual short-term memory is aided by cues presented after the visual information. To test the theory, they conducted a study where participants were presented with an array of colored squares to remember. After the array disappeared, an arrow was presented on half of the trials to cue the location of the square the participants needed to identify on the recognition test that followed. For the other half of the trials, arrows pointed to all locations, indicating that any of the squares could be tested in the recognition test that followed. Consistent with the theory to be tested, Matsukura et al. predicted that accuracy on the recognition test would be higher on the trials with the single arrow cue than on the trials with arrows indicating all locations in the array for the memory test. Thus, they made the hypothesis that memory would be better when studied items were followed by specific cues than when studied items were not followed by specific cues. Their results were consistent with their hypothesis: Participants were more accurate in identifying the squares they had seen when the location was cued than when it was not. Thus, their study supported the hypothesis that cues presented after studied visual information can improve short-term memory.

Suppose you were conducting a literature review on the development of mathematical concepts and you found that a researcher had suggested the theory that understanding of mathematical operations (e.g., addition, subtraction) is innate (something children are born with). Can you think of a way to make a theory-driven hypothesis for a study that tests this theory? Think about how the study would be conducted, and then use the theory to make a hypothesis about the outcome of the study (an example of how this could be done is presented at the end of the Test Yourself section).

Data-Driven Hypotheses

Another way in which researchers can make hypotheses about a study is by examining the specific findings of previous studies that are similar and generalizing the findings to their study. Hypotheses made in this way are considered data-driven hypotheses because they are made based on data from previous studies. This type of hypothesis involves **inductive reasoning** because the researcher is taking a specific result from another study and using it to make a more general prediction for the research question of interest. For example, suppose researchers are interested in causes of insomnia. In their literature review, they come

Inductive Reasoning: using specific information to make a more general prediction

across a study that found that people who report high levels of anxiety also report getting less sleep per night. From this study's results, they may conclude that anxiety is related to insomnia and make the hypothesis for their study that a relationship between level of anxiety and number of hours of sleep will be found.

A recent study by Schnall, Benton, and Harvey (2008) provides an example of a hypothesis based on data from previous studies. These researchers were interested in the connection between emotions and moral judgments. Previous studies had shown that when participants were induced to feel disgust (e.g., exposed to a bad smell), they more harshly judged an action as immoral than control participants who did not experience the disgusting situation (Schnall, Haidt, Clore, & Jordan, 2008). Schnall et al. hypothesized from these results that, if feelings of cleanliness were induced, the opposite effect should occur: Participants should judge actions less harshly. They conducted two experiments to test this data-driven hypothesis. In both experiments, one group of participants was primed with the concept of cleanliness, while another group was not primed with this concept. Participants then judged the actions of others in a set of moral dilemmas (e.g., keeping money in a found wallet). Results indicated that participants who experienced the concept of cleanliness in the study rated the actions in the dilemmas less harshly than participants who were not primed with the concept. Thus, Schnall et al. supported their data-driven hypothesis with the results of their study.

Descriptive and Causal Hypotheses

Regardless of where the information comes from, hypotheses will either attempt to describe behavior or make a causal prediction about behavior. This distinction maps on to the different types of research questions described above: descriptive and causal. Which type of research question is being asked will also dictate which type of hypothesis is made: a **descriptive hypothesis** or a **causal hypothesis**. If researchers are interested in the causes of behavior, they will state a prediction about a particular cause of behavior, typically as a difference in groups or conditions that differ based on the cause being studied. For example, if researchers have the research question "Does drinking caffeine on the day of an exam cause an improvement in test performance in college students?" then their hypothesis may be that a group of students who are asked to drink caffeine the day of an exam will have higher test performance than a group of students who are asked not to drink caffeine. If, however, the researchers are interested only in whether certain behaviors occur together or wish to document the occurrence of a particular behavior, they are likely to have a descriptive research question and a descriptive hypothesis. For example, if researchers have the research question "Do students who score low on an exam also have high levels of anxiety?" then their hypothesis may be descriptive, such that a relationship between these behaviors is predicted (i.e., when these behaviors are measured together, students with lower test performance will have higher anxiety scores). As you will see in the next chapter, descriptive and causal hypotheses are also tested with different types of research designs.

Descriptive Hypothesis: a prediction about the results of a study that describes the behavior or the relationship between behaviors

Causal Hypothesis: a prediction about the results of a study that includes the causes of a behavior

---

CHAPTER SUMMARY

Reconsider the questions from the beginning of the chapter:

- How do researchers develop a research question? Research questions come from many sources, including researchers' curiosity. However, research questions should be relevant to current knowledge in the field of study and answerable using scientific methods. A literature review will help researchers know if their research question fulfills these criteria.

- How do researchers conduct a literature review? A literature review is a thorough review of research done in an area of study. Searchable databases, such as PsycINFO, are useful for conducting a literature review.

- What are some useful resources for a literature review? Searchable databases that provide researchers access to empirical and review journal articles include PsycINFO, PubMed, and ERIC. Google Scholar may also be useful in locating these sources.

- What will you find in a literature review? A thorough literature review will produce journal articles that researchers can use to understand what types of research questions will add to knowledge in a field of study, what methods researchers are currently using to answer those research questions, and the theories or past results in an area that will help researchers develop hypotheses for their studies.

- What are the different types of research articles and how are they organized? Research articles are either empirical, review, or theoretical. Empirical articles describe a study conducted by the authors of the article. Review articles summarize results and methods from a particular area of study. Theoretical articles discuss new or revised theories of behavior in an area of study.

- How do we use a literature review to make hypotheses? Researchers can use theories described in journal articles to develop hypotheses, or researchers can use past studies' results to develop a hypothesis about the outcome of their study.

- What are the different types of hypotheses that a researcher can make? A researcher can make theory-driven and data-driven hypotheses.

THINKING ABOUT RESEARCH

A summary of a research study in psychology is given below. As you read the summary, think about the following questions:

1. What type of hypothesis (theory-driven or data-driven) did the authors make?

2. Do you think this is a causal or a descriptive hypothesis? How do you know?

3. Can you state the authors' research question? From the description of the study, where did this research question seem to come from?

4. If you were to conduct a literature review for their research question on PsycINFO, how would you proceed? Describe the steps you would take.

5. Write an Abstract for the study in your own words that adheres to APA guidelines.

6. If you were to read an APA-style article describing this study (which you could do by finding the reference below), in which section would you find information about the paragraphs the participants read during the study? In which section would the authors report what statistical test they conducted? In which section would they indicate if their hypothesis was supported?

Study Reference

Vohs, K. D., & Schooler, J. W. (2008). The value of believing in free will: Encouraging a belief in determinism increases cheating. *Psychological Science, 19,* 49–54.

Purpose of the Study. Vohs and Schooler (2008) were interested in the effects of a belief in determinism (i.e., believing that events in a person's life are not under their control) on moral behaviors. Their interest stemmed from recent findings from neuroscientists that our behaviors may be caused by factors out of our control (e.g., our genes, the functioning of our brain, our environments, etc.). They reported that a previous study (Mueller & Dweck, 1998) had found that children exert less effort in a task if they are told that their failure in a difficult task they had previously completed was due to their intelligence level rather than their level of effort. From this finding, Vohs and Schooler reasoned that a belief in determinism may negatively affect behavior. Thus, in their study, they predicted that exposure to a deterministic argument would result in more cheating behaviors than if this belief was not promoted.

Method of the Study. Thirty college students participated in the study. Participants were randomly assigned to read one of two paragraphs taken from the same book. One of the paragraphs suggested that scientists believe that free will is an illusion. The other paragraph discussed consciousness and did not mention the topic of free will. All participants were then asked to complete a set of math problems, presented one at a time on a computer screen. Participants were asked to complete each problem. They were also told that the computer program had an error such that the answers to some of the problems may appear with the problem and that they should try to solve the problems on their own (they could make the answer disappear by pressing the space bar when the problem appeared). The researchers measured the number of times the participants pressed the space bar as a measure of cheating behavior (more presses means less cheating).

Results of the Study. The results indicated that the group that read the determinism paragraph pressed the space bar less often (about 5 times during the study) than the control group (about 10 times during the study) that read the consciousness paragraph. Figure 2.5 displays the mean space bar presses for each group.

Figure 2.5   Mean Number of Space Bar Presses for Each Group

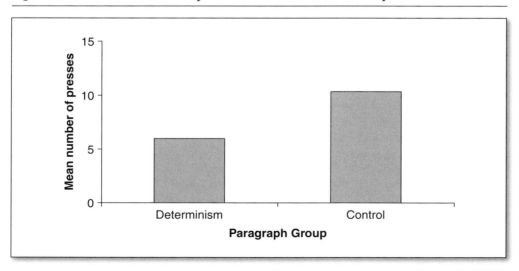

SOURCE: Results from Vohs and Schooler's (2008) study.

Conclusions of the Study. From their results, Vohs and Schooler (2008) concluded that a belief in determinism (i.e., free will is an illusion) causes more immoral behavior (e.g., cheating) to be exhibited by individuals.

COMMON PITFALLS AND HOW TO AVOID THEM

Problem: Using inappropriate search engines—students often use common search engines such as Google, Yahoo, and Wikipedia to search for information about psychological research, which is unreliable and incomplete.

Solution: Use databases such as PsycINFO, ERIC, and PubMed to search for primary source journal articles about psychological research.

Problem: Use of inappropriate sources—sometimes students include sources in literature reviews that are either not peer reviewed or are not the most relevant sources for the research question of interest.

Solution: Check the type of publication for sources (this information is provided by PsycINFO) to ensure that sources included in a literature review are the most appropriate for the research question.

Problem: Hypotheses stated too generally—students often state hypotheses for studies too generally without addressing specific aspects of the study.

Solution: Attempt to state hypotheses as specifically as possible, including variables of the study when appropriate (see Chapter 4 for more information on variables)

Problem: Focus on full text articles—oftentimes students will focus a literature review too heavily on articles with full text access online, missing important studies for their topic.

Solution: Be sure to conduct a thorough literature review, even if that means walking over to the library to pick up a hard copy of an article that does not have full text available online.

Problem: Only reading the Abstract—because the Abstract contains a summary of the article, students sometimes believe that they can fully understand the article by just reading the Abstract.

Solution: Abstracts are written to provide a short summary of the article and may not fully represent the method or results of a study. Thus, it is important to read through the entire article when conducting a literature review. In addition, you should never cite a source that you have not fully read.

TEST YOURSELF

1. For the information listed below, indicate in which section(s) of a journal article it should be found.

   (a) Average scores for different groups in a study

   (b) Number of participants in the study

   (c) Researchers' hypotheses

   (d) Comparison of results of present study with results of previous studies

   (e) Summary of the instructions given to the participants

2. Describe how theory-driven and data-driven hypotheses are made.

3. Explain why the research question below is not an appropriate research question for psychological research:

   Does every human being have a soul?

4. What is a "peer-reviewed journal article," and how does it differ from an article you might find in a popular magazine?

5. What is a literature review, and why is it an important part of the research process?

6. Explain the differences between a database such as PsycINFO and a search engine such as Google.

Answers: 1a. Results, 1b. Method—Participants, 1c. Introduction and Discussion, 1d. Discussion, 1e. Method—Procedure. 2. Theory-driven hypotheses are made using predictions of a theory for a research study. Data-driven hypotheses are made by generalizing results from past studies to the results of a research study. 3. This is an inappropriate research question for psychological studies because it would be difficult to observe behaviors to answer this question. In other words, it is a question that cannot be answered by scientific methods, because there are no clear behaviors that are seen as indicative of a soul. 4. A "peer-reviewed journal article" is typically an article written to describe a research study to inform other researchers what has previously been found in an area of psychology. "Peer reviewed" means that the article has been reviewed by experts in the area before publication to improve the article and make a recommendation about publication. An article in a popular magazine would likely provide a short summary of the study and may not accurately reflect the original article. Thus, magazine articles are considered secondary (rather than primary) sources. 5. A literature review is a review of previous research in an area to allow a researcher to conduct research that does not replicate what has previously been done and to allow researchers to make accurate predictions about a study's outcome. 6. PsycINFO will yield peer-reviewed articles about research. Google will yield other types of information (such as popular magazine articles) that are considered secondary sources that may not be reliable.

Example of Theory-Driven Hypotheses for Innateness of Mathematical Operations (From the Section "Theory-Driven Hypotheses"): To determine that something is innate, you would need to test infants who are very young and have not had enough experience with objects to develop understanding of mathematical operations such as addition and subtraction. You could then test these infants in a study, where you show them objects of a set number that they are habituated to (no longer show interest in), occlude the objects with a screen, and then either add an object or remove an object behind the screen so that the infant can see the object being added or subtracted. You then remove the screen and show them the objects, but show them an incorrect number of objects based on the operation. If the infants show interest (indicating something that was not expected by the infants) in what they are shown, this can be seen as evidence that the infants understand what they should have seen after the operation was performed. Thus, the theory-driven hypothesis for this study is that infants will look longer when the number of objects does not match the operation than when the number of objects does match the operation.

A study like this was performed by Wynn (1992), where her findings indicated that infants as young as 5 months looked longer when the number of objects did not match the operation than when the number of objects shown was correct based on the operation. Wynn argued that these results support the theory that understanding of addition and subtraction operations is innate.

CHAPTER 3

How Psychologists Use the Scientific Method

Observation Techniques and Research Designs

CONSIDER THE FOLLOWING QUESTIONS AS YOU READ CHAPTER **3**

- How do psychologists observe behavior?
- What are some common techniques for observing and recording behavior in different situations?
- How do psychologists use observations to learn about behavior?
- What questions about behavior do the different research methods allow psychologists to answer?
- Which research method is best when asking about the cause of behavior?

$\mathbf{I}$magine that you work in a busy corporate office. One day your boss comes to you for advice. It was found that productivity in the office tends to decline later in the afternoon and he or she wants to find a way to increase productivity during this time period. Your boss's suggestion is that having a cappuccino machine in the office lunchroom may cause workers to drink more coffee after lunch, giving them more energy to be more productive in the afternoon. You have been asked to use your knowledge of research methods to find out if the suggestion is a good one. How would you conduct a study to provide the advice your boss is looking for?

In this chapter, we discuss the methods psychologists use to learn about behavior. This chapter will provide an overview of some of the main observation methods and research designs used in psychological research to illustrate how psychologists apply the scientific methods described in Chapter 1 to the study of behavior. Figure 3.1 illustrates the steps involved in the research process while designing the study. The choice of observation technique and research design is made by the researcher. This choice depends on the type of behavior that is of interest and what kinds of questions one wants to answer about the behavior. **External** and **internal validities** also play a role in these choices. External validity is the degree to which the behavior observed in the study is realistic, would occur naturally, and can be generalized

37

External Validity: the degree to which the results of a study apply to individuals and realistic behaviors outside the study

Internal Validity: the degree to which a study provides causal information about behavior

beyond the boundaries of the study to other individuals and situations. How much external validity a study has can be important because the goal of research is to gain knowledge about behavior that applies to a large group of individuals in their everyday lives, not just the individuals who participated in the study with the restrictions on the situation the study included. In other words, the conclusions need to generalize beyond the study itself. Some of the observation techniques and research designs that psychologists use tend to allow for higher external validity than others. However, in many cases, the higher the external validity in a study, the lower the internal validity.

Figure 3.1   Steps in the Research Process: Designing the Study

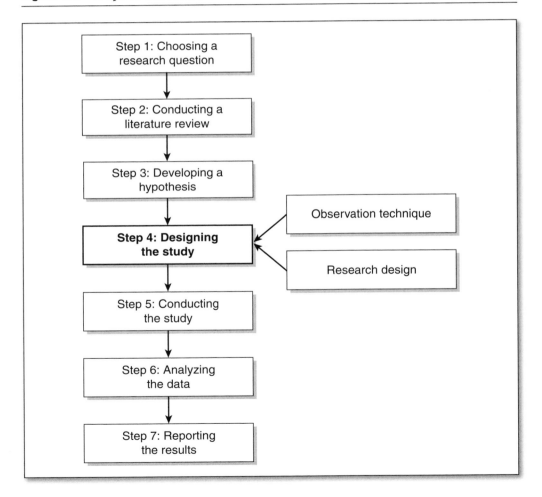

Internal validity is the degree to which a study provides a good test of a causal hypothesis, where alternative explanations of the data can be ruled out. A study with high internal validity provides causal information about behavior. To increase the internal validity of a study, a researcher controls for extraneous factors that can affect the observations. With more control over the factors in a study, internal validity will increase, but behavior may become more artificial and lower the external validity of that study. As we discuss the different types of studies that can be conducted by psychologists, you will see that internal and external validities are important concepts in research.

Another important issue in observing behavior is making sure that the observations are *reliable*. For some observation techniques, this means making sure observers are categorizing behaviors the same way. For other techniques, this means making sure that different items on a survey or questionnaire designed to measure a specific behavior all provoke similar responses from the research participants. In other words, reliability in a survey means that the participants' responses are similar from item to item or from one time they complete

Reliability: the degree to which the results of a study can be replicated under similar conditions

the survey to the next. Thus, **reliability** is important to consider when you design a study and choose an observation technique, but how you increase reliability will depend on the observation technique you are using.

OBSERVATION TECHNIQUES

How do psychologists observe behavior? When researchers are planning to observe a behavior, they must first decide how they are going to define that behavior. This is the **operational definition** of the behavior. An operational definition of an abstract concept (depression, memory ability, etc.) allows the researcher to define it for the purpose of measurement. Thus, an operational definition is a definition of an abstract concept that makes it concrete for the purpose of the research study. If "social behavior" is of interest, the researcher may define this as "the number of people who spend time in groups," "the number of times an individual approaches another individual to interact with him or her," or "the score on a questionnaire that asks about social behaviors." There are clearly many ways to define a particular behavior for

Operational Definition: the definition of an abstract concept used by a researcher to measure or manipulate the concept in a research study

observation. Researchers choose an operational definition for behavior that they expect will provide the best (i.e., most valid) method of learning about the behavior they are interested in. In other words, they define the concept so that it can be measured by a specific behavior (or set of behaviors). The techniques described in the following sections are different ways in which psychologists have observed behavior. As you will see, the choice of technique is linked to the operational definition the researcher is using. See Table 3.1 for a comparison of these techniques.

TABLE 3.1 Comparing Observation Techniques		
Technique	**Definition**	**Realism**
Naturalistic observation	Observing individuals' behavior in their normal environments	High Decreases if observers fail to be unobtrusive
Surveys/questionnaires	Individuals respond to items in written form or on the Internet	Moderate Decreases with self-monitoring, certain question wording, and responses controlled by scale used
Systematic observation	Collection of systematic behaviors in controlled tasks	Low Due to control of task situation
Archival data	Using available records to collect observations	Varies with type of record

Naturalistic Observation

A recent popular show on the Animal Planet cable network called *Meerkat Manor* follows packs of meerkats as they interact with each other, with other packs of meerkats, and with the environment they live in. The show is narrated to make it more entertaining, but the behaviors displayed on the show are observed as the animals exhibit them naturally in their normal environment. In other words, the researchers for the show use **naturalistic observation** to learn about meerkat behaviors. Naturalistic observation is used when a researcher wants to learn about behavior that naturally occurs for an individual without influencing the behavior. The goal of naturalistic observation is to be unobtrusive so that the researcher does not affect the observed individuals' behavior. Naturalistic observation is often used by researchers interested in observing the behavior of animals in their natural environment or children who are in specific environments (both natural and contrived).

_____ ⚬ _____

Naturalistic Observation: a data collection technique involving noninvasive observation of individuals in their natural environments

To understand behaviors observed with naturalistic observation, a researcher must develop a coding scheme to categorize the behaviors the participants exhibit. This allows the researcher to quantify (i.e., count) and summarize the behaviors for the group of individuals observed. The coding scheme will depend on the operational definition of the behavior the researcher is using. In other words, the behaviors the researcher has indicated are part of the operational definition become categories of behaviors in the coding scheme. For example, if researchers are studying helping behaviors with naturalistic observations, they may define helping behavior as approaching someone who appears to need help (e.g., has dropped something, needs help opening a door, has a broken-down car, etc.) and offering help or acting to help the person. Thus, observers may sit on a university quad and count behaviors they observe that fit into categories such as "asking someone if they need help," "helping someone pick something up," "giving someone directions when asked." This allows researchers to quantify the different behaviors they see. The researchers can then describe helping behaviors according to their coding scheme to indicate the frequency of helping behaviors overall for this situation and group of individuals and which types of behaviors occur more often than others.

The primary advantage in using naturalistic observation to study behavior is that the behavior is likely to be more realistic than with some of the other techniques. This can increase the external validity of a study. However, this technique has its disadvantages. It can sometimes be difficult to be unobtrusive. The presence of an observer can easily change the behavior of the individuals being observed. This is an issue that has come up for the *Meerkat Manor* show. Camera crews follow the meerkats closely all the time to record their behaviors for the show, and their presence may have affected the behaviors they observe. Thus, researchers using this technique must take great care to ensure that they are not influencing the behavior they are observing simply by being present in an individual's environment. Another drawback to naturalistic observation is that it can be very time-consuming. The observers must wait for the behavior they are interested in to be exhibited by the participants. Thus, this technique can be more time intensive and consume more resources than other observation techniques. A third disadvantage is that if there are multiple observers (observing the same or different individuals), they must be trained and checked to ensure that they are collecting their observations in the same way. They must be coding the same behavior the same way. This is known as **interrater reliability** (how similarly the observers are coding the data). In the helping behaviors study described above, it is likely that more than one person would observe on the quad (either at the same time or at different times) to allow enough helping behaviors to occur. If the observers code the behaviors differently (e.g., one observer counts bending over to help as "helping someone pick something up," while another observer only counts this behavior if someone actually picks up something someone dropped), the internal validity of the study will decrease because the observers will have different operational definitions of the behaviors.

Interrater Reliability: a measure of the degree to which different observers rate behaviors in similar ways

Chiang (2008) provides a recent example of a study that used naturalistic observations. In this study, 32 children with autism were observed to investigate aspects of their spontaneous communication. The children were videotaped in their natural environments (classrooms at their school), while they completed normal, everyday activities (lunch, free time, academic activities, etc.). In the article reporting the study (published in the journal *Autism*), Chiang described the coding schemes developed to summarize and understand the communication behaviors that were seen in the tapes viewed by the observers (speech or writing, vocalizations that were not identified as words, eye contact, common gestures such as hugging, waving, or nodding, etc.). The interrater reliability (above 80%) is also reported to provide evidence that the observers were coding the data in a similar manner. Chiang concluded that children with autism exhibit a range of communicative behaviors across the different settings and suggested a model for future studies of spontaneous communication in autistic individuals. The issue of intrusiveness can be considered for this study. How much did the presence of the video camera affect the participants' behavior? Were participants aware of the video camera? If so, were they more self-conscious or uncomfortable about their behavior because of its presence? The issue of obtrusiveness should be considered whenever naturalistic observations are used in a study.

Surveys/Questionnaires

The other data collection techniques we will discuss are more obtrusive than the naturalistic observation technique because they involve some type of interaction with the research participants. One of these techniques commonly used in psychological research is asking individuals about specific behaviors in a survey. (Although the terms *survey* and *questionnaire* are sometimes used in different contexts in research, in this text I will use these terms interchangeably.) **Survey research** is often conducted to measure mood, attitudes about a topic, or frequency of certain behaviors through self-reports from the participants. Typically, surveys contain a number of questions that ask the research participant to rate the presence or frequency of his or her own thoughts or behaviors. When surveys are used, participants are often asked to use a response scale (e.g., 1 to 5 or 1 to

Survey Research: a research study that uses the survey observational technique to measure behavior

Closed-Ended Response Scale: participants respond to survey questions according to the response options provided by the researcher

7) or response category (e.g., often, sometimes, not very often, never) that matches how they feel about a behavior or how likely they are to exhibit the behavior. This means that the participants are limited in the types of responses they can make to the survey items. In other words, the survey uses a **closed-ended response scale** because only certain responses are valid responses to the items. The scale in Table 3.2 was designed to assess how likely one is to discuss one's emotions and disclose personal problems to others. Scores on this scale have been shown to be related to higher self-esteem and general satisfaction with one's life (Kahn & Hessling, 2001). The Distress Disclosure Index provides an example of a closed-ended response scale, as a 5-point scale is given for responses.

TABLE 3.2 Distress Disclosure Index

1. When I feel upset, I usually confide in my friends.	1 Strongly disagree	2	3	4	5 Strongly agree
2. I prefer not to talk about my problems.	1 Strongly disagree	2	3	4	5 Strongly agree
3. When something unpleasant happens to me, I often look for someone to talk to.	1 Strongly disagree	2	3	4	5 Strongly agree
4. I typically don't discuss things that upset me.	1 Strongly disagree	2	3	4	5 Strongly agree

5. When I feel depressed or sad, I tend to keep those feelings to myself.	1 Strongly disagree	2	3	4	5 Strongly agree
6. I try to find people to talk with about my problems.	1 Strongly disagree	2	3	4	5 Strongly agree
7. When I am in a bad mood, I talk about it with my friends.	1 Strongly disagree	2	3	4	5 Strongly agree
8. If I have a bad day, the last thing I want to do is talk about it.	1 Strongly disagree	2	3	4	5 Strongly agree
9. I rarely look for people to talk with when I am having a problem.	1 Strongly disagree	2	3	4	5 Strongly agree
10. When I am distressed, I don't tell anyone.	1 Strongly disagree	2	3	4	5 Strongly agree
11. I usually seek out someone to talk to when I am in a bad mood.	1 Strongly disagree	2	3	4	5 Strongly agree
12. I am willing to tell others my distressing thoughts.	1 Strongly disagree	2	3	4	5 Strongly agree

SOURCE: Kahn and Hessling (2001).

Another way to design a survey is to ask participants to respond to questions on an **open-ended response scale**. In other words, they can respond in whatever way they wish to the questions you asked them. Analyzing the data from an open-ended response scale would also require the development of a coding scheme, because the responses are **qualitative** rather than **quantitative**. Such coding schemes have been developed by researchers

Open-Ended Response Scale: participants respond to survey questions in any manner they feel is appropriate for the question

Qualitative Data: nonnumerical participant responses

Quantitative Data: numerical data

for some validated surveys used frequently in certain types of research. Using a closed-ended response scale allows the researcher to collect quantitative responses (i.e., numerical responses), so no coding scheme is needed for closed-ended scales. Surveys are often administered using pencil and paper or (as is becoming more frequent) over the Internet via Web site.

Researchers are often interested in testing the validity and reliability of the surveys and questionnaires they use. Checking the validity of a survey means making sure that the questions asked are really about the behavior the researcher is interested in. If a survey is designed to measure someone's level of anxiety, the questions have to be written to ask about behaviors that are related to anxiety, or the survey would not be measuring what it was designed to measure. In other words, does the survey actually measure the construct it was designed to measure? Checking the reliability of a survey means making sure that the responses you get from an individual at one point in time are similar to the responses you get from the same individual at another point in time. If an individual's responses change drastically from time to time, even though the attitude or behavior being measured by the survey does not change, you will not get an accurate measure of that attitude or behavior. A more detailed discussion of the validity and reliability of surveys is presented in Chapter 9.

Using a validated survey typically gives a researcher observations of behavior that are a step ahead of the other techniques discussed because the validity and reliability of a survey will already have been tested and the survey revised (if necessary) to maximize its accuracy. The primary disadvantage of using surveys to observe behavior is that the observations are considered self-reports, which means that they may not be accurate representations of a person's behavior. Individuals do not always view their behavior accurately and may report who they think they are on a survey and not who they actually are. Participants may also want to portray themselves more positively to the researcher and intentionally respond in a way that achieves that goal (i.e., they self-monitor). This is called *social desirability*, and it can bias the results of a survey or questionnaire. Thus, researchers must be careful in interpreting behaviors observed with this technique, as they may not be accurate representations of individuals' behaviors.

The Beck Depression Inventory-II (BDI-II; Beck, Steer, & Brown, 1996) and Beck Anxiety Inventory (BAI; Beck & Steer, 1993) are two commonly used surveys in psychological research on mood. These surveys contain items that ask individuals about the intensity of certain feelings and the intensity of specific behaviors related to depression and anxiety, respectively. For example, the BDI-II contains 21 items and asks respondents about feelings of sadness, being punished, and lack of interest in sex and behaviors such as difficulty in sleeping and changes in eating habits. Many studies have used the BDI-II to measure depression or the BAI to measure anxiety, and the reliability and validity have been frequently tested.

Interviews. Surveys can also be administered as **interviews** such that individuals respond to questions orally. Interviews can be done face-to-face, over the phone, or in focus groups. Like naturalistic observations, observing behaviors with interview data requires the researcher to develop a coding scheme to understand the behaviors described or exhibited in the interview. An advantage of interviews is that you can ask about a specific behavior instead of waiting for the individual to exhibit the behavior spontaneously (as in naturalistic observations). Another advantage is that if the interview is structured to allow flexibility, different questions can be asked depending on the response that is given. For example, if a participant responds that a question particularly applies to him or her, the interviewer can follow up that response with additional questions on the topic tailored to the type of response made.

Interviews: a data collection technique that involves direct questioning of individuals about their behaviors and attitudes

Focus groups are becoming a popular way to conduct interviews to learn about individuals' attitudes toward a societal issue, political candidate, or consumer product. Interviewing people in groups uses fewer resources and can sometimes elicit responses from individuals who may be more reluctant to voice an opinion when they are asked on their own. When reluctant individuals hear that others have an opinion similar to their own, they may be more likely to voice their opinion. However, this can also be a limitation to the use of interviews: If they are conducted in groups, individuals may go along with the group rather than voice an opinion that differs from others (Ashe, 1955). In other words, conformity of responses occurs. Interviewees may also self-monitor during interviews, meaning that they can respond according to how they wish to appear to others instead of how they actually are (i.e., the social desirability bias can occur). Another drawback to the use of interviews is that the way a question is asked can affect the response that is given. Thus, great care must be taken in writing questions for interviews.

A recent study by Creasey and Ladd (2005) used interviews of individuals to investigate the relationship between parental attachment and conflict resolution behaviors in current romantic relationships. To understand attachment style to their parents, research participants were interviewed about their relationships with their parents. Responses were then coded to categorize individuals according to different types of attachments that children have with their parents. Creasey and Ladd reported that the success of conflict resolution strategies with a romantic partner depended on the type of attachment individuals had with their parents.

Systematic Observation

Systematic observations are typically used when the researchers want to exert the highest amount of control over behavior. In other words, the observations are obtrusive and can often affect the behavior being studied. Thus, systematic observation is often used to study behaviors that are least likely to be affected by the process of measuring them. Examples of these behaviors are often cognitive or biological in nature (e.g., memory accuracy, problem-solving speed, firing of a neuron, activity in a particular brain area). However, systematic observation can be used to study behaviors in other areas of psychology as well. A recently developed method for studying automatic social attitudes called the Implicit Association Test, or IAT (Greenwald, McGhee, & Schwartz, 1998) uses systematic observation of reaction times of participant responses to sets of word or picture stimuli to measure one's unconscious prejudicial attitudes. In the IAT, the speed with which people respond to items after certain associations have been formed is recorded to determine if some judgments take longer than others. The IAT works by associating a specific response to different dimensions of a concept (e.g., press the right key when you see a female name and the left key when you see a male name; press the right key when you see items a teacher might use and the left key when you see items a firefighter might use). The concepts are then combined (e.g., press the right key when you see a female name or an item used by a firefighter and the left key when you see a male name or an item used by a

Systematic Observation: data collection technique where control is exerted over the conditions under which the behavior is observed teacher). The assumption is that longer responses with one combination of concepts (e.g., female names and firefighter items both requiring a right-key response) than the other combination (e.g., female names and teacher items both requiring a right-key press) may reveal unconscious social biases people may have that they are either unaware of or consciously suppress when asked explicit questions about their beliefs (e.g., Is it appropriate for a woman to become a firefighter?). Figure 3.2 illustrates the IAT procedure. You can also try out the IAT procedure for yourself at http://implicit.harvard.edu.

Figure 3.2   Simplified IAT Procedure

	Gender-Key Association	Occupation-Key Association	Common Associations Provide Baseline Condition	Test of Biased Association— Slower Responses Than Baseline Indicate Bias
Response-Dimension Pairing	Male (left key) Female (right key)	Teacher (left key) Firefighter (right key)	Male/firefighter (left key) Female/teacher (right key)	Male/teacher (left key) Female/firefighter (right key)
Stimuli (With Correct Response)	John (left) Mary (right) Angela (right) Steve (left)	Ladder (right) Books (left) Hose (right) Pencil (left)	Henry (left) Desk (right) Truck (left) Heather (right)	Rick (left) Book (left) Axe (right) Judy (right)

SOURCE: Greenwald, McGhee, and Schwartz (1998).

NOTES:

1. Conditions with keys (right, left) reversed (e.g., male with right key, female with left key) are also used.

2. Longer response times for bias test trials indicate unconscious social biases.

Because a high degree of control can be exerted on the measurements of behaviors observed using systematic observations, they typically add to the internal validity of a study. The situation in which the behaviors are measured is typically controlled to eliminate influences on the behaviors that are not the focus of the study. Thus, systematic observations are often collected in a laboratory setting, where distractions of normal life are minimized and tasks are presented and completed on a computer to maximize accuracy. The drawback of this level of control is that the behaviors being studied may be artificial. In other words, external validity can be lower for systematic observations than other data collection methods, though these observations may have better internal validity.

Using Archival Data

Sometimes when researchers have questions about behavior, they find that those behaviors they are interested in have already been observed. In other words, the data they wish to analyze to answer their research question already exist. Someone else has collected them. For example, if researchers are interested in health-related behaviors, they may wish to use existing hospital records as their observations. An example of this type of study was done in Pueblo, Colorado, a few years ago (Bartecchi et al., 2006). Pueblo is a small town with two hospitals at which residents of the town and surrounding area receive medical care. After the town passed a smoking ban, researchers decided to look at hospital records to compare the number of hospitalizations for heart attacks during the year and a half before the smoking ban began (as a way to determine the number of heart-related illnesses that occurred when people were allowed to smoke in public places) with the number of hospitalizations for heart attacks that occurred during the year and a half after the smoking ban started. They found that the number of hospitalizations for heart attacks decreased significantly during the year and a half after the smoking ban and concluded that the decrease in public smoking was related to this decrease (by comparing heart attack hospitalization rate change for comparable areas without a smoking ban over the same period of time). The use of hospital records in this study is an example of how researchers use **archival data** as an observation technique.

Many archival data sets are collected by agencies on a periodic basis. A quick Web search will show summary results for many of these observations. For example, one can find data related to presidential approval ratings, consumer confidence, consumer spending, and opinion polls. Figure 3.3 shows approval ratings (percentage of people who approve of the

Figure 3.3 Approval Ratings for President George W. Bush

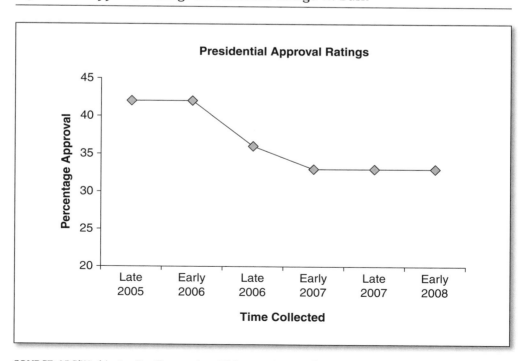

SOURCE: ABC/Washington Post Data retrieved February 17, 2008, from www.pollingreport.com/BushJob.htm.

—————————— ❦ ——————————

Archival Data: a data collection technique that involves analysis of preexisting data

job the president is doing) for President Bush over a 2-year period near the end of his presidency. Currently, a Web search will yield periodic ratings for President Obama. Presidential approval ratings are collected and published frequently each year by many news agencies. Many of these data sets are collected by governmental agencies and are available to researchers who wish to analyze the data on their own. Corporations may also make archival data sets available to researchers who wish to study such workplace behaviors as work productivity and absenteeism.

Archival data offer researchers a means of collecting data quickly. Few resources are needed, as the data are collected by another agency or institution. However, archival data offer the researcher no control over the circumstances under which the data are collected, the sampling technique used, or the measures used to observe behavior. Researchers using archival data also have no control over how the data are coded, which can make comparisons difficult across groups or areas if data are coded differently by different organizations.

—————————— ❦ ——————————

Content Analysis: an archival data collection technique that involves analysis of the content of an individual's spoken or written record

Content Analysis. **Content analysis** is a specific type of archival data observation technique that involves analysis of what someone has said (as in a speech or interview) or written (as in a book or article). This may involve analyzing the transcript of a speech someone gave, a written document, or a recorded statement. In content analysis, a researcher is analyzing a record of what someone has said or written in the past; thus, no interaction takes place between the research participant and the researcher. A coding scheme must be developed by the researcher to determine which behaviors will be considered in the analysis. This type of analysis can be resource intensive and time-consuming. Table 3.3 contains some examples of behaviors that psychologists might want to observe. For each behavior, consider how

---

TABLE 3.3   Thinking About Observations

For each behavior listed below, consider how you might observe the behavior using (a) naturalistic observation, (b) surveys and questionnaires, or (c) systematic observation. Be sure to operationally define the behavior before you describe how the observations would be collected. Also consider the limitations of each observation method as you choose one for each behavior.

1   How do humans (or animals) solve a problem?
2   How do people react to bad news?
3   What types of people are most likely to disclose personal problems to others?
4   How do groups of children organize themselves to complete a task?
5   What behaviors characterize people with attention deficit disorder (ADD)?
6   What types of brain activity result when one consumes caffeine?

psychologists might use each of the observation techniques described in this chapter to measure the behavior.

TYPES OF RESEARCH DESIGNS

Research design types differ based on the type of question the researcher wants to answer. In addition, **variables** (i.e., a behavior, situation, or characteristic that can differ from individual to individual) are used in different ways in each design type. Variables can be numeric and vary continuously from person to person or can be categorical so as to group individuals into different categories that can be compared. The behavior of interest in a study is typically one variable (or more) that is of primary interest in a research study. Observations in a study constitute what is called a **dependent** or **response variable**.

Dependent variables are measured in every research study. For some designs, only a single dependent variable is measured, and the behavior is examined descriptively or causally (if the researcher is interested in a causal relationship and uses an experiment to study this relationship). Other designs examine relationships between multiple dependent variables. Thus, how a dependent variable is measured depends on the observation technique, and what is learned about a dependent variable depends on the type of research design used.

> **Variable:** an attribute that can vary across individuals
>
> **Dependent/Response Variable:** a variable that is measured or observed from an individual

Each of the observation techniques described earlier can be used in any of the major research designs; however, practically speaking, some types of observations are much more common in some designs than in others. Examples of the most common observation techniques used in each design will be described as each one is discussed. In addition, some of the more common designs are discussed in more detail in Part II of this book. Note also that you may see the term *research design* applied to many aspects of a design. Here the term applies to the major categories of research designs that are used by psychologists to answer different types of research questions. What follows is a description of the major research designs used in psychological research with some examples of these designs.

Case Studies

In 1970, a woman walked into a welfare office in Southern California with her daughter Genie. After the woman was interviewed, it became clear that although Genie appeared to be about 6 or 7 years old, she was in fact 13 years old and had no language abilities. Her parents had kept her locked in her bedroom every day since she was very young. Genie did not attend school and had not been exposed to enough language from her family to learn how to speak. After Genie's situation was discovered, psychologists became interested in her case and hoped to learn from her about the development of language and whether it can occur at such a late age in a child (Fromkin, Krashe, Curtiss, Rigler, & Rigler, 1974). Genie became the subject of intensive study by a number of individuals. From the case study of Genie, evidence was gained for a critical period of language development, because Genie was raised with little language interaction with others and had difficulty learning language after she was rescued.

The goal of a **case study** is to gain insight into and understanding of a single individual's (or just a couple of individuals') behavior. Case studies can also be conducted for a group of individuals, such as an agency or institution. Typically, a case study will involve intensive observation of an individual's naturalistic behavior or set of behaviors. Thus, researchers often use naturalistic observations, interviews, or archival data (especially in the case of a famous individual) to learn about the individual's behavior, although some case studies have also included systematic observations and surveys to learn about an individual. Case studies are often exploratory studies, such that a researcher is learning about a behavior when little is known about it (e.g., unusual symptoms of a new disorder).

> **Case Study:** a research design that involves intensive study of particular individuals and their behaviors

Some of the more well-known case studies conducted by psychologists have been with individuals who suffered a brain injury. Researchers study such individuals after their brain injury both while they are still alive (if possible) and after their death. Behaviors these individuals exhibit are then connected to the brain injury they suffered, which can be explored more extensively after their death. Physiological psychologists have gained a lot of important knowledge about brain functions through case studies of these individuals. A famous case is that of H. M. (typically these patients are identified by initials only or a pseudonym to keep the findings confidential for these individuals). H. M. suffered damage to a brain area known as the hippocampus during a surgery in 1953 that was done to help reduce his epileptic seizures (Hilts, 1996). As a result of the surgery, H. M. could no longer remember new experiences for longer than a few minutes. Through extensive study of H. M., psychologists have learned that the hippocampus is an important structure for encoding or retrieving memories of events because H. M. lost the ability to retrieve memories of things that happened after his surgery (even though he still had access to memories of events he experienced before his surgery). From case studies of H. M. came a new set of questions about the hippocampus and exactly what function it serves in memory. In addition, researchers found that H. M. could improve on tasks over time, indicating that certain types of new memories were still available to him. For example, a recent study (Bohbot & Corkin, 2007) found that his ability to learn a spatial memory task was quite good, despite having severe amnesia (his memory for things he experienced lasts only a few minutes). Case studies of H.M. are still conducted today. Although he died in 2008, H. M.'s brain will continue to be studied to further our understanding of the importance of specific brain areas in cognitive functioning.

Other case studies have used archival data or content analysis of a document to better understand an individual's behavior. For example, Lester (2006) recently examined the diaries of a man who committed suicide in an attempt to identify specific events in his life that may be connected to his choice to kill himself. Abramson (1984) conducted a case study of the sexual behaviors of a woman who called herself "Sarah" after receiving a letter from her. "Sarah" had been abused (physically and sexually) as a child and was recovering from those traumas at the time she wrote to Abramson, a psychologist at the University of California, Los Angeles. Abramson then conducted interviews with "Sarah" to better understand how individuals recover from such traumatic experiences. Abramson learned a good deal about psychological resilience and recovery in an individual despite traumatic childhood events.

Case studies can even be done after a person has died. When Albert Einstein died in 1955, portions of his brain were preserved to allow it to be studied. Since then scientists have examined these brain sections to look for ways in which Einstein's brain may differ from brains of other people. One difference that has been found is that Einstein's brain contains many more neuron cells in a section of his brain's cortex than the brains of control participants that were used as a comparison (Anderson & Harvey, 1996). In addition, a section of Einstein's brain appears to have been improperly formed, allowing connections between areas of the brain that are not connected in other people's brains (Witelson, Kigar, & Harvey, 1999). These differences may account for the intellectual abilities Einstein possessed, but simply examining Einstein's brain will not allow researchers to make such strong conclusions. Instead, these studies allow researchers to start hypothesizing about which brain areas or characteristics may be important for advanced intellectual abilities, and these hypotheses can then be tested in further studies (see Figure 3.4).

Figure 3.4   Case Studies Can Provide a Unique View of an Individual

SOURCE: Copyright by S. Harris, www.sciencecartoonsplus.com/galpsych2.htm.

Case studies typically focus on rare or unusual cases to gain some information about a behavior that is not exhibited by all individuals. This means that the behaviors examined in case studies often cannot be generalized to all individuals. Because of the reduced generality of the behaviors, case studies do not allow for strong tests of the cause of the behavior (experiments are best for that—as explained in a later section), and researchers must be careful about drawing conclusions about the causes of the behaviors they are studying. However, case studies can give researchers a "starting place" for investigations of a behavior or a set of behaviors. Thus, they serve an important purpose in psychological research, drawing attention to new research questions that can be further explored with additional studies.

Correlational Studies

Correlational Study: a type of research design that examines the relationships between multiple dependent variables, without manipulating any of the variables

Predictor Variable: the dependent variable in a correlational study that is used to predict the score on another variable

Outcome Variable: the dependent variable in a correlational study that is being predicted by the predictor variable

Is insomnia related to depression? Do students who watch more TV have lower grade point averages (GPAs)? Do children who play violent video games behave more violently? Each of these questions can be explored in a **correlational study** (correlation means relationship). Correlational studies allow a researcher to examine relationships between variables and predict values for one variable from values on the other variable(s) if a relationship is found. If a predictive relationship is examined, the variable that is used to make the prediction is called the **predictor variable**, and the variable that is being predicted is called the **outcome variable**. Thus, the goal of a correlational study is to determine if different behaviors are connected and occur together. This type of study, however, still does not allow us to determine if one variable *causes* another to occur (again, only well-designed experiments allow researchers to test causal relationships). All we can learn from a correlational study is if two variables covary (i.e., change together—up, down, or in opposite directions from each other). Then researchers may be able to predict one variable from another.

Positive Relationship: a relationship between variables characterized by coupled increases in the two variables

Negative Relationship: a relationship between variables characterized by an increase in one variable that occurs with a decrease in the other variable

Scatterplot: a graph showing the relationship between two dependent variables for a group of individuals

If a relationship is found in a correlational study between two variables, it can take one of two forms: a **positive relationship** or a **negative relationship**. A positive relationship means that the values on the variables change in the same direction (up and down) at the same time. A negative relationship indicates that as values on one variable increase, the values on the other variable decrease. Figure 3.5 illustrates each type of relationship that might exist between GPA and the number of hours an individual watches TV per week. The graphs in Figure 3.5 are called **scatterplots**.

Figure 3.5 Positive (A) and Negative (B) Relationships Between Number of Hours of TV Watched and GPA

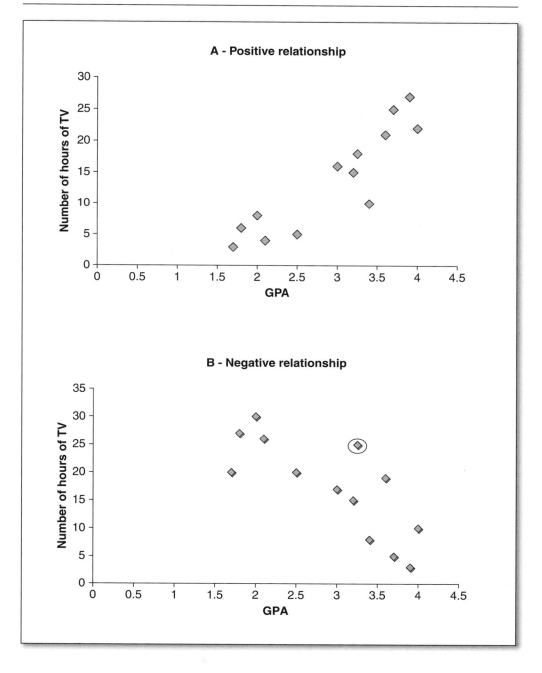

In a scatterplot, one variable is placed on the *x*-axis, and the other variable is placed on the *y*-axis. The data points in the graph represent the scores on the two variables for each individual (horizontally for the first variable and vertically for the second variable). Thus, the data point that is circled in Panel B shows that one individual in this study reported watching 25 hours of TV per week and had a GPA of 3.25. You may also notice that there are very few data points below 1.0 on the GPA scale in the graph. This may be because very few students in college have GPAs lower than 1.0 (if they do, they do not remain in college very long).

Remember that a relationship between these variables does not mean that watching TV will *cause* one to have a higher or lower GPA or that having a higher or lower GPA will *cause* one to watch more TV. It is quite possible that a third variable (e.g., lack of interest in academic topics, a poor academic environment while growing up, good background in academic topics that are covered in TV shows) is causing the number of hours of TV watched and GPA to change. This is called the **third-variable problem** and it is the reason that researchers cannot determine causation from correlational studies.

Third-Variable Problem: the presence of extraneous factors in a study that affect the dependent variable can decrease the internal validity of the study

---

Experiments

Have you ever wondered why it took so long for scientists to learn that smoking causes cancer? People have been smoking for hundreds of years, and medical science has been studying the effects of smoking on health for many decades. Yet warnings on cigarette packages did not appear until 1966, and claims about smoking causing lung cancer were tentative for many years. Scientists could show that smoking and cancer were linked but could not show that smoking caused cancer in humans in a definitive way. The reason these findings were tentative for so long is that ethically it is very difficult (if not impossible) to conduct an **experiment** to examine whether smoking *causes* cancer in humans. An experiment involves manipulating the presumed causal variable known as the **independent variable**. This means that in the smoking experiment, one group of people would be assigned to smoke and a similar group of people (similar in age, weight, health, diet, etc.) is not allowed to smoke. Obviously, researchers cannot force people to smoke (especially, if they have a hypothesis that it is harmful to them) or force people to never smoke. Thus, it has been very difficult (and has taken many correlational studies and animal experiments) to show that smoking is a cause of lung cancer, but this example illustrates what is required to test causal hypotheses: experiments.

Experiment: a type of research design that involves manipulation of an independent variable, allowing control of extraneous variables that could affect the results

Independent Variable: a variable in an experiment that is manipulated by the researcher such that the levels of the variable change across or within subjects in the experiment

---

As mentioned above, a key aspect of experiments that allows tests of causal relationships is the manipulation of the independent variable (or independent variables—an experiment can contain more than one independent variable). The independent variable is the factor that the researcher thinks may affect the observed behavior. Thus, data are collected from the participants in an experiment under at least two different conditions. The data from these conditions are then compared with one another to see if there are differences caused by the independent variable manipulation. These different conditions make up the **levels of the independent variable**. For example, an experiment may involve subjecting one group of participants to treatment for depression, while another group receives no treatment. In this case, the treated group is the

Levels of the Independent Variable: different situations or conditions that participants experience in an experiment because of the manipulation of the independent variable

Experimental Group: the group of participants in an experiment that experience the treatment level of the independent variable

Control Group: the group of participants in an experiment that do not experience the treatment level of the independent variable

experimental group, because they receive the treatment condition, whereas the nontreated group is the **control group**, because they receive no treatment. Comparison of depression scores (the dependent variable in this experiment) for the two groups would allow the researcher to determine if the treatment was helpful (scores for the treatment group are higher than the control group's), harmful (scores for the treatment group are lower than the control group's), or makes no difference (scores for the treatment and control groups are similar). Another way to conduct this experiment would be to use two different treatments (e.g., talk therapy vs. drug therapy) for the two groups. In this case, there is no control group; both groups of participants receive some type of treatment. Comparison of the scores for the two groups in this experiment would indicate which of the two therapies was more helpful or if they are similar. In fact, this comparison is a key feature of an experiment. The goal in an experiment is to examine the effect of the independent variable on the dependent variable. We do that by comparing the data observed in the different levels of the independent variable; thus comparison tells us if the independent variable has an effect. In other words, the comparison across the levels of the independent variable provides the test of the hypothesis.

Another key feature of experiments is the control of factors that could affect the results but are not part of the independent variable(s) manipulated. These extraneous factors are called **confounding variables**. If confounding variables are not controlled, the causal relationship between the independent and dependent variables will be unclear. For example, in the depression examples discussed earlier, the severity of the depression the participants have before the experiment could be a confounding variable because participants with more severe depression may show less improvement with therapy than participants with less severe depression. If the participants with more severe depression are inadvertently assigned to the therapy group in the first example or to one of the therapy groups in the second example, they may show no effect of therapy, even if an effect does exist. In other words, the severity of the depression may mask the causal relationship between therapy group and depression at the end of the study. Thus, the researcher should control for this factor in the experiment, perhaps by **randomly assigning** participants to groups. The control aspect of experiments is discussed further in Chapter 11.

---------------- ❧ ----------------

Confounding Variable: an extraneous factor present in a study that may affect the results

Random Assignment: participants are randomly assigned to levels of the independent variable in an experiment to control for individual differences as an extraneous variable

Systematic observations and surveys are the most common observation techniques used in experiments. These observation techniques allow for more control over the measurement of behavior than the other techniques (see Table 3.1). The IAT procedure described earlier (and in Figure 3.2) provides an example of the use of systematic observation in an experiment. An independent variable in an experiment using the IAT procedure is the type of word (or image) pairing the participant is responding to. The dependent variable is often the amount of time the participants take to respond to the word pairings.

Quasi-Experiments

In some cases, researchers want to compare the behavior of groups of individuals but are unable to manipulate the characteristic on which the groups differ. For example, suppose you wanted to compare the behavior for older and younger adults. You cannot randomly assign individuals to be of a specific age, so age cannot be a manipulated variable. This means that you lose some control over alternative explanations of the data, because participants are not randomly assigned to the groups. In this example, if younger and older adults differ on the measured behavior, age may have caused the difference or something that varies with age (e.g., experiences of different generations with technology) may have caused the difference. Thus, conclusions from **quasi-experiments** must be more tentative than conclusions from experiments, where a true independent variable is manipulated. However, quasi-experiments involve group comparisons just as experiments do, and data from quasi-experiments are often analyzed the same way as they are analyzed in experiments (see Chapter 14 for more on data analysis). The key difference between experiments and quasi-experiments is that the random assignment of participants to groups is missing in a quasi-experiment (Shadish, Cook, & Campbell, 2002).

---------------- ❧ ----------------

Quasi-Experiment: a type of research design where a comparison is made, as in an experiment, but no random assignment of participants to groups occurs

Some studies also have less control over conditions under which data are collected in a repeated-measures design. For example, suppose a researcher is interested in the change in attitude regarding trust of politicians after taking a political science class. In this study, attitude would be measured before and after the class in what is called a **pretest-posttest design**. If attitude changes from pretest to posttest (either getting better or worse), this change may be either because of the class or because of other events that occurred in the time between the tests (e.g., a political scandal may have occurred in this time). Thus, the causal relationship between the political science class and attitude change is less clear. For this reason,

---------------- ❧ ----------------

Pretest-Posttest Design: a type of research design (often a quasi-experiment) where behavior is measured both before and after a treatment or condition is implemented pretest-posttest designs (that do not include a control group) are considered quasi-experiments. Other types of quasi-experimental designs are considered in Chapter 12.

CHAPTER SUMMARY

Reconsider the questions from the beginning of the chapter:

- How do psychologists observe behavior? There are some common techniques used by psychologists to observe behavior described in this chapter.
- What are some common techniques for observing and recording behavior in different situations? The common techniques used by psychologists to observe and record behavior are naturalistic observations, surveys/questionnaires, systematic observations, and archival data.
- How do psychologists use observations to learn about behavior? Each technique can be used in different research designs to allow psychologists to answer different types of questions about behavior.
- What questions about behavior do the different research methods allow psychologists to answer? Different research designs (e.g., case studies, correlational studies, experiments, and quasi-experiments) allow researchers to ask different questions about behavior. Case studies allow descriptive questions to be answered for a single individual or institution. Correlational studies allow descriptive and predictive questions to be answered about behavior. Quasi-experiments and experiments allow comparisons among groups, with experiments answering causal questions about behavior.
- Which research method is best when asking about the cause of behavior? Experiments are the best method to use when asking causal questions about behavior.

THINKING ABOUT RESEARCH

A summary of a research study in psychology is given below. As you read the summary, think about the following questions:

1. The study below is described as an experiment. What aspects of the method indicate that the researchers used an experimental research design?
2. Describe the variables in this study (independent variable and levels, dependent variable).
3. Based on the description, which observation technique do you think the researchers used in this study? In what way did their design avoid some of the disadvantages of this technique? What disadvantages of this technique are possibly affecting their results in this study?
4. What types of extraneous variables should the researchers be concerned about in this study?
5. How would you judge the external validity of this study?

Study Reference

Lee, L., Frederick, S., & Ariely, D. (2006). Try it, you'll like it: The influence of expectation, consumption, and revelation on preferences for beer. *Psychological Science, 17,* 1054–1058.

Purpose of the Study. The researchers examined preferences for beer under conditions that varied in terms of when information about an ingredient of one of the beers was given: before tasting, after tasting but before preferences were indicated, and never (no information was given to one group about the ingredients). The ingredient given is one that most people think should make the beer taste worse. The research question was whether the timing of the ingredient information would affect the preference for the beer by influencing one's expectation of taste of the beer. Preference for the beer with the undesired ingredient should be lower in any condition where the information influences the preference.

Method of the Study. Pub patrons in Massachusetts were asked to participate in a taste test of two types of beer labeled "regular beer" and "MIT brew." The "MIT brew" contained a few drops of balsamic vinegar (the vinegar apparently changed the flavor of the beer very little). Participants were randomly assigned to one of the three groups that differed according to when information was given: blind group (no information given), before-tasting group (information given before tasting), and after-tasting group (information given after tasting but before preference was indicated). All participants were given a small sample of each beer to taste. They were asked to indicate which of the two beers they preferred.

Results of the Study. In the blind condition, the "MIT brew" was preferred more often (about 60% of the group) than the before condition (only about 30% of the group), indicating that ingredient information had an effect before tasting. However, the "MIT brew" was also preferred more often in the after condition (just over 50% of the group) than in the before condition and was not preferred less often than the blind condition, indicating that when ingredient information is given after tasting, it does not affect preference. Figure 3.6 presents the means of the three groups.

Figure 3.6   Results of the Beer-Tasting Study

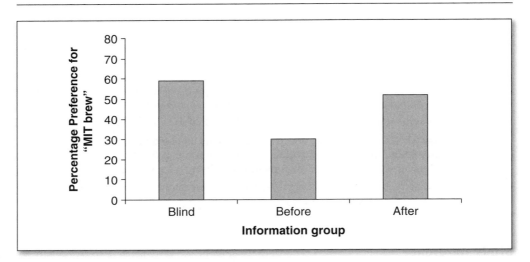

SOURCE: Results from Lee, Frederick, and Ariely's (2006) study.

Conclusions of the Study. The researchers concluded that the timing of information about a beer-drinking experience affects preference for the beer. Their results indicated that when information about the beer ingredient was given before the participants tasted the beer, it affected their tasting experience (and their preferences), but when information was given after the participants tasted the beer, it did not affect their experience or their preference. More generally, this study showed that our expectations of our perceptual experiences affect how we judge those experiences.

COMMON PITFALLS AND HOW TO AVOID THEM

Problem: Concluding cause without manipulation—nonexperimental studies are sometimes interpreted as providing causal information.

Solution: To test causal relationships, an experiment with a manipulated independent variable is needed.

Problem: External validity versus internal validity—some view external validity as more important than internal validity in all psychological research studies.

Solution: Be aware that high internal validity is required to test causal relationships but that internal and external validity typically trade off in psychological studies.

Problem: Use of control groups in experiments—students sometimes incorrectly believe that all experiments require a control group.

Solution: Remember that control groups are important in experiments if a single treatment is being evaluated or the effectiveness of multiple treatments is being tested, but control groups are not required in every type of experiment.

TEST YOURSELF

Match each research design below with its appropriate description

1. Experiment
2. Case study
3. Correlational study
4. Quasi-experiment

(a) Design that focuses on observing just one or a few individuals

(b) Design that will allow one to look for relationships between measured variables

(c) Best design for testing a causal relationship

(d) Design that allows comparison of groups but does not contain a true independent variable

5. Reread the scenario described at the beginning of the chapter about increasing work productivity. Use the concepts you read about in this chapter to design a study to test the boss's suggestion. Be sure to operationally define work productivity and decide what technique you will use to observe this behavior. Choose the research design that best fits the question you are trying to answer.

6. Suppose you are interested in testing the hypothesis "The herb ginkgo biloba causes one to have better memory."

   (a) What is the best research design to test this hypothesis? Why?

   (b) Describe the study you would conduct to test this hypothesis.

7. _____ validity indicates that a study's results can be generalized to other individuals and real-life situations. _____ validity indicates that a study's results provide causal information about the variables tested.

8. For each description below, indicate which observation technique was used:

   (a) Medical records of patients with depression are examined to determine how often these patients attempt suicide based on what type of treatment they received

   (b) Participants are asked to perform a task on a computer where they must unscramble sentences as quickly as possible—the amount of time it takes to complete the task on each trial is recorded

   (c) A series of statements regarding their alcohol consumption behaviors is presented to participants—they are asked to rate their agreement with each statement on a scale from 1 to 5

   (d) Students in a college class are observed to record the number of times they exhibit behaviors indicating lack of attention to the lecture

Answers: 1. c, 2. a, 3. b, 4. d, 5. There are lots of ways to test this. One example is to use a measurable work behavior (such as number of reports written in a week or number of clients served per day) as the operational definition of work productivity. The study could compare work productivity change (difference between work productivity before the study starts and work productivity during the study) for workers on different floors of the office (where one floor has the cappuccino machine and the other floor does not). Or work productivity could be measured for a week without the machine and then measured for a week with the machine and compared for the 2 weeks. Both designs involve a quasi-experiment. A true experiment would be difficult to conduct in the workplace. 6a. This is a causal hypothesis; thus, an experiment is the best design. 6b. A manipulated independent variable that includes random assignment of participants to a ginkgo biloba group and a control group that receives a placebo should be included. 7. External, Internal. 8a. archival data, 8b. systematic observation, 8c. survey/questionnaire, 8d. naturalistic observation.

Types of Variables

When you hear that someone is "intelligent," what does that mean to you? Do you think that the person gets good grades? Does the person excel in math and science courses? Does the person read a lot of books? Does it mean the person has a large brain? Or do you think that the person has an ability to solve complex problems quickly and easily? These are some of the same questions that psychologists have attempted to answer when they have tried to study intelligence, and each of the suggestions above has at one time or another been used by researchers as a definition of "intelligence."

The study of intelligence has a long history. Some attempts to measure intelligence in psychology have used intelligence tests that were designed to measure innate abilities that are not affected by culture or experiences (i.e., intelligence test scores were used as operational definitions of the concept of intelligence—see Chapter 3 for more discussion of operational definitions). Scores on these tests reflected a person's current ability level in reference to other people's abilities of the same chronological age. A score on these tests is called an intelligence quotient or IQ score. However, these tests are not always reliable or valid measures of innate abilities, and some psychologists have pointed out that these measures rely on a specific definition of intelligence that is expressed in the types of questions asked on the test.

More recently, other psychologists have suggested that there may be several forms of intelligence that can be measured in different ways. For example, Gardner (1999) suggested that intelligence comprises several different abilities. Some of the forms he proposed include the following: A person can be intelligent such that he or she has excellent verbal abilities (i.e., a good writer), mathematical and logical abilities (i.e., one excels at math and logical problems), or spatial abilities (i.e., one can navigate well or produce excellent drawings). Still other psychologists (e.g., Goleman, 1995) have suggested that people can have social intelligence (i.e., are skilled at interpersonal interactions) or emotional intelligence (i.e., can understand others' emotions and manage their own emotions well).

From this example of the measurement of intelligence in psychological research, you can see that how something is defined for the purpose of measurement can be controversial. Someone who may have exceptional spatial abilities may still be considered unintelligent from his or her score on a standard intelligence test, if the test is designed to measure other abilities. In other words, how one chooses to define the concept of intelligence will affect the outcome of that measure. Thus, the goal of a measure of behavior is important to consider when a researcher is choosing to measure an abstract concept such as intelligence. Some of the intelligence tests described above have been used to predict future performance, even though they were not designed for this purpose. Other types of tests, called aptitude tests, were developed specifically to predict future performance (such as the SAT or Scholastic Aptitude Test and ACT or American College Test that high school students take are used to predict their academic performance in college), and a person's score on these tests is often a fairly accurate prediction of his or her future academic performance. However, if one wishes to predict future success in life (e.g., type of job or salary), these tests may not be valid indicators because they were not developed for this purpose. These are some of the issues we will discuss in this chapter: the importance of how we measure and manipulate variables in a study and how these choices can affect how well the study tests a causal hypothesis (i.e., the internal validity of the study), applies to everyday behavior (i.e., the external validity of the study), and provides results that are reliable (Figure 4.1).

DEPENDENT VARIABLES

In Chapter 3, **dependent/response variables** were introduced as variables that are measured in a research study. In this chapter, we will discuss how dependent variables can be measured and how this affects **reliability** (how consistent the measurements are). Chapter 3 also introduced **operational definitions**, definitions of concepts that describe how they are measured or manipulated in a study. There are many ways to operationally define the abstract concepts, such as depression, anxiety, intelligence, and memory, that psychologists wish to study. Some of the specific types of measurements that are used when dependent variables are operationally defined in psychological research are described below.

—— ❧ ——

Dependent/Response Variable: a variable that is measured or observed from an individual

Reliability: the degree to which the results of a study can be replicated under similar conditions

Operational Definition: the definition of an abstract concept used by a researcher to measure or manipulate the concept in a research study

Figure 4.1   Steps in the Research Process: Designing the Study

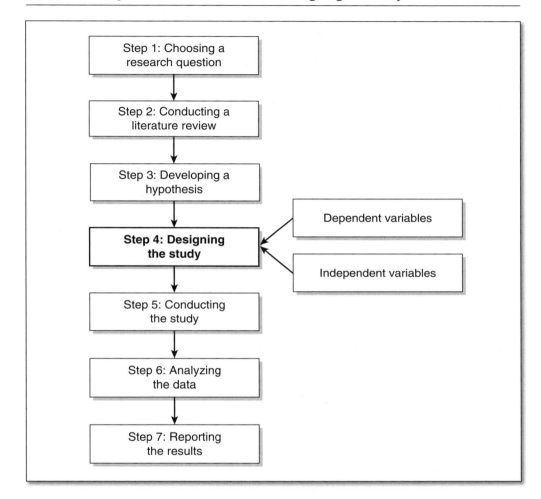

Scales of Measurement

As described above for the concept of intelligence, how a researcher measures the dependent variable in a study can be important. Different types of measures allow different questions to be asked about the behaviors. In addition, some types of measures will be more reliable than others. The choice of scale will also constrain the types of statistical tests that can be used to analyze the data. There are four primary scales of measurement for dependent variables: (1) nominal, (2) ordinal, (3) interval, and (4) ratio. Each of these scales is described below.

Nominal Scales. The simplest scale of measurement is a **nominal scale**, where nonordered categorical responses are collected. For example, if researchers are measuring a person's

---
❧

Nominal Scale: a scale of data measurement that involves nonordered categorical responses

Qualitative Data: nonnumerical participant responses

Quantitative Data: numerical data

---

current mood, they may ask the respondent to choose from categories such as anxious, happy, depressed, and angry. These categories are not ordered on any continuum; they are merely different categories that reflect a person's mood. Another example of a nominal scale is college major. Values on this scale are categories (e.g., English, Education, Psychology, Philosophy) that are not ordered in any particular way. Gender is another common nominal variable (e.g., male, female). The responses on a nominal scale do not involve numerical values; thus, nominal scales are considered **qualitative data** rather than **quantitative data**.

Ordinal Scales. When the response categories of a measure contain an ordering (i.e., can be ordered from lowest to highest) on a continuum of measurement, the measure is considered an **ordinal scale**. However, response categories on an ordinal scale are not assumed to be equally spaced on the continuum. They are merely ordered categories on the scale. For example, in measuring a person's mood, a researcher may ask respondents to rate their current anxiety level with possible response categories of "not at all anxious," "a little anxious," "fairly anxious," and "very anxious." These categories are ordered from lowest amount of anxiety to highest, but there is no implied equivalence between the "not at all anxious" and "a little anxious" response categories and the "a little anxious" and "fairly anxious" response categories. Thus, the response categories on this scale are not necessarily equally spaced. Another example of an ordinal scale might be asking students to indicate how often they consume alcohol during a typical week with response categories of "none," "once," "two to five times," and "more than five times." Again, these response categories are ordered from smallest to largest amount, but the difference between "none" and "once" is not the same as the difference between "once" and "two to five times."

❧

Ordinal Scale: a scale of data measurement that involves ordered categorical responses

---

Rank orderings of stimuli are also considered ordinal scales. For example, if preference for different products is being measured, the respondents may be asked to rank order (e.g., first, second, third, etc.) the products according to the ones they like more than the others. In rank orders, the difference between the first and second choices may be much larger or smaller than the difference between the second and third choices. Like nominal scales, ordinal scales involve qualitative data because the response values are not numerical.

Interval and Ratio Scales. Interval and ratio scales involve numerical response values; thus, they involve quantitative data. There are many measurement scales in psychology that are considered **interval** and **ratio scales**. Interval scales involve numerical categories that are equally spaced. Thus, a common interval scale is the **Likert Scale**, where respondents are asked how much they agree or disagree with a statement on a 1 to 5 or a 1 to 7 scale (where possible responses are any whole value between these endpoints). Responses from surveys are often measured on a Likert Scale with qualitative anchors provided to give the numerical values meaning (e.g., 1 = *item is least like me*, 3 = *item is somewhat like me*,

5 = *item is most like me*). However, the responses given by participants are the numerical ratings, with equal spacing between the different numbers on the scale.

Ratio scales also involve numerical measurements, but ratio scales allow a ratio comparison of values between individual scores. For example, a score of 50 on a ratio scale is twice as high as the score of 25. The amount of time to complete a task (sometimes called **reaction time**) is a common ratio scale used in psychological research. If one participant takes 250 milliseconds to complete a task and another participant takes 500 milliseconds to complete the same task, it can be said that the second participant took twice as long as the first participant. Accuracy for a task is also a ratio scale. In fact, measurement scales for distance, time, accuracy, height, or weight are ratio scales. For many ratio measurement scales (such as many of those listed above), 0 is the lowest value possible; however, some ratio scales do involve values lower than 0 (e.g., reaction times measured in a study can be negative, if the participant responds before the stimulus appears).

Temperature scales provide a good example of the difference between interval and ratio scales. Common temperature scales (Fahrenheit, Celsius) involve values of 0 that are not the coldest temperatures possible (anyone who has lived through a cold winter can tell you that negative temperatures are possible and can be unpleasant). In addition, Fahrenheit and Celsius temperature scales are interval scales because 20° is not twice as cold as 10° or four times as cold as 5°. The Kelvin scale for temperature, however, does include a 0 value that is the lowest possible value. The value of 0 on this scale indicates that it is the lowest temperature possible, and scores on the Kelvin scale are ratios of each other (e.g., 100 K is twice as hot as 50 K). Thus, the Kelvin scale of temperature is a ratio scale. See Table 4.1 for a comparison of the different measurement scales and some additional examples of each type of scale.

Correctly identifying the scale of measurement used for the dependent variable is an important step in conducting appropriate statistical analyses. Different scales may require different types of analyses in some designs. This issue will be discussed further in Chapters 7 and 14.

Interval Scale: a scale of data measurement that involves numerical responses that are equally spaced, but scores are not ratios of each other

Ratio Scale: a scale of data measurement that involves numerical responses, where scores are ratios of each other

Likert Scale: a scale of responses that measures a participant's agreement or disagreement with different types of statements, often with a rating from 1 to 5 or 1 to 7

Reaction Time: measurement of the length of time to complete a task

---

Validity and Response Scales

The choice of measurement can also affect the validity of a study (i.e., the study's accuracy in testing the researcher's hypothesis). For example, in many cases, the more response choices there are on the scale, the more accurate the measurement will be of the behavior that is being measured. If you think about measuring height with a ruler, you can see how

Scale	**Definition**	**Example**
Nominal	Unordered categories	University where degree was earned
Ordinal	Nonnumerical, ordered categories	Letter grades earned in a course (A, B, C, D, F)
Interval	Numerical categories without a true zero point	Ratings on personality surveys with values from 1 to 5
Ratio	Numerical categories with a true zero point	Age measured in days since birth

TABLE 4.1   Scales of Measurement

this works. Imagine you have a ruler that has increments marked only for every foot (1 foot, 2 feet, 3 feet, etc.). How accurate would your height measurement be if you used this ruler? The answer is "not very accurate," because you can only choose between values of 5 feet or 6 feet (or 7 feet for very tall people). If instead you use a ruler marked in inches, you can measure your height more accurately (5 feet 2 inches, 5 feet 7 inches, 6 feet 1 inch, etc.). The ruler with more values on it will give you more accurate measurements. Response scales for behavior work the same way. The more values on the scale, the more accurate (and thus, more valid) the scale will be.

In addition, if a poor operational definition of a concept is used, inaccurate conclusions from the data may also result. In this case, the measure has low **construct validity**. A measure with high construct validity will provide an accurate measure of the behavior of interest. In other words, has the researcher used an appropriate operational definition of the variable of interest? For example, suppose a researcher is interested in measuring anxiety in children who are 5 years old. It is unlikely that children this young will understand the items on a standardized anxiety questionnaire such as the BAI (Beck Anxiety Inventory; Beck & Steer, 1993) or the response scale for the BAI. Thus, if this questionnaire (and response scale) were used in a study with young children, the responses would likely be inaccurate and lower the validity of the study. While scores on the BAI may be a good operational definition of mood for adults, they are likely to provide a poor operational definition of mood for children. Thus, the BAI scores will have low construct validity in a study with children. For a study such as this, where mood responses from young children are required, it may be best to use a **nonverbal scale** to ensure that the children can provide valid responses. A series of faces with different expressions of mood may be a better (and more valid) measurement scale for mood responses in 5-year-olds. See Figure 4.2 for an example of a nonverbal response scale (also see Egan, Santos, & Bloom, 2007, for an example of a study that used a similar nonverbal response scale with children).

Construct Validity: indicates that a survey measures the behavior it is designed to measure

Nonverbal Scale: survey response scale that involves pictorial response categories for participants with low verbal skills (e.g., children)

Figure 4.2 Example of a Nonverbal Response Scale

When deciding on an appropriate operational definition to ensure that a study has good construct validity, a researcher can start by considering the **face validity** of a measure when it is chosen for a study. This means that, on the surface, the scale seems to measure what you think it does. For example, if you want to know how well someone performs a task under different conditions, an accuracy scale seems to be an intuitively good measure for this behavior. If you want to know about someone's mood, asking respondents about their mood seems as if it will measure what you want to measure. If items on a questionnaire seem to relate to the concept being measured, then the questionnaire has good face validity. We will consider more validity issues below as they relate to other variables in a research study.

Face Validity: on the surface, a study or scale appears to be intuitively valid

Reliability of Measurements and Response Scales

The choice of measurement can also affect the reliability of the data collected in a study. Some scales will be more reliable than others. For example, the reliability of a new survey is typically tested (in several ways) to ensure that responses will not change for a participant over time or across items on the survey, because the way survey items are written and the response scale chosen for a survey can affect the reliability of the scores on the survey. Typically, the reliability of a survey is tested by comparing scores for the same participants at different times or by comparing scores for the same participant on different parts of the survey. Reliability of surveys will be described further in Chapter 9.

Reliability is also an issue when a study involves multiple raters or coders of the behaviors of interest. The consistency of the recording of behaviors from different raters or coders is called **interrater reliability**. Interrater reliability was introduced in Chapter 3 with the naturalistic observation technique, as this form of reliability is most important with naturalistic observations. For example, in a study using naturalistic observations, there are typically multiple observers of the behaviors of interest,

Interrater Reliability: a measure of the degree to which different observers rate behaviors in similar ways either observing at the same time to ensure that all behaviors are recorded or observing at different times to allow the participants to be observed for longer periods of time. In studies with multiple observers, you want to be sure that the different observers are making observations in the same way. In other words, it is important to have good interrater reliability. Consider a study where children are being observed for aggressive behaviors using naturalistic observations of the children, while they are at recess at school. For the study, aggressive behaviors have been operationally defined as aggressive contact with another person or yelling at another person. During the observation period, a child is seen yelling at other children. One observer codes the yelling as aggressive behavior because the behavior fits the operational definition. However, another observer codes the yelling as nonaggressive behavior, because he or she saw that the child was yelling from a distance to be heard, not to be aggressive. In this case, the two observers have coded the same behavior in a different way, resulting in an inconsistency in the data. If the observers continued to code behaviors of other children this way, this inconsistency would decrease the reliability of the data. To make sure that the interrater reliability in a study is good (and the inconsistencies just described do not occur), observers must be well trained to code behaviors in the same way, and their interrater reliability should be tested by having each observer code the same set of behaviors to look for a strong positive relationship between the data coded by the different observers. In other words, high interrater reliability means that there is a high rate of agreement in the way the different observers are recording behaviors.

INDEPENDENT VARIABLES

Independent Variable: a variable in an experiment that is manipulated by the researcher such that the levels of the variable change across or within subjects in the experiment

---

All research studies include at least one dependent variable, because the dependent variable is the measure of the behavior that is being observed. However, a subset of studies, classified as experiments, also includes an **independent variable**. In Chapter 3, we discussed experiments and how they differed from other research methods (i.e., they include an independent variable that is manipulated and a comparison of the levels of the independent variable to test the hypothesis). Here we will discuss some different ways that independent variables can be manipulated in a study and how the manipulation of independent variables can affect the validity of a study.

Types of Manipulations

There are three ways in which an independent variable can be manipulated to create levels of the independent variable: (1) as the presence and absence of a treatment or situation, (2) as a type of treatment or situation, and (3) as the amount of a factor in a treatment or situation.

Presence/absence variables typically include two levels, with one level being the presence of something and the other level being the absence of that thing. For presence/absence variables, the presence group is also called the experimental group and the absence group is called the control group (see Chapter 3 for more discussion of these concepts). The "something" that is manipulated could be a therapy (presence of therapy and absence of therapy), a drug treatment (presence of the drug and absence of the drug), or a time constraint for a task (presence of the time constraint and absence of the time constraint), depending on the type of study being conducted. Presence/absence variables are also called **bivalent independent variables** because they are independent variables that contain only two levels. Remember that an independent variable must have at least two levels, so a bivalent independent variable is the simplest type of independent variable.

Presence/Absence Variable: a variable that involves a manipulation with a level that involves the treatment and a level that does not involve the treatment

Bivalent Independent Variable: an independent variable with two levels—a design is considered bivalent if it contains only one bivalent independent variable

Type variables include a different type of the "something" being manipulated in each level. For example, different types of drugs or therapies can be compared, different versions of an ad or product can be compared, or different types of instructions for a task can be compared. In each of these independent variables, all the levels include the factor being manipulated (drug, therapy, ad, product, instructions), but each level involves a different type or version of that factor.

Type Variable: a variable that involves a manipulation of types of a treatment

Amount variables involve a manipulation of the amount of a factor in each level. For example, an experiment can investigate the amount of a drug (i.e., dosage) that is optimal for relieving symptoms such that each level of a variable includes a different amount of the drug given to the participants. A common independent variable in memory research is the manipulation of the amount of time that passes between the study of material and the test on that material (i.e., a study-test delay) such that each level involves a different time delay (e.g., 5 minutes, 30 minutes, 2 hours, 1 day, 1 month, etc.). Whenever an independent variable contains three or more levels, it is considered a **multivalent variable** (i.e., multiple levels, more than two). See Figure 4.3 for a comparison of different independent variable manipulations.

Amount Variable: variables that include levels with a different amount of the treatment changing from level to level

Multivalent Variable: an independent variable that includes three or more levels—a design is considered multivalent if there is only one independent variable that contains three or more levels

Quasi-Independent Variables

So far in this chapter, we have been discussing true independent variables, or variables that are manipulated by the researcher. As described in Chapter 3, participants can also be separated into groups based on characteristics they already have. These groups create levels

Figure 4.3   Types of Independent Variable (IV) Manipulations

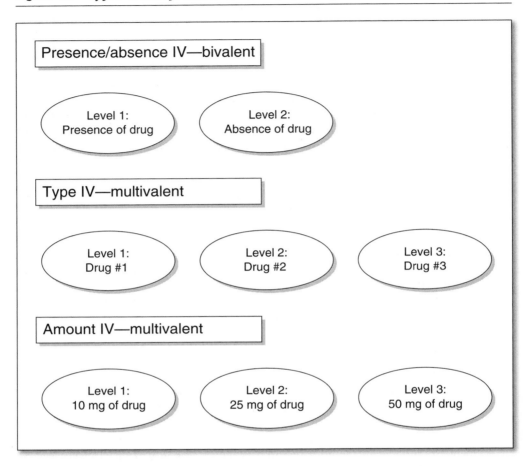

of a **quasi-independent variable** (also called a **subject variable**) based on characteristics that a researcher is unable to manipulate. The groups can then be compared in the same way as groups that are randomly assigned are compared. Some examples of common quasi-independent variables used in psychological research include gender, age, personality types (e.g., introverts and extroverts), and ethnicity. Any characteristic that you can measure or observe from the participants can be used to group those participants and create a quasi-independent variable in a study.

Quasi-Independent/Subject Variable: variable that allows comparison of groups of participants without manipulation (i.e., no random assignment)

The use of quasi-independent variables is very common in psychological research studies. However, researchers must be cautious when including these variables, because the causal relationship between the quasi-independent and dependent variables is not always as clear as it is with true independent variables. Without the manipulation by the researcher, it is always possible that additional factors (that are not part of the quasi-independent variable) are causing differences (or lack of differences) to occur between the groups. Thus, a researcher must always consider these additional factors when drawing conclusions from these factors.

For example, consider a study that compares different age groups on completion of a memory task to determine if memory declines as people age. Suppose the researcher for this study presented the items the participants were to study on a computer screen and then asked them to judge items presented on the computer screen as items they studied or not (i.e., they received a recognition test). The older participants in this study perform worse on the memory task than the younger participants. The researcher concludes that recognition memory of this type declines as people age. However, it is also possible that instead of having a deficit in memory abilities, the age group difference was due to the older participants having less familiarity with computers, making more errors in completing the computer task, and showing lower performance on the memory task due to their lack of experience with computers. The difference in computer experience between the two groups is one of those additional factors that must be considered here (and ruled out, if possible) before the researcher can conclude that the older participants had worse memory. In other words, the causal relationship between age and memory abilities has become clouded by the difference in computer experience between the two groups. Had the researcher been able to randomly assign the participants to the different age groups (or matched the participants based on previous experience with computers), this additional explanation of the results could have been ruled out more easily. Therefore, it is important to remember that the causal information gained from quasi-independent variables is not as clear as it is from true independent variables, and the researcher must be more cautious when interpreting differences across groups that were not manipulated (i.e., assigned) by the researcher. See Figure 4.4 for a comparison of true independent and quasi-independent variables.

VALIDITY AND SOURCES OF BIAS

In this chapter, we have been discussing how the variables we examine in a study, as well as how we choose to measure or manipulate them, can affect the validity of the study. In fact, there are several different types of validity to consider when designing a study, and each has different implications. We have already considered choosing variables based on face validity (i.e., intuitively, does the variable seem to do what it should) and how a poor operational definition of a concept can lower the construct validity of a measure, but there are a few other types of validity that researchers should consider when designing a study. Some of the more common forms of validity and sources of bias that threaten these forms of validity are discussed below. Examples of these sources are provided in Table 4.2.

Internal Validity

Much of our discussion of validity has focused on **internal validity**. A study with good internal validity provides a good test of a causal hypothesis and controls for those extraneous factors that could affect the data but are not of interest in the study. In other words, a study with good internal validity will provide a good test of a causal relationship by

Figure 4.4   Independent and Quasi-Independent Variables

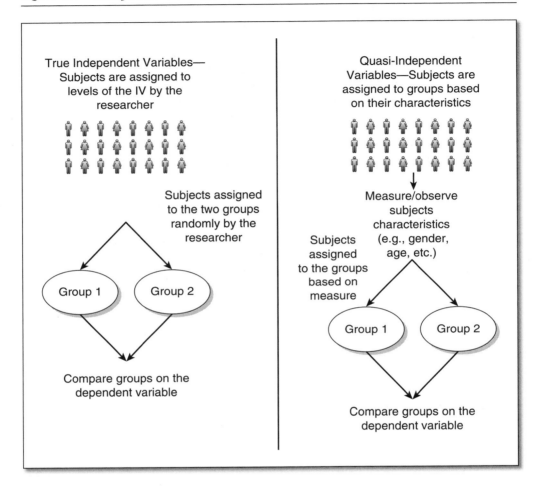

TABLE 4.2 A Summary of Sources of Bias			
Bias	**Definition**	**Examples**	**Type of Validity Threatened**
Group differences	Participant groups are not equated on characteristics that can affect the data	Gender, previous knowledge or experience with the task, current mood state	Internal

Bias	Definition	Examples	Type of Validity Threatened
Order effects	Order of conditions in a within-subjects design can affect data collected in different conditions	Easy versus difficult tasks, positive versus negative experiences	Internal
Testing effects	Multiple testing sessions—first testing affects subsequent testing	Practice effects, fatigue effects, accumulated knowledge of the task	Internal
Regression toward the mean	Extreme scores unlikely to recur	High score on test in class with low average grade, low score on test in class with high average grade, professional athlete has high-performing year compared with average performance	Internal
History	Historical event affects posttest in pretest-posttest study	9/11 attacks occur during study, economy declines during study, new law is passed	Internal
Maturation	Natural changes in participants occur over course of study	Participants' cognitive abilities improve with age, illness symptoms improve over time	Internal
Attrition/mortality	Participants fail to complete a study	Participants drop out of different conditions in unequal numbers, characteristics of participants who remain in study are different from those who drop out, creating bias	Internal and external
Hawthorne effect	Studying participants can change their behavior	Workers' productivity improves when they know they are being studied, participants perform better in a memory study than they would outside the study	External

removing alternative explanations of the data (besides the independent variable). The discussion of different research designs in Chapter 3 indicated that the best way to test a casual relationship is to use the experimental method. Thus, well-designed experiments typically have higher internal validity than other research designs. The best way to design a good experiment (or even a good quasi-experiment) is to control for sources of bias that can make the causal relationship less clear (i.e., other factors besides the independent variable that might affect the dependent variable). These sources of bias are often called

— ❧ —

Internal Validity: the degree to which a study provides causal information about behavior

Confounding Variable: an extraneous factor present in a study that may affect the results

confounding variables (see Chapters 3 and 11 for more discussion of confounding variables). There are several common sources of bias that can lower the internal validity of a study. A researcher would be wise to keep these in mind when designing a study in order to control for or minimize these threats to internal validity.

Experimenter Bias. The first source of bias we will discuss is one that can be caused by the researcher. **Experimenter bias** occurs when a researcher inadvertently treats groups differently in the study due to knowledge of the hypothesis for the study. For example, suppose an instructor is trying out a new type of assignment in a class that she thinks will help students learn a topic better than her old method. To test the effectiveness of the new assignment, she gives the assignment to one section of her class and the old assignment to another section of her class. She then compares the test scores of the two groups, with each section receiving the

— ❧ —

Experimenter Bias: a source of bias in a study created when a researcher treats groups differently (often unknowingly) based on knowledge of the hypothesis

same exam. If the section with the new assignment scores higher than the section with the old assignment, there are several possible reasons that this may have occurred. One explanation is that the new assignment is more effective than the old assignment in helping students learn the material. Another explanation is

that there may be group differences (e.g., better students in the new assignment section) that caused the results, because the students were not randomly assigned to the two sections. A third explanation is that there may have been experimenter bias in the study. In other words, because the instructor expected the new assignment section to perform better, she may have unknowingly been more enthusiastic with these students or encouraged them more than the other section. Alternatively, the instructor may have exhibited experimenter bias in the opposite manner by spending more time teaching the material to the old assignment section

— ❧ —

Single-Blind Design: procedure used to hide the group assignment from the participants in a study to prevent their beliefs about the effectiveness of a treatment from affecting the results

Placebo: a sugar pill given to the control group in a drug study to allow all groups to believe that they are receiving a treatment

Double-Blind Design: procedure used to control for experimenter bias by keeping the knowledge of the group assignments from both the participants and the researchers who interact with the participants

because she expected them to have more trouble learning the material. Either situation represents experimenter bias in the study.

To counter experimenter bias, a blind procedure can be used in a study to hide the group assignment from the researcher and prevent inadvertent bias from occurring. A **single-blind design** is used to combat effects of subjects' knowledge of their group assignment. For example, when the effectiveness of a drug is tested, the control group typically receives a **placebo** to equate beliefs of effectiveness of treatment across groups. In a **double-blind design**, both the participants and the researchers who interact with the participants do not know which participants are assigned to the different groups. Thus, the instructor from the assignment study above could have used a double-blind design by trying out her assignment in a colleague's class or having a guest lecturer who is unaware of her hypothesis teach the material of interest. With this alternate procedure, the researcher who made the hypothesis does not interact with the participants during the course of the study.

Testing Effects. **Testing effects** can be an issue when multiple testing sessions occur in a study. They are more likely to occur in studies where participants are tested more than once or complete a task over a series of trials. Thus, testing effects are more likely in **within-subjects** experiments than **between-subjects** studies, as participants' behavior is measured under all levels of the independent variable(s) in within-subjects experiments (see Chapter 11 for more discussion of between-subjects and within-subjects experiments). Testing effects occur when an initial test affects data collected on subsequent tests. For example, in many tasks, participants will improve over time due to practice effects. The more time participants spend completing a task

Testing Effects: occur when participants are tested more than once in a study with early testing affecting later testing

Within-Subjects Variable: each participant experiences all levels of the variable

Between-Subjects Variable: each participant experiences only one level of the independent variable

Counterbalance: a control used in within-subjects experiments where different participants are assigned in equal numbers to the different orders of the conditions

(either across multiple levels of an independent variable or across many trials in a study), the more easily they will complete the task due to experience with the task. Of course, the opposite can occur with extreme numbers of trials or many repeated testing sessions in a study. Participants can become fatigued over time, and their performance on a task will decline over many repeated exposures to a task. Testing effects can be avoided in a study by minimizing the number of trials of a task as much as possible and **counterbalancing** levels of a within-subjects independent variable (see Chapter 11 for more discussion of counterbalancing). When questionnaires are used in a study, different items may be used on different versions of the measure to minimize testing effects over repeated completions of a questionnaire. Testing effects will also be discussed in the "nuts and bolts" chapters as they apply to specific types of studies: surveys in Chapter 9, experiments in Chapter 11, and quasi-experiments in Chapter 12.

Regression Toward the Mean. **Regression toward the mean** occurs when participants obtain an extreme score (high or low) on a questionnaire or task at one testing session but regress toward their mean score at another testing session. In other words, "regression toward the mean" means that extreme scores are not likely to recur. Regression toward the mean can be problematic in studies where a test or

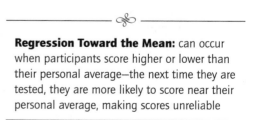

Regression Toward the Mean: can occur when participants score higher or lower than their personal average—the next time they are tested, they are more likely to score near their personal average, making scores unreliable

questionnaire is given more than once. If a participant scores very high or very low on the test the first time it is taken but obtains a more average score the next time the test is taken, it can make comparison of scores across conditions of a study difficult. Is the change in score due to the independent variable, or is it due to regression toward the mean? This can be a difficult question for a researcher to answer, but the more times the participant is tested, the more information a researcher will have about the answer to this question.

Consider an example of regression toward the mean in sports (there are many good examples of this concept in professional sports). On September 1, 2004, a baseball player named Ryan Howard made his major league debut with the Philadelphia Phillies. He hit well that year and stayed with the team, playing more often and finally starting at first base in 2005 when Jim Thome went on the disabled list with an injury. In 2006, Howard hit so well that he posted a batting average of .313 (i.e., he got a hit 31.3% of the times he batted, which is very good for a major league player, especially a young player) and won several awards, including the National League MVP award. The following year, although still a good player, Howard's batting average fell to .268, a value closer to his current overall average of .280 (retrieved May 21, 2008, from the Phillies Web site: http://philadelphia.phillies.mlb.com). Ryan Howard's batting average hit an extreme high in 2006 but returned closer to his overall average the following year (his average the previous year in 2005 was .288, also closer to his overall average of .280). Thus, he experienced regression toward the mean for his batting average after achieving an extreme batting average score in 2006.

Regression toward the mean can occur in a similar way in research studies where other types of behavior are measured. Have you ever received a surprisingly good score on an exam in a class that you were not doing very well in, or a disappointingly low score on an exam for a class where you had an A on previous assignments or exams? In each of these cases, it is likely that you scored closer your mean score in the class on the next exam or assignment due to regression toward the mean. Now suppose that your instructor for this class was trying out a new teaching technique in the middle of the semester by comparing scores on the first and second exams to determine if the scores increased with the new teaching technique implemented between the first and second exams. What would your extreme score do to the instructor's data in the test of the new teaching technique? The answer is that it would lower the validity of the test. It would be harder for the instructor to know if the change in scores on the second test is due to the new teaching technique or due to regression toward the mean.

Regression toward the mean is a difficult source of bias to remove from a research study. The best way to minimize its effects is to use random assignment to conditions for between-subjects variables and to use several repetitions of the test for within-subjects variables. Random assignment should spread regression toward the mean across the different groups so that it does not cause group differences. Using several repetitions of the test (e.g., having participants complete the test more than once for each level of the independent variable) will allow scores closer to each participant's true mean to occur in each condition. With a single testing for each level, you may end up with an extreme score for one of those levels. Trimming extreme scores from the data (when possible) will also help minimize regression toward the mean as a source of bias (see Chapter 7 for more information about trimming outliers). Splitting a group in half based on high and low scores can also control for regression toward the mean. Finally, using a large number of participants in a study (exactly how many depends on the type of study and the types of variables being tested) can help minimize the effect of a single extreme score on the data.

History. In studies that occur over a period a time, a few different sources of bias can occur during the time period. For example, suppose a researcher is conducting a study to compare different treatments for depression. The treatments typically take time to implement. During this time period, the effects of the treatments (if there are any) will occur. However, effects of other factors may also occur. One example is the effects of historical events (i.e., **history effect**). These events can be experienced by a large group of individuals or personally experienced by individuals. For example, suppose that during the time the depression study was being con-ducted, the economy took a turn for the worse and many people were losing their jobs and having difficulty paying bills. In this case, the historical event (the economy declining) could affect the depression levels of participants in the study, making it difficult

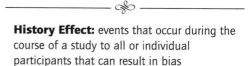

History Effect: events that occur during the course of a study to all or individual participants that can result in bias

to detect positive effects of the treatments being tested. Alternatively, individual partic-ipants in the study could experience personal events that affect their level of depression (loss of a loved one, a promotion at work, etc.). Thus, history of the participants (either shared or personal) can affect the data in the study and reduce the internal validity.

Effects of history (and other sources of bias that occur over time) are most likely to occur in pretest-posttest designs. In Chapter 3, pretest-posttest designs were described as designs where participants are tested both before (pretest) and after (posttest) the implementation of a treatment or other type of variable. The best way to minimize effects that occur over time in a pretest-posttest design is to include a control group that takes the pretest and posttest at the same time as the experimental group but does not receive the treatment given to the experimental group. On average, effects of history (and other sources of bias) should occur equally for the experimental and control groups, allowing the researcher to see the effects of the treatment in the experimental group based on a comparison of the groups.

Maturation. Another factor that can affect a study conducted over a period of time is **maturation**. Maturation occurs when participants exhibit natural changes over the course of a study. This can include actual maturation, as in developmental studies where individ-uals are observed at different ages, or other types of changes that occur to individuals over a period of time. For example, in the study described above to test several treatments for depression, suppose there are two groups of depressed participants: one group receives a drug therapy for 12 weeks, whereas the other

Maturation: natural changes that occur to the participants during the course of a study that can result in bias

group receives a talk therapy for 12 weeks. Suppose also that both groups showed the same amount of improvement over the 12-week period in their symptoms of depression. One possible interpretation of these data is that both treatments are equally effective in improv-ing symptoms of depression. However, another possible interpretation of these data is that symptoms of depression improve on their own without treatment (e.g., participants may become more hopeful about their lives if they know they are being treated) and that nei-ther treatment is actually effective. In other words, maturation affected the data such that the participants improved as a natural consequence of factors that occurred during the 12 weeks in which the study was done.

As described above, the best way to minimize effects of maturation is to include a control group that does not receive the treatment to allow a comparison of groups that have similar experiences except for the treatment. In the treatment of depression study, this means adding a third group that has depression tested at the start of the 12 weeks and at the end of the 12 weeks but does not receive any treatment for their depression. (They should also be told that they are on the waiting list for receiving therapy so that any effects of knowing they will be receiving treatment can occur for the control group as well.) If the control group shows the same improvement as the two treatment groups, then maturation has likely occurred and participants have improved on their own and not as a result of the treatments. However, if the treatment groups show improvement above and beyond any improvement shown by the control group, then these improvements can more confidently be interpreted as due to the treatment the participants received.

Attrition. **Attrition** (also called **mortality**) occurs when participants drop out of a study after completing only part of the study. This is much more likely to occur in long-term studies that are conducted over a period of time. Attrition results in data being deleted from a study (or a portion of a study). The particular problem with participants dropping out during a study is that it is possible that the participants who drop out of a study may have different characteristics from the participants who remain to complete a study, thus biasing the full set of data toward participants with the characteristics required for completing the study.

—————— ❧ ——————

Attrition/Mortality: occurs when participants choose not to complete a study

For example, in the depression treatment study, suppose that some of the participants in the study drop out during the 12-week period and do not return for the posttest. It is possible that these participants who have chosen not to complete the study did so because they have worse depression symptoms than the participants that remained in the study (i.e., someone who is highly depressed may be less likely than someone who is not as highly depressed to return to the study to take the posttest). In this case, the data obtained in the study will tell the researcher about the effects of treatment for individuals who are moderately depressed and not for individuals who are severely depressed because the severely depressed participants dropped out. It is also possible that participants will drop out of this study because their depression symptoms improve and they feel they no longer need to continue treatment. Without knowing the cause of the attrition, the results of the study are even more difficult to interpret. Thus, attrition has reduced the validity of the data by making it only generalizable to moderately depressed individuals.

As with the other sources of bias described above that occur over a time period, attrition is best handled by inclusion of a control group. This will spread the attrition (on average) across the groups, allowing the researcher to make group comparisons to test the effect of the independent variable. However, the problem of generalizing the data to the larger population of interest (e.g., all individuals with depression symptoms) still remains. This is a problem with external validity (do the results generalize outside the study?), though, rather than one of internal validity that would occur if different numbers of individuals dropped out from the different groups, making the groups more unequal. We will consider issues of external validity in the next section.

External Validity

External validity is the degree to which a study measures realistic behaviors and a study's results can be generalized beyond the study (i.e., to other individuals and situations). In other words, if participants behave in a research study the way they would in their everyday lives, then the study has good external validity. The results of the study can be generalized to behaviors, conditions, and individuals who were not specifically tested in the study. As described above, external validity can be reduced by attrition, but there are also other factors that can reduce the external validity of a study. For example, as more control is imposed over sources of bias that reduce internal validity, the more external validity tends to suffer. When researchers include controls for internal sources of bias, they are typically restrict-

External Validity: the degree to which the results of a study apply to individuals and realistic behaviors outside the study

ing the situation under which the behavior of interest will be expressed. Thus, the behavior may become more artificial and specific to the study being conducted. In other words, the behavior observed in the study becomes less like behavior that occurs in the participants' everyday lives.

For example, suppose a researcher was interested in the effects of work environment on work productivity. In the study, room size and the presence or absence of a window in the room are manipulated (i.e., these are the independent variables). The participants are asked to perform a task where they have to insert blocks of varying shapes into slots in a box for a 30-minute time period. At the end of the 30-minute period, the number of pegs correctly inserted is counted for each participant as a measure of work productivity (i.e., number correct on the peg task is the operational definition of work productivity). The mean number of pegs correctly inserted is compared for the different room types. The study is conducted as a typical laboratory experiment such that the independent variables of interest are manipulated across room type, but the rooms are the same in all other ways.

Think about the internal and external validity of this study for a moment. The study appears to be fairly high in internal validity because the work environment is kept constant except for the manipulation of the two independent variables. The task is simple enough not to be affected by individual differences in ability. In other words, the study provides a good test of the hypothesis that room size and presence/absence of a window affect work productivity. However, one might question the external validity of the study. The peg task might be a realistic type of task for a factory worker but may not be a good example of a daily task for an office worker. Thus, the results of the study may only generalize to a portion of all workers. In addition, the partici-

Hawthorne Effect: a source of bias that can occur in a study due to participants changing their behavior because they are aware that they are being observed

pants in the study know that they are participating in a study and may adjust their behavior accordingly. They may, for example, work harder than they would in their job because they know that they are being observed. Or, alternatively, they may not work as hard as they do in their job because they know that the task is just for a research study, and their performance does not affect them personally as it might in a job environment. This is known as the **Hawthorne effect** (see discussion below).

Now consider a similar study conducted in a factory by the factory's manager. Employees are placed in the different working environments as in the study described above (the rooms vary by size and whether or not a window is present). They complete their normal factory line task as usual. After a 30-minute period in the new environment, the factory manager counts up the number of assemblies completed by each employee to compare the different environments. The study described here is considered a **field experiment**, because the experiment (independent variables are still manipulated as in the laboratory experiment described above) is conducted in a naturalistic environment (i.e., in the "field").

------------ ✀ ------------

Field Experiment: an experiment conducted in the participants' natural environment

Consider the internal and external validity of this experiment compared with the one described above. The external validity seems to be higher in the field experiment, because the factory workers' normal job task is used as the operational definition of work productivity. The behavior observed is more naturalistic for these workers. In addition, they are in their normal environment with other workers and normal factory sounds, making it more likely that they will exhibit more naturalistic work behaviors. However, several sources of bias have now been introduced into the experiment that might threaten the internal validity. Interactions with other coworkers are no longer controlled and could be different for different individuals across the experimental conditions. Noise is also a factor that might contribute to work productivity. It is not controlled across the room conditions in the field experiment as it is in the laboratory experiment. Thus, in this example with comparable laboratory and field experiments, the more controls there are that increase the internal validity in these experiments, the lower the external validity of the behaviors observed in the experiments.

Note that both studies described above are experiments. While experiments are typically higher in internal validity (and lower in external validity) than other research designs, this is not always the case and different types of experiments can vary greatly in internal validity based on the number of sources of bias controlled for by the researcher. For example, in each of the above experiments, changes could be made in the method or design to increase internal or external validity as needed. How carefully a study is designed can make a big difference in how high the internal and external validity is, regardless of the research design employed. The design of the study can alter a participant's perception of the study, leading to a change in behavior that is less realistic simply because the participant knows that he or she is being observed. This issue will be discussed further below.

The Hawthorne Effect. The *Hawthorne effect* is a term coined by Landsberger (1955) as he was analyzing a set of studies conducted at the Hawthorne Plant, a factory that produced products for the Western Electric Company in the 1920s and 1930s in Chicago. Researchers conducted studies in the factory to determine the effects of different lighting conditions on worker productivity. The researchers found that all the lighting conditions they tried increased the workers' productivity. In other words, by simple virtue of being studied, the workers' behavior changed. Other possible explanations have been offered for the results of this study (see Adair, 1984; Bramel & Friend, 1981), but the idea that studying individuals can change their behavior is now known as the Hawthorne effect. The act of studying individuals can alter their behavior and affect the results of a study, reducing its validity.

A related concept known as **demand characteristics** can also affect the validity of a study. Demand characteristics occur when participants in a study attempt to "figure out" the purpose of the study and change their behavior based on their view of the purpose of the study. The participants' understanding of the study's purpose can be correct or incorrect, but they change their behavior based on whatever notion they have of the purpose (either to exhibit behavior that is consistent with what they think the researcher expects or to exhibit

> **Demand Characteristics:** a source of bias that can occur in a study due to participants changing their behavior based on their perception of the study and its purpose

behavior different from what they think the researcher expects). This is a concept related to the Hawthorne effect, as demand characteristics occur as a result of a participant's participation in a study.

One way to deal with the Hawthorne effect (and demand characteristics) is to observe the participants unobtrusively. This can be done using the naturalistic observation technique. However, this is not always possible for all behaviors. Another way to deal with the Hawthorne effect is to make the participants' responses in a study anonymous (or confidential). This may alleviate some of the effects of this source of bias. Deception may also be used to hide the purpose of the study. These issues will also be addressed in the context of ethical standards for research with human participants in Chapter 5.

Sources of Bias Specific to a Field of Study

Some sources of bias are specific to a field of study. As a researcher becomes more familiar with an area of psychological study, these sources of bias become more clear, and ways to control for them can be built into the studies that one designs. For example, in some memory research where study-test delay time is not an independent variable of interest, it can become a source of bias. Suppose that a researcher is interested in comparing two study conditions for their effect on memory ability. If one condition takes longer to complete, it is possible that the study-test delay will be longer in this condition than the study condition that can be completed in a shorter amount of time. Thus, memory researchers must consider the delay time in designing studies to ensure that different conditions are matched on this factor. Visual acuity is often controlled for in visual-perception experiments by requiring participants to have normal or corrected-to-normal vision. Each area of research will have its own sources of bias. As you become more familiar with a particular area of research, you can often learn about these sources of bias by examining the methods of other researchers to identify controls they have used to remove this bias.

CHAPTER SUMMARY

Reconsider the questions from the beginning of the chapter:

- What is a variable? A variable is an attribute, situation, or behavior that can change from individual to individual.

- What are the different types of variables that researchers consider in their studies? Dependent variables are measured from individuals and are present in all research studies. Confounding variables are variables that may affect the dependent variables in a study but are not of interest to the researchers (i.e., can bias the results). Independent variables are variables manipulated by the researcher in an experiment. Quasi-independent variables are present in quasi-experiments and experiments. They are similar to independent variables in that they involve a comparison of groups, but they are not manipulated (i.e., levels are not randomly assigned).
- Which type of research method contains an independent variable? Why? Experiments contain independent variables because experiments involve the manipulation of a variable that allows for additional control of confounding variables.
- How do reliability and validity affect the results of a study? Having good internal validity in a study means reducing bias that can affect the results and providing a good test of the hypothesis. Having good external validity means studying behaviors and obtaining results that generalize to individuals beyond the study in their everyday lives. Having reliable data in a study means having results that would occur again in a similar situation.
- What are some factors that affect the validity of a study, and how can a researcher control these factors? Several common sources of bias have been discussed in the chapter. Some are common to particular types of designs or behaviors. To control these sources of bias, researchers should first identify possible confounding variables in a study and then design the study in the best way to avoid having these variables bias the results.

THINKING ABOUT RESEARCH

A summary of a research study in psychology is given below. As you read the summary, think about the following questions:

1. Identify the two independent variables. For each independent variable, indicate if it was manipulated between subjects or within subjects.
2. Identify the two dependent variables. Which two behaviors of interest are operationally defined by these dependent variables (one for each dependent variable)?
3. Consider the internal validity of this study. Does the study appear to provide a good test of the research question stated in the Purpose section? Why or why not?
4. Consider the external validity of this study. Are the memory behaviors exhibited in the study realistic? Why or why not?
5. Would you characterize this study as higher on internal validity, external validity, both?
6. Why do you think the researchers had the control group complete unrelated tasks during the time the "forget" group was completing the tasks for the filler lists? In what way does this aspect of their procedure improve the design of their study?

Study Reference

Smith, S. M., & Moynan, S. C. (2008). Forgetting and recovering the unforgettable. *Psychological Science, 19,* 462–468.

Purpose of the Study. The debate regarding repressed and recovered memories motivated this study. Researchers have argued about whether emotional or traumatic memories can be forgotten and then recovered at a later time when the appropriate retrieval cues are available (see McNally, 2003). In addition, some researchers (e.g., Loftus, 1993) have argued that recovered memories might actually be false memories. Laboratory research regarding false memories has confirmed that false memories can be created. However, little research has examined the notion that emotionally charged memories can be forgotten and subsequently recovered. This current study was designed to test this notion.

Method of the Study. Students from an introductory psychology course participated to fulfill a course requirement. All participants studied categorized lists. During the study phase, they were presented with the category name (e.g., Tools) and 10 exemplars of that category. Participants wrote down each exemplar and rated its category typicality on a scale from 1 to 10. Three target lists were presented among many filler lists. The target lists were neutral (Tools), memorable and emotional (Curse words), and emotional but not memorable (Diseases). All participants saw the same lists. After the study phase, the control group (about half of the participants) completed some unrelated tasks. The experimental "forget" group (the other half of the participants) received additional tasks involving the filler lists (but not the three target lists) to focus them on the filler lists and away from the target lists (i.e., make them more likely to forget the target lists). All participants then received a free recall test of the category names (Tools, Curse words, etc.) to determine what they had forgotten. Finally, all participants received a cued-recall test where they were given the category names (Tools, Curse words, etc.) and asked to recall as many category exemplars as they could that they had seen earlier in the experiment.

Results of the Study. In the free recall test, a "forget" effect was shown for all three target lists. Memory performance for the category names was lower in the "forget" group (4% for Diseases, 23% for Tools, and 40% for Curse words) than in the control group (20% for Diseases, 59% for Tools, and 75% for Curse words). In the cued-recall test, the groups showed similar levels of memory performance for the category exemplars (about 6.5 out of 10 for the Diseases, about 6.0 out of 10 for Tools, and about 8.5 out of 10 for Curse words), indicating recovery of the memories for all types of target lists. See Figures 4.5 and 4.6 for mean memory task performance.

Conclusions of the Study. The results of the study showed that items, even memorable and emotional items such as curse words, can be forgotten (on the free recall test) and then recovered with appropriate retrieval cues (cued-recall test). Thus, the study provides support from a laboratory study that emotional memories can be inhibited and then recovered at a later time.

COMMON PITFALLS AND HOW TO AVOID THEM

Problem: Confusing independent and dependent variables—students often get confused about which variable is which.

Solution: Remember that dependent means "relies on" and that must always be the variable that could change due to the "cause" or independent variable—thus, the dependent variable is the variable that is the behavior of interest measured from the participants and analyzed by the statistical tests.

Figure 4.5 Mean Free Recall of Categories

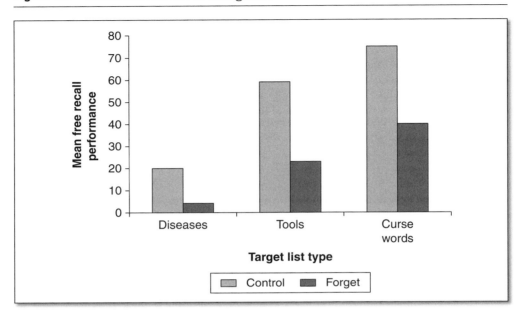

SOURCE: Results from Smith and Moynan's (2008) study.

Figure 4.6 Mean Cued Recall of List Items

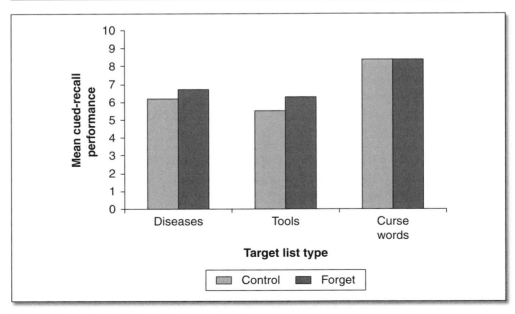

SOURCE: Results from Smith and Moynan's (2008) study.

Problem: Confusing independent and quasi-independent (subject) variables—students also have difficulty identifying a true independent variable that has been manipulated.

Solution: One method of identifying independent variables can be used for studies with different groups. For these studies, look for random assignment to levels for true independent variables that will indicate that a manipulation was made by the researcher.

Problem: Correctly identifying sources of bias—students sometimes have difficulty identifying sources of bias that can affect a study's results.

Solution: First identify the research design type (experiment, correlational study, etc.) and then consider sources of bias that are common for that design type; also consider the study from the participants' perspective and think through how their responses may be influenced by factors other than the variables of interest in the study.

Problem: Confusing scales of measurement—students sometimes have trouble distinguishing between different scales of measurement.

Solution: Consider first whether the scale involves categories or numbers. That will limit the scale to either a nominal/ordinal (categories) or interval/ratio (numbers) scale. If the scale contains categories, consider whether the categories can be ordered from highest to lowest (ordinal) or not (nominal). If the scale involves numbers, determine whether the scale has a true zero point that indicates the absence of the variable being measured (ratio) or not (interval).

TEST YOURSELF

1. For each dependent variable below, indicate if it is measured on a nominal, an ordinal, an interval, or a ratio scale:

    (a) The amount of money you paid in tuition this year

    (b) Your hobbies from most important to least important to you

    (c) Whether you plan to go to graduate school (yes or no)

    (d) Your last exam score as a measure of your performance on the exam (as percentage accuracy)

    (e) How much you are enjoying this class (on a 1 to 5 scale)

    (f) A list of your current career options

    (g) Your class standing (freshman, sophomore, junior, or senior)

2. For each of the following measures about aspects of beer, match each measure with the correct measurement scale: nominal, ordinal, interval, or ratio

    (a) How dark the beer is with choices of lager (lightest), ale (medium light), porter (medium dark), and stout (darkest)

    (b) How long it takes one to identify the type of beer one is drinking

    (c) Which brewery made the beer with choices of Yuengling, Leinenkugel, Blue Moon, Sam Adams, and Coors

    (d) How much someone likes a beer being tasted on a scale of 1 to 5

3. For the study described below, indicate all the information you can about how the independent variable was manipulated.

> A psychologist conducted a study to compare the effect of different types of displays on participants' interest in a task. All participants in the study were asked to complete a set of math problems in the laboratory. Half of the participants just saw the text of the problem presented on the screen in black and white and typed in their answer on the computer keyboard. The other half of the participants saw the text of the problem in different colors, and small pictures that helped illustrate the problem were included. At the end of the task, all participants rated their interest in completing the task on a 1 to 10 scale.

4. For the study described in (3), list any possible sources of bias you can think of that might threaten the internal validity of the study and explain how the bias could affect the results of the study.

5. For the study described in (3), evaluate the external validity of the study. How could this study be redesigned as a field experiment?

Answers: 1a. ratio, 1b. ordinal, 1c. nominal, 1d. ratio, 1e. interval, 1f. nominal, 1g. ordinal. 2a. ordinal, 2b. ratio, 2c. nominal, 2d. interval. 3. Independent variable = type of problem display, type independent variable, bivalent independent variable, manipulated between subjects. 4. With a between-subjects design, the primary concern is with group differences. Thus, one might be concerned about group differences for interest in math and ability (which can also affect interest). If group differences exist in math interest before the study, they will cloud the test of the independent variable effect on the dependent variable. 5. The external validity could be improved with more realistic math problems and classroom situations. A field experiment could be done by designing different texts that present math problems in the different formats and by asking students to use them in the classroom. Tests could also be designed for classroom use with the different presentation formats.

Ethical Guidelines for Psychological Research

CONSIDER THE FOLLOWING QUESTIONS AS YOU READ CHAPTER 5

- Why do we need ethical guidelines for research?
- How were ethical guidelines for psychological research developed?
- Were the Milgram (1963) and Zimbardo (1974) studies ethical? Why or why not?
- What are the current ethical guidelines for human participants?
- What is an institutional review board (IRB), and what purpose does it serve?
- What are the current ethical guidelines for animal subjects?
- How do ethics influence the way we report research?

In 1932, in Tuskegee, Alabama, the U.S. Public Health Service began a research study to investigate the course of syphilis in the human male. The researchers recruited 399 African American men who had previously contracted syphilis. The men were told that they had "bad blood" and that they could receive free health care by coming to the clinic where they were studied. None of the men were informed that they had syphilis by the researchers, and none of the men were treated for the disease (Brandt, 2000).

At the time the study started, the treatment for syphilis was dangerous and was not always effective. Thus, the researchers of the Tuskegee syphilis study were interested in better understanding the damage that the disease did to the men as it progressed to help determine if treating the disease was better than not treating it. By 1947, however, penicillin had become available as a safe and effective treatment for syphilis. Yet the researchers of the Tuskegee syphilis study did not end their study until 1972 and did not make penicillin available to the participants to treat the disease.

Through this study, the researchers learned a good deal about the progression of the syphilis disease. They learned about the different stages of the disease and about the many symptoms that accompany the disease. These symptoms include rashes, warts on the genitalia, and pus-filled skin pox. Later stages involve damage to the internal organs, including dementia when the brain deteriorates in some patients.

The researchers who were responsible for the Tuskegee syphilis study believed for the most part that their study was ethical (Brandt, 2000). They thought the medical knowledge about syphilis that would be gained was an important contribution to science. In addition, they argued that the men in the study were not being harmed by the study. The participants had already contracted syphilis, so the researchers believed that they were not doing anything to worsen the disease. The participants were also receiving free medical examinations that they could not have afforded on their own. In addition, in 1969, the Centers for Disease Control (CDC) reaffirmed the need for the study after concerns about the ethics of the study were raised. They also won the approval of the American Medical Association (AMA) for the study.

Do you agree with the attitudes of the researchers of the Tuskegee syphilis study that their study was not harmful to the participants in the study? If you answered "no" and believe it was harmful, *why* do you think it was harmful? In what way did the study harm the research participants? The answers to these questions have been a major point of discussion among psychologists and medical researchers for the past 50 years or so, as changes in the way society views the ethics of research on human participants has taken place. These changes in ethical guidelines for research have been motivated in large part by the discussion of studies such as the Tuskegee syphilis study, where it is clear to many people that the researchers did not meet their ethical obligations. In this chapter, we will discuss the historical context for ethical guidelines that provide the motivation for current ethical standards, the current guidelines for research with humans and animals, and the role of an institutional review board in the research process. See Figure 5.1 for an indication of the steps in the research process to which ethics are relevant.

HISTORICAL CONTEXT FOR ETHICAL GUIDELINES

Why do we need ethical guidelines for research in psychology? There are several reasons that researchers are held to ethical standards, but the most important one is that researchers are not always able to be objective about the effects of a study on the participants and whether or not a study will be harmful to the participants. In addition to the Tuskegee syphilis study, there are a few other important examples of studies that were conducted to advance scientific knowledge but also may have harmed the research participants in the process. Some particularly heinous examples are the experiments conducted by the Nazis on World War II concentration camp prisoners.

Nuremberg Code

At the end of World War II, the world learned of the atrocities the Nazis had committed during the war. Among their horrific acts were experiments conducted on concentration camp inmates. These experiments were conducted by scientists interested in learning about the limits of the human body and mind. Many of the experiments were designed to better understand the conditions soldiers are able to endure in war and involved participant exposure to extreme temperatures, infections, and noxious chemicals (Schuler, 1982). The subjects of these

Figure 5.1   Steps in the Research Process: Ethical Guidelines

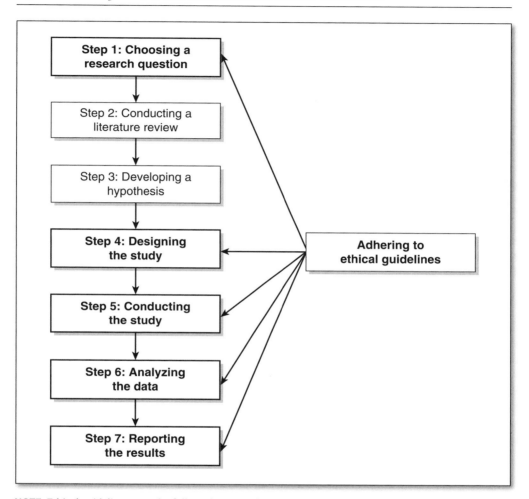

NOTE: Ethical guidelines must be followed at several steps in the research process.

experiments were forced to participate as prisoners in the Nazi concentration camps. The details of the experiments became public during the Nuremberg trials held between 1945 and 1949, where Nazi officers and officials were tried for war crimes (see Figure 5.2). The **Nuremberg Code** was developed by officials involved in the trials (judges, medical experts) as a result of what was learned about the Nazi experiments and was an early attempt to specify ethical standards for research with human participants.

Nuremberg Code: set of ethical guidelines developed for research with human participants based on information gained during the Nuremberg trials after World War II

Figure 5.2   Experiments Conducted on Nazi Concentration Camp Prisoners During World War II Prompted the Development of the Nuremburg Code of Ethics

SOURCE: Copyright by Jupiter Unlimited, www.jupiter unlimited.com.

———————— ✺ ————————

Informed Consent: obtaining consent from participants for participation in research after the participants have been informed about the purpose, procedure, and risks of the research

Coercion: forcing participants to participate in research without their consent

The Nuremberg Code focuses on the issues of **informed consent**, which is informing participants about the study and then gaining their consent for participation, and **coercion**, where participants' right to refuse or end participation in a study is taken away. The Code also includes other important ethical guidelines that are still part of the ethical guidelines psychologists currently adhere to. The Nuremberg Code states the following (Schuler, 1982):

1. Participation in research is voluntary, and participants must be given information about the risks involved in the research (i.e., informed consent and freedom from coercion).

2. The research must contribute to scientific knowledge and be conducted by qualified researchers.

3. The researchers must avoid unnecessary harm, take precautions against risk, ensure that benefits outweigh the risks of the study, and terminate the study if unforeseen harm comes to the participants.

4. The participants have the right to discontinue their participation in the study (i.e., freedom from coercion).

APA Code

In 1953, the American Psychological Association (APA) codified its own ethical standards for the field of psychology, including psychological research (Schuler, 1982). (The European Federation of Psychologists' Association, www.efpa.eu, and several other international psychologists' associations have developed similar ethics codes that have been adopted by other countries.) Many of the elements in the APA code overlapped with the main elements of the Nuremberg Code described above. Two additional elements were included in the guidelines for research: (1) the researchers must reduce harm due to **deception**, which is misleading the participants about the study's purpose or procedures, and (2) the researchers must ensure the confidentiality of participant data. However, the original APA code left the responsibility for overseeing research studies to the researchers, and several researchers used the weighing of benefits against risk element to justify harmful studies by claiming that the studies were highly beneficial. In some psychological studies, the researchers have argued that the important knowledge gained in the study justified the risk to the participants. Two well-known examples of research

———————— ✺ ————————

Deception: misleading participants about the purpose or procedures of a research study conducted by psychologists that many have argued stretched the APA ethical standards are described below: the Milgram (1963) obedience study and the Zimbardo (1973) prison study.

Milgram (1963) Obedience Study. During the Nuremberg trials, several defendants argued that they were not responsible for their wartime actions because their actions were carried out to follow orders of their superiors. This defense led social psychologists to some interesting research questions. How strong is the power of authority? Does a person need to have sadistic tendencies in order to harm another person, or is an order from an authority figure enough to cause someone to commit these actions? Stanley Milgram became interested in these questions and wondered how many people would harm another person simply because an authority figure told them to do so. Milgram designed a study to investigate these research questions that examined the effect of an authority figure on participants' behavior. In his study, participants were recruited to administer a memory task to a second participant. The second participant was actually a **confederate** in the study. In other words, the second participant was not an actual participant; instead, the confederate acted a part in the study to make the participants believe that he or she was just another participant in the study.

Confederate: a person who is part of a research study but acts as though he or she is not, to deceive the participant about the study's purpose

The confederate was placed behind a screen and attached to electrodes in the participants' presence. After that point, the participants could hear the confederate but could not see him during the study. The participants were then asked to read word pairs to the confederate for a later memory test. The participants administered the memory test by reading a word and asking the confederate to choose the word it was paired with in the study list from four choices. Each time the confederate answered incorrectly, the participants were instructed to deliver an electric shock to the confederate by pressing a button on a console placed in front of them. For each wrong answer, the participants were told to increase the level of shock delivered. Shocks were not actually delivered to the confederate, but participants were led to believe that they were actually shocking the confederate. The confederate cried out after some of the shocks as if in pain and was silent for the more severe shock levels. The buttons on the participants' console were labeled such that the shocks appeared to increase in intensity with each incorrect answer. If participants resisted (verbally or nonverbally), an experimenter in a white lab coat (i.e., an authority figure) encouraged them to continue, with statements increasing in strength as more resistance was displayed (see Figure 5.3).

Figure 5.3   An Experimenter and Participant as in the Milgram (1963) Study

SOURCE: Copyright by Jupiter Images, www.jupiterimages.com.

NOTE: The photograph shows that an experimenter in a lab coat served as the authority figure and encouraged the participants to continue the study if they were hesitant to administer electric shocks to the "learner" confederate.

At the start of the study, Milgram asked other social psychologists how many participants they thought would continue the experiment to the end, where the shocks were labeled "danger" and "XXX." Most predicted that only the very cruelest participants (less than 2%) would administer all the shocks. However, the results of Milgram's study showed that almost two thirds of the participants administered all the shocks, and none of the participants checked on the confederate without asking permission first. This study showed that the presence of an authority figure greatly influences people's behavior, to the point where people may harm another person when ordered to do so.

Milgram justified his study by arguing that although the participants were deceived in the study, they did not experience long-term harm from the study. The participants were fully debriefed after the study to show that no harm had been done to the confederate. In addition, vital knowledge about human behavior was learned. The social psychologists Milgram had surveyed at the start of the study had been unable to predict the results of the study. Thus, new knowledge was gained about the effect of authority figures on behavior. However, critics of the study argued that the stress of the situation and deception of the participants were too great and were psychologically harmful (Schuler, 1982). Furthermore, it is unclear whether the participants felt they could withdraw from the study if they wished, given that every time they protested the experimenter told them they were required to continue.

Imagine how you would feel if you were a participant in the Milgram study and learned that you were willing to shock another person simply because a stranger in a lab coat told you to. How would that knowledge change the way you felt about yourself? Milgram countered the criticisms with a survey of the participants after the study that showed that a large majority of them were "glad" or "very glad" to have participated, despite the stressful situation they experienced in the study. Despite Milgram's arguments, an exact replication of the Milgram study is unlikely to meet the ethical standards for research currently in use in psychology (but see Burger, 2009, for a description of a recent modified replication that was also covered on the ABC News show *Primetime*).

Zimbardo (1973) Prison Experiment. Another famous study that was criticized for stretching ethical standards for research was conducted by Phillip Zimbardo at Stanford University in the early 1970s. Zimbardo was interested in how the roles we are given in a society affect our behavior toward others. He created a mock prison in the basement of the psychology building at Stanford and randomly assigned students to play the role of prisoner or guard in the mock prison. He carefully screened the participants to ensure that they were all similar in terms of intelligence and personality characteristics. Thus, the only difference between the prisoner and guard groups was the role they were assigned to play in the prison experiment.

Zimbardo created conditions for the prison that were as realistic as possible. He had the participants assigned as prisoners publicly arrested by campus police before they were placed in the prison. They were given prison clothes to wear and assigned a number. They remained in the prison 24 hours a day for the length of the experiment. Small cells were built in the prison area to confine the prisoners for much of their time. The guards were given uniforms and worked set shifts at the prison, returning to their student lives during their off hours.

Zimbardo had planned for the prison experiment to take place over 2 weeks but stopped the study after only a few days, when he realized that the study had become harmful to the participants. Some of the prisoners had extreme stress reactions and had to be released. Several of the guards became cruel and forced the prisoners to engage in embarrassing behaviors. However, none of the participants ever asked to stop the experiment. Both groups of participants, prisoners and guards, had lost the reality that they were participants in an experiment and were greatly affected by the situation they were placed in during the experiment.

Zimbardo followed ethical guidelines in designing the experiment. He considered alternate ways of studying the effects of the prisoner/guard roles, received informed consent from all the participants before beginning the study, and discussed the purpose of the study and its benefits (a process called **debriefing**) with the participants after the study ended (Zimbadro, 1973). He also stopped the experiment earlier than planned to avoid further harming the participants (see www.prison exp.org for more information on this study provided by Zimbardo). However, critics of the

———————— ✂ ————————

Debriefing: discussing the purpose and benefits of a research study with participants, often done at the end of the study

study claimed that the participants should not have been placed in such a stressful situation in the study. Furthermore, given the powerful influence of the prison context, it was difficult for those involved in the study to be objective about the effects of the study. Zimbardo himself admitted to being influenced by the context of the prison study, feeling like a prison warden at times when the study was taking place (Reiniger, 2001).

CURRENT ETHICAL GUIDELINES FOR HUMAN PARTICIPANTS RESEARCH

Due to the criticism leveled at studies such as Milgram's and Zimbardo's, the APA Ethics Code has been revised several times to ensure that researchers include a thorough debriefing of the participants, more clearly define the conditions under which deception may be used, and include specific guidelines for research with animal subjects. See Table 5.1 for a summary of the current APA Ethics Code guidelines for research.

In addition to the APA Ethics Code, federal ethical guidelines exist that must be adhered to at all institutions that receive public funds. After the Tuskegee syphilis study became public, the U.S. Government formed a committee to discuss appropriate ethical guidelines for medical and psychological research. The committee produced the Belmont Report (National Commission for the Protection of Human Subjects of Biomedical and Behavioral Research, 1979, p. 200), which lists the responsibilities of researchers as they conduct research with human participants and the rights of those participants before, during, and after a study (a copy of the full report can be viewed at www.nihtraining.com/ohsrsite/guidelines/belmont.html). The Belmont Report provides the set of ethical guidelines that researchers in psychology must adhere to. Three major principles are described in the report that outline the responsibilities of researchers: (1) *respect for persons*, (2) *beneficence*, and (3) *justice*. We will consider how

TABLE 5.1 Summary of the APA Ethics Code for Research	
APA Code	**Ethics Issues Addressed**
1. Research should be approved by the researcher's IRB, where applicable.	IRB approval
2. Research must include an informed consent process, including the following: (a) purpose of the research (b) expected duration of the participants' participation (c) procedures used in the research (d) participants' right to decline to participate and withdraw participation at any time and the consequences of withdrawal (e) foreseeable risks of the research to the participants (f) benefits of the research (g) confidentiality rights of the participants (h) incentives for participation (i) whom to contact for questions or concerns	Informed consent
3. In addition to (2), if the research involves an experimental treatment, the participants must be informed that it is experimental, how participants will be assigned to groups, the available alternative treatments, and the compensation they will receive for participation.	Informed consent Reduce harm
4. In addition to (2), if the research involves video or audio recording of the participants, they must be informed ahead of time if it does not compromise the research to do so.	Informed consent Confidentiality
5. Incentives for participation must be reasonable so as not to be coercive.	Coercion
6. If the research involves deception, the researchers must determine that the deception is necessary and justified and explain any use of deception to participants as soon as possible at the completion of the study. Researchers may not use deception that is expected to cause physical pain or severe distress.	Deception Reduce harm
7. Thorough debriefing must be given for the study. If it is not possible to give debriefing immediately, researchers must protect against participants' harm.	Reduce harm
8. If researchers become aware of unexpected harm to participants, they must take reasonable measures to reduce harm, including termination of the study if necessary.	Reduce harm

APA Code	Ethics Issues Addressed
9. The following are rules to be remembered while doing research with animals: (a) adhere to federal and local guidelines for care and treatment of animals (b) involve trained personnel (c) minimize discomfort to the animals (d) painful or stressful procedures must be justified and only used when alternative procedures cannot be used (e) use anesthesia and prevent infection when surgical procedures are used (f) terminate animals quickly with minimal pain if termination is necessary	Animal research ethics
10. Researchers must report data accurately and correct errors if they are discovered.	Ethics in reporting research
11. Researchers must properly cite others' ideas and work when reporting research.	Ethics in reporting research
12. Publication credit can be taken only for work the authors have performed, and credit order should be determined according to the contribution of each author.	Ethics in reporting research
13. Data should be shared with other researchers to allow verification of results.	Ethics in reporting research

SOURCE: American Psychological Association (2002).

these principles translate to ethical guidelines for psychological research in the section below. Table 5.2 also provides an overview of the application of these principles to psychological research.

Respect for Persons

The first principle of the Belmont Report, respect for persons, refers to the treatment of participants in research studies. Informed consent is an important element of this principle, and it includes informing the participants about the nature of their participation in a study, including what the participants will do in the study, the purpose of the study, any risks associated with the study, benefits of the study, information about alternative treatments (if applicable), and the participants' rights during the study (especially their right to withdraw

TABLE 5.2	Applications of the Belmont Report Principles
Principle	**Application**
Respect for persons	Provide information about the study before it begins (nature of participation, purpose, risks, benefits)
	Obtain voluntary consent from participants after they are informed (i.e., informed consent)
	Give participants opportunity to ask questions
	Inform participants of right to withdraw
Beneficence	Reduce risk of harm to participants
	Potential benefits of the study must outweigh risks
	Inhumane treatment of participants is never justified
Justice	Selection of participants must be fair
	All participant groups must have opportunity to receive benefits of research
	No participant groups may be unfairly selected for harmful research

---

Consent Form: a form provided to the participants at the beginning of a research study to obtain their consent for the study and explain the study's purpose and risks, and the participants' rights as participants

from the study and their right to ask questions about the study). It is the researchers' responsibility to ensure that the participants have the ability to understand the information they are given during the informed consent process. Often, researchers will provide a **consent form** that includes the information listed above about the study that the participants can read and sign before their participation in the study. Special protections must be provided for participants who may not have the ability to fully comprehend the information (e.g., children, persons with certain types of disabilities or illnesses). The amount of protection needed depends on the risk of harm to those individuals and the benefits of their participation.

As part of the informed consent process, research participants must volunteer to participate in the study after they are informed about the study as described above. This creates a dilemma for participants who may feel coerced to participate in the study. For example, the rights of participants who are prisoners must be carefully considered to reduce any implied coercion the participants may feel to participate. This may also be an issue when students are included in a research study where the instructor is a researcher for the study. In this case, the instructor needs to make it clear in the informed consent process that the participants have the right to refuse to participate without it affecting their evaluation in the course. If non-English-speaking participants are included, a translated version of the informed consent information must be provided. If children or other individuals with legal guardianship are included as participants, informed consent must be obtained from the legal guardian, and assent for their participation must be obtained from the participants.

The assent process must explain what the participants' participation will entail and must be explained in a way that the participants can understand what they are being asked to do.

Beneficence

Beneficence refers to the reduction of risk of harm to the participants as compared with the benefit of the study. In other words, a **risk-benefit analysis** should be conducted to ensure that the benefits of a study outweigh the risks to the participants. In addition, the risk of harm to the participants should be reduced as much as possible when designing a study. There are many types of risks that must be considered in psychological research. Physical risk is an obvious factor but is an issue in only a small number of studies. More common are risks to psychological health and reputation and social standing. Some studies may be emotionally upsetting to participants or cause them stress (as the 1963 Milgram study did). If they are asked to consider difficult or traumatic experiences during an interview or in answering a questionnaire, participants can experience psychological harm in a study. In some studies, negative mood induction may occur to compare mood states. Thus, altering participants' mood may also psychologically harm them. Risk to participants' social standing may occur if their **confidentiality** is breached in disseminating a research study. Thus, it is the researcher's responsibility to maintain the participants' confidentiality at all times during the research process.

Risk-Benefit Analysis: weighing the risks against the benefits of a research study to ensure that the benefits outweigh the risks

Confidentiality: it is the researcher's responsibility to protect the participants' identity and right to privacy (including participant responses) during and after the research study

The risks described above are weighed by the researcher against the benefits of the study to society to ensure that the benefits outweigh the risks. The researcher must determine what the likely benefit of the study is, determine the likely risks to the participants—often by reviewing past studies conducted in a similar manner to determine their impact on the participants—and describe the study in terms of its potential benefit to justify whatever risks may befall the participants during the study. Thus, studies with the potential to gain important knowledge may have increased risks as compared with studies with lesser potential benefits. However, inhumane treatment of participants is never justified, and the researcher is responsible for determining what conditions may be too harmful to participants to include in a study.

Justice

Fair selection of participants is covered by the justice principle. Researchers are responsible for ensuring that all participants have a fair chance of receiving potentially beneficial treatments in research (e.g., treatments for specific mental illnesses or conditions), as well as ensuring that potentially harmful conditions are not exclusively administered to a specific group (as it was when treatment was withheld from African American men with syphilis in the Tuskegee study). Special considerations must be provided for groups that may be easier to manipulate (e.g., individuals with illnesses, low-income individuals). For example, suppose that you are a researcher conducting a study in a geographical area where there are many economically disadvantaged individuals (e.g., a low-income area of a large city, a developing country). As compensation, you plan to offer the participants $50 to participate in your extensive study (e.g., you plan to interview the participants extensively and observe them for a period of time). Compensation of $50 is a reasonable amount to offer U.S. students for this type of participation, so you offer the same amount to the low-income participants in your study. However, $50 will have a different value to low-income individuals than it would to middle-class individuals. Even if the participants did not want to participate in your study, they may feel compelled to participate to earn the $50, which may feed their family for a period of time. Thus, many would consider this type of compensation coercive to the low-income participants. These individuals may feel that they have less choice in participating because they are in greater need of the compensation than higher-income individuals. These issues must be considered by researchers to ensure that the selection of their participants is fair. If a participant group is to be excluded from a research study, there must be a scientific justification for the exclusion.

An Example

Consider a recent study by Mihai et al. (2006). These researchers were interested in testing a possible treatment for alcohol abuse. After long-term alcohol abuse, individuals may experience delirium tremens. These episodes can include hallucinations, disorientation, motor tremors, and severe anxiety. The treatment Mihai et al. were interested in involved videotaping patients with severe alcohol dependence while they were experiencing a delirium tremens episode.

Patients who were hospitalized with delirium tremens were recruited for inclusion in the study. To be eligible, patients had to have severe alcohol dependence for at least 3 years and consume a large quantity of alcohol per day. Consent to videotape the patients was obtained from the patients' families. Patients were videotaped during their delirium tremens episode with a psychiatrist and a medical assistant present. Consent for the study was obtained from the patients themselves at some point after videotaping. After the patients had recovered from their delirium tremens episode (9 to 27 days later), they were randomly assigned to one of two groups. One group of patients (the experimental group—see Chapter 3) was shown the videotapes of their episodes with a psychiatrist explaining the symptoms and their connection to the alcohol abuse. The other group (the control group—see Chapter 3) was given the choice to erase their tapes or to view them after 6 months had passed. None of the patients in the second group had viewed their videotapes before a 6-month follow-up occurred.

Each month for 6 months after the beginning of the study, the patients were tested for relapse rates, number of days per week they drank, and number of drinks they had on each day they drank. Results indicated that the group that viewed their videotapes showed lower relapse rates, fewer drinking days per week, and fewer drinks per drinking day than the group that did not view their videotapes. Mihai et al. (2006) concluded that the videotape treatment was effective in reducing relapse in patients with alcohol dependency.

Based on the ethical guidelines described above (see Tables 5.1 and 5.2), what are the ethical issues involved in this study? What issues should the researchers consider before they conduct this study? One issue you may consider is the coercion of the participants. Initial consent for the study was obtained from the patients' families instead of from the patients themselves. Consent was not obtained from the patients before videotaping took place. However, the researchers may have felt that the patients were not in a position to provide consent during their delirium tremens episode. Instead, they destroyed the videos of any patient who refused to consent after the videotaping took place. Another issue is the participants' confidentiality. The videotapes of the participants' delirium tremens episodes provide a lasting record of a difficult and potentially defaming episode in the participants' lives (see Broyles, Tate, & Happ, 2008, for a more thorough discussion of ethical issues involved in videotaped records collected in research). Where the videotapes are stored, who is allowed access to them, and what happens to them when the study is concluded are all important issues in this study. In fact, the researchers reported destroying the videotapes at the conclusion of the study (if they had not already been destroyed prior to this time at the participant's request) to protect the confidentiality of the participants. A third issue is the harm the study procedures may bring to the participant and whether the risk of harm outweighs the benefit of the study. The participants in the study may have experienced stress, anxiety, or other negative emotions while viewing the videotapes of their delirium tremens episodes. However, the researchers may have argued that the possible benefit of finding an effective treatment for alcohol abuse may outweigh the negative emotions experienced by the participants in the study. This is a difficult question best answered by society at large: When is the discomfort of a few worth knowledge that may aid many? We will return to this question later in the discussion of animal research ethics.

INSTITUTIONAL REVIEW BOARDS

In response to reported abuses of research ethics, the U.S. Department of Health and Human Services (DHHS) currently requires all institutions where research is conducted (universities and colleges, hospitals, companies, etc.) to have an **institutional review board (IRB)** to oversee the research conducted at that site or by researchers affiliated with that institution and

Institutional Review Board (IRB): a committee of knowledgeable individuals who oversee the ethics of research with human participants conducted at an institution

ensure that ethical guidelines are adhered to in research with human participants (DHHS, 2005). This policy applies to all institutions that are subject to federal regulations. The IRB reviews all research proposed at the institution to provide a more objective evaluation of the ethics of a study. The IRB is made up of at least five members with backgrounds sufficient to ensure qualified review of the research proposals. If the IRB finds ethical problems with a proposed study, the board can instruct the researcher to revise the study or simply disapprove the study. In other words, before researchers can conduct a study, they must first receive approval from their IRB.

There are three categories of review by IRBs. The category for a study is determined by the amount of risk there is to the participants in the study. Riskier studies require more careful and thorough review. The three categories of IRB review are (1) *exempt*, (2) *expedited*, and (3) *full review*.

Exempt Studies

Exempt studies are those studies that have the smallest amount of risk involved. They are typically studies that involve educational or cognitive testing of participants, where there is no physical or psychological risk and little or no risk of loss of social standing if confidentiality were to be breached. Archival studies where the individuals cannot be identified in the data also fall into the exempt category. Research conducted in educational settings for educational purposes also qualifies for exempt review. Studies that fit into this category are typically given a brief review and then assigned exempt status, which means that they are exempt from further review as long as the procedures of the study do not change in the future.

Expedited Studies

The DHHS identified a category of expedited review for studies that involve minimal risk (DHHS, 2005). Expedited studies need be reviewed by only one member of the IRB, which speeds the process of review. Expedited studies may involve a small amount of physical or psychological risk. For example, studies involving noninvasive medical procedures (measurements of heart rate, galvanic skin response, brain-wave activity, etc.), collection of blood by normal means (finger stick, venipuncture, etc.), video- or audiotaping of observations, and survey or questionnaire studies with minimal emotional impact are typically given expedited review.

Full-Review Studies

Studies with the highest amount of risk receive full review by the IRB, meaning that each member of the IRB will review the research proposal. Studies requiring full review are often studies where a special population has a risk of harm, such as studies with particular risk to children or other individuals who may not be capable of providing informed consent on their own. Studies involving invasive medical procedures or high psychological risk, as with deception that could cause stress or questionnaires about behaviors that could cause emotional distress, typically require full IRB review.

Criteria for IRB Approval

IRB members use a set of criteria to evaluate research proposals and ensure that the research meets the ethical guidelines described in the Belmont Report (U.S. DHHS, 2005). The criteria are as follows:

1. The researcher will minimize unnecessary risk to the participants.
2. The risk in the study is justified by the potential benefits of the study.

3. The selection of the participants is fair and appropriate for the study.

4. An informed consent process is included in the study and can be documented by the researchers.

5. The researcher will monitor collection of the data to ensure the safety of the participants during the course of the study.

6. The privacy and confidentiality of the participants will be protected by the researcher.

7. If a special participant group is included in the study, procedures must be included to protect the rights of these participants.

A research proposal sent to the IRB for review must address each of these elements. Individual IRBs may have their own proposal form that researchers must complete to allow all elements of the criteria to be addressed clearly in the proposal.

Deception and Debriefing

In addition to the criteria listed above, the APA Ethics Code (APA, 2002) requires sufficient justification for studies involving deception and a debriefing process in all studies. If a study makes use of deception, the researcher must justify why the deception is necessary and why alternative procedures that do not use deception cannot be employed. The deception cannot be used if it will cause physical or severe psychological harm. Note, however, that there is a difference between deception and not fully disclosing the study's purpose. In many cases, researchers do not fully disclose the purpose of the study to reduce **demand characteristics**, where the participants may alter their behavior based on their perception of the study's purpose or hypothesis (see Chapter 4 for more discussion of demand characteristics). For example, in research testing a type of memory called *indirect memory*, researchers may not call the test a memory test, because they do not want the participants to intentionally retrieve studied items during this test. In other words, indirect memory tests involve a form of memory that is used unintentionally. In studies of indirect memory (Roedger & McDermott, 1993), participants are given a study session and then a task that they are to complete as quickly as possible (e.g., identify a word flashed very quickly on the computer screen) with studied items included in the task. No mention is made of the study episode when the indirect memory test is given, and participants are often told that it is an unrelated task. This is done to discourage participants from using direct memory in the test (i.e., intentionally retrieving studied items). Indirect memory can be measured in these tests by the faster speed with which participants identify words they have studied versus items not studied. This is a procedure commonly used in research I have conducted on indirect memory (e.g., McBride, Coane, & Raulerson, 2006). Describing the indirect memory test in general or alternative terms that reduce demand characteristics

Demand Characteristics: a source of bias that can occur in a study due to participants' changing their behavior based on their perception of the study and its purpose is not the same as deceiving the participants, and the IRB will view these situations differently when reviewing a study for approval.

Most studies involve a debriefing process to fully explain the purpose of the study to the participants and the knowledge that the study will contribute, including expected results of the study. However, if the study uses deception, the debriefing process must thoroughly explain the nature of the study and the deception used, including the purpose of the deception in the study. The goal of the debriefing process is to allow the participant to leave the study with a positive attitude toward the research. Thus, if the participant has been stressed during the study, part of the debriefing process should attempt to reduce this stress. If the participant's mood has been negatively altered by the study, an attempt should be made during the debriefing process to restore the participant's mood state before the study began. The participants are also provided with an opportunity to gain new knowledge about their behavior in the debriefing through the explanation of the study provided by the researcher and through questions they may wish to ask about the study.

An Example

Consider the ethics of the following social psychology study: To investigate the effects of personal-space invasions on physiological behaviors, Middlemist, Knowles, and Matter (1976) arranged an interesting field experiment of urination behaviors in college males. They conducted their experiment in a men's restroom at a university, such that men using the restroom were selected as participants, and a **field experiment** (see Chapter 4 for a discussion of field experiments) was conducted. Three urinals in the restroom were arranged so that men entering the restroom were forced to use (1) the end urinal with a confederate next to them (the urinal at the other end had a "being cleaned" sign and a bucket and sponge placed on it), (2) the end urinal with a confederate two urinals away (the middle urinal had the sign), or (c) the end urinal with no confederate nearby (both of the other urinals had signs). An experimenter in a stall measured the time it took for the participant to begin urination and the length of time he urinated. Participants were never informed that they were participating in a research study. The researchers found that the participants in the condition with the confederate at the urinal next to them took longer to begin urination and urinated for a shorter duration than the other two conditions, indicating that invasion of personal space affects physiological behaviors.

Field Experiment: an experiment conducted in the participants' natural environment

Imagine that you are a member of the IRB reviewing this study before it is conducted. What issues might you have with the research? What are the risks to the participants in this study? Do you feel that the risk to the participants outweighed the benefit of the knowledge gained? Why or why not? Can you think of any other way that this study could be designed to reduce the risks to the participants? One issue that you may have noticed is that no informed consent process or debriefing took place because the participants were never informed that they were involved in a research study. The informed consent process would likely have affected the participants' behavior, but a debriefing process may have alleviated any psychological discomfort caused by the presence of the confederate, especially in the condition with a confederate at the next urinal. However, the researchers may have argued that the process of debriefing the participants may have embarrassed them, thus causing harm. These are the sorts of issues that are considered by the members of an IRB as they review research.

CURRENT ETHICAL GUIDELINES FOR NONHUMAN ANIMAL SUBJECTS

Psychological research sometimes involves animal subjects (see Figure 5.4). Animals are often used as subjects when study procedures are considered too invasive or difficult to conduct with human participants. Important knowledge regarding basic human behaviors such as hunger, thirst, sensory processes, and learning has been gained through animal research in psychology (APA, n.d.). However, research with animal subjects represents a minority of the studies conducted in the field of psychology. Only about 7% to 8% of all psychological research involves animal subjects, mostly with bird and rodent subjects (APA, n.d.). Monkeys and other primates are rarely used in psychological research—only about 5% of animal studies in psychology involve primates (APA, n.d.). Yet just as there are guidelines for research with human participants, there are ethical guidelines that researchers must adhere to in research with animal subjects as well. The APA Ethics Code (APA, 2002) defines specific criteria that must be met for animal studies regarding justification of the study, personnel involved in the study, care and housing of the animals in the study, acquisition of the animals for the study, and procedures used in the study.

Figure 5.4 **Rats Are a Common Species Used in Psychological Research With Animals**

SOURCE: Copyright by Jupiter Unlimited, www.jupiter unlimited.com.

Justification

According to the APA Ethics Code (APA, 2002), justification of research with animal subjects must include a clear scientific purpose for the study. This ensures that frivolous studies with animals will not be conducted. Any study with animal subjects must be shown to contribute important knowledge of behavior (for humans or other animals). The researcher must also justify the use of the specific species chosen for the study and why that species is best suited to the study. In other words, how will a study with that species contribute knowledge about behavior that can be generalized beyond that species? Researchers must consider alternative species and justify why animals are needed to the study. Just as in research with human participants, a risk-benefit analysis must be conducted to justify the research. The greater the risk of harm to the subjects, the greater potential benefit there must be from the study.

Personnel

The APA Ethics Code (APA, 2002) indicates that only trained and experienced personnel may be involved in research with animal subjects. Any researcher involved with a study involving animals must be trained in the procedures to be used in the study to ensure that quality research is conducted and that effects on the animals can be properly anticipated. Researchers must also have knowledge about the specific species being studied to properly care for the animals during the course of the study.

Care and Housing of the Animals

Researchers and the institutions where the research is conducted are responsible for the proper care of the animal subjects before, during, and after a research study has been conducted. The Animal Welfare Act (U.S. Department of Agriculture [USDA], 2007) provides specific standards for the acquisition, housing, and care of animals in the United States. Other countries also have specific standards for the care of animals that are used in research. The APA Ethics Code (2002) specifically states that researchers in psychology must meet or exceed the USDA guidelines for care of animals. Animals are to be provided with humane care and housing conditions that keep the animals in good health. Enrichment of the animals' environment is also encouraged.

Acquisition of the Animals

The APA Ethics Code (2002) describes criteria in a separate section of the guidelines to outline how animals used in psychological research may be ethically obtained. Animals not bred by the researcher's institution must be obtained in a manner that follows USDA regulations and local ordinances. Researchers must ensure that proper care of the animals is maintained during transport to the facility. Animals taken from the wild must be obtained humanely and lawfully. Finally, rules regarding the use of endangered or threatened species must be followed.

Procedures Used in the Study

Researchers must treat animals humanely during the study procedures. If the animals will experience pain, their discomfort should be minimized as much as possible. For example, animals must be given anesthesia during surgical procedures, and these procedures may be conducted only by trained researchers. As described above, greater risk of harm to the animals requires greater justification of the study. Studies that harm animal subjects must have a greater potential to contribute important knowledge. Animals must be monitored during the study to look for unanticipated negative effects. For example, if food is withheld from the animal for a period of time during the study, the researchers must stop the study if the animal's body weight falls below a set criterion to ensure the health of the animal. Finally, animals cannot be released into the wild at the completion of the study, as it may be unsafe for the animals and the ecosystem into which they are released. Researchers conducting field studies in the wild must take care not to disturb the ecosystem in which they are observing.

Institutional Animal Care and Use Committee

The IRB equivalent for research with non-human animal subjects is the **Institutional Animal Care and Use Committee (IACUC).** Just as IRBs oversee research conducted with human participants, IACUCs oversee research conducted with nonhuman animal subjects at an institution. Thus, IACUC members must have knowledge of the APA Ethics Code regarding animal subjects, federal guidelines regarding the care and treatment of animals, and research procedures used in past studies with animals. Research proposals must be reviewed and approved by the IACUC before research with animals may commence.

Institutional Animal Care and Use Committee (IACUC): committee of knowledgeable individuals that oversees the ethics of research with nonhuman animal subjects at an institution

For proposals of animal research, justification of the research is a particularly important issue. As discussed above, the risk-benefit analysis of research with human participants is important in justifying the need for the study and any risks the participants may experience as a result of the study. The benefit of the knowledge gained by the study must outweigh the risks to the participants. However, in the case of animal research this can be more difficult to determine. Human participants can refuse consent or choose to withdraw from a study if they wish. They can verbally indicate to the researcher if they are experiencing high levels of stress or pain during the study to alert the researcher to stop the study (as occurred in the Zimbardo, 1973, prison study). Animal subjects do not have the choice to participate in a study and cannot terminate their participation during the course of a study. Animals cannot verbalize their discomfort level to the researcher, and it may be unclear how much discomfort an animal is experiencing during a study. Finally, some studies require that the animal be sacrificed to more closely examine brain tissue or other physiological aspects of the animal. Thus, justification of a study with animal subjects is an extremely important part of the approval process. The issue of when discomfort to a few is worth a great benefit to the many, especially when the few have no choice but to endure the discomfort, is one that is debated by both psychologists and society at large.

An Example

As an example of ethical considerations for animals in psychological studies, consider a study reported by Nuseir, Heidenreich, and Proudfit (1999). Nuseir et al. were interested in the effects of an injection of a drug that reduces pain into a specific area of the brain to determine if that area of the brain is involved in pain perception. Rats were used as subjects in the experiment. Each rat was immobilized, injected with the drug, and then subjected to a heat source applied to its tail. A control group received a saline solution instead of the drug as a comparison group. The time it took for the rat to flick its tail (indicating it felt the heat on its tail) was measured for the rats. If the rat did not flick its tail within 10 seconds, the heat source was terminated to prevent burning of the rat's tail. At the end of the experiment, the rats were anaesthetized and injected with a lethal drug before brain removal. Tissue samples of the rats' brains were then analyzed to map the exact site of drug injection. Results indicated that although the tail flick response time was slower for the drug group than the saline group initially, over time the responses were quicker, indicating that the drug had worn off. Thus, the area of the brain the researchers were interested in was involved in pain perception in the rats.

What should the researchers consider in this study to ensure that their study meet ethical guidelines for research with animals? Did you notice any aspects of the study in the description above that shows the researchers included methodological details to make their study more ethical? You may have noticed, for example, that the researchers terminated the heat source after 10 seconds when the rats did not flick their tail to prevent harming them. They also anaesthetized the rats before removing their brains so that they would not feel any pain. In fact, the published report of the study contains a section titled "Animal Care and Use" that indicates that the study adhered to ethical guidelines for animal research and that efforts were made to reduce the rats' suffering (such as the procedures described above). What would need to change in the above study in order to include human participants? Would the same knowledge be gained if human participants were used instead? Why not? Should there be similar ethical guidelines for human and animal subjects? Why or why not? These are ethical issues that psychologists continue to ask themselves as research is designed to answer important societal questions.

ETHICS IN REPORTING RESEARCH

In addition to the treatment of participants/subjects in a study, the APA Ethics Code (2002) contains sections outlining ethical guidelines for reporting research in an ethical manner. Two primary issues are addressed in these sections: (1) errors in the data that are reported (either intended or unintended) and (2) **plagiarism**. These issues are just as important to the scientific process as the treatment of participants/subjects.

Plagiarism: claiming another's work or ideas as one's own

As you have seen, the scientific method relies on reports of previous studies for hypothesis development, designing valid methods, and anticipating negative consequences of study procedures on participants. Thus, the reports of psychological research must be accurate, or future research will decrease in validity, an effect that can ripple through the literature for many years. Researchers are ethically bound to report data accurately. If an error is discovered in their report, the researcher must correct the error or make it known if correction is not possible.

Credit must also be given for information contained in the reports of research. Thus, researchers must properly cite the source of information they give in research reports. This includes both word-for-word reports from others (your university likely has a student code of conduct that forbids and punishes this type of plagiarism) and summarized representation of another's ideas. You have seen such citations throughout this text that provide sources for the information it contains. Research reports (even those that may not be published) must always cite sources for theories, methods, data, and other topics an author describes that came from another source.

Violation of either of the above ethical guidelines (data errors or plagiarism) can seriously damage one's career. There have been several famous examples of such violations that damaged the standing of researchers in the scientific community. One such recent example was reported in 2006, when Woo Suk Hwang, a well-known cloning researcher in South Korea, reported false research on the cloning of human stem cells (Bhattacharya, 2006). Hwang reported being the first scientist to clone human stem cells, an important accomplishment given the utility of stem cells in the treatment of medical problems and the difficulty researchers face in obtaining stem cells. Hwang reported his research in the prestigious journal *Science* (Hwang, Rho, et al., 2005; Hwang, Ryu, et al., 2004). However, Hwang and his research team were actually not successful in cloning stem cells as they reported, a discovery made by a probe of his work. He is now facing criminal charges in South Korea and has irreparably damaged his scientific career. From this example, you can see that false data reports can have very serious consequences. You are probably more likely, however, to be concerned about the second issue discussed here: plagiarism. Plagiarism can be intentional or unintentional; however, both are serious ethical violations, as they both involve taking credit for someone's work or ideas. Students should exercise caution when writing about psychological research in their own reports to ensure that their own words are used and that information is properly cited. If you have any doubts about your own writing, it is always a good idea to check with your instructor to make sure your writing does not contain plagiarism.

CHAPTER SUMMARY

Reconsider the questions from the beginning of the chapter:

- Why do we need ethical guidelines for research? As described in this chapter, ethical guidelines are needed to define the appropriate treatment of subjects in psychological research.
- How were ethical guidelines for psychological research developed? Current ethical guidelines were derived over the years as the original Nuremberg Code was revised and adopted by the American Psychological Association (APA) and the U.S. Government in the Belmont Report.
- Were the Milgram (1963) and Zimbardo (1974) studies ethical? Why or why not? Due to the level of deception and stress caused by the situation participants experienced in the Milgram study and the level of stress experienced by the "prisoners" in the Zimbardo study, many researchers believe that these studies were not ethical.

- What are the current ethical guidelines for human participants? Current ethical guidelines for psychological research are summarized in Table 5.1.
- What is an institutional review board (IRB), and what purpose does it serve? The IRB oversees research conducted at each institution. In cases where the researchers may not be the most objective judge of the ethics of their study, the IRB provides a more objective review of the ethics of psychological research.
- What are the current ethical guidelines for animal subjects? Current ethical guidelines for animal subjects are also summarized in Table 5.1.
- How do ethics influence the way we report research? Ethical guidelines for reporting research necessitate accurate reports of results and proper citation of sources.

THINKING ABOUT RESEARCH

A summary of a research study in psychology is given below. As you read the summary, think about the following questions:

1. What are some ethical issues for this study regarding informed consent?

2. What steps do you think the researchers of this study would have taken to obtain informed consent from the research participant in order to conduct an ethical study?

3. What steps should the researchers take to protect the confidentiality of the participant in this study?

4. Do you think it would be ethically appropriate for the researchers in this study to administer the reinforcements themselves? Why or why not?

5. How can the researchers reduce possible harm to the participants in this study?

6. If you were an IRB member reviewing this study, what information would you ask the researchers to provide to allow you to determine the risk-benefit analysis for this study?

Study Reference

Baker, J. C., Hanley, G. P., & Mathews, R. M. (2006). Staff-administered functional analysis and treatment of aggression by an elder with dementia. *Journal of Applied Behavior Analysis, 39,* 469–474.

Purpose of the Study. A behavior analysis study was conducted to examine the use of noncontingent reinforcement (i.e., reinforcement that does not depend on performance of a specific behavior) as a means of reducing aggressive behavior in elderly persons with dementia to prevent injury to the elderly persons or to the care staff. The noncontingent reinforcement in this study involved allowing the participant to have a break from the prompting of a hygiene routine that the participant disliked as reinforcement for ending aggressive behavior during the routine. In one condition of the reinforcement phase of the study, the reinforcement was not contingent on the participant's behavior, because the breaks occurred on a timed schedule in this condition, regardless of when aggressive behavior occurred. This condition was compared with a second condition that involved reinforcement contingent on the participant's behavior (i.e., negative reinforcement): A break was provided whenever the participant was aggressive during the hygiene routine after aggressive behavior had ceased.

Method of the Study. A 96-year-old woman with dementia due to Alzheimer's disease was the only participant in the study. The participant had a history of severe aggressive behavior toward care staff at her residence. The participant was observed before or after mealtimes while she was not being restrained. Observation sessions occurred in the participant's bathroom and lasted 3 to 5 minutes each. The dependent variable was aggressive hitting operationally defined as "forceful contact with a closed or open fist with a staff member" (p. 470). Hitting behaviors were measured within each 10-s interval of each of the observation sessions. Interrater reliability ranged from 96% to 100%. The independent variable was the condition under which the aggressive behavior was measured: during the noncontingent reinforcement treatment or in a contingent reinforcement condition. In the contingent reinforcement condition, the care staff member involved in the study allowed a 10-s break from the bathroom routine each time aggressive hitting occurred and had ceased. In the noncontingent reinforcement condition, a 10-s break was given from the bathroom routine every 20 s regardless of the participant's behavior. The participant completed several sessions in the noncontingent reinforcement condition first. Once aggressive behavior was reduced to low levels, she completed several sessions in the contingent reinforcement condition as a comparison. Then, several sessions of the noncontingent reinforcement condition were conducted again.

Results of the Study. Low levels of hitting were observed in the first set of noncontingent reinforcement condition sessions (mean percentage of intervals where hitting occurred was 9%). Levels of hitting were shown to decline across sessions in this condition. Hitting increased when the comparison contingent reinforcement condition was introduced ($M = 46\%$) but decreased again when the noncontingent reinforcement condition was reintroduced ($M = 9\%$) with hitting reduced to 0 for the last few sessions of the study.

Conclusions of the Study. This study showed that noncontingent reinforcement can be used to reduce aggressive behavior in elderly persons with dementia, thus reducing the possibility of harm to the elderly persons and their care staff.

COMMON PITFALLS AND HOW TO AVOID THEM

Problem: Confusing deception with full information—there can be confusion about what qualifies as deception in psychological research.

Solution: Holding back some information about the study does not usually qualify as deception. In many cases, researchers do not fully inform participants about the purpose of the study to prevent demand characteristics. Deception typically involves a more direct manipulation of the participants' understanding of the study.

Problem: Failure to identify risks—researchers often fail to see the possible risks to the participants in their own study.

Solution: Assume that there are always risks to the participants in a study. Sometimes these risks are minimal, such as boredom or fatigue. You should also think carefully about the different elements of the ethical guidelines (confidentiality, deception, informed consent, etc.) to attempt to identify situations where these elements could cause possible harm to the participants.

Problem: Inadequate debriefing—sometimes students designing a research study do not properly debrief participants at the end of a study.

Solution: Be sure to include a thorough debriefing for your study. It is your responsibility to ensure that participants do not have a negative experience in your study, and the debriefing is your opportunity to ensure that participants leave with as positive a view of the study as possible. Be sure to explain why the study was conducted to enrich the participants' understanding of psychological research. Also include information about where they can have further questions answered or learn about the final results if they wish.

TEST YOURSELF

1. Suppose you wanted to replicate the Milgram (1963) study to adhere to ethical guidelines currently in place for psychological research. What changes would you need to make to the procedure (described in this chapter) in order to conduct the study ethically?

2. Given what is described in this chapter regarding the informed consent process, make a list of information about your modified Milgram (1963) study (see Question 1) that should be provided on a consent form for participants.

3. Why is the debriefing process especially important in studies that involve deception?

4. Write a debriefing statement that you think might be appropriate for the Middlemast et al. (1976) study on male urination described in the chapter.

5. Which of the following is part of the ethical guidelines for research with human participants?
   (a) No identifying information may be collected from the participants during the study.
   (b) Participants can withdraw from the study at any point before the study begins, but not after that point.
   (c) Participants must be informed about the study's procedures before they are asked to give consent for their participation.
   (d) All of the above.

6. Which of the following is part of the ethical guidelines for research with animal subjects?
   (a) Only trained personnel may be involved with the research.
   (b) Discomfort of the animals must be minimized as much as possible.
   (c) Use of animals and the particular species of animal used must be strongly justified for the study.
   (d) All of the above.

7. The _____ provides a set of ethical guidelines provided by the U.S. Government that must be adhered to by all researchers conducting studies with human participants.
   (a) Nuremberg Code
   (b) APA Ethical Code
   (c) Belmont Report
   (d) IACUC

8. At the conclusion of a study with animal subjects, the researcher
   (a) must provide for the care of the animals for the rest of their lives
   (b) may release the animals into the wild to live the rest of their lives
   (c) must use those animals for additional research studies before any new animals can be obtained
   (d) (a) and (c) only

Answers: 1. As mentioned in the chapter, Burger (2009) conducted a modified replication of this study in conjunction with ABC News' *Primetime* show. To make the study ethical (and have it approved by his IRB), he made the following changes: (a) shock labels only went to 150 volts, at which point the confederate first objected verbally to the shocks, (b) participants were prescreened to rule out individuals who might be more greatly affected by the stressful conditions of the study, (c) right to withdraw from the study was emphasized (once verbally and twice in writing) to make this right more salient to participants, and (d) the experimenter was a clinical psychologist who immediately stopped the study at the first sign of excessive stress from the participant. 2. The consent form should include the following: a statement that the participant is being asked to volunteer for research, that his or her participation is voluntary and he or she has the right to withdraw at any time without penalty, the purpose and the procedures of the study, the risks (including possible stress) and benefits of the study, and information about whom the participants can contact if they have questions or concerns about the study. 3. The debriefing process is especially important for research that involves deception because the goal is that participants leave a study with as positive an impression of the research as possible. In addition, participants have the right to a thorough explanation of the study. Explaining why the deception was necessary is important in achieving these goals. 4. Answers will vary, but debriefing for this study should explain that the purpose of the study was to investigate natural physiological responses that occur to most individuals due to an invasion of personal space. It should also include information that the participant's data will be kept completely confidential, that the participant has the right to withdraw from the study at any time (especially if an informed consent process did not take place before the study), and information about whom the participants may contact if they have further questions or are feeling uncomfortable about participating in the study. 5. c, 6. d, 7. c, 8. a.

Sampling

> **CONSIDER THE FOLLOWING QUESTIONS AS YOU READ CHAPTER 6**
>
> - What is the difference between a population and a sample?
> - Why do we need to sample?
> - What is the difference between probability and convenience samples?
> - Which types of samples will reduce sampling error more than other types?
> - In what situations would a researcher need to use a convenience sample?
> - How do psychologists use the Internet to sample?

Suppose you read in a magazine that 98% of women who responded to a survey reported being dissatisfied with their marriage and 75% reported having affairs. Would you conclude from this survey that 98% of all married women are unhappy being married? Would you believe that 75% of married women have affairs? Why or why not?

It is hoped that by now you have begun to recognize that not all research produces valid results and that whenever you are presented with statistics, such as those above about married women, you should be at least a little skeptical (even if the statistics seem believable) because there are many factors that can influence the observations collected in a study. How the study was conducted can tell you a lot about whether the results can be generalized to a larger group of individuals beyond the participants who participated in the study. We discussed some of these possible sources of bias in Chapter 4. In this chapter, we will consider another possible source of bias in research studies: the sampling technique.

To give you an example of how sampling can affect a research study's results, consider the survey results described above. Hite (1987) reported these survey results in her book *Women and Love*. However, only 4.5% of the women that received Hite's survey responded to it (Reiniger, 2001; Wallis, 1987). This means that very few of the women who were contacted completed the survey (4,500 out of 100,000 contacted for her survey). Her low **response rate** may help explain her results. Because individuals have a choice to complete a survey or not, the 4.5% who chose to complete the survey may have been different from the other women who chose not to complete the survey, resulting in a sample that did not represent how most women feel about the issues in the survey. For example, it is possible that the women who completed Hite's survey were particularly unhappy about their relationships and were compelled to complete the survey to express their dissatisfaction.

To further investigate this issue, ABC News conducted a survey in 2004 that showed that only 14% of women who responded to their survey reported having an affair outside of a committed relationship. In their sample, 92% of the people who were asked to complete the survey did so (1,380 out of 1,501 contacted for the survey). In other words, the ABC News survey's results were more likely to be similar to the responses of all American women (if all American women could have responded) than the results of Hite's survey, because the **response rate** was much higher in the ABC News survey. Thus, the higher response rate (i.e., a larger percentage of those contacted completed the survey) makes it more likely that the ABC News results better reflect the attitudes of American women, even though fewer individuals completed this survey than Hite's (1987) survey.

Response Rate: the percentage of people out of the total number available who respond to a survey

In this chapter, we will consider the effect of sampling techniques on the results of research studies, discuss several common sampling techniques used in psychological research, and compare different sampling techniques based on their potential to contribute bias to the study and the practicality of their use in a study (Figure 6.1).

POPULATIONS AND SAMPLES

The goal of psychological research is to learn about behavior that applies to a group of individuals. The group can be all humans, all Americans, or all Europeans who have high levels of anxiety. The group a researcher wants to learn about depends on the study being conducted and the research question the study is designed to answer. This group is called the **population**. The population is typically a fairly large group of individuals. Thus, even though it is the population we want to learn about, it is usually impossible to test the entire population in a research study. There are often too many individuals in a population to include in a study, and researchers would have a difficult time locating each individual and persuading them to participate. Therefore, researchers select a **sample** of individuals from the population to serve as the participants in their study (Figure 6.2). This allows the researchers to learn about the population from the sample selected from it and to have a participant sample that is small enough that all individuals in the sample can participate in the study. The actual size of the sample will depend on the type of study and the resources that researchers have for collecting data from their sample. In studies where individuals must participate one at a time (as in some experiments using systematic observations—see Chapter 3), the sample

Population: a group of individuals a researcher seeks to learn about from a research study

Sample: the group of individuals chosen from the population to represent it in a research study

Figure 6.1   **Steps in the Research Process: Creating a Sample**

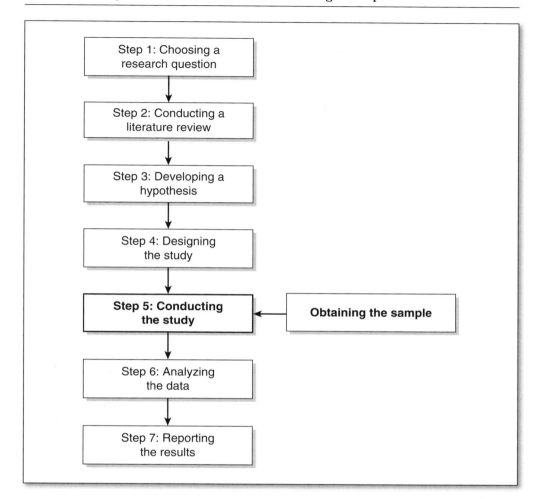

may be smaller than in studies where individuals can participate simultaneously (as in correlational studies using surveys for data collection—see Chapter 3).

Regardless of the size of the sample obtained, the goal in participant sampling is to choose individuals for the sample who will represent the behaviors and attitudes of the entire population. In other words, you want to choose individuals who will provide similar observations overall to the observations you would see in the population if you were able to study the entire population. Any difference in the observations between the sample and the population is called **sampling error**. All research studies will have some amount of sampling error because the sample will never give you the same observations as the entire population would. The best a researcher can do is to minimize the sampling error as much as

Figure 6.2   A Sample Is Chosen to Represent the Population in a Study

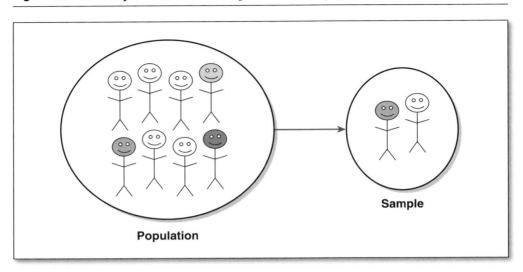

possible. One way to reduce sampling error is to choose a sampling technique that will give you the most representative sample for the population you want to learn about. We will begin with **probability samples**, where individuals have a specific probability of being chosen from the population. Probability samples are most likely to be representative of the population, so you should use these samples whenever it is feasible to do so. However, as you will see below, it is not always practical to use a probability sample. In many cases, a **convenience sample** (also called a **purposive sample**; Shadish et al., 2002) is needed. In convenience samples the probability of an individual being chosen from the population cannot be determined, because individuals are not chosen randomly. Thus, the sample may not represent the population as well as a probability sample but can be obtained more easily than a probability sample. Table 6.1 provides an overview of the sampling techniques discussed to help you choose the best sampling technique for a study.

Sampling Error: the difference between the observations in a population and in the sample that represents that population in a study

Probability Sample: sample chosen such that individuals are chosen with a specific probability

Convenience/Purposive Sample: sample chosen such that the probability of an individual being chosen cannot be determined

PROBABILITY SAMPLES

Probability samples can reduce the amount of sampling error that exists in a study. Thus, it is important to use a probability sample when sampling error is likely to be large. Sampling error will increase whenever observations differ greatly from participant to participant in a sample or when a sample is chosen such that a segment of the population is not represented in the sample. For example, in small samples it is more likely that data will

TABLE 6.1	Overview of Sampling Techniques			
Technique	**Characteristics**	**Example**	**Advantages**	**Disadvantages**
Probability samples	Probability of choosing an individual in the population is known.			
Simple random	Each member of the population has an equal probability of being selected using random sampling.	Students are chosen randomly from list of all students at a university.	Reduces sampling error by choosing from all members of the population to best represent the population	Difficult to ensure that each member of a large population can be chosen in a sample
Cluster	Clusters of individuals are identified and then a subset of clusters is randomly chosen to sample from.	Doctors who work at hospitals are chosen for a sample by identifying all hospitals in different areas of the United States and then randomly choosing 10 hospitals in each area of the United States to sample from.	Makes it easier to choose members randomly from smaller clusters to better represent the population	Can ignore segments of the population that are not in the clusters chosen for the sample
Stratified random	Members of a population are selected such that the proportion of a group in the sample is equal to the proportion of that group in the population using random sampling.	Registered voters are randomly selected from lists of Democrats and Republicans to equal the proportion of registered Democrats and Republicans in the United States.	Reduces bias due to an identified characteristic of the population by equating proportions in the sample and the population for that characteristic to better represent the population	Similar to simple random—can be difficult to ensure equal probability of being chosen from a large population
Convenience/ purposive samples	Probability of choosing an individual in the population is NOT known.			

(Continued)

TABLE 6.1 (Continued)

Technique	Characteristics	Example	Advantages	Disadvantages
Haphazard/ volunteer	Members of population are chosen based on convenience and on who volunteers.	Sample is chosen from students who volunteer to complete an extra credit assignment in their psychology course.	Easier to obtain than probability samples	May not represent the population well due to selection bias because random sampling is not used
Quota	Members of population are selected such that the proportion of a group in the sample is equal to proportion of that group in population	Volunteers are recruited from students in a psychology course such that the gender breakdown in the sample is the same as the gender breakdown of all students at the school.	Easier to obtain than probability samples and allows for better representation of a characteristic of the population	May not represent the population well due to selection bias because random sampling is not used

---

Simple Random Sample: sample chosen randomly from the population such that each individual has an equal chance of being selected

Cluster Sample: sample chosen randomly from clusters identified in the population

Stratified Random Sample: sample chosen from the population such that the proportion of individuals with a particular characteristic is equivalent in the population and the sample

differ from participant to participant. We will consider three different types of probability samples that researchers can consider when sampling error is likely to be high: **simple random samples**, **cluster samples**, and **stratified random samples**.

Simple Random Samples

A simple random sample is a sample in which each member of a population has an equal chance of being selected for the sample. Thus, if a population has 100 individuals, the chance of any one individual being selected for the sample is 1 in 100 or 1%. In most cases, using a simple random sample will give you the most representative sample possible for the population you are interested in, because the process of random sampling is less likely to over- or underrepresent any particular subgroup of the population than any other selection mechanism. The key to using a simple random sample is to find a way to choose individuals from the population such that they all have an equal chance of being selected. Suppose that the population for a study is all students at your university or college. If you want to choose a sample of 1,000 participants from this population, you could obtain a list of all the students at your school and choose 1,000 of them at random by having a computer generate a list of random numbers that correspond to numbers in your list of students. Many programs, such as Microsoft Excel, can do this for you. You can then contact each of the 1,000 students chosen randomly from the list to participate in your study (Figure 6.3).

Figure 6.3 Simple Random Sample

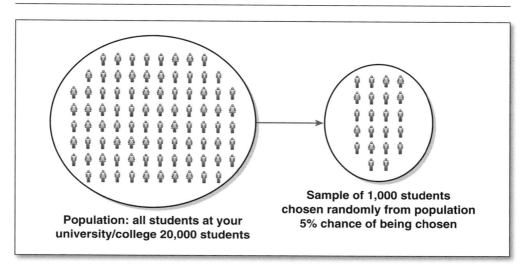

Population: all students at your
university/college 20,000 students

Sample of 1,000 students
chosen randomly from population
5% chance of being chosen

NOTE: Each individual in the population has an equal chance of being chosen.

However, simple random samples can be difficult to obtain for large populations. Suppose that you want to generalize the results of your study to *all* college students, not just the ones at your school. In this case, your population will be very large, and you will not have access to all the individuals in the population to choose them with equal probability. A simple random sample is not practical for this population, and another sampling technique is a better choice.

Cluster Samples

A better way to sample all college students is to use a cluster sample. In a cluster sample, clusters of individuals (e.g., all students at each university/college) are first identified. Then a subset of the clusters is chosen to sample from (e.g., 25 of the universities/colleges on the list). Finally, individuals can be chosen at random from each of the target clusters in the subset (e.g., by randomly choosing 20 students from the list of all students at each of the 25 universities/colleges in the target cluster subset). Cluster samples allow researchers to obtain a probability sample from a large population more easily than they would with a simple random sample, because the list from which individuals are selected is more manageable and easier to obtain (i.e., it is easier to obtain lists of students at 25 universities/colleges than to obtain lists of students at *all* universities/colleges) (Figure 6.4).

Figure 6.4   Cluster Sample: Clusters Randomly Chosen From a Population

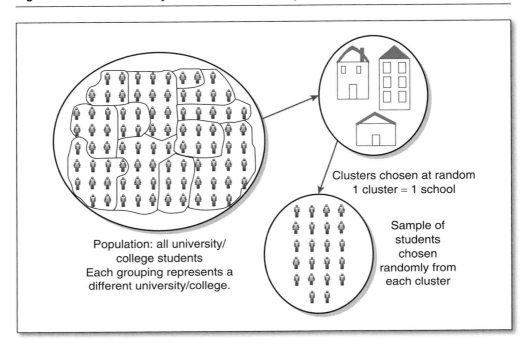

Population: all university/
college students
Each grouping represents a
different university/college.

Clusters chosen at random
1 cluster = 1 school

Sample of
students
chosen
randomly from
each cluster

From this example, you may be thinking that cluster sampling still seems rather difficult. However, cluster samples can be used more conveniently by using a hierarchy of clusters. For the example above, suppose that you were not able to obtain lists of all the students at each of the 25 universities/colleges that make up your target clusters. In this case, you could add a level of clusters to your sampling technique. For example, instead of sampling randomly from the lists of all students at the 25 target universities/colleges, you could identify a course at each university/college chosen at random from the class list for the current semester and use the students in each class as your sample from that cluster. By using the classes as another level of clusters, you make the sampling job easier and still obtain a random sample from your population.

A disadvantage of cluster sampling is that a portion of the population may be missed in the sample, giving the researcher a sample that is not fully representative of the population. For example, suppose that all (or most) of the schools chosen at random as target clusters in the example above happened to be in the southern United States. In this case, significant portions of the population (college students in the other parts of the country or other countries) would be underrepresented in the sample. One way to fix this problem is to use another level of clusters in the sampling procedure that first groups schools by area before target cluster schools are chosen. Another solution to this problem is to use a stratified random sample.

Stratified Random Samples

A stratified random sample is used when researchers want to make sure that their sample contains equivalent percentages of individuals from subgroups as exist in the population. For example, approximately 60% of U.S. college students are female, and 40% are male. Thus, if you are interested in the population of U.S. college students in your study and you want to ensure that the gender breakdown of students in the population is also represented in your sample, you would need to make sure that 60% of the students chosen at random from the population are female and 40% are male. This means that if your sample contained 100 students, 60 would be female, and 40 would be male. You could obtain lists of students organized by gender and randomly choose 60 females and 40 males from this list to obtain your sample. Using this method, your sample will best represent U.S. college students by gender. If your sample did not follow this gender breakdown, your sample might be biased, depending on how much gender affects the results of your study.

A stratified random sample could also be used to solve the problem of location bias in the example above. Suppose you determined the breakdown of college students by area of the United States thus: 30% on the East Coast, 25% on the West Coast, 20% in the South, and 25% in the Midwest. To ensure that your sample contains a similar breakdown by area and best represents the population of college students, you can use the percentages of students by area to draw your sample. In other words, you would randomly choose 30% of your sample from students on the East Coast, 25% of your sample from students on the West Coast, and so on. In this way, your sample will represent the current breakdown of students by area in the population (Figure 6.5).

CONVENIENCE SAMPLES

In many cases, researchers would have a difficult time obtaining probability samples for their studies. As mentioned above, probability samples require access in some way to the entire population to select individuals according to a predetermined probability value. This is not always easy to achieve. For some studies, use of a probability sample can be important when sampling error is likely to be large. This is especially true for studies where results may be influenced by demographic factors such as gender, ethnicity, or location of residence, or in studies where participants are likely to differ from one another in their behaviors or attitudes. Sue (1999) argued, for example, that when ethnicity is not considered in a sample, ethnic differences that may exist will be ignored. However, in other studies, these factors are less important and less likely to influence the results. In studies of basic cognitive functions, such as perception, memory, or psycholinguistics, demographic factors are often less influential, and a convenience sample can be used without too much sampling error affecting the results. A convenience sample allows researchers to obtain a sample more easily when choosing at random from the population (or from subsets of the population) is not possible or necessary.

If a convenience sample is used in a study, a researcher should be aware of the limitations of these samples. Convenience samples will likely increase the amount of sampling error in the study, lowering its **internal validity** by making a test of the hypotheses less accurate (Rosenthal

Figure 6.5   Stratified Random Sample

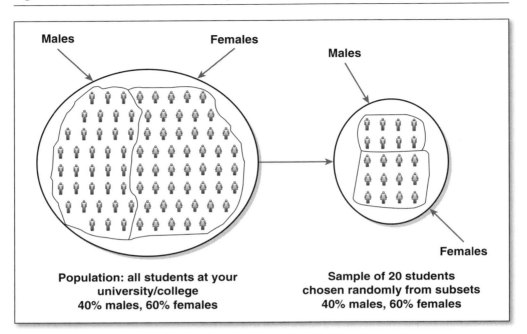

Population: all students at your
university/college
40% males, 60% females

Sample of 20 students
chosen randomly from subsets
40% males, 60% females

NOTE: Subsets of the population are identified based on demographics. A proportion of individuals is then randomly chosen from subsets to represent proportions in the population.

& Rosnow, 2008). This can occur because some of the characteristics of individuals who volunteer to participate in studies may act as confounding variables and cloud a causal relationship tested in a study. See Chapters 3 and 4 for more discussion of internal validity and Chapter 7 for discussion of sampling error. In addition, because individuals are not chosen with a known probability, it is less likely that a convenience sample will provide a good representation of the population in the study (a situation that leads to the increase in sampling error mentioned above). This makes it more difficult to generalize the results of the study to the population, lowering its **external validity**. See Chapters 3 and 4 for more discussion of external validity. External validity of a study should be considered when conclusions are drawn from results collected with a convenience sample.

The most common type of convenience sample used by psychologists is the **haphazard sample** (also called a **volunteer sample**). However, a **quota sample** is another type of convenience sample that is fairly common in psychological research.

Internal Validity: the degree to which a study provides causal information about behavior

External Validity: the degree to which the results of a study apply to individuals and realistic behaviors outside the study

Haphazard/Volunteer Sample: sample chosen from the population such that available individuals are chosen

Quota Sample: sample chosen from the population such that available individuals are chosen with equivalent proportions of individuals for a specific characteristic in the population and sample

Haphazard/Volunteer Samples

If you have ever participated in a research study at your school where you were recruited through a sign-up system (an online sign-up system, a sign-up bulletin board, etc.), then you have been part of a volunteer sample in a study. Volunteer sample studies recruit individuals from a population (e.g., students at your school) by recruiting individuals who a researcher has easy access to (such as asking students in certain types of classes to sign up for the research studies). The incentive for students to sign up for these studies may be a research requirement or extra credit points in their course or a monetary compensation. You may have such a requirement or extra credit opportunity in the class for which you were assigned this text. If you have ever been asked to answer some survey questions by someone at the grocery store or in front of the student union building, then you have seen another example of volunteer sampling. The survey takers approached individuals they had easy access to and asked for volunteers to complete their survey (Figure 6.6).

Volunteer samples are convenience samples because the probability of recruiting any individual from the population is not known due to a lack of random selection from the population or subset of the population. For example, when students at a university or college sign up to participate in psychological research studies, they are typically recruited from specific courses in which students are made aware of the research participation opportunities. Thus, the sample comes from students taking certain types of courses on campus (i.e., typically psychology courses). It is possible that these students are different from the students taking other courses on campus. In addition, the students are often given an incentive to sign up (e.g., credit

Figure 6.6   Haphazard/Volunteer Sample

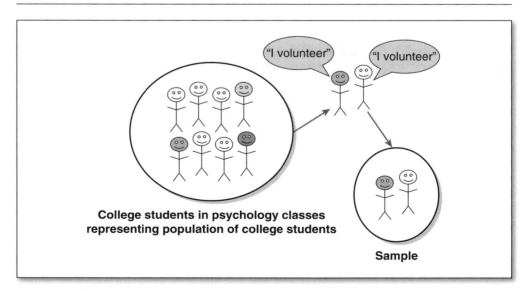

NOTE: Individuals are chosen from the population based on whom the researcher has easy access to and who volunteers from this group.

in a course, monetary payment). The incentives may be influential to certain types of students. For example, a small monetary compensation or course credit may be more motivating to some students than to others. This means that the entire population of students at a university or college may not be represented in the sample, making it more difficult to generalize the results from the sample chosen to the population a researcher wishes to learn about.

Volunteer samples are quite common in psychological research. They are used because they are typically the most convenient means of obtaining a sample for a study and in most cases do not greatly reduce the generalizability of the results of a study. See below for further discussion of this issue.

Quota Samples

Quota samples are similar to stratified random samples without the random selection from subsets of the population. As with a stratified random sample, the goal of a quota sample is to represent subgroups of the population in the same proportions in the sample as exist in the population. Thus, if researchers wish to examine attitudes about college work habits, they may be concerned with their participants' class level, as participants at different class levels may have different attitudes based on the amount of experience they have with college-level work. If the population of students at their school is 30 % freshmen, 20 % sophomores, 25 % juniors, and 25 % seniors, then the sample will contain the same breakdown of class level in a quota sample. However, unlike a stratified random sample, the quota sample will make use of convenience sampling techniques such as recruiting participants from a participant sign-up pool or asking students sitting in the library to fill out the survey. The researchers will keep track of the percentage of different class levels in their sample to ensure they equate the class-level breakdown in their sample to that in the population. Sampling will continue until the quota is reached for each class level.

COMPARISON OF PROBABILITY AND CONVENIENCE SAMPLING TECHNIQUES

As described above, the advantage of convenience samples is that they are easier to obtain than probability samples. The disadvantage is that they may not be truly representative of the population a researcher wants to learn about, lowering the external validity of a study. The importance of external validity in psychological studies has been debated for decades. Many researchers have argued that results from psychological studies using volunteer college students for samples are not informative about the behavior in the general population (e.g., Rosnow, Rosenthal, McConochie, & Arms, 1969; Sears, 1986). However, convenience samples may be a lesser problem in studies examining certain types of behavior that are likely to generalize beyond the study. In addition, the purpose of the study may be to examine what is possible in human behavior, even if that behavior may not occur in the real world for a large group of individuals (Mook, 1983). Remember that studies will differ in how basic and how applied they are, based on the goals of the researcher. The more basic the research, the more external validity may be sacrificed due to the control required to meet the goal of gaining causal information about behavior. Important knowledge can still be gained about human behavior from studies where it is unclear how well the results generalize to everyday behaviors and populations that go beyond college students (Oakes, 1972). This issue also highlights the importance of replication in the scientific process. Results that generalize to one population may not generalize to another population. Thus, it is important to consider both the population and the goal of the research when choosing a sampling technique.

One should also consider the difference between a "target" population and the "accessible" population. The "target" population is the population to which the researcher wishes to generalize the results of the study. The "accessible" population is the population that the researcher has available to sample from. For example, a researcher may wish to generalize the results of a study to all human adults or to all U.S. citizens. However, it is unlikely that these populations will be accessible to the researcher. It is more likely that a population of university students at the researcher's institution is accessible for sampling. In some cases, using an "accessible" population rather than the "target" population may affect the external validity of the study. However, in many situations, the results of a study that addresses a common behavior can be generalized to the "target" population as well.

RECRUITING PARTICIPANTS

Regardless of the type of sampling technique chosen, researchers must consider how to actually recruit the participants for a study. In other words, how will the participants be contacted to let them know about the study and what incentives will be offered for their participation? The issue of how to contact the participants to recruit them is related to the selection mechanism in some types of studies. For example, if you are randomly choosing participants from the phone book, it may make sense to contact them by phone. If you are randomly choosing participants from a list of students at a university, you may only be provided with certain types of contact information (e.g., campus or permanent addresses, e-mail addresses) that will limit the means available for contacting the participants. Many university and college psychology departments have participant pools available to researchers that provide a standard means of contacting participants for haphazard/volunteer samples (e.g., participant sign-up board or Web site). The means of contacting participants is an important issue, as it may affect the sample size obtained for a study. Researchers should carefully consider recruitment techniques that may be most effective for their population. For example, younger participants may be more likely to respond to e-mail contacts, whereas older participants may be more likely to respond to phone contacts. If you are considering recruiting acquaintances for a research study, the ethics of such recruitment should also be considered. For example, what is the best way to approach an acquaintance about participating in a study to maximize sample size but also reduce coercion?

Incentives can also have an impact on the sample size obtained. For established institution participant pools, there may be incentives built in to the recruitment process, such as completion of an assignment or extra credit in psychology courses. In these cases, an alternative assignment must also be available to students in the course to reduce coercion. Other incentives such as payment or entrance in a drawing may be also be possibilities available to researchers if the resources for these incentives exist. Again, coercion issues should be considered for these incentives as well. Not all studies require incentives; individuals may be willing to participate in short studies without such incentives (e.g., completing a short survey on the street). Longer and more arduous studies may require an incentive to recruit a sufficient sample size. However, as described above, this may also create a situation where the incentive or lack of incentive adds bias to the study.

USING THE INTERNET TO SAMPLE

Samples obtained using the Internet are becoming more frequent in recent psychological research. Many types of observation techniques can be used with **Internet samples**, including surveys and systematic observations. Experiments that require systematic presentation of stimuli can be reproduced for presentation on the Internet to individual participants. See http://psych.hanover.edu/research/exponnet.html for a list of current psychological studies being conducted on the Internet ("Retrospection," 2008). According to Birnbaum (2001), advantages of Internet samples over laboratory studies include use of larger and more diverse samples, fewer opportunities for bias due to experimenter interactions with participants, fewer constraints on the time and location of data collection, less time needed to collect a sample, and fewer researchers needed to supervise the study procedures. Many researchers have also shown that data collected with Internet samples produced similar effects to samples collected in the laboratory (Birnbaum, 2001; Krantz & Dalal, 2000).

❦

Internet Sample: sample chosen from the population by recruiting on the Internet

---

The studies comparing lab and Internet samples show that Internet samples tend to be more demographically diverse (Birnbaum, 2001). Thus, Internet sampling may yield samples that are better representative of large, general populations. However, there are some issues that researchers should be aware of when they choose to use an Internet sample (Birnbaum, 2001). For example, some smaller subgroups in the population may require extra work to include in the sample because the number with access to the Internet may be too small to allow for adequate sampling. Researchers may need to contact special-interest groups to recruit them for the study to achieve the best representation possible. In addition, it may be difficult to control who completes a study on the Internet, making stratified random and quota samples more difficult to obtain and making it difficult to monitor repeat participation from the same individuals. It may also be difficult to balance group size in between-subjects designs. Finally, it is more difficult to monitor participants during the study procedure to rule out sources of bias (such as distractions) for Internet samples. Nonetheless, Internet samples show great promise in making sampling easier for some types of psychological studies.

Providing incentives may be also be important for recruiting Internet samples. The type of incentive a researcher offers may affect the sample size obtained in an Internet sample more often than in studies where data collection is done in a laboratory or in other in-person environments because it may be harder to gain a participant's attention with an Internet study. On the other hand, the feeling of anonymity that comes with completing a study on the Internet may also be a benefit in recruiting Internet samples. Finally, Internet samples may be larger than samples obtained by other means; thus, researchers must also consider available resources when choosing an incentive for an Internet study.

CHAPTER SUMMARY

Reconsider the questions from the beginning of the chapter:

- What is the difference between a population and a sample? The population is the group of individuals a researcher wants to learn about. The sample is the subset of the population that participates in the study.
- Why do we need to sample? In most cases, it would be difficult or impossible to test the entire population in a study. Thus, a sample is used to represent the population in the study.
- What is the difference between probability and convenience samples? In probability samples, the probability of an individual being chosen from the population is known, and participants are chosen randomly from the population or a subset of the population. For convenience samples, the probability of an individual being chosen is not known, and the participants are chosen in a nonrandom manner.
- Which types of samples will reduce sampling error more than other types? Probability samples are typically more representative of the population and will have less sampling error.
- In what situations would a researcher need to use a convenience sample? In many cases, a population is too large to allow all individuals to be identified for sampling. Thus, a convenience sample is used. In other cases, the incentive for participation may apply only to a convenience sample.
- How do psychologists use the Internet to sample? The Internet is a useful tool for recruiting a representative sample that may be larger than a sample that is recruited in person.

THINKING ABOUT RESEARCH

A summary of a research study in psychology is given below. As you read the summary, think about the following questions:

1. Identify the most likely population of interest (i.e., "target" population) for this study based on the description below.
2. What sampling technique was used in this study?
3. Do you think the sample collected in this study provided a sample that was representative of the population of interest? Why or why not?
4. What are some of the disadvantages of the sampling technique used in the study?
5. Suppose this study had been conducted with a simple random sample of the population of practical nurses and social workers licensed in the state of Massachusetts. Describe how a simple random sample might have been obtained for this study.
6. What would be the advantages and disadvantages of using the simple random sample you described in (5) above?

Study Reference

Barnett, R. C., Marshall, N. L., & Singer, J. D. (1992). Job experiences over time, multiple roles, and women's mental health: A longitudinal study. *Journal of Personality and Social Psychology, 62,* 634–644.

Purpose of the Study. The study examined the connection between women's judged job quality and their mental health (anxiety and depression). The researchers further examined how a woman's family role affected the relationship between job quality and mental health. They predicted that over time, as women judged their job quality to decrease, their mental health would decrease (i.e., depression and anxiety would increase). They further predicted that this effect would be reduced in women with family roles (partner, mother).

Method of the Study. A sample of 403 women was chosen from the population of practical nurses and social workers licensed in the state of Massachusetts. The researchers used the registers of licensed professionals to identify the population and select their sample. Women on the register were selected at random for the sample. The sample was also chosen such that it matched the population in terms of race, partnership status, and parental status by selecting individuals in these categories according to the proportions that existed in the population. The participants completed three interviews, one per year for 3 years. At each interview, the participants completed a survey regarding their job-role quality in terms of the rewards of and concerns they had about their jobs. They also completed surveys regarding their depression and anxiety levels.

Results of the Study. The results of the study indicated that if the quality of a woman's job role decreased over the 3-year period, distress level (anxiety and depression) increased (i.e., mental health declined). However, this finding was evident only for women who were single and did not have children.

Conclusions of the Study. The results of this study show that a reduction in judged job quality is linked with a reduction in mental health (with regard to anxiety and depression) for women in helping professions (such as nurses and social workers) who do not also have a family role (partner or mother). The authors concluded that women with family roles can still reap mental health rewards even if their job quality declines.

COMMON PITFALLS AND HOW TO AVOID THEM

Problem: Confusion of "volunteer" sample and consent—the use of the term *volunteer sample* can be inaccurately interpreted as a sample that consents to participate.

Solution: Remember that ethical guidelines require informed consent for research studies. The choice of sampling technique does not negate this obligation. All participants in the sample, regardless of the type of sample, have a right to informed consent.

Problem: Devaluation of volunteer samples—students often believe that if a study uses a volunteer sample, it is flawed.

Solution: While it is true that volunteer samples may not provide the most representative sample for some populations, they typically do not lower the external validity of a study very much and are quite common in psychological research. Consider the behavior that is examined in a research study before judging whether the sample may generalize. In many cases, the behavior can be generalized beyond the volunteer sample that was tested.

TEST YOURSELF

1. In what ways are probability samples preferable to convenience samples?

2. Despite the superiority of probability samples, why do many psychological studies use convenience samples?

3. Suppose you were conducting a survey study to learn about drinking behaviors for the population of students at your school with a quota sample. In your sample, you want to be sure that you represent the population according to year in school and gender. Describe how you might choose your sample for this study and how your survey would be administered.

4. What are some advantages to collecting samples using the Internet?

5. In a _____ sample, individuals are chosen at random from the population, but are chosen in proportions equivalent to proportions that exist in the population (e.g., 90% right handed, 10% left handed).

    (a) simple random

    (b) haphazard

    (c) quota

    (d) stratified random

6. In a _____ sample, individuals who volunteer from the population are chosen for the sample.

    (a) simple random

    (b) haphazard

    (c) quota

    (d) stratified random

7. Sampling error is

    (a) a type of sampling technique.

    (b) the difference in observations between the population and the sample.

    (c) an error introduced into a study by the researcher's bias.

    (d) none of the above.

Answers: 1. Probability samples are typically better representatives of the population they are drawn from because the probability of an individual being chosen is determined ahead of time and controlled through random sampling. 2. Many studies use convenience samples because it can be difficult to identify all the members of large populations to randomly select them. 3. There are several ways to do this, but the key is to use a convenience sample of students at the school in the same proportions as they exist at the school based on year-in-school and gender. These proportions will need to be known before the sample is selected. You will also need a recruitment technique (Internet with e-mail contact, surveys mailed to campus address, etc.) to describe how to administer your survey. 4. Internet samples tend to be more diverse than other samples; they can be collected using fewer resources and in a shorter period of time. 5. d, 6. b, 7. b.

Summarizing and Interpreting Data

Using Statistics

CONSIDER THE FOLLOWING QUESTIONS AS YOU READ CHAPTER 7

- How can we summarize a set of data to better understand it?
- What is the difference between the different measures of central tendency of a distribution (mean, median, and mode)?
- How do inferential statistics allow us to learn about populations from the data collected from a sample?
- How do we make hypotheses about populations?
- What can we learn from significance testing?

Based on a survey conducted by Gallup (Morales, 2008), a large majority of Americans (82%) believe that smoking is "very harmful." The survey was based on responses from 1,016 American adults by telephone. In other words, the researchers for this survey collected a random sample of American adults for their survey. Does this mean that if all American adults were given this survey, 82% of them would say that smoking is "very harmful"? The answer is "probably not," because the 82% reported is based on the sample, which represents the population but is unlikely to yield exactly the same values as the population. In other words, due to **sampling error**, the difference between observations in the sample and the population, the sample value is unlikely to equal the population value exactly (see Chapter 6 for more discussion of sampling error). In fact, researchers reported a margin of error of + or −3% for this survey. This means that they are 95% sure that if all American adults were surveyed, between 79% and 85% of them would say that smoking is "very harmful." But where did this margin of error of 3% come from, and why is it that the researchers cannot be 100% certain that the population value

Sampling Error: the difference between the observations in a population and in the sample that represents that population in a study

is in this range? The answers to these questions require a basic understanding of the principles of descriptive and inferential statistics, which will be covered in this chapter. The goal of this chapter is not to help you learn how to calculate the statistics. Calculations of statistics are described in the Appendix, and Chapter 14 covers use of the SPSS statistical software package. Instead, this chapter will help you understand the logic of how researchers use statistics to understand their data and test their hypotheses. Figure 7.1 shows where analyzing the data falls among the steps in the research process.

Figure 7.1   Steps in the Research Process: Analyzing the Data

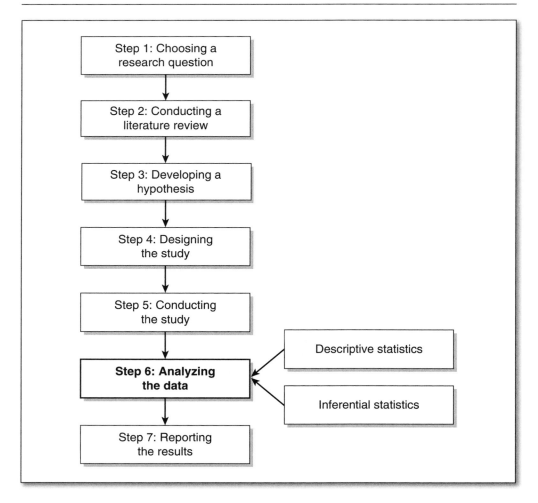

DESCRIPTIVE STATISTICS: SUMMARIZING THE DATA

Before we can understand how well our sample represents the population and whether our hypothesis was supported by the data, we need to first summarize what the data contain. It can be difficult to interpret what data reveal about behavior from just the raw data (i.e., the scores from each participant). Thus, researchers rarely report the raw data they have collected. Instead, researchers typically report **descriptive statistics** that summarize the set of data (also called

Descriptive Statistics: measures that help us summarize data sets

Distribution: a set of scores

Central Tendency: representation of a typical score in a distribution

Variability: the spread of scores in a distribution

a **distribution**). There are three main categories of descriptive statistics that help researchers summarize data. They are (1) the **central tendency** of the distribution, (2) the **variability** in the distribution, and (3) graphs or tables of the central tendency and variability.

Central Tendency

The central tendency of a distribution is a measure that indicates a *typical* score in the distribution. Three basic measures are commonly used to indicate the central tendency of a distribution: the **mean**, the **median**, and the **mode**. The mean is simply the calculated average score in the distribution (i.e., all the scores are added together and divided by the total number of scores in the distribution). The median is the middle score in the distribution, where half of the scores are above the median and half of the scores are below the median. The mode is the most common score (i.e., the one that appears most often in the distribution). Each of these measures can yield different values for any

Mean: the calculated average of the scores in a distribution

Median: the middle score in a distribution, such that half of the scores are above and half are below that value

Mode: the most common score in a distribution

given distribution, but they all represent a typical score in the distribution. Table 7.1 provides a comparison of the three measures of central tendency for two different distributions.

The mean is the most commonly reported measure of central tendency. It is also an important value for inferential statistical tests, as you will see below. However, the mean can be greatly affected by extreme scores in a distribution. High or low extreme scores will pull the mean value toward the top or bottom of the distribution's range because these extreme scores are included in the calculation of the average value. This is illustrated by the second distribution of scores in Table 7.1. The extreme score of "13" in this distribution pulls the mean toward it. The mean for this distribution is higher than the median or mode due to this extreme score. Thus, when a distribution includes several extreme scores, sometimes called **outliers**, researchers often report the median score in addition to or instead of the mean. One example of a distribution that is likely to include outliers is a distribution of salaries at a company. The majority of the workers at most companies earn a salary that

TABLE 7.1	Two Distributions and Their Measures of Central Tendency		
Distribution	**Mean**	**Median**	**Mode**
1, 3, 4, 4, 4, 5, 7	4	4	4
1, 1, 1, 1, 2, 2, 13	3	1	1

may be within a particular range (e.g., $30,000 to $60,000 per year). However, there are also likely to be a few top executives at the company who earn a salary much higher than this range (e.g., $800,000 per year). If you were to calculate the mean salary at the company, the top executives' large salaries would skew the mean higher than the typical salary in the company and make it appear as though typical salaries are higher than they really are. Thus, the median value is typically reported for salary distributions. Another example of this type of distribution is **reaction time** (i.e., how long it takes someone to make a response in a task). Reaction time distributions typically include scores that are clustered around an average score that represents the typical speed of response with a few scores that are longer than the rest. These longer scores often result from cases where people take longer than typical to respond or lose their attention focus in a task. Thus, these longer scores are extreme compared with the typical reaction time score in a distribution and draw the mean score higher when they are included.

Outliers: extreme high or low scores in a distribution

Reaction Time: measurement of the length of time to complete a task

The mode is often reported when the distribution includes frequencies of responses (i.e., nominal scales). For example, if a survey is given where people must choose their current mood from categories such as happy, sad, anxious, or excited, the mode is typically reported (e.g., most participants reported feeling anxious).

Variability

The variability of a distribution indicates how much the scores in the distribution differ from each other across the response scale. For example, if a 1 to 5 rating scale is given for survey items and most participants use the values from 2 to 4, the distribution will have low variability, as most of the scores are similar to one another and do not use the entire response scale. However, if the participants use all the values from 1 to 5 for their responses, the variability in the distribution will be higher. High variability can also occur in a distribution when some participants' responses differ greatly from other participant' responses. Figure 7.2 illustrates distributions with high and low variability. In the left graph, you can see that the scores are clustered close together, representing low variability. In the right graph, the scores are more spread out and do not cluster as much in the middle of the distribution.

Figure 7.2   Low and High Variability Distributions

As with central tendency, there are a few different measures of variability that researchers typically report for a distribution: **range**, **standard deviation**, and **variance**. The range is the most basic measure and is simply the difference between the highest and lowest scores in a distribution. However, the range ignores all the scores between the most extreme scores and therefore is a crude measure of variability. The standard deviation and variance are much more precise measures of variability. The standard deviation is a measure representing the average difference between the scores and the mean of the distribution. However, if you were to simply calculate the differences between the scores and the mean and add them up, you would find that the value is always 0. Thus, the standard deviation is determined by calculating the difference between each score and the mean, squaring those values, adding them up, and dividing by $n - 1$ (where n is the number of scores). See the Appendix for an example of this calculation. We divide by $n - 1$ because the scores are from a sample that represents the population (see Chapter 6), not from the population itself. This $n - 1$ value is called the **degrees of freedom** term, and it is used in the calculation of both descriptive and inferential statistics. Unlike the range, all the scores are considered in the calculation of standard deviation. The variance is simply the standard

Range: the difference between the highest and lowest scores in a distribution

Standard Deviation: a measure representing the average difference between the scores and the mean of a distribution

Variance: the standard deviation of a distribution squared

Degrees of Freedom: number of scores that can vary in the calculation of a statistic deviation squared. Standard deviation and variance measures are important for inferential statistical tests, as you will see below.

Graphs/Tables

❧

Frequency Distribution: a graph of a distribution showing the frequency of each response in the distribution

Bar Graph: a graph of the means for different conditions in a study where the bar height represents the size of the mean

Line Graph: a graph of the means for different conditions in a study where each mean is graphed as a point and the points are connected in a line to show differences between mean scores

Graphs (also called figures) and tables of data are useful tools for quickly summarizing data in a visual way. They can represent a **frequency distribution** for a data set, which indicates how often each score or category appears in a distribution. In a frequency distribution, the different responses are graphed on the x-axis (the horizontal axis) and the frequency of each response in the distribution is graphed on the y-axis (the vertical axis). Figure 7.3 illustrates a frequency distribution of letter grades in a methods course. Frequency distributions can be useful in quickly identifying whether there are outliers in a distribution of scores that may affect the measures of central tendency. Another way to represent a distribution in a graph or table is to include a measure of central tendency (typically the mean) in the graph or table. A table is organized to include the mean score for different conditions or groups in a study. A graph can be organized in the same way as a table but can be visually presented as a **bar graph** or a **line graph**. Figure 7.4 shows a bar graph and line graph for the mean scores in a study. In these graphs, the condition or group is indicated on the x-axis, and the mean score is indicated on the y-axis.

In Chapter 3, we discussed another type of graph that can be used to describe the relationship between two distributions called a **scatterplot**. As shown in Figure 3.5,

Figure 7.3 Frequency Distribution of Letter Grades in a Course

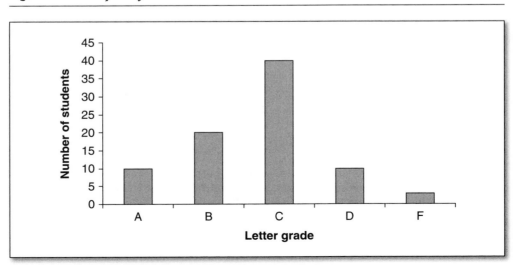

Figure 7.4 Bar and Line Graphs Showing the Comparison of Mean Memory Scores for Children and Adults

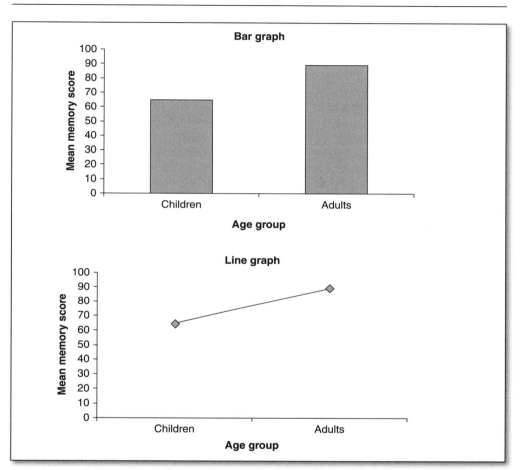

a scatterplot is a graph that includes data points from each participant in a study for two different dependent variables. One variable is plotted on the *x*-axis and one is plotted on the *y*-axis. For correlational studies with a **predictor** and **outcome variable** (see Chapters 3 and 10 for more discussion of these variables), the predictor variable is typically plotted on the *x*-axis, and the outcome variable is plotted on the *y*-axis. How well the data points cluster together in the graphs indicates the strength of the relationship between the two variables.

Scatterplot: a graph showing the relationship between two dependent variables for a group of individuals

Predictor Variable: the dependent variable in a correlational study that is used to predict the score on another variable

Outcome Variable: the dependent variable in a correlational study that is being predicted by the predictor variable

INFERENTIAL STATISTICS: TESTING HYPOTHESES

As indicated above, descriptive statistics help researchers summarize and understand their data. However, they are also useful in testing hypotheses about the populations researchers want to learn about. In some studies, researchers are interested in comparing means across groups of participants or conditions to test a hypothesis. Remember that the descriptive statistics that come from the sample will be similar to those that would be produced by the entire population, because the sample is chosen to represent the population in the research study. The sample statistics are often not exactly the same as those that would be produced by the population, however, because sampling error is always present. This is why we can never be 100% certain of what the population mean is just from looking at the sample mean (e.g., see the smoking survey study description at the beginning of the chapter). Without testing the entire population, we can estimate the population mean only with a particular level of

Inferential Statistics: a set of statistical procedures used by researchers to test hypotheses about populations

certainty. The more variability there is in the data, the more sampling error there is, and the less certain we are about the value of the population mean (i.e., the margin of error). Thus, researchers use **inferential statistics** to determine what can be learned about the population from the sample. As you will see below, descriptive statistics are an important part of the inferential process.

Hypotheses

We will begin our discussion of inferential statistics with the hypotheses that we are learning about from the statistical procedures. Recall from Chapter 2 that making a hypothesis is an important step in the research process. The literature review helps us determine what we should predict for the data in our study. In inferential statistics, this hypothesis made by the researcher is usually the **scientific or alternative hypothesis** (why it is called the alternative hypothesis will be become more clear as you read). The scientific or alternative hypothesis is the hypothesis either that an effect of the independent variable exists (for an experiment or quasi-experiment) or a relationship between the variables exists (for a correlational study). This hypothesis is stated in terms of an effect or relationship that

Scientific/Alternative Hypothesis: the hypothesis that an effect or relationship exists (or exists in a specific direction) in the population

Null Hypothesis: the hypotheses that an effect or relationship does not exist (or exists in the opposite direction of the alternative hypothesis) in the population

exists in the population because it is the population that the researcher wants to learn about. The **null hypothesis** is the opposite hypothesis to the scientific or alternative hypothesis: that an effect or relationship does not exist in the population.

We will consider an example to state these hypotheses more concretely. Imagine that you are conducting a study to examine the research question: *Do memory abilities change as people age?* (see Figure 7.3 for example data from such a study). You conduct a literature review (see Chapter 2 for discussion of how to conduct a literature review), and the previous studies you read seem to indicate that memory abilities do change as people age. Thus, an appropriate hypothesis for your study is: *Memory abilities change with age.* This becomes the scientific or alternative hypothesis for your inferential statistics. The scientific or alternative hypothesis is often denoted by H_a or H_1. Thus,

> H_1: *In the general population, memory abilities change with age.* OR *In the general population, different age groups have different mean memory scores.*

The null hypothesis (denoted by H_0) makes the opposite prediction: that *memory abilities do not change with age.* Thus,

> H_0: *In the general population, memory abilities do not change with age.* OR *In the general population, different age groups have the same mean memory scores.*

What we have considered above is called a **two-tailed hypothesis** because we are considering both possible directions of difference in the hypothesis. In other words, our alternative hypothesis above does not predict whether younger or older individuals will have higher memory scores. It simply states that the mean scores for younger and older individuals in the population will be *different*. It does not include a prediction about which population will have higher scores. However, for this study, you might find previous studies that indicate that as people age, their memory abilities decline. Thus, you could make a directional or **one-tailed hypothesis**. As a one-tailed hypothesis, our alternative hypothesis could be stated thus:

Two-Tailed Hypothesis: both directions of an effect or relationship are considered in the alternative hypothesis of the test

One-Tailed Hypothesis: only one direction of an effect or relationship is predicted in the alternative hypothesis of the test

> H_1: *In the general population, older individuals have lower memory scores than younger individuals.*

We could also make the opposite prediction (e.g., H_1: *In the general population, older individuals have higher memory scores than younger individuals*), but the hypothesis stated above is more likely to be consistent with the results of previous studies. For this alternative hypothesis, our null hypothesis must include any other possible outcome, so our null hypothesis is this:

> H_0: *In the general population, older individuals have higher memory scores than younger individuals or the memory scores of the two age groups are the same.*

For a one-tailed hypothesis, the null hypothesis contains the predictions of no effect or relationship *and* the effect or relationship in the direction opposite to that predicted in the alternative hypothesis. See the top portion of the flowchart in Figure 7.5.

One-tailed hypotheses are typically made only when a researcher has a logical reason to believe that one particular direction of the effect will occur. Thus, one-tailed hypotheses are often made when the other direction of the effect logically should not occur or does not

Figure 7.5   **Steps in Conducting Inferential Statistics Tests**

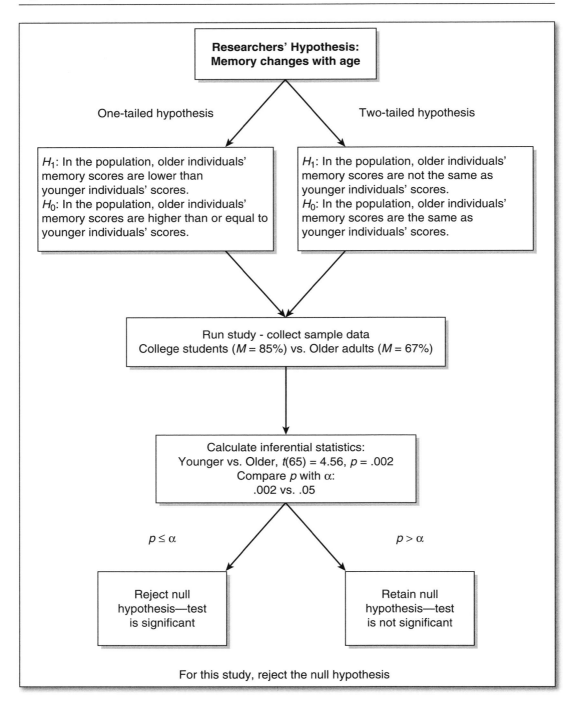

answer the research question. They may also be made when the literature review of an area indicates that one direction of the effect has been shown consistently over a number of research studies.

The study described above could also be done to look for a relationship between age and memory ability. In this case, the hypotheses would be stated with regard to relationships that might exist (or not) in the population. The two-tailed alternative hypothesis in this case would be this:

H_1: *In the population, age and memory scores are related.*

The null hypothesis would be:

H_0: *In the population, age and memory scores are not related.*

A one-tailed alternative hypothesis for a test about relationships would predict a specific relationship (positive or negative) between the variables, and the null hypothesis would predict no relationship or a relationship in the opposite direction of the alternative hypothesis.

An inferential statistical test provides a test of the null hypothesis for either one-tailed or two-tailed hypotheses. These tests allow researchers to determine if there is enough evidence to reject the null hypothesis for their study and accept the scientific or alternative hypothesis. This is why it is called the alternative hypothesis: It is the alternative to the null hypothesis. The evidence provided by the inferential test is the likelihood of obtaining the data in the study when the null hypothesis is actually true. That is what the inferential test focuses on: What is the chance of obtaining the data in this study when the null hypothesis is in fact true? If the chance is fairly high, then there is no evidence to reject the null hypothesis. In other words, there may not be an effect or relationship (although the test does not speak to this possibility specifically). If the chance is very low, then the researcher takes that as evidence against the null hypothesis, rejects it, and accepts the alternative hypothesis that there is an effect or relationship. *In other words, the decision to reject or not reject the null hypothesis is based on the probability of obtaining the data in the sample when the null hypothesis is true.* The strength of the effect or relationship and the amount of sampling error in the data are considered to determine this probability.

Now consider this inferential process more specifically in terms of populations and samples. When we choose a sample from a population, we are choosing one possible sample from this population. There are many other possible samples that could be chosen instead, and each sample would have its own mean. But if we considered all the possible sample means that could come from samples from this particular population, we would find that most of the sample means would be fairly close to the actual population mean and a few would be quite far away. Figure 7.6 represents a distribution of possible population means that can occur for a particular population. Notice that a few of the sample means are at the far ends of the distribution and are far off of the population mean, but most of the sample means are close to the actual population mean in the middle of the distribution. This distribution is called the **distribution of sample means** and is used to determine how likely it is that

Distribution of Sample Means: the distribution of all possible sample means for all possible samples from a population

Figure 7.6 Distribution of Sample Means From a Population When the Null Hypothesis Is True

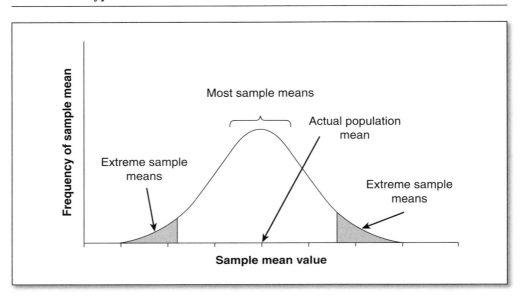

any sample mean will occur for a population. This distribution represents the different sample means that can occur when the null hypothesis is true. In fact, the exact probability of a sample mean falling into portions of this distribution can be determined and is a value obtained when the inferential statistical test is conducted. Thus, researchers know the likelihood that their sample mean would have occurred when the null hypothesis is true after they conduct their inferential test. This information allows them to determine if they have an extreme enough sample mean to decide that it probably did not come from this distribution (i.e., the chance is very small that it came from the distribution of sample means), and they can reject the null hypothesis, because their sample mean probably did not come from this distribution. This is the general logic used in significance tests, regardless of the type of test researchers conduct.

Significance Testing

How unlikely does a sample mean have to be before we decide it did not come from the distribution of sample means? That is a value determined by the researcher, and it is typically set at 5% or less. In other words, there has to be a 5% or less chance that the sample mean came from the distribution of sample means for a researcher to reject the null hypothesis. This probability value is called the **alpha level** (often denoted by the Greek letter α) in inferential statistics. It is the highest probability that a sample mean came from this distribution that still provides evidence against the null hypothesis. It is set by the researcher at a low value to allow rejection of the null hypothesis only when it is very unlikely that the sample mean came from the distribution of sample means for the null hypothesis. The probability of a sample mean occurring in the distribution of sample means is compared with the alpha level in an inferential test. Remember that most sample means occur near the actual population mean, so if the probability is high that the sample mean came from this distribution, then it is more likely that the null hypothesis is true. If the probability value (also called a *p* value) is equal to or lower than alpha, then the researcher rejects the null hypothesis as unlikely to be true. If the *p* value is higher than alpha, the researcher cannot reject the null hypothesis, as it be might true (again, the test

Alpha Level: the probability level used by researchers to indicate the cutoff probability level (highest value) that will allow them to reject the null hypothesis

***p* Value:** probability value associated with an inferential test that indicates the likelihood of obtaining the data in a study when the null hypothesis is true

Significant Test: the *p* value is less than or equal to alpha in an inferential test, and the null hypothesis can be rejected

does *not* provide evidence *for* the null hypothesis, only against it). If the *p* value is less than or equal to alpha, the test is said to be **significant**. In other words, a significant inferential test means that the null hypothesis can be rejected, the alternative hypothesis can be accepted, and the researcher can conclude that there is an effect or relationship for the data in the current study.

Consider the distribution of sample means again (see Figure 7.6). Suppose that an inferential test you conducted indicated that the probability of the sample mean when the null hypothesis is true is .70. This means that there is a 70% chance of obtaining your sample mean when the null hypothesis is true (i.e., there is a 70% chance that the null hypothesis is true given your data). In this case, it is very likely that the null hypothesis is true and you cannot reject it. However, suppose instead that the *p* value for your data was .03. This means that there is only a 3% chance of obtaining your sample mean when the null hypothesis is true. Your sample mean falls in the most extreme portion of this distribution. This portion of the distribution is called the **critical region** of the distribution. The darkened portions in Figure 7.6 indicate the critical regions for a two-tailed hypothe-

Critical Region: the most extreme portion of a distribution of statistical values for the null hypothesis determined by the alpha level (typically 5%)

sis, and the shaded portion in Figure 7.7 indicates the critical region for a one-tailed hypothesis. When your calculated statistic falls in this region, you can take this as evidence against the null hypothesis and reject it. For the *p* value of .03, the value will fall in the critical region of the distribution, indicating that your value is unlikely to occur when the null hypothesis is true. In other words, the chance of obtaining your data when the null hypothesis is true is very low, and you can be fairly confident that it is wrong in this case and reject it.

Now consider the study discussed above regarding the comparison of younger and older individuals' memory abilities. Suppose this study had been conducted comparing scores on a memory test for college students and older adults. In the study, the college students' mean

Figure 7.7 Distribution of Sample Means With Different p Values Represented

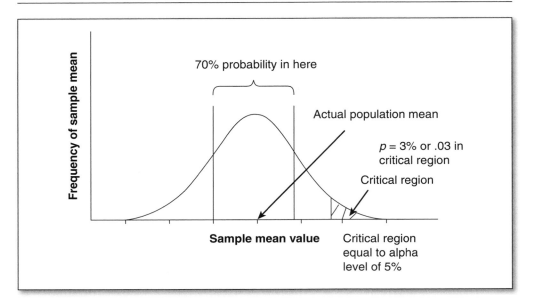

score was 85%, and the older adults' mean score was 67% (see Figure 7.5 for sample means). The inferential test will indicate the likelihood that these two sample means both came from the same population with a single mean (consistent with the two-tailed null hypothesis that the scores are the same for younger and older individuals) or from different populations with different means (consistent with the two-tailed alternative hypothesis that the scores are different for younger and older individuals). The p value given for the statistical test will indicate the chance of obtaining these means from the same distribution of scores (i.e., when the null hypothesis is true). As seen in Figure 7.5, for this study, the p value was .002, which means that the chance of obtaining these data when the null hypothesis is true is only 0.2%.

Statistic Distributions. The process just described is followed when an inferential statistical test is conducted. However, depending on the statistic being used, a researcher may be considering the difference between sample means or whether a relationship exists between distributions. Thus, instead of considering the probability of a single sample mean in the distribution of sample means, a distribution for the statistic being calculated is the distribution that is used to determine the p value. Different types of statistics are used for different measurement scales and research design types (see Chapter 4 for a discussion of measurement scales and research designs). The p value obtained represents the probability of obtaining that statistic in a distribution corresponding to the null hypothesis. Thus, the p value has the same meaning regardless of which statistic you are using. Figure 7.5 indicates how p values are useful in the process of conducting the statistical test. We will consider different types of statistics and when to use them more specifically in Chapter 14.

Significance Test Outcomes. Table 7.2 illustrates the different possible outcomes of a significance test. The columns represent the reality for the population being studied: Either the null hypothesis is true and there is no effect/relationship, or the null hypothesis is false and there is an effect/relationship. When a significance test is conducted, the researcher does not know whether the null hypothesis is actually true or false. However, the test is conducted to look for evidence that the null hypothesis is not true. If that evidence is found, the researcher can decide that the null hypothesis is false and reject it. This is the outcome represented in the first row of Table 7.2. If in fact the null hypothesis is actually false, the researcher has made a correct decision in the test, because the decision matches the reality about the null hypothesis. However, remember that the researcher will never know whether the null hypothesis is really true, so it is possible to make the wrong decision. Thus, the outcome to reject the null hypothesis in the first row under the column where the null hypothesis is really true is an error. The researcher's decision does not match the reality for the null hypothesis. This is called a **Type I error** and indicates that the researcher has rejected the null hypothesis when it is really true. The chance of making a Type I error is determined ahead of time by the researcher when an alpha level is chosen. Alpha is very often set at 5 % (or .05) by researchers. It is the standard alpha level used in psychological research. Thus, in tests with $\alpha = .05$, there is a 5 % chance of making a Type I error.

Type I Error: error made in a significance test when the researcher rejects the null hypothesis when it is actually true

The second row in Table 7.2 illustrates test outcomes for the other decision that can be made in the significance test: failing to reject the null hypothesis, which occurs when evidence against it is not found in the test. A correct decision is made in the test when the decision is to fail to reject the null hypothesis and it is really false (bottom right box). However, another type of error, called a **Type II error**, can be made when the null hypothesis is not rejected but is actually false. This means that an effect or relationship exists in the population but was not detected in the data from the sample. The chance of a Type II error is more difficult to determine. There are several factors that can influence the probability of a Type II error, including the alpha level chosen, the size of the effect or relationship, and the sample size in the study. The researcher can lower the chance of a Type II error by using an optimal sample size and making sure that the study is designed to maximize the effect or relationship being

Type II Error: error made in a significance test when the researcher fails to reject the null hypothesis when it is actually false

Power: ability of a significance test to detect an effect or relationship when one exists (equal to 1−the probability of a Type II error)

TABLE 7.2	Possible Outcomes of a Statistical Test	
Decisions	**Null Hypothesis Is Actually False**	**Null Hypothesis Is Actually True**
Reject the null hypothesis	Correct decision!	Type I error
Fail to reject the null hypothesis	Type II error	Correct decision!

studied. By keeping the Type II error rate low, you are increasing the **power** of your significance test to detect an effect or relationship that actually exists. Thus, it is important to keep Type II errors in mind as you design your study to conduct a powerful test of the hypothesis.

Up to this point, we have discussed inferential statistics generally as they can be applied to different types of hypotheses. Chapter 14 continues this discussion with the "nuts and bolts" of how to use the different statistical tests that are based on this hypothesis-test logic. For a discussion of how common statistics are calculated and how SPSS software is used to calculate and interpret the statistics, refer to Chapter 14.

Predicting the Null Hypothesis

As mentioned above, in many cases, the alternative hypothesis is also the researcher's hypothesis. The researcher predicts that an effect or relationship exists in the population. However, in some cases, the researcher may wish to predict that an effect or relationship does not exist in the population. Is this an appropriate thing for a researcher to do when using inferential statistics? Many would argue that it is not appropriate for a researcher to predict the null hypothesis because significance tests do not provide evidence for the null hypothesis. In fact, most papers that are published in psychological journals describe studies that showed significant results (Greenwald, 1975), because it can be difficult to draw strong conclusions from studies that do not show significant results. However, power analyses can be used to estimate the chance of a Type II error occurring and the null hypothesis being falsely retained. While any single study with nonsignificant results will not be sufficient to provide support for the null hypothesis, a series of studies that have a reasonable level of power to detect effects (80% or higher is the generally accepted level, Cohen, 1988) that all show the same nonsignificant results may provide some support for the null hypothesis. Thus, if researchers want to predict the null hypothesis, they must be prepared to conduct several studies in order to obtain some support for their hypothesis. Greenwald (1975) also argued that a bias against the null hypothesis can result in researchers' ignoring studies that do not find significant effects (which can be caused by the bias against publishing them). In addition, because it is important that theories of behavior can be falsified (see Chapter 1), it is sometimes necessary to predict the null hypothesis in order to truly test a theory. Finally, several researchers (e.g., Cohen, 1990, 1994; Loftus, 1993) have suggested alternatives to significance testing as a means of interpreting data to get around this issue.

CHAPTER SUMMARY

Reconsider the questions from the beginning of the chapter:

- How can we summarize a set of data to better understand it? Data can be summarized with descriptive statistics. Measures of central tendency indicate a typical score in a distribution. Measures of variability indicate the spread of the scores in a distribution. Graphs and tables can also provide a visual summary of the data.
- What is the difference between the different measures of central tendency of a distribution (mean, median, and mode)? The mean is the average of the scores in the distribution. The median is the middle score in the distribution. The mode is the most frequent score in a distribution.

- How do inferential statistics allow us to learn about populations from the data collected from a sample? Inferential statistics estimate sampling error to adjust for how well the sample represents the population in hypothesis tests. Then an inferential statistic is calculated from the sample values with an estimate of sampling error included in the calculation. For each statistic, a p value is determined that indicates the likelihood of obtaining the sample data when the null hypothesis is true. If the p value is less than or equal to alpha, this is taken as evidence against the null hypothesis about the population, and it can be rejected. Otherwise, the null hypothesis about the population must be retained. See Figure 7.5 for an illustration of this process.
- How do we make hypotheses about populations? Null and alternative hypotheses about populations are stated for studies as either comparisons of conditions or predictions about relationships.
- What can we learn from significance testing? We can determine if there is enough evidence against the null hypothesis to reject it and conclude that the alternative hypothesis is true.

THINKING ABOUT RESEARCH

A summary of a research study in psychology is given below. As you read the summary, think about the following questions:

1. What research design is used in this study (i.e., experiment, quasi-experiment, correlational study, case study)? Describe any independent and dependent variables in the design.

2. Should the authors make one-tailed or two-tailed hypotheses for their statistical analysis? Explain why.

3. State the null and alternative hypotheses for this study.

4. Suppose the test the researchers conducted to compare the "explicit zero" and "hidden zero" conditions provided a p value of .043. Assuming they used an alpha level of .05, what decision should the researchers make regarding the null hypothesis for this comparison?

5. For the decision made in (4) above, suppose that the null hypothesis is actually true. What type of error have the researchers made in this case?

6. Explain why other researchers should attempt to replicate the results of this study under similar conditions. What benefit is there to replication in psychological research?

Study Reference

Magen, E., Dweck, C. S., & Gross, J. J. (2008). The hidden zero effect: Representing a single choice as an extended sequence reduces impulsive choice. *Psychological Science, 19,* 648–649.

Purpose of the Study. Because impulsivity is negatively related to important variables (academic achievement, social adjustment, etc.), the authors conducted a study to investigate how the way choices are presented to people affects impulsivity. They investigated the use of what is called a "hidden zero" presentation of choices, where people are asked to choose between two options, but the portions of the options where they receive nothing are not explicitly stated (e.g., Would you rather have $5 today or $6 in 6 months?). This is how choices are typically presented to participants in studies examining this type of impulsivity. However, because other research (e.g., Tversky & Kahneman, 1981) has shown that the way choices are presented to people can influence their choices, the authors decided to compare the "hidden zero" presentation described above with an "explicit zero" presentation. In the "explicit zero" presentation, the cases where the person receives nothing is explicitly stated (e.g., Would you rather have $5 today and $0 in 6 months or $0 today and $6 in 6 months?).

Method of the Study. An Internet sample completed a questionnaire where they either made choices in the "hidden zero" condition or they made choices in the "explicit zero" condition. The choices were between small dollar amounts ($2 to $8.40), where a small amount was offered today or a slightly larger amount was offered after a delay (7 to 140 days). Two samples completed the questionnaire. One sample was told that the choices were hypothetical, whereas the other sample was told that they would receive one of their choices from the study chosen at random. Half of each sample completed all choices with the "hidden zero" condition and the other half of each sample completed all choices with the "explicit zero" condition. Impulsiveness was measured by the number of smaller, sooner choices made by each participant.

Results of the Study. Results were similar for the two samples (hypothetical and real money choices), so results are presented for both samples together. Impulsivity was found to be significantly lower in the "explicit zero" condition (overall mean number of sooner choices was 5.26) than in the "hidden zero" condition (overall mean number of sooner choices was 7.69) of the study.

Conclusions of the Study. The results of the study indicated that the presentation of choices affected the measured impulsivity of the participants. When an "explicit zero" case was included in the choice, people were less impulsive than when the zero case was not explicitly stated. The authors concluded that the mere mention of the "downsides" of choices (i.e., the zero cases in the choices) can decrease impulsivity in the choices.

COMMON PITFALLS AND HOW TO AVOID THEM

Problem: Supporting the null hypothesis—students often make the error of stating that the null hypothesis is supported with a nonsignificant result.

Solution: Always remember that hypothesis testing procedures with inferential statistics are designed to provide evidence against the null hypothesis, never to support it. When a decision to retain the null hypothesis is made, this simply means that there is not enough evidence to reject it, not that it is supported by the data.

Problem: Stating that results "prove" the hypothesis is true—students sometimes make the mistake of stating that statistical results prove that an effect exists or that a hypothesis is supported.

Solution: Remember that any single study cannot prove something is true in psychological research. Hypotheses are supported by the data but are never proven true or false, because it is always possible that a Type I or Type II error has occurred. It is a good idea to avoid using the word "prove" when you report results of a psychological study.

Problem: Ignoring the power of the test—researchers sometimes do not consider the power of their tests carefully enough, concluding that a nonsignificant result can be relied on with the same certainty as a significant result.

Solution: Remember that although the Type I error rate is set as alpha by the researcher (usually .05 in psychological studies), the Type II error rate is typically unknown at the start of a study and is usually much higher than .05. Thus, researchers should not view nonsignificant results with the same level of certainty as significant results.

TEST YOURSELF

1. Suppose you conducted a study to test the hypothesis that social pressure affects memory accuracy. You set up a study where participants view a video of a person robbing a convenience store. Then half of the participants watch a video of other "participants" discussing the crime. In reality, the "participants" in the video are part of the experiment, and some of the details of the crime that are discussed are inaccurate. The actual participants are told they should consider other people's perspectives on the crime because it is difficult for any one person to accurately remember all the details. The other half of the participants do not view the video discussion of the crime but are also told that it is difficult for any one person to accurately remember all the details of the crime. Thirty minutes after viewing the original crime video, all participants are given a recognition memory test about details of the crime. For this study, answer the following questions:

   (a) What are the independent and dependent variables?

   (b) State the alternative and null hypotheses for this study.

   (c) Suppose you collected the data for this study, calculated the appropriate statistic to compare the means for the two groups (see Chapter 14 for discussion of statistical test appropriate for this design) and obtained a *p* value of .013 for the statistic. What decision should be made (assuming $\alpha = .05$) about the null hypothesis? What can you conclude about the independent variable from this decision?

   (d) Now suppose that in reality, the null hypothesis is true. What type of decision have you made in (c): correct decision, Type I error, or Type II error?

2. Suppose you conducted a study to determine if some people have the ability to predict which of two cards a poker player has been dealt for a poker hand. The study involves a single sample of people who claim to be "better than average poker players." In the study, all participants are asked to view a poker player being given a card from the dealer. They are asked to judge from the player's reaction whether the card is a card dealt to the player that will "complete a four of a kind hand" or "not complete a four of a kind hand." They complete 100 judgment trials, and their overall percentage accuracy is calculated. In other words, across all trials, the participants have a 50% chance of being correct if they have no ability to interpret the player's "poker face" (i.e., they are guessing). If they are able to interpret the player's poker face, the participants should perform better than chance (50%) in correctly choosing which type of card the player has been dealt.

   (a) Should a one-tailed or two-tailed test be used for this study? How do you know?

   (b) State the null and alternative hypotheses for this study.

   (c) Suppose that the test statistic calculated for this study yields a *p* value of .18. What decision should be made with regard to the null hypothesis (assume $\alpha = .05$)? What can the researcher conclude about the poker players' abilities?

   (d) Suppose that in reality poker players are able to predict another player's hand with better than chance accuracy. In this case, what type of decision was made in (c) above?

3. Explain the difference between Type I and Type II errors that can be made in significance testing. Which type of error has probability equal to alpha?

Answers: 1a. IV = video condition (view crime discussion video or not), DV = recognition memory score. 1b. This is a two-tailed test (no prediction is made about which group will score better), so for H_1: in the population, the video condition affects recognition scores, for H_0: in the population, the video condition does not affect recognition scores. 1c. Reject the null hypothesis because $p < \alpha$—the independent variable (viewing the discussion of the crime with false information or not viewing the discussion) has an effect on memory accuracy. 1d. If the null hypothesis is true and you reject it, you are making a Type I error. 2a. A one-tailed test should be used, because the researcher is predicting that people will be better than chance ($> 50\%$) if they have poker abilities, but less than chance does not indicate poker abilities. 2b. H_1: in the population, "better than average" poker players will guess the type of card chosen at a rate higher than 50%, H_0: in the population, "better than average" poker players will guess the type of card chosen at a rate lower than or equal to 50%. 2c. $p > \alpha$, so the null hypothesis must be retained. The researcher cannot conclude that the poker players can predict another player's hand at better than chance accuracy. 2d. This would be a Type II error, because the null hypothesis was retained when in reality it is false. 3. Type I errors occur when a researcher rejects a null hypothesis that is actually true. Type II errors occur when a researcher fails to reject a null hypothesis that is actually false. The probably of a Type I error is set by alpha.

CHAPTER 8

Reporting Research

CONSIDER THE FOLLOWING QUESTIONS AS YOU READ CHAPTER 8

- What are the different ways that psychologists present research?
- How do we write an APA-style article? What information goes in each section of the article? How do we format the article?
- What is an appropriate format for an oral presentation of research?
- How do we prepare a conference-style poster presentation of research?

Once you have completed your first research project, you may be asked to present the study to a group. You may be asked to write an American Psychological Association (APA)–style article, give an oral presentation, or prepare a poster presentation of your research. This is how psychologists communicate with each other about research that they have conducted. It is an important part of the scientific method to tell others about your study and its results. This is how knowledge accumulates and science progresses.

You should already be somewhat familiar with an APA-style article by reading the published journal articles that other psychologists have written. However, the focus up to this point in the text has been on how to read and understand these articles. In this chapter, we will focus more on how to write one of these articles as a researcher who has completed a study and is getting ready to present it to others. We will also discuss the other common forms of presentation: the oral presentation and the poster presentation. Oral and poster presentations are common at conferences as methods of presenting research one has completed. They are sometimes given before an APA-style article is written for publication and, thus, represent the most up-to-date findings in an area. There are many undergraduate conferences that are held regionally each year, and your college may hold its own as well. Thus, as a student you are more likely to be involved in an oral or poster presentation if you present research outside your class. However, all the presentation styles will help you learn how to organize the presentation of research, and writing APA-style articles should also help you better understand journal articles that others have written. We will begin with the APA-style article as a mode of research presentation (see Figure 8.1).

Figure 8.1   Steps in the Research Process: Reporting the Results

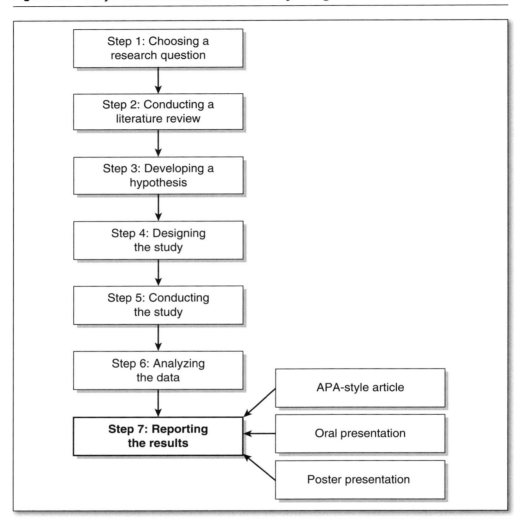

APA-STYLE ARTICLE WRITING

As you have seen in the journal articles you have read (and from the description of these articles in Chapter 2 of this text), APA-style articles follow a particular organization style. APA style refers to the writing style proposed by the American Psychological Association (APA, 2010) for research articles in psychology and related fields. There are other formatting styles for research articles, but APA style is the most commonly used style in psychology, and most psychological journals require submission of articles for publication to be written in APA style. Figure 8.2 illustrates the formatting of an APA-style article that

Figure 8.2   Sample APA-Style Article

Does Delay Affect

Prospective Memory Accuracy?

Jackie K. Cavallo

Illinois State University

(Continued)

Figure 8.2 (Continued)

Abstract

The present experiment was designed to test the effect of delay on prospective memory. Prospective memory is remembering to complete a task in the future (Einstein & McDaniel, 2005). Previous studies that measured forgetting of prospective memory have reported mixed results. Thus, the current study tested the effect of delay in an attempt to clarify the effect. Delay between the presentation of the prospective memory instructions and the prospective memory cue was manipulated. Delays of 5 to 20 min were tested. Results indicated that prospective memory performance did not change as delay increased. Thus, there was no evidence that delay affects prospective memory for this range of delays.

Does Delay Affect Prospective Memory Accuracy?

Prospective memory (PM) is the act of remembering to perform a task at some point in the future (Einstein & McDaniel, 2005). More and more research is taking place on this topic. Researchers in this area have been examining the effect of delay on PM. In these studies, the delay between the PM instructions and the presentation of the PM cue was manipulated. Knowing how delay affects PM may indicate how similar PM is to retrospective memory (i.e., remembering something you have experienced in the past).

Previous studies have reported mixed results for the effect of delay on PM. For example, in a study by Nigro and Cicogna (2000), university students answered two standardized questionnaires. After completing the first questionnaire, participants were told to relay a message to the experimenter in charge of giving the second questionnaire. The message was the same for all participants. Random assignment was used to place the participants in one of three delay conditions: 10 min, 2 days, or 2 weeks. On seeing the second experimenter at their designated time, participants were to give the message. Results showed that PM accuracy was not affected by delay of the second session. However, Hicks, Marsh, and Russell (2000) did find an effect of delay on PM performance. They manipulated delay in a laboratory study of PM and found that PM performance increased from a delay of 2.5 min to a delay of 15 min. Thus, the effect of delay on PM is unclear.

Contrary to the results of Hicks et al. (2000), Meier, Zimmerman, and

(Continued)

Figure 8.2 (Continued)

Perrig (2006) found that PM performance decreased with longer delays. In their second experiment, they administered delays of 5, 15, and 45 min using two distractor tasks. Results suggested that as the delays got longer the PM accuracy decreased.

The purpose of the current study was to find out if delays between the PM instructions and the presentation of the PM cue significantly affect PM accuracy. Delays of 5, 10, 15, and 20 min were used. Based on the results of Meier et al. (2006) for delays in this range, I hypothesized that as delay increased, PM accuracy would decrease.

Method

Participants

The participants were 80 undergraduate students from a psychology department subject pool at Illinois State University. They completed the experiment voluntarily and received extra credit in their courses for their participation. Participants were randomly assigned to one of the four conditions—5-, 10-, 15-, or 20-min delay—with 20 participants per condition.

Design

A between-subjects design was used to examine the differences between the four delay conditions and PM accuracy. The independent variable was delay between instruction of the PM task and the PM cue. The levels of the independent variable were 5-, 10-, 15-, and 20-min delays. The dependent variable in the study was PM accuracy.

Materials

The stimuli consisted of categories and items that did or did not belong to a specific category given. The stimuli were drawn from Battig and Montague's (1969) category norms. There were 11 categories presented to the participants with exemplars: fruit, vegetable, human body part, metal, fish, flower, city, color, sport, musical instrument, and places to sleep. There were 280 category and exemplar pairings in the experiment, divided into four blocks of trials. Trials were numbered for participant accuracy in recording judgments on the record sheet. Half of the exemplars belonged to the category presented, whereas the other half did not belong. The participants were given response sheets numbered from 1 to 280. They circled "yes" or "no" on each trial according to whether or not the exemplar belonged in the category. Four PM cues appeared in the category-judgment trials: hotel, dormitory, library, and restaurant. Two of these cues were presented with a correct category, and two were presented with an incorrect category. The trials were presented with PowerPoint. In each trial, categories and exemplars were presented in the center of the computer screen.

Procedure

Participant sessions were run individually. Participants first read and signed an informed consent form. The ongoing task for the four conditions was to identify whether the item exemplar on the right of the screen belonged in the category presented on the left of the screen. In addition, the PM task for all participants was to mark an "X" next to the trial number when a building was displayed in

(Continued)

Figure 8.2 (Continued)

the trial. Both the ongoing and PM task instructions were read to the participant by the researcher. Ten practice trials followed. At that time, if participants had any questions, they were answered before the rest of the experiment continued.

Each of the 280 trials remained on the screen for 5 s. There were three breaks of 30 s between each block of trials. The four PM cues appeared within a minute period at the delay time for each delay group. At the end of the experiment, the participants were debriefed and thanked and received their course credit.

Results

The effect of delay on prospective memory accuracy was tested. A one-way analysis of variance (ANOVA) was run on the accuracy data with an alpha level of .05. Means and standard deviations for PM accuracy can be found in Figure 1. PM accuracy in all conditions was relatively low. We found that the effect of delay on PM accuracy was not significant: $F(3, 37) = 0.06$, $p = .98$.

In addition to PM accuracy, we analyzed the ongoing task accuracy for each delay. With an alpha level of .05, a one-way ANOVA was used to analyze these data. Means and standard deviations for the ongoing-task accuracy can be found in Table 1. The ongoing-task accuracy was high in all conditions. Results indicated that the effect of delay on the ongoing task accuracy was not significant: $F(3, 37) = 1.44$, $p = .25$.

Discussion

The current study was designed to examine how the amount of time between the PM instructions and the presentation of the PM cue affects PM accuracy. The hypothesis was that as delay increased, PM accuracy would decrease. The results of the current study indicated that PM accuracy was not significantly affected by delay. The overall PM accuracy was low for all conditions. It was also found that delay did not affect the accuracy of the ongoing task. The overall ongoing-task accuracy was high in all conditions.

The present results are consistent with some previous studies that found no effect of delay on PM accuracy. An example of such a study is that of Nigro and Cicogna (2000), where they found no effect of delay for delays from 10 min to 2 weeks. In the current study, results consistent with Nigro and Cicogna's were found for delays from 5 to 20 min. However, the present results are inconsistent with those reported by Meier et al. (2006). They found significant effects of delay for delays of 5 to 45 min. The inconsistency could be due to the way delay was manipulated (e.g., no distractor task was used in the present study) or the shorter delays used in the present study.

This study examined the effects of delay on PM accuracy in the hope of better understanding factors that affect PM and how similar PM is to retrospective memory, which typically shows an effect of delay. The results of this study indicated no effect of delay on PM. Future studies should continue to explore delay as a possible factor that affects PM to allow us to fully understand how PM works.

(Continued)

Figure 8.2 (Continued)

Running head: DELAY AND PROSPECTIVE MEMORY ACCURACY   8

References

Battig, W. F., & Montague, W. E. (1969). Category norms for verbal items in 56 categories: A replication and extension of the Connecticut category norms. *Journal of Experimental Psychology Monographs, 80*(3, Pt. 2).

Einstein, G. O., & McDaniel, M. A. (2005). Prospective memory: Multiple retrieval processes. *Current Directions in Psychological Science, 14,* 286–290.

Hicks, J. L., Marsh, R. L., & Russell, E. J. (2000). The properties of retention intervals and their affect on retaining prospective memories. *Journal of Experimental Psychology: Learning, Memory, and Cognition, 26,* 1160–1169.

Meier, B., Zimmerman, T. D., & Perrig, W. (2006). Retrieval experience in prospective memory: Strategic monitoring and spontaneous retrieval. *Memory, 14,* 872–889.

Nigro, G., & Cicogna, P. C. (2000). Does delay affect PM performance? *European Psychologist, 5,* 228–233.

Table 1

Mean Ongoing Task Performance

Delay	Mean	Standard Deviation
5 min	.97	.05
10 min	.95	.04
15 min	.98	.04
20 min	.96	.03

(Continued)

Figure 8.2 (Continued)

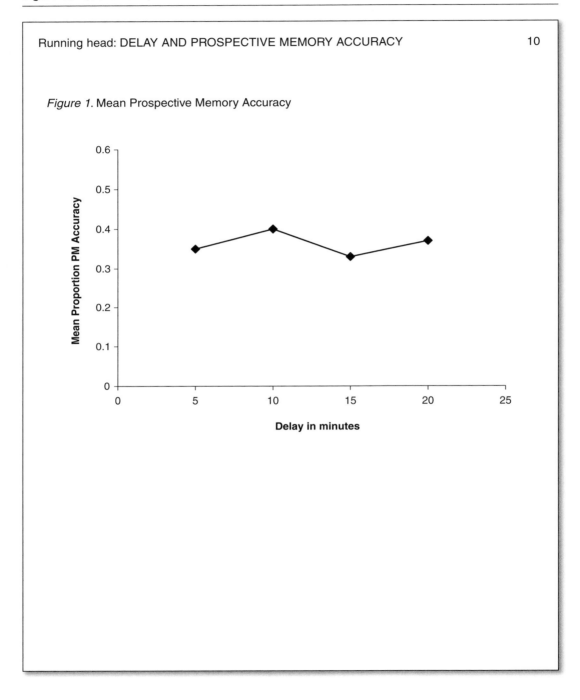

Figure 1. Mean Prospective Memory Accuracy

has been typed in by a researcher. We will discuss each section of the APA-style article and the information that should be included in each section. Some important APA style rules will also be covered to help you format your article as you type it. All information described in the section below is also covered in the *Publication Manual of the American Psychological Association* (APA, 2010). In addition, an article describing what belongs in the sections of an APA-style article that is also formatted in APA style is available at http://my.ilstu.edu/~dmmcbri/APAsample.doc.

Sections of an APA-Style Article

Title Page. The first page of your article will be the Title Page. It will include the title of the article, the authors' names, and the authors' affiliations centered on the page. Your title should be concise and informative. Someone should be able to determine the general topic of your study from the title you choose. The Title Page will also contain a running head that is a shortened version of the title (50 or fewer characters including spaces). The purpose of the running head is to include a shortened version of your title that runs along the top of every other page of a published article to identify the article within the journal. Take a look at an article published in APA style and you will see the running head in the top margin of every other page. The running head is typed in all capital letters and appears in the header on each page, left margin justified. Finally, the page number appears in the header, right margin justified, of every page in the article (including the Title Page, which is Page 1).

Abstract. The second page of your article will contain your Abstract. The Abstract should be a short paragraph (not indented) that describes the important aspects of your article. In other words, your Abstract should contain a sentence or two for each of the four major sections of your article: Introduction, Method, Results, and Discussion. For example, a sentence or two that explains the purpose of your article can begin your Abstract. A sentence or two that describes the method can follow. Be sure to describe the primary variables in your study. The primary result(s) should be described in a sentence or two, and your Abstract should end with the primary conclusion of the study. However, the length of your Abstract is limited (in most cases to 120 to 150 or fewer words), so you must be selective in what you discuss in your Abstract. Do not include too many details of the method, and do not include all results. If you use numbers in your Abstract, they should be typed in numerical form. Finally, the heading "Abstract" should be centered in bold at the top of the page.

Introduction. Your Introduction will begin on the third page of your article. Your full title (not the heading "Introduction") should be centered at the top of the page. Your Introduction should do several things. It should inform your reader about the general topic of your study (e.g., the bystander effect, visual short-term memory, therapeutic treatments for depression). Be careful not to begin your Introduction too generally. Your Introduction should not begin with statements about all of psychology or all human behavior. Begin by explaining what behavior your study will address and which aspects of that behavior are most relevant to your study. Be sure to indicate what your research question is. You should also review relevant background studies that tell your reader what is already known about your research question and how it has been studied previously. Be careful not to simply summarize the background literature. Instead, you should only discuss aspects of these studies that are particularly relevant for the development of your study.

Your Introduction should become more specific as it progresses, with some details about your study's design being discussed (e.g., simply indicating the variables that were studied) to inform the reader how your study addresses your stated research question. State your hypotheses toward the end of your Introduction. Be sure to explain (briefly) why you are making those hypotheses, tying them to the background literature you discussed earlier in your Introduction. One of the main purposes of your Introduction is to make the argument that your study will contribute important knowledge to the topic area you have chosen and that you are justified in making the hypotheses you are making. In other words, if you have written a good Introduction, your reader should have a good idea what your hypotheses are before you state them and be convinced that they are the best hypotheses to make for your study. By the time readers reach the end of your Introduction, they should also be convinced that the study you are describing is important and worthy of reading. Be sure to keep your argument in mind as your write your Introduction.

Method. The Method section begins on the next line after your Introduction ends. To begin the Method, you should type the heading "Method" in bold centered on the page. Do not begin a new page for the Method section. A general rule of thumb to use in deciding what information to include in your Method section is enough information that researchers could replicate your study if they wanted to. For example, your Method section should contain a description of your stimuli or survey but should not include the type of writing instrument used by your participants (unless it is relevant to the design of your study). The Method section has four subsections: Participants, Design, Materials or Apparatus, and Procedure. Each subsection should begin with the subsection heading left justified and in bold. You may not need to include each subsection in every Method section you write. If you take a look at some different journal articles published in APA style, you will see that some authors choose to combine some of these subsections, and in very short articles (e.g., Short Reports of the journal *Psychological Science*), the subsections are all combined into one Method section that contains the relevant details of all the subsections. In addition, in many articles, you may see that the Design section has been omitted or combined with the Materials section.

Participants. In the Participants subsection, describe the relevant details of the participants or subjects in your study (humans are typically referred to as "participants" and nonhuman animals as "subjects"). For example, how many participants participated? How were the participants recruited? How were they compensated? Who were the participants? Were they college students or individuals living in retirement communities? Or did the researcher use Sprague-Dawley rats as subjects? Also include demographic information about the participants that is relevant to your study, such as gender breakdown, socioeconomic status, education level, and age. How participants were assigned to study conditions (e.g., randomly) should also be indicated in this section.

Design. Although not explicitly listed in the *APA Publication Manual* (APA, 2010), the Design subsection is often included by authors for studies with more complex designs (e.g., experiments) to improve the clarity of the method. The Design subsection describes the variables in your study and how they were measured and manipulated. Be sure to indicate any independent and dependent variables included in your study. Describe levels of any independent variables. In other words, provide operational definitions of the variables in the Method. In many cases, the materials used in the study (e.g., stimuli, questionnaires) are too closely tied to the design to separate them, and the author will combine these two sections.

Materials/Apparatus. The Materials or Apparatus subsection contains information about what was used to run the study. Any stimuli or questionnaires presented in the study should be described in this subsection, including the origin of these materials and number of items. Assignment of stimuli to conditions is also described in this section. If complex equipment is used in a study, this section may be labeled "Apparatus," or the author may include a separate Apparatus section.

Procedure. The Procedure subsection describes what the participants/subjects experience in the study in chronological order. Information about the instructions they were given in the study and the tasks they performed should be included. Timing of any stimulus presentations should be described in the Procedure. In addition, how the participants/subjects were assigned to conditions should be included for studies that are experiments, and debriefing should be described for studies that involve deception. A statement indicating that participants/subjects were treated according to ethical standards is often included in this section.

Results. The Results section begins on the next line after the end of the Method section. Do not begin a new page for the Results section. The section begins with the heading "Results" centered on the page in bold. The Results section will state the dependent variables that were analyzed and the tests used to analyze them. The alpha level for the statistical tests should be given, and the tests that were run should be described. You should make statements about the results, indicating what differences or relationships were found, with support for the statements provided by the statistical values. For example, your Results section may contain a statement such as "The difference between the two age groups was significant, $t(65) = 4.56$, $p = .002$, with older participants scoring higher ($M = 85.00$, $SD = 7.89$) than younger participants ($M = 67.00$, $SD = 7.32$)." Notice that the statistics are not the focus of the sentence. The difference is the focus, with support provided by the t and p values and the mean values for each condition. Also note that statistical values are generally rounded to two decimal places. Be sure to format statistics according to APA style, with italics for statistics, degrees of freedom provided, and spaces surrounding equal signs. Consult the *Publication Manual* (APA, 2010) for APA style for specific statistics.

The Results section should also include any tables or figures that help illustrate the important results of the study. Choose one or the other for any set of results. Do not provide both a table and a figure for the same results. Figures may take the form of one of the graph types described in Chapter 7 (e.g., line graph of means, bar graph of means, scatterplot). Be sure to refer to the table or figure in the text of the Results section. However, tables and figures are positioned near the end of the typed article. They are not embedded in the text of the Results section. All figures should have a figure caption that is typed above the Figure. See Figure 8.2 for examples of formatted tables and figures in APA style.

Discussion. The last section of text in your article is the Discussion section. Begin the section with the heading "Discussion" on the next line after your Results section ends. The Discussion section should continue where your Introduction left off, beginning with a review of the hypotheses and some statements about whether these hypotheses were supported and which results provide that support. The Discussion section should also contain a comparison of your results with those from past studies, especially the studies you described in the Introduction section. For example, are your results consistent with those from previous studies? If not, why not? Limitations of the study should also be discussed in this section of the article. However, be careful not to argue that the study was conducted poorly. You are still making an argument (as you did in the Introduction) that the study contributes to scientific knowledge. As part of that argument, you can point out issues your study does not address or limitations of the research method chosen for the study, and you may also wish to suggest directions for future studies in your area of research based on the results you found. Your Discussion section should end with a summary paragraph, describing what you learned overall from the study.

References. The Reference section provides a complete listing of all the sources cited in the article. The references are listed in alphabetical order by the last name of the first author. All subsequent authors are listed in the reference in the order in which they appear in the publication. You should also provide the publication year, title of the source, where the source was published, and additional information about the publication source. For example, a reference for the journal article described in the Thinking About Research section at the end of the chapter should appear as follows:

Geraerts, E., Bernstein, D. M., Merekelbach, H., Linders, C., Raymaekers, L., & Loftus, E. F. (2008).

Lasting false beliefs and their behavioral consequences. *Psychological Science, 19,* 749–753.

See the References section of Figure 8.2 for some additional examples of reference formatting. Begin a new page for the Reference section. Reference organization packages, such as RefWorks and EndNote, can help you format source references into APA style.

Multiple-Study Articles

For some APA-style articles, you may be describing multiple related studies in one article. For multiple-study articles, you should include one Introduction section that provides background for all your studies, a Method for each study, a Results section for each study, and a general Discussion section that describes conclusions for all the studies combined. The Method and Results sections of each study should be preceded by headings that indicate the study number, such as "Study 1" or "Experiment 1" centered on the page. A new hierarchy of headings should follow for the Method, Results, and subsections of the Method. Method and Results headings now are left justified in bold in multiple-study articles, and the subsections of the Method are indented with the paragraph and end with a period. See the *Publication Manual* (APA, 2010) for additional information about formatting multiple-study articles.

Research Proposals

In some situations, researchers must write a proposal for a research project before they conduct the study. Proposals are typically written to convince someone else that a research project should be conducted. The purpose may be to obtain grant funds to conduct the project or to propose a project for a class. To write a research proposal, the APA-style structure described above is generally followed, but a few modifications are made to account for the fact that the study has not yet been completed. For example, the Results section typically contains a plan for the analysis of the data and predicted results for the study. Likewise, the Discussion section contains a discussion of what may be learned in the cases where the hypotheses are supported and not supported. In addition, the details of the study (method details, etc.) are described in the future tense (e.g., "The participants will be recruited from a population of university students."), because the study will take place in the future.

General Formatting

When you type your APA-style article, you should format it according to the following APA style guidelines. The entire article should be double spaced. Use 1-inch margins all around the pages. Type the running head in the top left header and page number in the top right header of each page. Use past tense when you describe any study (including yours) that has already been completed. For example, state "The participants volunteered . . ." rather than "The participants will volunteer . . ." or "The participants are volunteering . . ." The only exception to this rule is if you are writing a proposal of a research study that has not yet been conducted. In this case, use future tense to describe the study. Always use past tense to describe details of published studies. Minimize use of the passive voice in your writing. Instead, use the active voice. For example, state "Williams and Jones (2006) manipulated the stimulus presentation." instead of "The stimulus presentation was manipulated by Williams and Jones (2006)."

When you present numbers in your article, use words for numbers less than 10, and numbers for values 10 and above, unless the number is a measurement, statistical value, or a value representing the sample, for which you should always use numbers. In addition, all numbers in the abstract should be in numerical form. Any number that begins a sentence should be presented as a word. Numbers that are used in lists (Study 1, Study 2; Group 1, Group 2, etc.) should be given in numerical form. Check the *APA Publication Manual* (APA, 2010) for more rules regarding use of numbers. If you use abbreviations in your article, you must define the abbreviation the first time you use it. For example, on the first page of this chapter, I defined American Psychological Association (APA) and then used this abbreviation throughout the chapter. APA style provides for a few exceptions for some abbreviations that do not need to be defined, such as *M* for mean, min for minute, and so on, when they are presented with a value.

Citation Format

It is important to cite the sources where you obtain information for your article. You should cite sources for definitions of concepts, review of previous studies, sources for stimuli or questionnaires, and so on. APA-style citation format is to include the last names of the authors in the order that appears in the publication and then the year of publication. For articles with five or fewer authors, list all authors the first time you cite the article. If you cite a source with three or more authors a second time or more than five authors at any time, include just the last name of the first author and et al. to indicate there are other authors. For single- or double-author articles, continue to cite all authors' last names.

Sources can be cited by naming the authors in the text and including the publication year in parentheses. An example of a citation of this type is "Hamilton and Mayes (2006) stated that . . ." Alternatively, the entire citation can be provided in parentheses to indicate the source of a statement. An example of a citation of this type is "Prospective memory is defined as remembering to perform a task at a future time (Einstein & McDaniel, 2005)." Note that this statement is not a quote from the Einstein and McDaniel article. It is a summarization of the definition in the writer's own words. Quotes are rarely used in psychological articles, but if you do include a direct quote from a source, you should also include the page number on which you found the quote in the article. Also note that the word "and" is used for citations where the authors are directly referred to in the text, whereas an "&" is used for citations enclosed in parentheses. Remember to include a full reference for each citation in the Reference section.

Proper citation of sources is an important part of avoiding **plagiarism** (taking credit for someone else's work or ideas). Any description of another study or of someone's theory must include the citation of the source of the study or theory to give proper credit to the sources' author(s). In addition, presenting another author's written work verbatim or in a manner similar to the written form produced by the author without quotations also constitutes plagiarism. Thus, students should be extremely careful when writing from sources to ensure that quotation marks or original writing is included.

───────── ⚘ ─────────

Plagiarism: claiming another's work or ideas as one's own

ORAL PRESENTATIONS

The most common venue for oral presentations of psychological research is a psychological conference. While you may not experience psychology conferences as an undergraduate student, there are many conferences held each year to showcase research conducted by undergraduate students. Your college or university may hold one of these each year. There are also regional conferences such as the Mid-America Undergraduate Psychology Research Conference (MAUPR) and undergraduate psychology conferences in many U.S. states (e.g., ILLOWA Undergraduate Psychology Conference for Illinois and Iowa) that may be of interest to you. Compared with poster presentations, oral presentations of research studies are less likely to be given by undergraduate students at conferences, although the class for which you were assigned this text may have such an assignment.

Preparing an oral presentation of a research study is not very different from writing an APA-style article. The primary differences are that you present the information orally to an audience, and there is usually a time limit, so you must work out ahead of time how much information you can reasonably include in the presentation. The type of information you present, however, is very similar. You should begin an oral presentation by introducing the main concepts (e.g., the bystander effect, visual short-term memory, therapeutic treatments for depression), and then present your research question and review what is already known about the research question. You should present hypotheses for your study. You should then explain the method of the study and review the results, typically using tables or figures to illustrate the main results. Finally, you should state conclusions of the study, including whether the hypotheses were supported (or not) by the results and what you learned from the study. Throughout the presentation, you should cite sources for your information, just as you would in an APA-style article.

Organization is very important for an oral presentation, just as it is for a paper presentation of research. You must present a coherent argument for your study and your hypotheses. In fact, it can be more difficult to organize an oral presentation, because you must choose carefully what information to present to fit into the time limit you are given. For example, many conference-style oral presentations are limited to 10 or 15 minutes. Thus, presenters must be very clear in what they present to make themselves understood by their audience in such a short time. A good oral presentation will be accompanied by visual aids, typically presented as PowerPoint slides. Visual display of information is much more important in oral and poster presentations because audience members must absorb the information more quickly than if they can take the time they need to read and understand a written paper.

POSTER PRESENTATIONS

As with oral presentations, you are most likely to encounter a poster presentation of psychology research at a psychology conference. You may also have been assigned a poster presentation for the course you are taking that assigned this text. Poster presentations are essentially mini-APA-style articles that are condensed to allow a visual presentation rather than a text presentation. They contain the same information as an oral presentation but may be even further condensed according to the space allowed for the poster. See Figure 8.3 for an example of a poster presentation of research. Notice that each of the main APA-style sections is included as well as visual presentations of stimuli and results. Bullet points are used in many places instead of full sentences to make the poster more easily read and to save space.

The organization of a poster presentation should be as visual as possible. Include examples of sample stimuli and organize sections so that they flow. Include a title and authors at the top of the poster. The body of the poster is often organized into segments to make information easier to find and comprehend. Place the introductory information at the left of the poster and then direct the flow of information down each segment, with new segments placed to right. See the example poster in Figure 8.3 for the organization style used in a poster.

During a poster presentation, the authors typically stand by their poster, prepared to offer a short summary to interested viewers and answer questions viewers may have as they read the poster. If you are preparing to give a poster presentation, it is a good idea to think through what you will say ahead of time so you give clear and concise descriptions of the research study described in the poster.

Figure 8.3 Poster Presentation of Research

Picture superiority in conceptual implicit memory tests

Dawn M. McBride & Jeremy K. Braithwaite
Illinois State University

Abstract

The present study examined picture superiority in conceptual implicit memory tests. In two laboratory experiments, university students completed category production tasks for studied words and pictures with levels of processing study tasks. In both experiments, item-specific processing was emphasized to test the distinctiveness view of picture superiority effects. Percentage of target responses data were analyzed with Analysis of Variance, which indicated significantly greater target completions for words than pictures with both semantic and graphemic study tasks in the implicit tests. Results are not consistent with the distinctiveness view of picture superiority effects.

Introduction

The current study was designed to clarify mixed findings regarding the picture superiority effect (i.e., better memory for pictures than words) in conceptual implicit tests. Transfer appropriate processing (TAP) theory (Morris, Bransford, & Franks, 1977) predicts picture superiority for explicit and conceptual implicit memory tests based on the overlap of conceptual processing for pictures from study to test. Picture superiority is typically found in explicit memory tests. However, mixed findings regarding picture superiority in conceptual implicit tests have been reported.

Alternatively, the distinctiveness view of picture superiority (Mulligan, 2006) predicts that picture superiority should not be found in implicit tests, because implicit tests do not typically require item-specific processing for retrieval. Thus, studies that have failed to find picture superiority in these tests are consistent with the distinctiveness view.

In the current study, we attempted to increase picture superiority in conceptual implicit memory tests by including a level of processing manipulation (Exps. 1 & 2) and using retrieval cues that were associated with only one item (Exp. 2). Semantic study and single-item retrieval cues should increase the item-specific processing in the task. Thus, if the distinctiveness view explains picture superiority, a picture advantage should be found in these conditions. However, if TAP theory explains picture superiority, a picture advantage should be found with graphemic study due to the increase in conceptual processing for words with semantic study.

Research Questions
• *Is there a picture superiority effect in conceptual implicit tests, as TAP theory predicts?*
• *Does an increase in item-specific processing cause a picture superiority effect in conceptual implicit tests, as the distinctiveness view predicts?*

Method

Participants
• Exp 1: 197 undergraduates
• Exp 2: 124 undergraduates

Design
•Exp 1: Level of processing (semantic/graphemic) X item type (picture/word/unstudied) X Memory test instruction (implicit/explicit)
•Exp 2: Level of processing (semantic/graphemic) X item type (picture/word/unstudied) - implicit test only

Materials
• Pictures or associated word labels were studied in counterbalanced sets
• Memory test cues consisted of a category label and a one-letter (Exp. 1) or two-letter (Exp. 2) stem in a single random order
• For Exp. 2, only one item could be used to complete each test cue

Procedure
• Participants studied words and pictures with semantic (rate pleasantness) or graphemic (count vowels or rate drawing complexity) instructions
• Explicit test instructions were to complete test cues with item studied (Exp. 1 only)
• Implicit test instructions were to complete test cues with first item thought of, timed by beeps every 3 s (both experiments)

Test Cue Examples

FRUIT - l_____ (Exp. 1)   FRUIT - le_____ (Exp. 2)

Results

EXP 1 - Explicit Test

EXP 1 - Implicit Test

EXP 1 - Summary
Picture superiority was found in the explicit test for graphemic study only. Word superiority was found in the implicit test for both study tasks. A level of processing effect (semantic > graphemic) was found in both tests.

EXP 2 - Implicit Test

EXP 2 - Summary
Word superiority was found for both study tasks in Exp. 2. A level of processing effect (semantic > graphemic) also found.

Discussion

No evidence of picture superiority was found in the conceptual implicit tests, despite attempts to increase item-specific processing in the test. These results do not provide support for the distinctiveness view of picture superiority effects.

TAP theory, however, can provide an explanation of the results of the two experiments. TAP theory predicts that whenever the processing from study to test overlaps, memory will increase for studied items. Pictures automatically require conceptual processing to interpret (Weldon & Roediger, 1987), and thus, have an advantage whenever the memory test requires conceptual processing (as in explicit and conceptual implicit tests). However, semantic study removes this picture advantage, because it allows for conceptual processing of words that would not automatically occur.

In Exp. 1, the TAP predictions were supported for the explicit test: Picture superiority was found for the graphemic study task, but memory was similar for pictures and words for the semantic study task.

The implicit test results do not seem to follow the TAP predictions. According to TAP theory, explicit and conceptual implicit tests should show similar results with regard to picture superiority. However, in our implicit tests, a letter stem was provided with the retrieval cues to increase item-specific processing. This may have increased the perceptual processing of the word retrieval cues that occurred in the implicit tests, giving words the advantage. Thus, the implicit results in the current study may still be consistent with TAP theory predictions.

A third experiment conducted recently supports this explanation of these results. When the letter stems were removed from the retrieval cues in the implicit test given in Exp. 1, picture superiority was found.

NEW EXP - Implicit Test - No letter stems

Related Papers

• McBride & Dosher (2002). A comparison of conscious and automatic memory processes for picture and word stimuli: A process dissociation analysis. *Consciousness and Cognition, 11*, 423-460.
• Mulligan (2006). Conceptual implicit memory and the item-specific-relational distinction. In *Distinctiveness and Memory*, Oxford University Press.
• Weldon & Roediger (1987). Altering retrieval demands reverses the picture superiority effect. *Memory & Cognition, 15*, 269-280.

CHAPTER SUMMARY

Reconsider the questions from the beginning of the chapter:

- What are the different ways that psychologists present research? Psychologists present research as written reports, oral presentations, and poster presentations.
- How do we write an APA-style article? What information goes in each section of the article? How do we format the article? An APA-style article is organized into sections that present the background and purpose of the study (Introduction), Method of the study, Results of the study, and conclusions of the study (Discussion). Additional format information is described in this chapter and in the APA Publication Manual (APA, 2010).
- What is an appropriate format for an oral presentation of research? An oral presentation is organized according to the major sections of an APA-style article, but presented orally, and often employs visual aids such as PowerPoint slides.
- How do we prepare a conference-style poster presentation of research? A poster presentation is also organized according the sections of an APA-style article, but provides a more visual representation of the most important information that is presented in those sections.

THINKING ABOUT RESEARCH

A summary of a research study in psychology is given below. As you read the summary, think about the following questions:

1. Notice that the sections of the following summary are identical to the four main sections of an APA-style article. Describe the four subsections of the Method and describe what the authors of this article likely included in each Method subsection of their article beyond what is already described below.
2. Read the Results section below and determine what is missing that should be included in an APA-style Results section.
3. Use the means provided in the Results section below to create an APA-style figure or table to present the means. Be sure to include a figure caption if you create a figure.
4. Use PsycINFO (or another search tool) to find the reference for the Loftus (2005) review article published in *Learning and Memory*. Be sure to locate the reference that is the most appropriate for the citation. Type the reference in APA style.
5. The study described below involved deceiving the participants. Explain how deception was used in the study and describe how the authors should design the study to adhere to ethical guidelines. Also indicate in which section of the APA-style article they should report the ethical aspects of the study.

Study Reference

Geraerts, E., Bernstein, D. M., Merekelbach, H., Linders, C., Raymaekers, L., & Loftus, E. F. (2008). Lasting false beliefs and their behavioral consequences. *Psychological Science, 19,* 749–753.

Purpose of the Study. Numerous previous studies have shown that false memories can be created for life events that were never experienced (see Loftus, 2005, for a review). However, previous research has not addressed the question of how these false memories affect the future behavior of participants. The current study planted a false memory in participants that they had become ill after eating egg salad when they were children. Their behavior with regard to egg salad was then tested 1 week and 4 months later.

Method of the Study. Undergraduate students were randomly assigned to either an egg salad group ($n = 120$) or a control group ($n = 60$). All participants completed three study sessions. At the first session, the participants completed a questionnaire regarding their food preferences and experiences, including whether they had ever been sick as a child from egg salad and how much they liked egg salad. Data for participants who had actually gotten sick from egg salad as children (as verified by their parents, $n = 5$) were omitted from the study. At the second session that occurred 1 week later, participants received feedback about their responses to the questionnaire. The feedback was false, but the participants were told that a computer generated the information they were given based on their responses to the questionnaire. The egg salad group were told that they had gotten sick from egg salad as a child. The control group was not given this information. Participants then completed another series of questionnaires, including a memory belief questionnaire to determine whether they believed they had gotten sick from egg salad as a child. Finally, participants were placed in a room for a false debriefing session with various foods present, including egg salad sandwiches. The type of sandwich participants chose was recorded. Four months after the first session, the participants were contacted to take part in a taste test study. They were asked to rate various foods on an 8-point scale, including egg salad sandwiches. Finally, participants were given the opportunity to eat the leftover food. The number of egg salad sandwiches was again recorded.

Results of the Study. Participants in the egg salad group were first divided into believers and nonbelievers, based on their responses to the memory-belief questionnaire. This division created three groups of participants for comparison: egg salad believers ($n = 41$), egg salad nonbelievers ($n = 58$), and control participants ($n = 58$). Results showed that fewer participants in the two egg salad groups ($M = 7\%$ for believers, $M = 4\%$ for nonbelievers) ate egg salad sandwiches at the second session than the participants in the control group ($M = 33\%$). The believer and nonbeliever groups did not differ. For the third session, participants who were believers ($M = 11\%$) ate fewer egg salad sandwiches than participants in the control ($M = 44\%$) and nonbeliever groups ($M = 37\%$). None of the groups differed in the mean number of other sandwiches eaten at either session. (*Note*: The means in this section were estimated from Figure 2 in the article.)

Conclusions of the Study. The results showed that exposing participants to a false belief about a life event (e.g., getting sick from egg salad as a child) affected their future behavior with regard to the objects of the event (e.g., they ate fewer egg salad sandwiches). Over time, this effect was evident for the believers, but not for the nonbelievers. These results indicate that future behavior is affected by a false belief, but the effect will dissipate over time if the false belief is not well accepted by the participants.

COMMON PITFALLS AND HOW TO AVOID THEM

Problem: Misuse of citations and quotes—students tend to overuse quotes in research reports and incorrectly cite sources.

Solution: Remember that quotes are rarely used in psychological reports. Instead, you should summarize another author's ideas in your words, being careful not to plagiarize other authors' writing. Always cite sources for ideas, definitions, theories, methods, and so on that come from another author.

Problem: Incorrect use of verb tense—students often use the wrong verb tense to describe their studies.

Solution: If you are reporting a study that has already been completed, use the past tense to describe the study (yours or someone else's). If you are writing a research proposal, use the future tense to describe a study that will be completed in the future.

Problem: Providing too many details of background studies—writing a full summary of a past study in the Introduction of a research report

Solution: The goal of the Introduction is to motivate the study you did (or will do), not to provide a full review of all the studies done in an area. Thus, you should describe only the most relevant background studies in your Introduction (i.e., those that help motivate your study or your hypotheses) and only describe aspects of those studies that help you make the point you want to make.

Problem: Describing background literature from secondary sources—students often use secondary sources (see Chapter 2 for more information) for literature reviews leading to problems with misrepresentation of the primary source

Solution: In your Introduction, be sure to describe primary sources you have read in reviewing background literature. This will allow citations of the primary source and more accurate presentation of background studies. You should never cite sources that you have not read.

Problem: Focus on statistics in Results section—making statements about the statistics instead of the effect or relationship tested

Solution: Remember that statistical values should be used to support statements about effects or relationships, not as the focus of your statements. For example, indicate that the effect of the independent variable on the dependent variable was significant and support this statement with statistics. Do not make statements that the statistic itself was significant or not significant.

TEST YOURSELF

1. In which section of an APA-style article would you include the following information about your study?

   (a) Statements of hypotheses

   (b) Graphs of the means for each condition

   (c) A description of the questionnaire the participants completed

   (d) The number of participants or subjects in the study

   (e) A citation for a published source

   (f) Instructions that were given to the participants

2. Which of the following is true about formatting an APA-style article? (Choose all that apply.)

   (a) Two-inch margins should be used.

   (b) The entire article should be double spaced.

   (c) Tables and figures should be embedded into the Results section.

   (d) You need to provide citations only when you quote from a source.

   (e) You should begin a new page for the References section.

3. For the citation examples below, indicate which ones display correct APA style:

   (a) Regia-Corte and Wagman (2008) reported that participants perceived a slope to be more difficult to stand on when wearing a weighted backpack.

   (b) In a review of how scientific thinking skills develop (Corinne Zimmerman) reported many studies that support this theory.

   (c) The list-strength effect is exhibited when stronger items (studied for a longer time, studied to a deeper level, etc.) in a list produce better memory than weaker items (Verde, 2009).

   (d) The method used in the current study is based on the method described by Garrison (Feb, 2009).

4. Place the following APA-style sections into the correct order in which they should appear in a manuscript: Results, Introduction, Procedure, Discussion, Abstract, References, Title Page, Participants.

5. Which of the following illustrates correct APA style for references of journal articles?

   (a) Reese-Weber, Marla (2008). A new experimental method assessing attitudes toward adolescent dating and sibling violence using observations of violent interactions. *Journal of Adolescence, 31,* 857–876.

   (b) Reese-Weber, M. (2008). A new experimental method assessing attitudes toward adolescent dating and sibling violence using observations of violent interactions. *Journal of Adolescence, 31,* 857–876.

   (c) Marla Reese-Weber (2008). A New Experimental Method Assessing Attitudes Toward Adolescent Dating and Sibling Violence Using Observations of Violent Interactions. *Journal of Adolescence, 31,* 857–876.

   (d) Reese-Weber, M. (March, 2008). A new experimental method assessing attitudes toward adolescent dating and sibling violence using observations of violent interactions. *Journal of Adolescence, Vol. 31,* pp. 857–876.

6. Explain how an oral presentation differs from a poster presentation.

Answers: 1a. Introduction and Discussion sections, 1b. Results section, 1c. Method section, Materials subsection, 1d. Method section, Participants subsection, 1e. any of the major sections can contain a citation: Introduction, Method, Results, Discussion—the Abstract may also contain citations, 1f. Method section, Procedure subsection. 2. Only (b) and (e) are true. 3. a and c are correct. 4. Correct order: Title Page, Abstract, Introduction, Participants, Procedure, Results, Discussion, References. 5. b, 6. An oral presentation provides an oral description of the major sections of a research report, typically with visual aids such as PowerPoint. There is often a time limit for oral presentations. Poster presentations provide a visual report of a research study, including each major section of the report. Authors are typically on site to provide oral summaries or more detailed information about the study the poster describes.

PART II

The Nuts and Bolts of Research Methods and Analysis

The Nuts and Bolts
of Survey Research

In the beginning of October, 2008, the press began to report that Barack Obama's U.S. presidential campaign was gaining momentum and John McCain's campaign was lagging behind. How did the press know that this was happening? In other words, before there is actual voting behavior to measure, how does the press (and the candidates) know whether an election campaign is succeeding? The answer is that they conduct surveys to determine what people think of the presidential candidates and whom they plan to vote for. For example, ABC News reported on October 22, 2008 (http://abcnews.go.com/PollingUnit/Politics/story?id=6087668&page=1, accessed June 2, 2009), that 54% of likely voters supported Obama, with only 43% of likely voters supporting McCain. These results were based on a phone survey, where land line and cell phone numbers in the continental United States were randomly selected to be called for the survey. The goal of the survey was to measure voters' attitudes about the presidential candidates because the election had not yet taken place, and votes had not yet been made.

Surveys are a common observation technique used in psychological research, but it can be difficult to construct a valid survey. In fact, this is one of the most important issues to consider when designing a new survey: how to maximize the validity of the scores from the survey. Consider surveys you may have taken for fun in a magazine or online. They may have asked you questions such as "What is your favorite color?" and "If you could be any animal, what would you be?" to tell you about your personality. How valid do you think these surveys are? Does your favorite color or preferred animal really indicate aspects of your personality? This is what researchers try to determine when they test the validity of the scores from a survey. In addition, how much can be learned from a survey if people's responses change each time they take the survey (e.g., your favorite color this month is purple, but last month you were really into blue)? Wording of the questions, choice of response scale (see Chapter 4 for more discussion of response scales), and sampling technique used can all affect the validity and reliability of the survey results. Thus, this chapter will describe the "nuts and bolts" of survey research, including issues that affect the validity and reliability of surveys that researchers should consider as they construct a survey (Figure 9.1).

Survey Research: a research study that uses the survey observational technique to measure behavior

---

Figure 9.1 Steps in the Research Process: Designing the Study

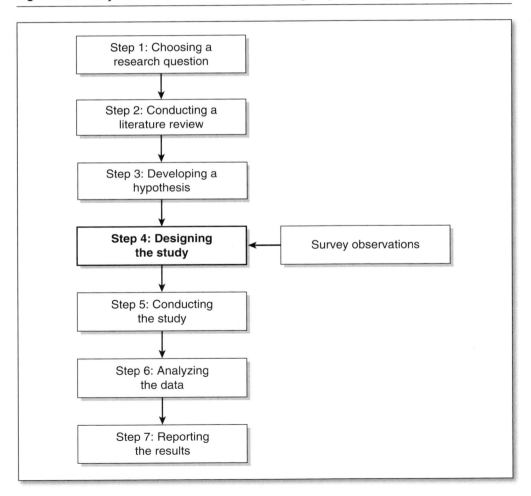

ANSWERING RESEARCH QUESTIONS WITH SURVEYS

Using surveys to learn about behavior is fairly common in personality, clinical, counseling, industrial-organizational, and social psychology. In these areas of psychology, surveys allow a researcher to learn about behaviors that would be difficult or impossible to directly observe in the behaviors of the participants: their thoughts and attitudes. In other words, surveys allow a researcher to obtain self-reports from participants about the behaviors and attitudes they report. They can also be used to ask people to describe other people's behaviors (e.g., parents describing their children's behaviors, teachers describing their students' behaviors). Surveys can be short, such as a single question, or they can be very long, containing hundreds of items. Longer, standardized surveys are often called questionnaires, but many psychologists use these terms interchangeably.

The majority of survey research is conducted to answer **descriptive** or **predictive research questions**. For example, "How do Americans (or people in the United Kingdom or people in Canada, etc.) currently feel about the economy?" is a descriptive question about an attitude that can be answered by administering a survey to Americans (or individuals in another country) with questions about the economy. Or a researcher could instead ask the question "Can Americans' (or others') consumer behaviors be predicted from how they currently feel about the economy?" In this case, the goal is to determine if a predictive relationship exists between the attitudes collected from the survey and the consumer behaviors of Americans. In some cases, researchers use surveys to test causal relationships in experiments. For example, suppose a researcher wants to answer the **causal research question**, "Which of a series of treatments causes the largest reduction in depression symptoms?" This researcher might conduct an experiment to compare the therapies' effect on scores from a depression questionnaire, such as the Beck Depression Inventory II (BDI-II), where the survey is used to measure the dependent variable of depression symptoms. Another example of experiments that involve surveys is in testing the effect of new products on consumer behaviors and attitudes. This type of research is often done by presenting participants with different products or different variations of a product and asking them to complete a short survey about each product. Thus, although surveys are used most commonly to describe or predict behavior, they can be used to test a variety of research questions. The difference between these types of questions is based on the researcher's goals for the study.

Descriptive Research Question: a research question that asks about the presence of behavior, how frequently it is exhibited, or whether there is a relationship between different behaviors

Predictive Research Question: a research question that asks if one behavior can be predicted from another behavior to allow predictions of future behavior

Causal Research Question: a research question that asks what causes specific behaviors to occur

CREATING A SURVEY

For many behaviors of common interest in psychology, a researcher will be able to find a questionnaire that has already been developed, tested, and validated for use in asking participants about these behaviors. There are two good sources for standardized questionnaires that may contain the type of survey you are looking for. One is called the Health and Psychosocial Instruments (HAPI) database. If your institution's library connects to the EBSCO database, you may find HAPI through your library's Web database. The other source is called the Mental Measurements Yearbook (also available through EBSCO if you have access to that database). Each of these sources contains references to standardized questionnaires on different topics, and in some cases, the questionnaires themselves are available on the sites. For example, there are many standardized questionnaires that measure various mood states of interest.

There are also situations where a researcher would like to ask participants about their thoughts and behaviors on a topic for which a questionnaire has not yet been developed and/or tested. In these cases, researchers may need to develop their own questionnaires to ask questions about a specific topic that has not yet been investigated with a survey. This is an area of psychological research called **psychometrics**, which involves the development, validation, and refinement of surveys and tests for measuring different psychological constructs, such as intelligence and aspects of personality (Vogt, 2005). When a new survey or test is developed, it is important that the validity and reliability of the measure be tested. Thus, we will next discuss some important issues that can affect the validity and reliability of surveys that should be considered when a new survey is being developed.

Psychometrics: area of psychological research that involves the development, validation, and refinement of surveys and tests for measuring psychological constructs

---

Survey Questions

The types of questions included in a questionnaire can affect the validity (see Chapters 3 and 4 for more discussion of validity) of the scores from the questionnaire by influencing the responses of the research participants. Thus, it is important to write questions carefully so as to reduce bias in responses. To ensure that your survey includes the best set of questions, it is a good idea to pilot sets of questions to determine the specific wording that is most easily understood by your participants.

Dillman (2000) makes several important suggestions to researchers writing survey questions. For example, consider how your participants will perceive the question. Are the questions confusing? Will it be unclear how the participants should respond in some cases? If you ask a question such as "When you go to the movies, do you tend to go with your friends, family, or on your own?" it will be unclear how a participant who does not go to the movies should respond. Consider whether participants will be able to recall the behaviors you are asking about. If you ask older adults a question such as "When you were a child, how many days a week did your parents talk about finances in your presence?" it may be difficult for participants to remember an accurate response. Avoid double-barreled questions that are actually two questions in one, where each question may require a different answer. For example, a question such as "Do you often get depressed and talk to others about it?" is actually two separate questions: "Do you get depressed?" and "If you get depressed, do you talk to others about it?" In addition, avoid loaded questions that assume too much (e.g., "When you talk about depression to your friends, whom do you speak to about it?"). In summary, strive to create simple and clear questions that can be unambiguously interpreted by the respondents. Researchers should consider these issues when they write questions to ensure that the questions will elicit valid responses from the participants.

Types of Survey Response Scales

When researchers write a survey, an important decision they need to make is the type(s) of response scales that will be included in the survey. As described in Chapter 3, question responses can be either **open-ended** or **closed-ended**. Open-ended responses allow the participants to respond in any way they feel is appropriate for the question. An example of an open-ended question is "How do you feel today?" For this question, participants may respond with a single word describing their current mental state or they may write a longer response that describes several aspects of their current mental state. Closed-ended questions provide a set of responses that the participants must choose from. For example, if the question above were followed with choices of "happy," "sad," "excited," "anxious," and "frustrated," the question would become closed-ended, because the participants are asked to choose one of the given responses for the question. A

Open-Ended Response Scale: participants respond to survey questions in any manner they feel is appropriate for the question

Closed-Ended Response Scale: participants respond to survey questions according to the response options provided by the researcher

Likert rating scale (i.e., rating agreement on a 1 to 5 scale) is another example of a closed-ended response scale (see Chapter 4 for more discussion of Likert Scales). The choice between these two response options will determine the type of data you collect with your survey. Collecting open-ended responses will require a coding scheme to be developed to categorize the different types of responses made. Collecting closed-ended responses involves use of one of the different types of measurement scales described in Chapter 4. Specifically, nominal, ordinal, or interval scales can be used, depending on the type of response options given to the participants.

If you choose to include closed-ended response scales in your survey, Dillman (2000) suggests following a similar process in the wording of questions. Consider how your participants will view the response choices you provide. Will the response categories be confusing to your participants or bias the way they respond? For example, if you ask "How much TV do you watch each day?" you may bias the response you get from participants with different types of closed-ended response categories. Giving choices of "(a) less than 1 hour per day, (b) 1 to 2 hours per day, or (c) more than 2 hours per day" may lead participants to respond differently than choices of "(a) less than 5 hours per day, (b) 5 to 7 hours per day, or (c) more than 7 hours per day." Carefully consider the number of response categories provided to the participants. Including too few choices can bias the participants' responses, but including too many choices may confuse the participants. However, more response options allows for more variable responses, which can increase the validity of the scores (see Chapter 7 for more discussion of the importance in variability in data distributions) so researchers should carefully consider the number of response options provided. Also, consider that the use of ordinal response scales, such as those described above, may not provide choices that match the participants' exact behavior. Thus, an open-ended ratio scale that allows participants to report the exact number of hours of TV they watch per day may be accurate.

Some other considerations: Avoid response categories that overlap, but make sure that categories are comparable and unbiased. Include equal numbers of positive and negative response categories. Try to include response categories that allow a response for all possible behaviors and attitudes. Decide if you will include neutral and/or undecided response categories to allow participants to indicate when they have no opinion on a topic. Consider how the respondents will interpret the response categories you have provided. If a rating scale is used, be sure to provide labels for the endpoints and perhaps the midpoint of the scale. Piloting your questions with the response categories can help determine the best categories to include in your survey (Figure 9.2). See Table 9.1 for some examples of different types of response scales.

Validity of Scores From a Survey

The concept of validity has been discussed in several contexts in the different chapters of this text. In Chapter 4, **construct validity** as it pertains to response scales was introduced. Construct validity is particularly relevant to survey research because a survey with construct validity is one that accurately measures the behavior it was designed to measure. Some

TABLE 9.1 Examples of Different Types of Response Scales for Survey Questions	
Response Scale	**Examples**
Open-ended	How do you feel today?
	_____
	What is your political affiliation?
	_____
	Why did you decide to go to college?
	_____
Closed-ended	How do you feel today? __ Happy __ Sad __Anxious __Excited __ Frustrated Indicate where your political affiliation falls on the following scale: X X X X X Liberal Neutral Conservative Rate how strongly you wanted to go to college when you were a high school senior: 1 2 3 4 5 6 7 Weak Neutral Strong Desire Desire

Figure 9.2 Consider the Response Choices You Include in Your Response Scale

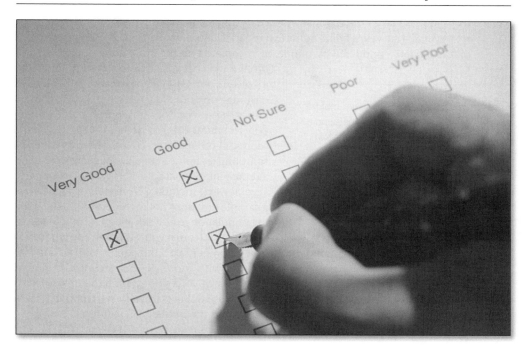

SOURCE: Copyright by Getty Images, www.gettyimages.com.

researchers have argued that all tests of validity of scores from a survey contribute to the construct validity of the survey (e.g., Messick, 1995). However, the method researchers use to test the validity of the scores from a survey depends on the goals they have for the research study in which the survey is used. For example, the validity of a survey may allow a researcher to test a theoretical assumption about behaviors. Alternatively, testing the validity of the scores from a survey may allow a researcher to determine if the survey can be used to predict related behaviors.

Construct Validity: indicates that a survey measures the behavior it is designed to measure

If researchers are designing their own survey, it is very important that they write survey items carefully to ensure that they address the behaviors they are intended to measure. This will help maximize the validity of the scores from the survey. Issues related to sampling, discussed in Chapter 6, can also affect the validity of the scores from a survey. A biased sample that does not accurately represent the population of interest can reduce the validity of the survey measure. For example, the survey described at the beginning of the chapter about which candidate voters supported was conducted by calling people with only landline or cellular telephones. Thus, the sample may have been biased such that people who were unavailable to answer their phone at the time they were called for the survey were excluded. In addition, **nonresponse errors** can decrease the validity of the scores from the survey measure in a similar way by biasing the sample. Nonresponse errors occur when individuals chosen for the sample choose not to respond to the survey. Thus, even when an appropriate sampling technique is used, nonresponse errors can still occur, making the sample less representative. However, if a survey is being administered in a laboratory setting, as compared with a survey that is mailed, conducted by phone, or completed on the Web, nonresponse errors are less problematic because a different sampling technique is involved. Nonresponse errors are a particular type of **coverage error** that occurs when the sample that completes the survey does not represent the entire population to which the researchers wish to generalize the scores. In other words, coverage errors occur when the sampling technique used is not successful in collecting a representative sample. This type of error can occur in several ways, including from nonresponse errors, from a sample that does not include a particular subgroup of the population (e.g., a sample of mostly males or mostly females), or from a volunteer sample where volunteers

Nonresponse Error: a sampling error that occurs when individuals chosen for the sample do not respond to the survey, biasing the sample

Coverage Error: a sampling error that occurs when the sample chosen to complete a survey does not provide a good representation of the population

are different from individuals who do not volunteer (e.g., individuals with strong feelings on a topic respond to a survey, but individuals with more neutral feelings do not respond). Coverage errors can reduce the external validity of your survey, such that responses from the sample do not generalize to the population a researcher wishes to learn about. See Chapter 6 for more discussion of sampling techniques and their effects on validity.

Previously validated surveys can be useful to researchers. If used with the same population for which they were validated, previously tested surveys can be used with more confidence and the knowledge that they will measure the intended behaviors with reasonable accuracy. However, if you must validate your own survey, there are some different ways this can be done. One method of validation is to examine relationships between your survey and other measures of the behaviors of interest, such as other surveys that have already been validated or direct observations that indicate the behaviors of interest (e.g., seeking counseling for mood problems, voting for a particular candidate or issue, exhibiting social behaviors). This is called **criterion-related validity**, and it is based on the relationship between your survey and the criterion measures or behaviors that have previously been used as operational definitions of the behavior of interest. Often, a researcher will test the criterion-related validity of a survey to determine if the survey can predict other behaviors. For example, the SAT (Scholastic Aptitude

Criterion-Related Validity: determining the validity of the scores of a survey by examining the relationship between the survey scores and other established measures of the behavior of interest

Test) and ACT (American College Test) are used as college entrance exams because the criterion-related validity of the scores on these tests has been tested with academic achievement in college. In some cases, these tests do predict academic achievement (e.g., first-year college GPA [grade point average], Coyle & Pillow, 2008); however, they have not been found to predict all types of academic achievement (see Sackett, Kuncel, Arneson, Cooper, & Waters, 2009, for a recent review of research on this issue). Thus, their validity may be limited to certain types of academic measures.

Another threat to the validity of survey responses is the willingness of respondents to accurately represent their true attitudes and behaviors in their responses. In some cases, participants completing a survey may alter their responses to present themselves in a more positive way. This effect is called the social desirability bias and can be present when surveys are used to measure behavior or attitudes from individuals. One way researchers have sought to deal with social desirability bias in survey responses is to include a measure of this bias such as the Marlowe-Crowne social desirability scale (Crowne & Marlowe, 1960). These measures include items designed to test a respondent's

Social Desirability Bias: bias created in survey responses from respondents' desire to be viewed more favorably by others, typically resulting in overreporting of "positive" behaviors and underreporting of "negative" behaviors

level of social desirability such that the bias can be measured within the sample. Social desirability measures are typically included along with the main survey.

Reliability of Responses

The reliability of responses to a survey is also important to determine because unreliable surveys will reduce the validity of the scores of a study. If participants respond to the questions in a different way at different times or respond in different ways to different sets of similar questions in the survey, the researcher will not be able to draw accurate conclusions from the survey responses. Thus, using a measure with high reliability will increase the likelihood of high validity for a study that includes a survey. One way to increase the reliability of scores on a survey is to use a longer survey. Surveys with more items will typically yield more reliable scores than shorter surveys. Shorter surveys tend to be less reliable, because an unusual response on a single item can skew the results quite a bit. However, with more items on a survey, a single unusual response will not affect the results as much. In addition, there are different types of reliability that are of interest depending on the purpose of the study. Two common types of reliability that are important to consider for a survey are discussed below.

Test-Retest Reliability. **Test-retest reliability** means that the scores on a measure are consistent over time. If a questionnaire has good test-retest reliability, then each time a person takes the questionnaire, his or her scores should be similar. Test-retest reliability is typically determined from the relationship between the same individual's scores on a questionnaire when he or she takes the questionnaire at different points in time. For example, if you were designing a new questionnaire, you might check its test-retest reliability by having a group of participants take the questionnaire once, recording their scores, and then have them take the questionnaire again 2 months later. If the scores from the first time they take the questionnaire are positively related to the scores from the second time they take the questionnaire 2 months later (with a strong relationship between the two), then the questionnaire has good test-retest reliability. However, getting the same participants to take a questionnaire twice can be problematic for two reasons: (1) participants may not come back the second time, and the sample size will be reduced—an issue known as **attrition/mortality** (attrition was introduced

---------- ✌ ----------

Test-Retest Reliability: indicates that the scores on a survey will be similar when participants complete the survey more than once

Attrition/Mortality: occurs when participants choose not to complete a study

Testing Effects: occur when participants are tested more than once in a study with early testing affecting later testing

---

as a form of bias in Chapter 4) and (2) having participants take the same questionnaire more than once can change their results through **testing effects**—these occur when taking a test or questionnaire once affects future scores on the scale (testing effects were also introduced in Chapter 4). Thus, other methods of evaluating the reliability of a questionnaire have been developed to deal with these problems. In addition, there may be occasions when researchers expect to find changes in scores over time based on changes in personality or attitudes as individuals develop or events that individuals may experience (e.g., starting a new job, getting married) between testings. Thus, test-retest reliability may only be desirable for some surveys tested with specific populations.

Internal Consistency of Scores. **Internal consistency** of scores indicates how similar scores on the different items of a survey are to one another. This is another means of evaluating the reliability of the scores on a survey. One way to determine internal consistency is to examine the correlation between scores for subsets of items. In other words, the items on the questionnaire are split into two halves or sections and the relationship between the scores on the two sets of items is tested. This is called **split-half reliability**. If a strong, positive relationship exists between the scores on the two sets of items, then the questionnaire has good split-half reliability. The advantage of split-half reliability as a method of testing the reliability of a questionnaire is that you can test the reliability with a single testing of a group of participants. You do not need to retest the participants and wait for the second set of results. However, split-half reliability provides a fairly crude measure of reliability and can depend on how the items are divided in the survey.

---------- ✌ ----------

Internal Consistency: a form of reliability that tests relationships between scores on different items of a survey

Split-Half Reliability: method of testing scores' internal consistency that indicates if the scores are similar on different sets of questions on a survey that address similar topics

---

Another method of testing the internal consistency of scores is to examine the overall correlation between pairs of items. In other words, the relationship between the scores for each pair of items on a survey is calculated, and then a statistical averaging of these correlations is determined for the whole survey. This method is called **Cronbach's alpha (α)**, which is also the name of the statistical test that is used to calculate the overall correlation (Green & Salkind, 2007). Note that Cronbach's alpha is different from the alpha level used to set the Type I error rate in an inferential statistical test (see discussion of alpha level in Chapter 7). Cronbach's alpha is a commonly used measure of reliability of scores for a survey and is provided in many studies for the responses collected from a survey.

---------- ✌ ----------

Cronbach's Alpha (α): method of testing scores' internal consistency that indicates the average correlation between scores on all pairs of items on a survey

SURVEY ADMINISTRATION

Researchers have a few options for administering surveys. Surveys can be given in person using a paper form of the survey, by computer, or by interview. Surveys can also be administered by mail or by phone using a mailing or phone list to choose participants. These latter two methods have the disadvantage of high nonresponse rates that can create nonresponse errors as described above. Participants can easily ignore a mailing or choose not to answer the phone for numbers they do not recognize. Finally, as described in Chapter 6, surveys can be administered on the Internet (by Website or e-mail).

Recruiting participants and getting them to complete the survey can require extra steps. The more participants in your sample who are willing to complete the survey, the lower chance there will be of nonresponse error in your study. Dillman (2000) makes several suggestions for improving response rates of surveys. How the survey is presented can influence whether a participant chooses to complete the survey. Using printed fonts and formatting that make the survey easy to read will increase completion rates. Some of the controversy over the outcome of the 2000 U.S. presidential election occurred because the Florida ballot had a confusing format, which led to many voters reporting that they may have marked their ballot for a different candidate than they had intended to vote for. In addition, contacting participants multiple times will increase completion rates. For example, sending an introduction letter or e-mail before the survey is sent, sending personalized correspondence, sending information about the importance of the survey with the survey itself, and sending follow-up reminders will encourage participants to complete the survey. Finally, including an incentive (e.g., a small amount of money, a gift) will encourage completion.

CHAPTER SUMMARY

Reconsider the questions from the beginning of the chapter:

- What types of research questions can be answered with survey observations? Most surveys are used to answer descriptive or predictive research questions in correlational studies. However, if a survey is used to measure behavior in an experiment, then it can be used to answer causal research questions as well.
- How are surveys constructed? Surveys are constructed with questions or items that address behaviors and attitudes on specific topics. Open-ended or closed-ended items may be included. The goal is to construct the survey such that its validity and reliability are maximized. Thus, validity and reliability are typically evaluated for new surveys researchers construct.
- What makes responses for a survey valid? If survey scores truly represent the behavior the survey was designed to measure, then the responses on the survey have good validity.
- How is reliability tested for a survey? There are several methods for testing the reliability of the scores from a survey. For example, correlations between scores on different items of the survey can be measured. Alternatively, correlations between scores on the same survey taken at different times can be measured. Strong, positive correlations in these cases would indicate reliable scores on the survey.

- What are some different ways that surveys can be administered? Surveys can be administered in paper booklets to groups or individuals, as oral questions posed to groups or individuals, or on the Web to individuals.

THINKING ABOUT RESEARCH

A summary of a research study in psychology is given below. As you read the summary, think about the following questions:

1. Explain how the researcher assessed the construct validity of the scores of her survey.

2. Imagine that you have been tasked with creating a college major satisfaction survey to be used in a study like this one. Write three items for this survey that could be responded to on the 5-point Likert Scale (see Chapter 4 for a discussion of Likert Scales) described below for this survey.

3. How did the researcher evaluate the reliability of the scores on her survey? Based on the results, how reliable were the scores?

4. Some of the participants in this study completed the Academic Major Satisfaction Scale twice. Do you think testing effects were a concern in this study? Why or why not?

Study Reference

Nauta, M. M. (2007). Assessing college students' satisfaction with their academic majors. *Journal of Career Assessment, 15,* 446–462.

Purpose of the Study. The purpose of the study was the evaluation of a survey to measure college students' satisfaction with their major. The researcher wrote a 20-item survey called the Academic Major Satisfaction Scale (AMSS) with a 5-point response scale that asked participants to indicate their agreement with the items. The validity of the scores of the survey was then tested by various means in the study.

Method of the Study. College students with a declared major were participants in the study. They completed the AMSS in an initial session. The participants' declared majors were then recorded both at the initial session and again 2 years later to determine which participants had kept their major and which participants had changed their major. Declared majors were recorded from the student directory. Participants were also asked to complete the AMSS a second time 2.5 years after the initial session (by mail). Two samples of participants completed this procedure. The scores from the first sample were used to choose the best items for the final version of the AMSS. The scores from the second sample were used to evaluate the validity of the final version of the AMSS. Thus, the second sample of participants completed the 6-item version of the AMSS, instead of the initial 20-item version that the first sample completed. The second sample also completed additional measures to assess the validity of the AMSS based on relationships to other previously validated measures.

Results of the Study. The scores from the first sample were analyzed to determine the items with the highest item-to-total correlation (i.e., correlations between pairs of items were calculated and the items with the highest total correlations were determined). Six items were chosen from these analyses. Change in AMSS scores was also analyzed. Results indicated that satisfaction scores increased over time, particularly for participants who changed their major during the 2-year period. The scores from the second sample that completed the final 6-item AMSS were analyzed in several ways. First, the pairwise correlations between items was determined (also known as Cronbach's alpha—see this chapter for more discussion) and found to be high. Thus, the items appeared to measure a similar construct. In addition, AMSS scores were higher among participants who did not change their major than those who did. The AMSS scores were also positively correlated with several other related measures such as participants' GPA and scores on a career decision scale that assessed how competent the participants felt in this area. A negative relationship was found between AMSS scores and career choice anxiety.

Conclusions of the Study. The results of the study indicated that the 6 items chosen for the final version of the AMSS had good internal reliability (based on Cronbach's alpha) and predictive validity (based on differences across those who changed and did not change their major). In addition, the AMSS appeared to have good validity based on relationships between AMSS scores and other related measures. Thus, the researcher concluded that the AMSS may be a useful survey for assessing college students' satisfaction with their majors.

COMMON PITFALLS AND HOW TO AVOID THEM

Problem: Biased question/item wording—the wording of questions/items on surveys can affect the participants' responses.

Solution: When wording questions/items on a survey, consider how they will be interpreted by the participants. If participants could have different responses to different parts of a question/item, consider breaking the item into two items. If a question/item could be misinterpreted by a participant, consider rewording the item.

Problem: Equating survey responses with direct measures of behavior—overestimating the validity of self-report measures can occur.

Solution: Remember that survey responses are based on what the participants are willing to report about their behaviors and attitudes. In some cases, participants may feel the need to present themselves in a more positive way than they really are, reducing the validity of responses on the survey. In addition, it is also possible that participants see themselves differently than they really are. Thus, they do not intentionally mislead with their responses, but their responses still do not match their actual behaviors or attitudes.

TEST YOURSELF

1.   What types of research questions can be answered with surveys?

2.   Survey items that can be completed with any response chosen by the participant are called _____ questions, whereas survey items that must be completed with one of the response options provided by the researcher are called _____ questions.

3.   Describe two ways that reliability can be tested for a survey.

4. Rewrite the survey question to improve its clarity:
   Do you prefer dogs or cats? ___ dogs ___ cats

5. Given the outcome of the U.S. presidential election in 2008, evaluate the survey described at the beginning of this chapter. What aspects of the survey allowed the researchers to accurately predict the winner of the election?

Match each concept below with its correct definition.

6. construct validity

(a) participants are not restricted in the types of responses they can make to survey items

7. test-retest reliability

(b) a measure of reliability based on the average correlations between pairs of items on a survey

8. open-ended scale

(c) the scores are similar each time a participant takes the survey

9. testing effects

(d) the scores are indicative of the psychological construct the survey was designed to measure

10. Cronbach's alpha

(e) scores at later testings are affected by a participant's having taken the survey or test previously

Answers: 1. Most types of research questions can be answered with a survey if the behavior of interest can be observed through self-reports from the participants. However, most research using surveys addresses descriptive or predictive research questions. 2. open-ended, closed-ended. 3. Test-retest reliability is good when scores on a survey show a strong positive correlation for participants who take the survey multiple times over a period of time. Split-half reliability is good when sets of scores on a survey show a strong positive correlation. 4. The question requires a forced choice between two alternatives, neither of which may be liked by the respondent. There are several ways to improve the question, but one way might be to use the following question and response choices:

If you were to have a pet, which animal would you prefer?

_____ dog

_____ cat

_____ bird

_____ reptile

_____ other (please specify _____)

_____ I do not like pets

5. Several aspects of the survey allowed the researchers to accurately predict the election outcome. For example, a random sample of likely voters instead of all Americans meant that they were sampling from people who were likely to cast a vote in the upcoming election. The large sample size kept the sampling error in the study low. The inclusion of cell phone users made the sample more representative, because some individuals in the population may not have landline phones. 6. d, 7. c, 8. a, 9. e, 10. b.

CHAPTER 10

The Nuts and Bolts of Correlational Studies

CONSIDER THE FOLLOWING QUESTIONS AS YOU READ CHAPTER 10

- What types of research questions can be answered with correlational studies?
- What is the difference between correlational and causal hypotheses?
- What aspects of correlational studies prohibit testing causal hypotheses?
- How do correlational studies allow us to predict behavior?

For the past several years, the popular press has been recommending that to ward off dementia, older people should continue to engage in activities that exercise their minds, such as solving crossword puzzles and playing other word games (Brody, 1996). These recommendations are based on research showing that people who engaged in more cognitive activities were less likely to get Alzheimer's disease (Wilson, Scherr, Schneider, Tang, & Bennet, 2007). Note that this claim is based on a correlation between variables (i.e., frequency of Alzheimer's disease and level of cognitive activity). In other words, the researchers are claiming that one variable tends to be higher with the absence of another variable (Alzheimer's disease and frequency of cognitive activity) not that one variable (frequency of cognitive activity) causes another (lower incidence of Alzheimer's disease). Yet the media report recommendations as if a causal relationship exists. Is this appropriate?

The answer to this question is "maybe not." The research findings reported above suggest several possibilities. One possibility is the causal relationship suggested by the media: engaging in cognitive activity as we age prevents Alzheimer's disease. Another possibility, however, is that development of Alzheimer's disease reduces the cognitive activities of people, perhaps because these activities become more difficult as the disease begins to develop. Finally, a third possibility is that a third variable causes both greater cognitive activity and lower incidence of Alzheimer's disease. For example, genetic factors could cause both interest in cognitive activities (making it more likely that someone engages in these activities) and the predisposition (or lack thereof) to Alzheimer's disease. In other words,

—— ✂ ——

Correlational Study: a type of research design that examines the relationships between multiple dependent variables, without manipulating any of the variables

finding a correlational relationship among variables does not provide information about the causal relationship between those variables. This is the more important issue to consider when considering a **correlational study** (Figure 10.1).

Despite the lack of causal information, however, correlational studies do provide information that allows researchers to determine which variables should be considered when they design tests of causal relationships. This is especially important when manipulating a variable to test the causal relationship is difficult or impossible. The results described above regarding incidence of Alzheimer's disease suggested to

Figure 10.1   **Steps in the Research Process: Designing the Study**

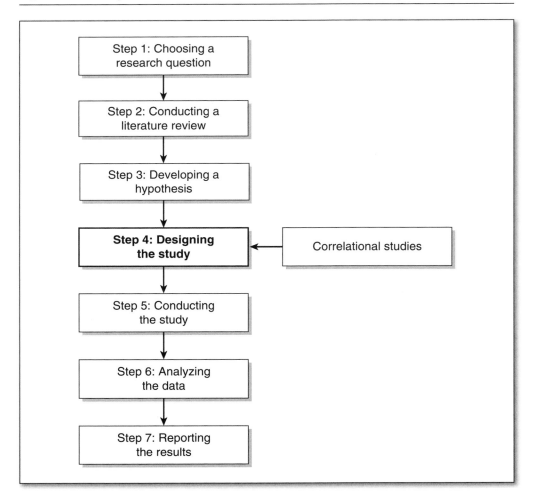

researchers that a causal relationship might exist between this factor and cognitive activities to allow additional studies to be done to provide further research examining possible causal relationships. For example, programs that include various cognitive activities can be tested to determine if they are effective in reducing the incidence of Alzheimer's disease (Szekely, Breitner, & Zandi, 2007). However, these studies will take time to complete, as Alzheimer's disease takes time to develop and currently can be confirmed only once someone has died.

RESEARCH QUESTIONS IN CORRELATIONAL STUDIES

Correlational studies are designed to address **descriptive** and **predictive research questions**. In other words, the researcher of a correlational study may be attempting to answer one type of descriptive research question regarding simple relationships between variables to determine if behaviors cooccur (see Chapter 2 for examples of other types of descriptive research questions). Alternatively, a researcher may conduct a correlational study with the ultimate goal of predicting one behavior from another behavior (e.g., predicting grades from number of hours of TV watched per week). Whenever a strong relationship exists between variables, prediction of one variable from other variables is possible. For correlational studies with predictive research questions, the variable that is used for the prediction is called the **predictor variable**, and the variable being predicted is called the **outcome variable**. If you have already read Chapter 9 on survey research (descriptive research questions are also discussed in Chapter 2), these two types of research questions probably sound familiar. In fact, most survey research involves a correlational study, and many correlational studies use surveys to measure behavior. Surveys are a very common observational technique in correlational studies. However, correlational studies may also involve naturalistic observations or systematic observations.

Descriptive Research Question: a research question that asks about the presence of behavior, how frequently it is exhibited, or whether there is a relationship between different behaviors

Predictive Research Question: a research question that asks if one behavior can be predicted from another behavior to allow predictions of future behavior

Predictor Variable: the dependent variable in a correlational study that is used to predict the score on another variable

Outcome Variable: the dependent variable in a correlational study that is being predicted by the predictor variable

Regardless of the type of observational technique used to measure behavior, the goal of any correlational study is to examine relationships between two or more measures of behavior. These relationships allow researchers to better describe the behaviors being studied or predict one behavior from another behavior. Hypothesized relationships are typically tested using correlational analyses (e.g., Pearson *r*) or regression analyses that allow predictions. See Chapter 14 for more discussion of these types of tests. A correlational study cannot, however, provide causal information about the relationship between the measures; it can only describe the relationship between the behaviors. As described in Chapter 3, this is due to the lack of manipulation of an independent variable in correlational studies and subsequent lack of control of other extraneous variables. Only an experimental study has these features, which allow a casual relationship to be tested.

Despite the lack of causal information, correlational studies do provide important information about relationships between variables in cases where manipulation is not possible. For example, to determine the link between certain behaviors (e.g., smoking) and poor health, correlational studies are often conducted, because manipulation of the behaviors that may cause poor health would be unethical. An experiment that examined this relationship might involve a researcher randomly assigning participants to smoke and others not to smoke. This study would be unethical if the researcher believes that smoking may be detrimental to health (e.g., animal studies have shown smoking to be harmful). It would be unethical to conduct a study where some participants are assigned to a condition that may be harmful to them. Thus, most of the research showing a link between smoking and long-term health in humans has involved correlational studies. Experimental studies providing evidence of a causal relationship between smoking and health have been conducted with animal subjects, illustrating how important animal studies can be in understanding certain kinds of everyday problems that humans face.

The key to understanding correlational studies is remembering that "correlation does not equal causation." The direction of the cause and effect relationship cannot be determined from a correlational study because none of the variables is manipulated in the study. For example, suppose researchers find a negative relationship between two dependent (i.e., measured) variables: number of hours of TV watched per week and grades in school for children.

They cannot conclude from this result that watching more TV causes lower grades. It is possible that this causal relationship exists between these measures, but it is also possible that having lower grades causes children to watch more TV because they are not spending that time doing homework or studying. In addition, Chapter 3 introduced the third-variable problem as an issue for correlational studies. Because correlational studies cannot control for extraneous variables in the

---
❧

Third-Variable Problem: the presence of extraneous factors in a study that affect the dependent variable can decrease the internal validity of the study

way that experiments can, it is always possible that a third variable (i.e., the **third-variable problem** discussed in Chapters 3 and 11) is responsible for the relationship between the measures. It is possible that parental influences have a causal relationship with both number of hours of TV watched and grades. Children with parents who force them to study for a certain amount of time per week and who reinforce good grades may also restrict the number of hours of TV their children watch. Conversely, some parents may encourage their children to watch TV with them and not encourage them to spend time studying or doing homework.

Figure 10.2 presents the three possible causal relationships that might exist for the example above. Consider what a researcher would need to do in order to tease apart these possible causal relationships to find out which one is accurate. To test Relationship A in Figure 10.2, the number of hours of TV the children watched per week would have to be manipulated (i.e., an experiment would need to be done) to determine its effect on their grades. In other words, some children might be assigned to watch no TV for a month and others might be assigned to watch a set number of hours of TV per week for that month, depending on how many groups the researcher wanted to compare. Then the TV watching

Figure 10.2   **The Different Types of Relationships That Might Exist Between Two Variables**

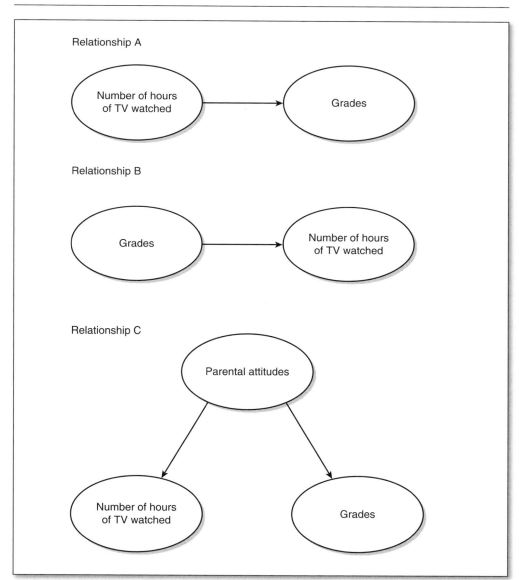

Relationship A

Number of hours of TV watched → Grades

Relationship B

Grades → Number of hours of TV watched

Relationship C

Parental attitudes → Number of hours of TV watched

Parental attitudes → Grades

groups would be compared on their average grades to determine if they differ. To test Relationship B in Figure 10.2, the children's grades would need to be manipulated (or at least the grades they are told they are earning), and then the grade groups could be compared for how much TV they watch per week. Testing Relationship C might be difficult; however, a researcher could assign parents to groups, where the groups are asked to encourage their children either to spend their time on academic tasks (such as doing homework and studying) or to spend their time watching TV. The researcher could then measure the children's grades and how much TV they watch after a period of time. Notice, though, that each of these tests of the different possible relationships requires an experiment to be conducted because a correlational study of these variables would reveal if a relationship between them existed but would not reveal the type of causal relationship that might be present.

If the study described above, however, found a relationship between the number of hours of TV watched per week and the child's grades, this relationship could be used to predict one behavior from the other for other individuals. The researcher's goal in conducting this study may have been to use the number of hours of TV watched that is measured for children entering elementary school to predict their future grades (i.e., there was a predictive research question) and, thus, evenly distribute children of different academic abilities across different classrooms. In this case, the number of hours of TV watched variable is a predictor variable, and the grades variable is an outcome variable. This relationship could also be used to screen children entering elementary school for gifted programs. In reality, the relationship between TV watching and grades is probably not as strong as is the relationship between grades and scores on certain types of standardized tests (e.g., intelligence questionnaires). Thus, school psychologists are more likely to use these tests to predict future grades for children.

CORRELATIONAL STUDY EXAMPLES

Correlational studies occur most frequently in personality, clinical and counseling, industrial-organizational, and social areas of psychology, but they can be used in any area of psychology where manipulation of a variable of interest would be difficult or impossible. Thus, as described above, correlational studies are used to answer descriptive and predictive research questions. The examples below highlight each of these types of questions.

Descriptive Studies

An example of a correlational study designed to describe the relationship between weather, mood, and cognitive abilities (e.g., ability to remember a short list of digits for a short period of time) was conducted by Keller et al. (2005, Study 1). Based on inconsistent findings in previous studies, their goal was to determine if a relationship existed in their study for these dependent variables, and if one was found, what type of relationship was present. The participants in this study completed a mood questionnaire and cognitive tasks at a single session. The weather was determined based on the temperature and barometric pressure (as a measure related to how much sunlight is present) reported by the National Climatic Data Center. In addition, activity level and time spent outside that day were considered in the data analysis. Keller et al.'s results indicated that there was no direct relationship between weather and mood. Instead, the relationship between weather and mood was *moderated* or changed by the amount of time the participants spent outside. In other words, a **positive relationship** was shown for people who spent more time outside that day (i.e., 30 minutes or more), meaning that as temperature increased, so did mood for these participants. However, a **negative relationship** was shown for people who spent less time outside that day, meaning that as temperature increased, mood decreased for these participants. Similar results were shown for the relationship between weather and cognitive abilities: A positive relationship was seen between the variables only for individuals who spent the most time outside that day. The researchers concluded that positive relationships do exist

Positive Relationship: a relationship between variables characterized by coupled increases in the two variables

Negative Relationship: a relationship between variables characterized by an increase in one variable that occurs with a decrease in the other variable

between weather and mood and weather and cognitive abilities but only when people spend a reasonable amount of time outside (more than 30 minutes a day).

Campbell, Bosson, Goheen, Lakey, and Kernis (2007) also conducted a correlational study to examine the relationship between narcissism (having an inflated self-image) and self-esteem because of suggestions that narcissists show high explicit self-esteem but actually have low self-esteem at an implicit level. Participants in the study completed a narcissism survey, an explicit self-esteem survey, and the Implicit Association Test (IAT) to measure implicit self-esteem (the IAT is a cognitive test that measures implicit attitudes based on the time it takes to respond to associated items—see Chapter 3 for more discussion of the IAT). Despite suggestions about the relationship between narcissism and implicit self-esteem, scores on the narcissism survey and the IAT were not related in the study. However, narcissism scores and explicit self-esteem scores were positively correlated. Thus, the researchers suggest that the idea that narcissists actually have implicit low self-esteem may not be accurate.

Predictive Studies

An example of a correlational study that was conducted to examine a predictive relationship between variables comes from Boger, Tompson, Briggs-Gowan, Pavlis, and Carter (2008). These researchers were interested in *predicting* expressed emotion in families from specific family characteristics to allow predictions of family dynamics from family characteristics. Expressed emotion is a measure that indicates how family members feel about one another and has been shown in past studies to be linked to the course of mental disorders in children and adults. The current study addressed whether expressed emotion can be predicted from family stress and functioning. Such a prediction might ultimately be useful in counseling situations to determine what types of treatments may be beneficial for different types of families. The study participants were mothers who completed surveys at different points in time. The measures of family stress and functioning included a survey regarding the quality of the parents' marital relationship, a report of stressful life events in the family, a survey regarding parenting stress, and a survey that assessed family expressiveness and conflict. The mothers also completed a survey that measured expressed emotion. Results indicated that of these measures of family stress, only family expressiveness (i.e., communication among family members) predicted expressed emotion (family members' attitudes toward each other). Outside stressors (such as stressful life events) did not predict expressed emotion. Thus, the study provided information about what factors do and do not predict positive and negative attitudes among family members.

Another study that examined factors that may predict a behavior focused on working alliance, which indicates how well clients and therapists are able to work together during therapy (Patterson, Uhlin, & Anderson, 2008). Previous studies have shown that working alliance is related to positive therapy outcomes. From these different studies, a prediction of working alliance in therapy could be made based on several measures previously found to be related to this behavior. Thus, Patterson et al. examined whether clients' preexisting expectations of counseling could predict their working alliance in a therapeutic relationship with a therapist. The participants were clients receiving therapy at a university counseling center. The participants completed a survey regarding their expectations about counseling before they started therapy. They then completed a survey regarding working alliance after their third therapy session. The results indicated that positive therapy expectations predicted good working alliance among the clients in the study. Thus the researchers concluded that therapists can use information about client expectations to tailor their therapeutic style so as to maximize working alliance in the therapeutic relationships with their clients.

Summary

The correlational study examples described above illustrate an important issue regarding this research design type: Despite similar methodologies (i.e., use of surveys or other dependent measures) and general goals (i.e., examining relationships), the specific research question being asked in the study will determine what is learned about the relationships among the variables. In some cases, the research question is descriptive in nature, such that the goal of the study is to examine if a relationship exists and, if one does exist, what form of relationship (e.g., positive or negative) exists between the variables. In other cases, the research question is predictive in nature, such that the goal of the study is to examine whether certain measures can be used to predict a behavior of interest. With knowledge about prediction, measures can be used in situations outside the study to predict behavior, as is done by colleges and universities to predict which applicants are most likely to succeed in college based on high school grades and entrance exam scores (e.g., the SAT [Scholastic Aptitude Test] or ACT [American College Test]).

CHAPTER SUMMARY

Reconsider the questions from the beginning of the chapter:

- What types of research questions can be answered with correlational studies? Correlational studies can answer descriptive or predictive research questions.
- What is the difference between correlational and causal hypotheses? Hypotheses tested in correlational studies are about describing or predicting behavior. Causal hypotheses predict a specific cause of a behavior.
- What aspects of correlational studies prohibit testing causal hypotheses? Correlational studies do not contain independent variables that are manipulated by the researcher.

Thus, the third-variable problem exists in correlational studies due to a lack of sufficient control of extraneous factors.

- How do correlational studies allow us to predict behavior? Regression analysis of the relationship between factors in a correlational study can test predictive relationships between variables (see Chapter 14 for more information on regression analyses).

THINKING ABOUT RESEARCH

A summary of a research study in psychology is given below. As you read the summary, think about the following questions:

1. Why do you think the researchers used a stratified random sample in this study instead of other possible sampling techniques (*Hint:* read or reread the section on stratified random sampling in Chapter 6)? How do you think this choice affected the validity of their study?

2. Explain why the research question asked in this study is predictive instead of merely descriptive.

3. List the dependent variables included in this study and indicate which were predictor and outcome variables.

4. In what ways did the researchers use correlations to answer their research question?

5. Describe a study that would test causal factors for marital satisfaction. How feasible would it be to ethically conduct your study?

Study Reference

Luo, S., Chen, H., Yue, G., Zhang, G., Zhaoyang, R., & Xu, D. (2008). Predicting marital satisfaction from self, partner, and couple characteristics: Is it me, you, or us? *Journal of Personality, 76,* 1231–1265.

Purpose of the Study. The purpose of this study was to evaluate how much the individual characteristics of each spouse and similarities between spouses predict marital satisfaction. Relationships between different questionnaires were tested to determine the contributions of the different factors to marital satisfaction scores on the Enriching Relationship Issues, Communication, and Happiness questionnaire (ENRICH; Fowers & Olson, 1993).

Method of the Study. A stratified random sample (based on city of residence) of 2,146 Chinese married participants completed several questionnaires. To obtain measures regarding individual participant personality characteristics, participants completed the Chinese Personality Assessment Inventory (CPAI; Cheung et al., 1996). Items on this survey require a yes/no response. To measure individual values, participants completed the Questionnaire of Value Orientation for Chinese (QVOC; Xin, 2001). Participants responded to items on this survey using a 6-point scale that indicated how strongly they agreed or disagreed with value statements. Spousal similarity within couples was determined from the difference between scores and correlation between the scores for the spouses on these two questionnaires. To measure marital satisfaction, participants completed the ENRICH (Fowers & Olson, 1993) questionnaire. Responses on this survey were completed using a 10-item Likert Scale indicating agreement or disagreement with the statements. Each of these questionnaires has been validated in previous research and has been shown to have good validity and reliability.

Results of the Study. Analysis of a specific predictive model of marital satisfaction tested the individual contributions of the spouses' scores on the CPAI and QVOC and the difference scores between spouses on these measures to the scores on the ENRICH questionnaire. Results indicated that individual characteristics and the correlation between spouse scores each independently contributed to marital satisfaction scores.

Conclusions of the Study. The authors concluded from this study that "whether individuals are happy or not in their relationship is a function of who they are, who their spouses are, and how much similarity they and their spouse share" (Luo et al., 2008, p. 1255). For example, high marital satisfaction could be predicted from an individual's having more intrinsic values (e.g., valuing responsibility) than extrinsic values (e.g., valuing money or power). The same was true of a spouse's values: High marital satisfaction could be predicted from a spouse's having more intrinsic values than extrinsic values. Finally, high marital satisfaction could be predicted for spouses who were similar in their personalities and values.

COMMON PITFALLS AND HOW TO AVOID THEM

Problem: Confusing correlation and causation—when correlations are presented between two factors, people often interpret the relationship as causal without a causal test.

Solution: As the story at the beginning of the chapter illustrates, reports of treatments should be carefully interpreted. This is particularly true for reports read in the media. Carefully consider the type of relationship that was tested in a study that is reported. If two factors simply cooccur, this does not indicate a causal relationship. To determine if a relationship between factors is causal, an independent variable must be manipulated in a study. A correlational study will not test a causal relationship; however, it may provide evidence of some type of relationship that researchers can further explore to determine the relationship's nature.

Problem: Confusion of different types of variables—it can be difficult to distinguish between independent and dependent variables.

Solution: Remember that for a variable to be an independent variable, it must be manipulated by the researcher. This means that unless a researcher has randomly assigned participants to the different conditions of the variable or each participant is completing all conditions of the variable, it is not an independent variable. (See Chapter 11 for more discussion.) However, dependent variables can be used as predictor variables to predict the score of another dependent variable, as described in this chapter.

TEST YOURSELF

1. Suppose you read a news report that a study was conducted where people who reported drinking green tea each day as part of their diet were less likely to be diagnosed with cancer over the 5 years in which the study took place. Why can't we conclude that drinking green tea makes one less likely to get cancer? Describe two possible explanations for the results reported from the study.

2. For the study described in (1), explain how the researchers could have done a study to test the causal relationship between drinking green tea and incidence of cancer.

3. Explain the difference between a descriptive research question and a predictive research question. Provide an example of each type of research question.

4. Identify the dependent variables included in the studies described in the Correlational Study Examples section of the chapter that are listed below. In addition, indicate which of these variables were predictor variables and which were outcome variables in the last two studies.

   (a) Keller et al. (2005)

   (b) Campbell et al. (2007)

   (c) Boger et al. (2008)

   (d) Patterson et al. (2008)

5. Suppose a study was conducted to examine the relationship between how often people exercise and how happy they are with their lives. Participants in this study were asked to report how many times a week they exercise for 30 minutes or more at a time and to complete a questionnaire with items that measure their quality of life (e.g., How many times in the past week do you remember feeling happy?). A positive relationship is found between number of times per week people exercise and their quality of life score. Answer the questions below about this study.

   (a) What are the dependent variables in this study?

   (b) Describe the three different types of causal relationships that could exist between the dependent variables you described in (a).

   (c) Explain why this study does not provide evidence for any of the causal relationships you described in (b).

Answers: 1. This is a correlational study. No independent variable was manipulated, and other possible factors that could affect cancer rates were not controlled for. Thus, we cannot conclude that drinking green tea has a causal relationship with cancer rates. It is possible that it does, or it is possible that people who are less likely to get cancer (e.g., no family history) are more likely to drink green tea (i.e., low cancer probability causes one to drink green tea). Finally, it is possible that a third variable (e.g., maintaining a healthy lifestyle) causes one to both drink green tea and have low likelihood of getting cancer. 2. An experiment would need to be conducted where the researcher randomly assigns participants to either drink green tea every day or to not drink any green tea (but perhaps to drink a similar-looking drink that they are told is green tea but is actually just colored water) and then records who gets cancer in order to compare cancer rates across the two groups. 3. A descriptive research question is one where a researcher is interested in whether a behavior occurs and how often it occurs. In a correlational study, a descriptive research question might be whether a relationship exists between two variables and what type of relationship exists. A predictive research question is one in which a researcher examines whether one variable can be predicted from one or more variables. Examples will vary. 4a. Weather as measured by temperature that day and barometric pressure that day, cognitive abilities, mood as measured by a questionnaire, activity level, and time spent outside that day; 4b. narcissism as measured by a survey, explicit self-esteem as measured by a survey, and implicit self-esteem as measured by the IAT; 4c. predictor variables—family stress and functioning measured by surveys, outcome variable—expressed emotion measured by a survey; 4d. predictor variable—expectations about counseling measured by a survey before therapy, outcome variable—client-therapist working alliance measured by a survey after therapy. 5a. How often people exercise measured by how many times per week they exercise for 30 minutes or more at a time and happiness measured by the score on the quality of life scale; 5b. more exercise may cause people to be happy, being happy could cause people to exercise more, or some third variable could cause both happiness and more exercise; 5c. no variable is manipulated in this study; thus, no causal relationships are tested. One of the variables (it would be easiest to manipulate the amount of exercise variable) must be manipulated (e.g., participants randomly assigned to different conditions of the variable) to test a causal relationship.

The Nuts and Bolts of Experiments

When our dog Daphne (see Figure 11.1) became a member of our family, she did not like to be left in the house without us. Whenever we went out, even for short periods of time, she would have "accidents" on the rug and engage in destructive chewing behaviors. She ruined a few small items of furniture and more than a few pairs of my husband's shoes. In an attempt to improve her behavior, we researched the issue and found several suggested "treatments" for this sort of behavior. We bought her a toy that held treats, accessed by chewing, that we could give her while we were away from home. We gave her some objects that we had used recently and smelled like us (e.g., an old T-shirt) to help her feel that we were nearby. We confined her to one room in the house to help her feel less anxious by being in a smaller space. Because we did not know which of these would best improve her behavior, we decided to try these "treatments" one at a time, five times each to make sure that the "treatments" were tested under different conditions (different days of the week, different times of day, etc.). After each trip away from home where one of these "treatments" was applied, we counted the number of "bad" behaviors there was evidence of in the house. We operationally defined (see Chapter 3 for more discussion of operational definitions) "bad" behaviors as soiling the floor or rug and chewing anything in the house that she was not supposed to. In other words, we used our knowledge of research methods to conduct an **experiment** to determine which "treatment" was most effective at stopping Daphne's "bad" behaviors while we were away from home. In most cases, an experiment would involve several individuals being tested (several dogs in this study), but

Figure 11.1   An Experiment on Daphne

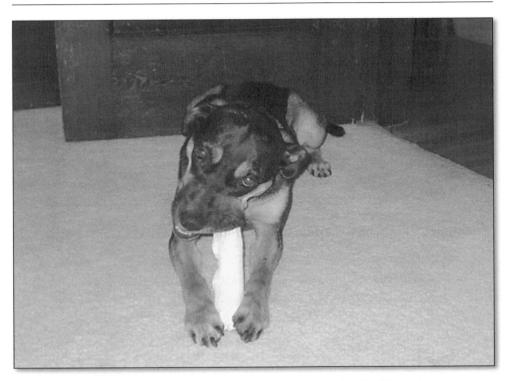

NOTE: This experiment helped determine the best "treatment" to stop her "bad" behaviors.

as we were only interested in how the "treatments" would affect Daphne, we used a small-*n* experiment to test the "treatments" (see Chapter 13 for more discussion of **small-*n* designs**). In this experiment, Daphne experienced all the "treatments," each at different times. We controlled for other possible explanations of her behavior by keeping her environment the same other than the "treatment" that was changing. We only tested the "treatments" when we would be away for 2 to 3 hours in the afternoon to keep the time she was left consistent across treatment conditions. Finally, we tested each treatment condition five times each to make sure that extreme behaviors that occurred during any single trip away from home would not bias the results. We wished to learn which "treatment" for Daphne would be most effective by comparing the "treatments" in terms of their effect on the dependent variable, her "bad" behavior. Through this experiment, we determined that the chew toy was most effective in reducing Daphne's undesirable behaviors.

❧

Experiment: a type of research design that involves manipulation of an independent variable, allowing control of extraneous variables that could affect the results

Small-*n* Design: an experiment conducted with one or a few participants to better understand the behavior of those individuals

If the example above sounds like something you may have tried in your life for yourself or a pet, then you may already be familiar with the concept of an experiment. Perhaps you have run an experiment to determine which study techniques work best in improving your exam scores. The experiments conducted by psychologists in their research follow the same principles as the example above. Different treatments or conditions of an independent variable are compared to determine whether those treatments or conditions differ in their effects on behavior and which of those treatments or conditions has the greatest effect on the behavior of interest.

In this chapter, we will discuss the "nuts and bolts" of experiments (Figure 11.2): how an experiment can increase the internal validity of a study, issues to consider for different types of independent variable manipulations, and what we can learn from more

Figure 11.2   Steps in the Research Process: Designing the Study

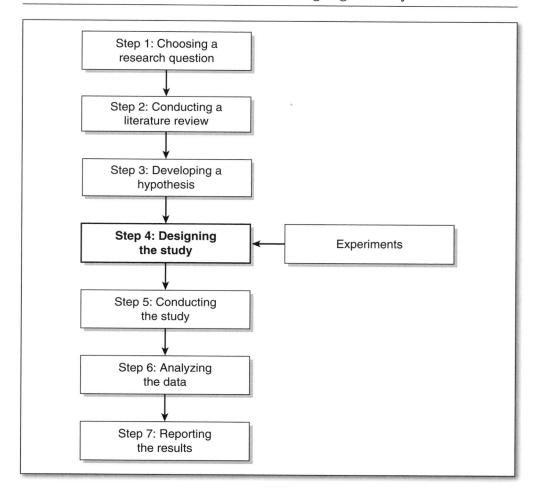

complex experiments that manipulate more than one independent variable. The discussion in this chapter will rely on your knowledge of concepts covered in Chapter 3; thus, you may wish to review the section on experiments in Chapter 3 before you read the rest of this chapter.

LEARNING ABOUT CAUSATION THROUGH MANIPULATION AND CONTROL

Remember from Chapter 3 that the experimental research design is the only type of research design that contains a true **independent variable** that is manipulated by the researcher. One aspect of an experiment that can seem confusing is the concept of manipulation. What does it mean to *manipulate* an independent variable? Generally, a manipulation of an independent variable involves researcher control of the administration of the levels of the variable to the participants. In other words, an independent variable is manipulated such that participants are randomly assigned to levels; the assignment is not based on any characteristic of the participants themselves. For example, a participant's gender, personality, and smoking status cannot be independent variables, because these characteristics are not randomly assigned for a participant by the researcher.

Independent Variable: a variable in an experiment that is manipulated by the researcher such that the levels of the variable change across or within subjects in the experiment

The manipulation of an independent variable in an experiment allows the researcher to learn about the causal relationship between the independent and dependent variables. In other words, manipulation of an independent variable in a study increases the internal validity of the study. Recall from Chapters 3 and 4 that a study with good internal validity is one that provides a good test of a causal hypothesis. Without the manipulation of an independent variable, it is very difficult to rule out other possible factors as causes of a change in the dependent variable. This is called the **third-variable problem** and must be considered in all studies. When researchers design an experiment, they already are controlling for extraneous factors that might affect the results of the study through the use of a manipulated independent variable. However, there are other ways that extraneous factors can affect the results of an experiment, and a researcher must identify these factors and design the experiment to control for these factors as best as possible. For example, even when an independent variable is manipulated, it is still possible that an extraneous factor (i.e., a **confounding variable**—see Chapters 3 and 4 for more discussion of confounding variables) changes systematically with the levels of the variable (time of day participants are run, slight alteration in instructions given by different experimenters, etc.). Thus, the researcher must design an experiment to control for the confounding variables as they may affect the results. Some specific types of confounding variables are discussed in Chapter 4.

Third-Variable Problem: the presence of extraneous factors in a study that affect the dependent variable can decrease the internal validity of the study

Confounding Variable: an extraneous factor present in a study that may affect the results

The manipulation of the independent variable can occur in two ways: the variable can be manipulated **between subjects** or **within subjects**. In between-subjects manipulations, each participant receives only one level of the independent variable. Participants are typically randomly assigned to the different levels of between-subjects variables. For example, a researcher interested in the effects of text format on learning can manipulate text format as a between-subjects variable by randomly assigning different students in a class to a hard copy version of the text and an online version of the text. **Random assignment** of participants to levels will allow random distribution of participant differences (study habits, academic achievement, etc.) across the levels, making it less likely that these participants' differences cause (and more likely that the independent variable causes) a difference across groups for the dependent variable being measured. Random assignment is accomplished when the researcher decides by chance which participants will be in the different groups in the study. In other words, random assignment is a means of controlling for participant differences across groups and will increase the internal validity of the experiment.

Between-Subjects Variable: each participant experiences only one level of the variable

Within-Subjects Variable: each participant experiences all levels of the variable

Random Assignment: participants are randomly assigned to levels of the independent variable in an experiment to control for individual differences as an extraneous variable

In within-subjects manipulations, each participant receives all levels of the independent variable. The researcher in the preceding example, who is interested in the effects of text format on learning, could manipulate text format within subjects by having each participant use each type of text for different chapters in the text. Random assignment is important for within-subjects variables in terms of the order in which participants receive the levels of the variable to control for possible **order effects** of the different levels of the variable. As in the example on the effects of text format, learning may be different depending on whether the participants receive the hard copy version or the online version of the text first. Order effects are a particular form of **testing effects**, with bias occurring because of multiple testings of a participant in a study.

Order Effects: occur when the order in which the participants experience conditions in an experiment affects the results of the study

Testing Effects: occur when participants are tested more than once in a study, with early testing affecting later testing

CONTROL IN WITHIN-SUBJECTS AND BETWEEN-SUBJECTS EXPERIMENTS

As described above, random assignment is an important means of control in an experiment for both between-subjects and within-subjects variables. However, each type of manipulation uses random assignment in different ways to control for different extraneous factors. There are also cases where random assignment may not be sufficient to control for these extraneous factors and additional controls may be needed. Thus, researchers must consider the types of extraneous factors that may be present in an experiment when they decide whether to use a between-subjects or within-subjects independent variable. These issues are discussed as they apply to each type of manipulation.

Between-Subjects Experiments

As described above, randomly assigning participants to different groups in a between-subjects manipulation controls for individual differences across the groups that might affect the data independently from the independent variable. In fact, the presence of individual differences across groups is the greatest concern for between-subjects experiments. In experiments where individual differences are likely to be present and a small sample size is used, random assignment may not be sufficient to control for these differences. In this case, the researcher has two additional means of controlling for individual differences. The first is to manipulate the independent variable as a within-subjects variable. This will allow participants to serve as their own controls and individual differences across groups are no longer of concern. However, for some variables, order effects may be more problematic and make between-subjects manipulation preferable. Thus, the second means of control is to use a **matched design** for between-subjects experiments. In a matched design, participants are matched on a characteristic that may contribute to group differences. Then each participant within a matched set is randomly assigned to different groups.

Matched Design: a between-subjects experiment that involves sets of participants matched on a specific characteristic with each member of the set randomly assigned to a different level of the independent variable

For example, consider a recent study by Hanlon and Roberson (2006). They conducted a series of experiments to investigate causes of documented difficulties young children encounter when learning color words. Different groups of children were taught color words under different feedback conditions to compare effects of feedback type on learning of the color words. However, the researchers were concerned about the effects of children's age and current vocabulary abilities on the learning of the color words. Thus, they created matched sets of participants who were matched on age and vocabulary abilities, and randomly assigned one member of each matched set to a different feedback condition. The matched sets allowed the researchers to control for the extraneous factors of age and vocabulary abilities that otherwise may have differed across groups and caused differences in the learning scores for the condition groups that were not caused by the feedback conditions themselves. Due to this control for group differences, the researchers were able to conclude that feedback that corrects the child's errors in using color words allows the child to learn the color words faster than other forms of feedback.

Another way to ensure that participants in the groups are matched on some characteristic is to measure that characteristic (e.g., years of education, socioeconomic status, language abilities) during the experiment and compare the groups in an additional analysis. This comparison will indicate if the groups are similar or different on that characteristic. However, if the groups are different, you are then left with the possibility that this difference affected your results. Thus, if you are concerned that a group difference is likely to affect your results, it is best to either use a within-subjects manipulation or match your participants before you assign them to the groups. Alternatively, if a between-subjects design is preferred, statistical tools can be used to account for group differences in the analysis of the data.

Within-Subjects Experiments

The primary concern of within-subjects variables is the order in which the participants receive the different levels of the independent variable. Because the participants receive all levels of the independent variable, it is possible that order of the levels can affect the dependent variable measure. For example, suppose that a within-subjects variable in an experiment involves a task difficulty manipulation such that all participants receive both an easy task and a difficult task. The order in which they receive these tasks can certainly affect the outcome of the study. If participants receive an easy task first and then a difficult task, they are likely to view the difficult task as more difficult than they would if they had received it before the easy task. The opposite situation will likely occur for how they view the easy task, depending on whether the easy task is first or second (i.e., they may view it as "easier" if they complete the difficult task first than if they complete the difficult task second).

To solve the problem of order effects for within-subjects manipulations, a researcher will typically **counterbalance** the order of the levels within the study. This means that different groups of participants will receive different orders of the levels of the independent variable. For example, in the experiment described earlier, half of the participants would receive the easy task first, and half would receive the difficult task first with participants assigned in equal numbers to the two different orders. Random assignment to orders or an alternative

Counterbalance: a control used in within-subjects experiments where equal numbers of participants are randomly assigned to different orders of the conditions

form of assignment may be used. Using different orders of the levels will counterbalance the order effects across the participants. The different orders can also be compared to determine if order effects exist, which is likely for this example.

Counterbalancing is relatively easy when there are only two conditions that participants will experience in an experiment. However, many experimental designs involve more than two conditions, making counterbalancing a little more difficult for within-subjects manipulations because all the orders must be included in a full counterbalancing. To illustrate this issue, consider a within-subjects experiment with three conditions: A, B, and C. There are six possible orders in which participants can experience these three conditions: ABC, BCA, ACB, CBA, CAB, and BAC. To fully counterbalance these three conditions, you would need six different orders of the conditions and numbers of participants in multiples of six in order to make an equal number of participants randomly assigned to each of the six possible orders of conditions. Already, the counterbalancing is becoming rather complicated. What happens when you have four conditions in the experiment (e.g., two independent variables, each with two levels)? The counterbalancing for a simple factorial experiment with four conditions is very complicated. To simplify the counterbalancing in such a case, a partial counterbalancing technique, called a **Latin Square**, can be used instead. In a Latin Square, the number of orders used in the experiment is equal to the number of conditions in the design, and each condition is in each ordinal position (i.e., first, second, third, fourth) exactly once. Latin Squares can be useful for within subjects designs where independent variables have the same number of levels.

❧

Latin Square: partial counterbalancing technique where the number of orders of conditions used is equal to the number of conditions in the study

---

For example, an experiment with four conditions (A, B, C, and D) can use a Latin Square to include four different orders of the conditions. Each of these conditions will be first once, second once, and so on, within the order structure. Thus, the order for a Latin Square would be ABDC, BCAD, CDBA, and DACB (see Grant, 1948, for the procedure to create a Latin Square for a design with any number of conditions). In this order structure, you can see that each condition serves in each ordinal position once. The researcher would then randomly assign each participant to one of these orders, requiring fewer orders of conditions in the experiment and lower multiples of participants to run in the experiment.

EXPERIMENT EXAMPLES

Although any area of psychological research may include experiments, there are areas of psychology where experiments are used more often than in others. In cognitive, biological, social, and (in some cases) developmental research, one is most likely to encounter the experimental research design. Other areas of psychological research do include experiments, but manipulation can be difficult or impossible for some factors of interest (e.g., clinical conditions or personality types). Thus, these examples come from areas where experiments are more likely to be used and will illustrate how experiments are used in different areas of psychology as well as some of the experimental concepts (e.g., control) that are described in this chapter.

Cognitive Example

Cognitive psychology includes the study of basic processing of information from the world around us. Cognitive psychologists study memory, perception, language processes, and decision making. Much of the research in these areas is focused on understanding factors that influence these processes and how they operate. Thus, experiments are a very common research design for cognitive psychologists.

As an example of how experiments are used to investigate basic processes in perception, consider a study conducted by Ehinger and Brockmole (2008). These researchers investigated the effects of the color of the objects in a visual scene on a person's ability to detect objects in the scenes. In their first experiment, participants were shown complex visual scenes (e.g., cars driving across a bridge), where a letter "T" or letter "L" had been inserted into the scene. The participants' task was to press a key when they found the letter in the scene. The participants' reaction time to complete the task was recorded for each scene (i.e., the dependent variable). In particular, the researchers were interested in the effect of the color conditions on the participants' ability to learn the location of the inserted letter in the scene for scenes that were repeated (as compared with scenes that were novel). Thus, participants were assigned to one of three color conditions: (1) a color-consistent change condition, where the colors of objects in the scene were changed from their original color in a consistent manner, with repeated scenes showing the same changed colors; (2) a color-inconsistent change condition, where the colors of objects were changed from their original color inconsistently, with repeated scenes showing different color schemes for the objects; (3) and a control condition, where the colors of objects did not change from the original colors in the scenes. In other words, a between-subjects experiment was conducted.

To control for some possible group differences, participants with normal or corrected vision (wearing glasses or contacts) and normal color vision served as participants. In addition, to control for possible order effects of the stimuli, the scenes were displayed in a random order. The participants were also asked to focus on the middle of the screen and press a key when they were ready to view a scene to control for lapses of attention in the task. These types of controls are typical for laboratory experiments.

Ehinger and Brockmole (2008) found that the participants got faster at detecting the letters across repeated scenes (i.e., they learned the locations), but this learning did not differ across the color conditions, indicating that there was no evidence that color affected the participants' abilities to detect the letters in the scenes. Because of the lack of an effect shown in this first experiment, the researchers conducted three further experiments with similar conditions to add support to their findings (see Chapter 7 for more discussion of results consistent with the null hypothesis). Their additional experiments supported the results of their first experiment: Color condition did not affect learning of the letter location in the scenes. The researchers concluded that color of objects does not seem to be an important factor in detection of objects in real-world visual scenes.

One thing you may be asking yourself is how realistic it is to see letters randomly placed in a complex visual scene of everyday life. For example, we expect to see letters on signs as we are driving, but they generally do not appear randomly around us. In addition, the colors of objects in a visual scene do not generally change as we are experiencing it. Thus, despite the high level of internal validity in this experiment provided by the controls for confounding variables, the external validity may not be high enough to conclude that color does not affect detection of objects in a visual scene experienced in everyday life. However, to provide a good test of the causal effect of color on object detection, the controls used in this experiment are necessary, and external validity must sometimes be sacrificed to provide good causal tests. (See Chapter 4 for more discussion of the trade-off of internal and external validities.)

Biological Example

Biological psychology (also called neuropsychology if it involves brain function) investigates the role of biological factors in behavior. Thus, experiments are often employed in this area of psychology to determine causal relationships between biology and behavior. In many cases, participants are asked to perform different tasks while brain function that corresponds to these tasks is recorded to better understand where brain activity occurs for different behaviors. In other types of studies, brain function in animals is manipulated to observe the causal effect of the manipulation on a behavior of interest. In other words, the brain (or other biological) activity can be either the dependent variable or the independent variable in the experiment.

Lui and Rosenfeld (2008) conducted a study of the former type. They were interested in the brain activity that occurs when people lie about a crime they have committed. They conducted an experiment with three groups of participants. One group was asked to perform a mock crime that involved pretending to steal two of five items. The second group was asked to perform a mock crime that involved pretending to steal three of the five items. The third group was the control group and was not asked to perform the mock crime but was presented with the five items. All participants had their brain activity recorded during a session before the crime where they were asked to provide truthful answers to the question "Have you stolen this?" when the items were presented on a computer screen. The "truth" session provided baseline truth recordings. After the crime sessions, all participants were asked to answer the question again for items presented on the screen, but the two crime groups were asked to lie about whether they had stolen the items. "Stolen" items and irrelevant items were included in the "lie" session. Brain activity was recorded during the "lie" session for all participants. A comparison of brain activity in the "truth" and "lie" sessions allowed the researchers to determine if different brain activity occurs when participants are lying.

Several controls for confounding (i.e., extraneous) variables were included in the experiment. All participants were presented the five items before the experiment to make sure that all groups were equally familiar with the items. Practice trials were also included in the sessions to make sure that participants were performing the task correctly before brain activity was recorded.

The results of the study showed that the brain activity that occurred during the "lie" session for the crime group that pretended to steal two items differed for the items that they pretended to steal during the crime session and irrelevant items that they did not pretend to steal. In other words, brain activity was different when participants in this group were lying. The researchers were able to identify 12 of the 14 participants in this group based on brain activity alone. However, participants in the crime group that pretended to steal three items did not show a difference in brain activity for "stolen" items and irrelevant items in the "lie" session. The researchers concluded that in this group, the majority of the items were stolen, which may have caused the participants to pay less attention to the "stolen" items when they were presented. Finally, the control group showed no differences in brain activity for items during the "lie" session, as expected. The researchers concluded that recording of brain activity can help detect when people are lying in some situations.

As in the previous example, although internal validity for this study was high, one might argue that the task the participants were asked to perform is not very realistic. Participants may not have been as motivated to lie about stealing the items in the study situation as they would have been if they had actually stolen them. They also may not have had as much anxiety in the study as they would have had after committing an actual crime. Thus, despite designing a study that provided good causal information about the link between brain activity and lying, the study's results may not generalize to situations in which an actual crime had been committed. This study provides another good illustration of how internal and external validity can trade off in psychological studies. With more internal validity, some external validity may need to be sacrificed within the study.

Another consideration for this experiment is exactly what the researchers are learning about brain activity and lying. Studies that show that certain brain areas are active during particular tasks or behaviors must be interpreted with caution. Just because a brain area was active while the participants in this study were lying, does not necessarily mean that this brain activity always occurs when people are lying (e.g., there may be individual differences in lying experiences that can result in different brain activity for some individuals) or that this brain activity indicates that someone is lying (e.g., it may mean they are just thinking about lying). In other words, one should consider other possible explanations for the results when one interprets the findings of psychological studies. In fact, Lui and Rosenfeld (2008) pointed out some of these limitations of their method when interpreting the results of their experiment.

Social Example

Experiments in social psychology have been described in the other chapters of this text. In Chapter 3, the implicit association test (IAT) was described as an example of systematic observation where word associations are manipulated and the participants' speed at reacting to the words is measured (see Figure 3.2). In Chapter 5, the Zimbardo (1973) experiment, where a randomly assigned role as a prisoner or guard in a mock prison affected participants' behavior, was described as an example of a study that may have violated ethical standards. Thus, if you have read these chapters, you have already encountered some examples of the use of experiments in social psychology. The example presented in this chapter will elaborate on the IAT procedure with an experiment that used this procedure to test the unconscious biases of participants.

Recall from Chapter 3 (see Figure 3.2) that the IAT procedure measures reaction times of participants when they make judgments for combinations of concepts with the same key press (e.g., press the right key when you see items that are female and items that a firefighter might use; press the left key when you see items that are male and items that a teacher might use). Longer reaction times to uncommon associations (e.g., female and firefighter) indicate implicit biases (e.g., against female firefighters) that the participant may have.

Ahern and Hetherington (2006) used the IAT to evaluate implicit attitudes toward the concepts of "thin" and "fat." Pictures of individuals were presented to represent thin and fat concepts. Words were presented to represent positive and negative concepts. Participants first completed trials associating a specific key with a concept (e.g., thin—right key, fat—left key; positive—right key, negative—left key). After the key association trials, the participants were given blocks of test association trials, where each concept pair (i.e., thin-positive, fat-negative or thin-negative, fat-positive) was presented with the same key. Thus, the independent variable was the concept pairing (match with stereotype, such as thin-positive, or mismatch with stereotype, such as fat-positive). A comparison of the different test association trial reaction times indicated the implicit bias of the participants. For example, if participants are faster for the thin-positive, fat-negative block than the other concept pairing block, then this indicates that they have an implicit bias toward thin as positive and fat as negative.

The blocks of test association trials for each concept pairing were counterbalanced in this within-subjects experiment to control for order effects of the presentation of the concept pairings. In other words, half of the participants completed the thin-positive, fat-negative pairing block first, and the other half of the participants completed the thin-negative, fat-positive pairing block first. In addition, the pictures used were as similar as possible for pose of the individual pictured, clothing worn by the individual pictured, activity being performed in the photo by the individual pictured, and emotional expression of the individual pictured.

Figure 11.3 illustrates the IAT results of the experiment. The analyses indicated that reaction time was faster for the thin-positive, fat-negative concept pairing than for the reverse pairing. This result indicates that overall, the participants showed a negative bias toward the concept of fat and a positive bias toward the concept of thin, with a large majority of the participants having this bias (86%). The researchers did not find any evidence that the IAT scores correlated with any explicit measure they collected, including body dissatisfaction and body mass index (a measure of weight as a proportion of height). Thus, the researchers concluded that the positive bias toward thin and the negative bias toward fat is very strong in the population tested.

Developmental Example

Whereas many studies in developmental psychology are quasi-experiments because of the inclusion of age as a subject variable (see Chapters 12 and 13 for further discussion), some developmental psychologists are also interested in exploring how causal relationships change across age groups. Thus, some researchers conduct experiments that contain a true independent variable and age as a subject variable.

Figure 11.3   **Results of the Ahern and Hetherington (2006) Implicit Association Test (IAT) Experiment**

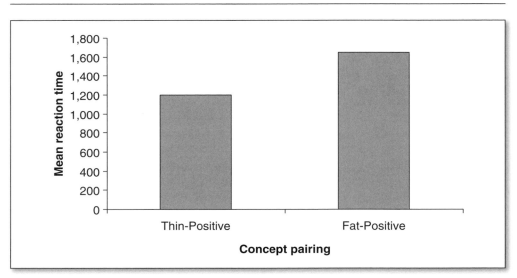

An example of this type of study was conducted by Hund and Plumert (2003). These researchers were interested in how memory for the location of objects is influenced by the similarity of objects and whether this relationship is the same for different age groups. They tested 7-, 9-, and 11-year-olds and adults in an experiment that manipulated the similarity of target objects. The participants in the experiment were asked to learn the location of objects in a model house. The objects were placed on dots in different sections of the house to help the participants learn the locations. Then the dots were removed, and the participants were asked to place the objects in the locations they remembered the experimenter placing them during the learning phase of the experiment. Half of the participants in each age group were shown objects in the same category (e.g., vehicles) placed in the same section of the house (i.e., location was related to object similarity). The other half of the participants in each age group were shown objects that were randomly placed in different sections of the house (i.e., location was not related to object similarity). Location errors (i.e., how far the participant placed the objects from their original positions) were recorded for the two object-type groups.

The researchers randomly assigned the participants to object-type groups to control possible group differences. The objects were also placed in the house in a random order to control for possible order effects in the placement of the objects.

The results of the study indicated that although older participants made fewer errors, participants in all age groups placed related objects closer together (i.e., had greater location error) than unrelated objects. This difference across object-type groups was present for all age groups, indicating that location memory relies on the similarity of objects for individuals from age 7 years through adulthood. In other words, "information about what objects are influences memory for where objects are located." (Hund & Plumert, 2003, p. 946). However, remember that age is a subject (or quasi-independent—see Chapter 12 for more discussion) variable that was not manipulated. Thus, any differences found for age groups (e.g., fewer errors for older participants) cannot be fully interpreted as a causal effect because of the absence of a manipulation for this variable. This limitation exists for all developmental designs that compare age groups as a subject variable, even if another manipulated variable is included in the design, as in the Hund and Plumert experiment.

FACTORIAL DESIGNS

Many of the experimental examples we have discussed in this and other chapters of the text involve a single independent variable, where the goal of the experiment is to compare the observations for the different levels of the independent variable. However, many

Factorial Design: an experiment or quasi-experiment that includes more than one independent variable

experiments conducted by researchers are **factorial designs**, meaning they contain more then one independent variable. The primary advantages of a factorial design over simpler experiments is that a researcher can be more efficient in testing the effects of multiple independent variables in one experiment and can also examine the effects of the

---------- ❧ ----------

Levels of the Independent Variable: different situations or conditions that participants experience in an experiment because of the manipulation of the independent variable

Main Effect: test of the differences between all means for each level of an independent variable in an ANOVA

Analysis of Variance (ANOVA): analysis of variance test used for designs with three or more sample means

Interaction Effect: tests the effect of one independent variable at each level of another independent variable(s) in an ANOVA

interactions of those independent variables on the dependent variable. Thus, many experiments conducted by psychologists are factorial designs.

In factorial designs, the comparison of means for the **levels of one independent variable** is the test of the **main effect** of that independent variable (see Chapter 3 for more discussion of levels of an independent variable). In other words, the main effects will indicate the independent causal effect of each independent variable in a factorial design. The main effect is one type of effect tested in an **analysis of variance (ANOVA)**, which is the type of statistical analysis used most often for a factorial experiment (see Chapter 14 for further discussion of ANOVA). The other type of effect tested in an ANOVA is an **interaction effect**. The interaction effect tests the effect of one independent variable for each level of another independent variable to determine how the independent variables *interact* to affect the dependent variable. Thus, a test for an interaction effect compares the differences of the levels of one independent variable across the levels of another independent variable.

To make the concept of an interaction more concrete, consider the factorial design in Figure 11.4. This design contains two independent variables, IVA and IVB, each with two levels. The columns indicate levels of IVA, and the rows indicate levels of IVB. The cells indicate the conditions created by combining the levels of the two independent variables. To

Figure 11.4   **Diagram of a General Factorial Design With Two Independent Variables (IV), Each With Two Levels**

determine the overall means for a level of an independent variable (i.e., the means compared in a main effect), the researcher can average the means for the cells in the columns and the rows. Main effects are determined by comparing the level means for each independent variable (i.e., comparing means for the rows and comparing means for the columns). To examine the interaction effect, the researcher must consider the differences between rows or columns. For example, one way to look at an interaction effect would be to consider the difference between $A1B1$ and $A1B2$ and compare it with the difference between $A2B1$ and $A2B2$. If those differences are not similar, then there is an interaction effect. In other words, the effect of IVB depends on whether you are looking at the $A1$ level or the $A2$ level of IVA.

It may take some time to understand interactions, so we will consider an example to further illustrate the concept. Suppose that the design illustrated in Figure 11.4 corresponds to independent variables of mode of study presentation (IVA) and mode of test (IVB) in a memory experiment. Figure 11.5 presents the variables and the levels of each variable, as well as the conditions created by the combination of these levels. In addition, means for each level of the independent variables and conditions are included. To determine main effects for study presentation mode, the condition means for each of the conditions that involve visual study would be averaged and compared with the average of the condition

Figure 11.5   **Diagram of a Specific Factorial Design With Two Independent Variables, Each With Two Levels**

NOTE: M stands for mean.

means that involve auditory study (i.e., column averages). In other words, the main effect of study mode would involve a comparison of 62.5 (for visual) and 67.5 (for auditory). This procedure would be similarly followed to determine if there is a main effect of mode of test by averaging the means for the conditions in each row. The main effect for test mode would involve a comparison of 67.5 (visual) and 62.5 (for auditory). There are several ways by which the means for the conditions may create an interaction between mode of study presentation and mode of test. Often, creating a graph of the condition means will illustrate an interaction best. If the lines in a bar graph are not parallel, then this may indicate an interaction between the independent variables (the effect also needs to be confirmed by inferential statistics—see Chapters 7 and 14 for more discussion). The most likely scenario for this experiment is that when study mode and test mode match, memory is best. Thus, the independent variables are most likely to interact according to Panel 1 in Figure 11.6, and this graph illustrates the interaction shown in the condition means in Figure 11.5. You can see in this graph that the mean memory score is highest for the visual study and visual test condition and for the auditory study and auditory test condition. Memory scores are lower when the study and test modes do not match.

Another way these independent variables might interact is with similar memory scores for visual study regardless of test mode but different memory scores for auditory study depending on test mode. Panel 2 in Figure 11.6 illustrates this scenario. The reverse scenario could also occur with similar scores for auditory study conditions but different scores for visual study conditions depending on test mode. Finally, these independent variables could interact such that the memory scores are different for the two test modes at both levels of study mode. Panel 3 in Figure 11.6 illustrates this possibility. Each of these outcomes represents an interaction effect between study and test mode variables. Graphs are useful in determining the type of interaction that occurred and should be followed up with additional statistical tests to determine exactly where the differences between the conditions in the interaction are in order to best describe the interaction effect. The follow-up statistical tests are called **simple effects tests**. These tests are described further in Chapter 14.

Interactions between independent variables can reveal interesting effects of the variables beyond what is seen in the main effects of each variable. For example, in the results shown in Panel 1 of Figure 11.6, there would be no main effects of the independent variables (if you average the two means for visual study and for auditory study, you get similar values; if you average the two means for visual test and for auditory test, you get similar values), but there is a clear interaction of these variables. If study mode had been the only independent variable included in the experiment with a visual test, the results may have led the researchers to conclude that presenting study information visually will provide for better memory of the information later. However, this would be an incomplete picture of how memory works. The addition of the test mode independent variable to the experiment provides a lot more information than either the study mode or test mode variables provide in a single independent variable experiment. Thus, factorial experiments can provide researchers with much more information about behavior.

⚜

Simple Effects Tests: statistical tests conducted to characterize an interaction effect when one is found in an ANOVA

Figure 11.6   Examples of Different Types of Interaction Effects

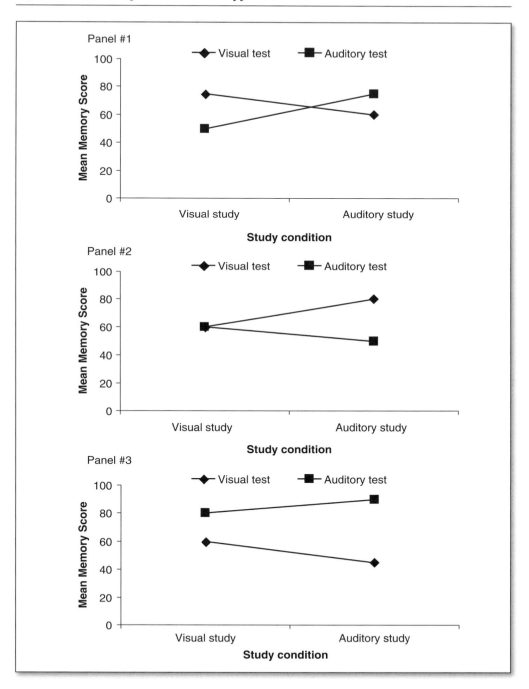

Another example may help illustrate the concept of an interaction further. Suppose that you work for a company that makes ice cream. Your boss has tasked you with the job of finding out if two proposed changes will affect ice cream sales by conducting an experiment to test the effects of these changes on consumer preferences. One proposal is to add more chocolate chips to the chocolate chip flavor of the ice cream. The other proposal is to use real vanilla in all the ice cream flavors (currently, the company uses artificial vanilla flavoring). Both proposals will cost the company money, so they want you to determine if either proposal will increase consumer preference for the ice cream to decide if these additions are worthwhile. Thus, your experiment will include two independent variables: Chocolate chip ice cream with (1) type of vanilla (artificial or real) manipulated and (2) amount of chips manipulated (current amount or 30% more chips). Figure 11.7 illustrates this design. You collect ratings of the ice cream from a group of 100 consumers, each of whom rates each type of ice cream on a scale of 1 to 7 for desire to purchase the ice cream. In other words, your design is a within-subjects design, as all participants will rate all the ice cream conditions (in different counterbalanced orders).

Figure 11.8 includes hypothetical mean ratings for each ice cream condition. Marginal means are also included for each level of the two independent variables. Looking at the marginal means, it appears as though the two independent variables

Figure 11.7 Diagram of the Ice Cream Experiment Design

NOTE: IV stands for independent variable.

Figure 11.8   Hypothetical Means for the Ice Cream Experiment

Type of vanilla : Amount of chips:	Artificial	Real	
Current	3	3	3
30% More	3	6	4.5
	3	4.5	

each independently affected the participants' ratings. For type of vanilla, the real vanilla received a mean rating of 4.5, whereas the artificial vanilla received a rating of only 3. The amount of chips variable shows similar results: Participants gave higher ratings to the ice cream with 30% more chips ($M = 4.5$, where M is the mean) than with the current level of chips ($M = 3.0$). Thus, if you just looked at the main effects, you might be tempted to recommend that your company implement both the proposals for all flavors of ice cream. However, looking at the condition means indicates something different. All the condition means show a rating of 3.0 for the ice cream, except in the real vanilla/30% more chips condition, where the mean rating was much higher than the other conditions ($M = 6.0$). In other words, the two variables interacted in such a way that this single condition seemed to result in the most preferred type of ice cream. Changing from artificial to real vanilla did not affect the ratings if the amount of chips stayed the same. Likewise, adding 30% more chips did not affect ratings if artificial vanilla was used. Only the combination of real vanilla and 30% more chips resulted in high ratings for the ice cream. This description of the interaction of the two independent variables provides the clearest picture of the results. Based on the interaction shown in the conditions means, your recommendation should be to only implement both proposals together for the chocolate chip ice cream (at least until more flavors can be tested to determine how these factors affect other flavors). This example illustrates the importance of interactions in factorial designs.

CHAPTER SUMMARY

Reconsider the questions from the beginning of the chapter:

- What aspects of an experiment make it different from other research designs? Experiments contain an independent variable that is manipulated and allows for control of alternative explanations of the results. Thus, experiments are the best research design for testing causal relationships.
- What aspects of experiments allow for greater internal validity than other research designs? The manipulation of a variable (independent variable) and the additional controls for confounding variables allow for greater internal validity in experiments than other types of research design.
- What are the different ways that independent variables can be manipulated to allow comparisons of conditions? Independent variables can be manipulated by type of something, amount of something, or the presence/absence of something (see Chapter 4 for more discussion of this aspect of independent variables). They can also be manipulated between subjects, where each participant receives only one level of the independent variable, or within subjects, where each participant receives all levels of the independent variable.
- What is an interaction between independent variables? An interaction can occur between independent variables such that the effect of one independent variable depends on which level of the other independent variable one is looking at. For example, an independent variable can show a difference between levels for Level 1 of another independent variable but show no difference between levels for Level 2 of the other independent variable.

THINKING ABOUT RESEARCH

A summary of a research study in psychology is given below. As you read the summary, think about the following questions:

1. What aspects of these studies allow us to define them as experiments?
2. Consider the designs of the two experiments. What is the independent variable in Experiment 1? What are the levels of the independent variable? How does the design change in Experiment 2?
3. Were the independent variables in these experiments manipulated between subjects or within subjects? How do you know?
4. Do the results shown in Figure 11.9 indicate an interaction effect? Explain your answer.

Study Reference

Lakin, J. L., Chartrand, T. L., & Arkin, R. M. (2008). I am too just like you: Nonconscious mimicry as an automatic behavioral response to social exclusion. *Psychological Science, 19,* 816–822.

Purpose of the Study. How do people behave after they have been excluded from a social group? The authors conducted two experiments to answer this question. For Experiment 1, they hypothesized that one thing people do after they have been excluded is to unconsciously mimic

Figure 11.9   Mean Proportion Mimicking Time by Exclusion Group and Type of Confederate

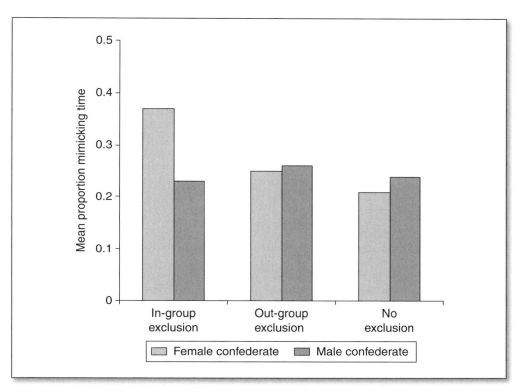

SOURCE: Based on results from Lakin, Chartrand, and Arkin's (2008) study.

others to increase social interactions in a low-cost, low-risk manner. For Experiment 2, they hypothesized that people will specifically mimic those who are part of the group that excluded them and that this mimicry is based on a need to belong.

Experiment 1

Method of the Study. There were 40 participants in Experiment 1. The participants played a Cyberball game online that involved receiving the ball at different points during the game. The game was computer controlled, but participants were led to believe that they were playing with other participants in the experiment. The participants were assigned to either an inclusion or an exclusion condition. Those in the inclusion condition received the ball as often as other players during the game. Those in the exclusion condition received the ball only a few times at the beginning of the game. Mimicry was tested after the game through interaction with an experimental confederate. The participant was asked to describe photos to the confederate. The confederate moved his or her foot during the photo-description task, and the participant's foot-moving behavior was videotaped during the task to look for mimicry of this behavior. The participants' foot-moving behavior was also videotaped during the time when they were alone before the confederate came into the room to determine how often the participants moved their feet before the foot-moving behavior was modeled by the confederate. Participants who consciously noticed the confederate's foot-moving behavior (as determined by a postexperiment questionnaire) were removed from the experiment ($n = 4$).

Results of the Study. Two experimenters coded the videos for number of seconds the participants moved their feet during the time they were alone (baseline) and the time they interacted with the confederate to determine a proportion of time they moved their feet during each time period. Effects of baseline foot movements were removed from the analysis when the comparison of the inclusion and exclusion conditions was made. The comparison of exclusion and inclusion conditions indicated that the participants in the exclusion condition ($M = .28$) mimicked the confederate for a longer time than the participants in the inclusion condition ($M = .17$), indicating that excluded individuals will unconsciously mimic others.

Experiment 2

Method of the Study. Experiment 2 included 164 female students. Participants in Experiment 2 played the Cyberball game described in Experiment 1. However, three conditions were included: (1) excluded by in-group (other female players), (2) excluded by out-group (excluded by male players), and (3) no exclusion (these participants did not play the Cyberball game—they completed a questionnaire during this portion of the experiment instead). All participants completed the interaction with the confederate in the second portion of the experiment. Half of the participants in each condition interacted with a female confederate (in-group confederate), and half of them interacted with a male confederate (out-group confederate). Participants who played the Cyberball game also completed a questionnaire asking how much they felt they belonged to the group when they played the game.

Results of the Study. Mean proportion mimicking time is shown in Figure 11.9 for each of the conditions. As illustrated in the figure, participants in the in-group exclusion condition mimicked more than those in the other conditions but only when the confederate was a member of the in-group (i.e., female). In addition, a further analysis showed that belongingness ratings were related to mimicry time only for participants in the in-group exclusion/in-group confederate condition.

Conclusions of the Study. The results from the two experiments supported the authors' hypotheses. Specifically, Experiment 1 showed that excluded individuals will unconsciously mimic another person, and Experiment 2 showed that this mimicry was most likely to occur when individuals encounter someone who is a member of the group that excluded them. Experiment 2 also showed that this mimicry was related to a need for belonging. The authors concluded that unconscious mimicry may fill a need in excluded individuals without expending cognitive resources or risking further rejection.

COMMON PITFALLS AND HOW TO AVOID THEM

Problem: Interpretation of causal results—not considering other possible explanations of results

Solution: Even in experiments where independent variables are manipulated, one must consider other possible explanations for the results, as it can be difficult to rule out all possible confounding variables in a single experiment.

Problem: Identifying true independent variables—the difference between true independent variables and subject variables can be confusing.

Solution: If the design is a between-subjects design, determine if the participants were randomly assigned to groups. If they were not, then the variable is probably a subject variable. Consider if the variable can be manipulated. Subject variables are often variables that cannot be manipulated. If the design is a within-subjects design, the variable is likely a true independent variable.

Problem: Identifying interactions—interactions can be difficult to identify and describe.

Solution: It is often helpful to create a graph of the condition means of a factorial design to determine if an interaction is present. If a line graph is created, an interaction can be seen in nonparallel lines.

Problem: Identifying the design of an experiment—independent and dependent variables can be difficult to identify.

Solution: It is often helpful to examine graphs or tables within a journal article to identify the design of an experiment. The dependent variable is typically identified from table captions or labels along *y*-axis. The independent variables are typically identified from table captions, legends in a figure, or labels along the *x*-axis.

TEST YOURSELF

1. What aspects of an experiment allow tests of causal relationships?

2. For each experimental description below, indicate which conditions an individual participant will receive (assume each independent variable (IV) has two levels):
   (a) IVA—within subjects
   (b) IVA—within subjects, IVB—within subjects
   (c) IVA—between subjects, IVB—between subjects
   (d) IVA—between subjects, IVB—within subjects

3. For the table of condition means below (means are mood scores), indicate which effects (main effect of type of therapy, main effect of length of therapy, interaction between type and length of therapy) are likely to be present. If an effect is present, indicate which levels or conditions were higher.

Therapy type:	Talk	Drug
Therapy length: 4 weeks	60	75
12 weeks	90	75

4. Create a graph of the results in (3). Be sure to correctly label the axes of your graph.

5. What is the advantage of using a Latin Square over full counterbalancing when counterbalancing the order of conditions in a within-subjects design? How many orders are used in a Latin Square?

6. Reread the example experiment about our dog Daphne presented at the beginning of the chapter to answer the following questions:

    (a) What is the independent variable, and what are the levels of this variable in the experiment?

    (b) Was the independent variable manipulated between subjects or within subjects?

    (c) What controls for confounding variables are described for this experiment?

    (d) If a researcher were interested in testing the effectiveness of the "treatments" for the population of all dogs, how would such an experiment be done?

7. Identify the independent and dependent variables included in the studies described in the Experiment Examples section and listed below. For any independent variable(s), also state the levels of the independent variable.

    (a) Ehinger and Brockmole (2008)

    (b) Lui and Rosenfeld (2008)

    (c) Ahern and Hetherington (2006)

    (d) Hund and Plumert (2003)

Answers: 1. Manipulation of an independent variable and control of extraneous variables. 2a. both levels of IVA, 2b. all four conditions (*A1B1*, *A1B2*, *A2B1*, and *A2B2*), 2c. only one of the four conditions (*A1B1* or *A1B2* or *A2B1* or *A2B2*), 2d. each with two conditions: either *A1B1* and *A1B2* or *A2B1* and *A2B2*. 3. No main effect of therapy type (each column has a mean of 75), main effect of therapy length (row means of 67.5 for 4 weeks vs. 82.5 for 12 weeks—longer has higher score), and interaction effect such that drug therapy has higher score for 4-week length, but talk therapy has higher score for 12-week length. 4. Latin Square will allow fewer orders to be used than a full counterbalancing—useful for designs with more than three conditions—number of orders = number of conditions. 5. See following example graph.

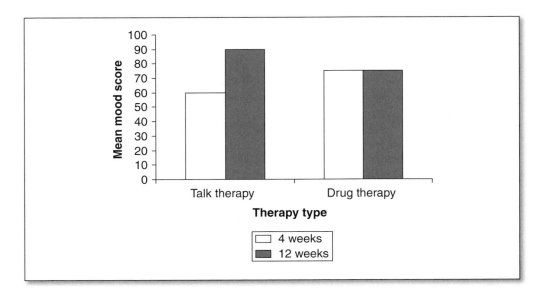

6a. The independent variable is the "treatment" for separation anxiety with levels of chew toy, our used objects, and confinement. 6b. Within subjects. 6c. Each "treatment" was used five times to control for length of time away and other possible variables that might change with our times away from home; the "treatment" orders were counterbalanced to control for order effects. 6d. This experiment would likely be done by choosing a sample of dogs that represent the population (see Chapter 6 for information about sampling techniques) and randomly assigning a portion of the sample to each of the treatments (e.g., 25 dogs to each treatment group). Confounding variables as described for the scenario in the chapter would be controlled for each treatment group (e.g., test all dogs for same length of visit away in same environment and at same time of day). This experiment would use a between-subjects design. The dependent variable could be measured in the same manner as the chapter scenario with the operational definition specified. 7a. independent variable = color condition; levels = color changed from original color of object with consistent colors across repeated scenes, color changed from original color of object with inconsistent colors across repeated scenes, original color of object with no color changes (control condition); dependent variable = time to find the inserted object. 7b. Independent Variable 1 = session; levels = "truth" session, "lie" session; Independent Variable 2 = lying condition during "lie" session; levels = mock crime with two items stolen, mock crime with three items stolen, no mock crime (control condition); dependent variable = brain activity during the sessions. 7c. Independent Variable 1 = concept; levels = fat, thin; Independent Variable 2 = concept pairing; levels = match (e.g., fat-negative), mismatch (e.g., fat-positive); dependent variable = reaction time for key press. 7d. independent variable = object locations; levels = organized by category, random organization; subject variable = age group with levels = 7-, 9-, and 11-year-olds and adults; dependent variable = location errors (difference between location object is placed in during the test phase and the object's original location in the study phase).

The Nuts and Bolts of Quasi-Experiments

CONSIDER THE FOLLOWING QUESTIONS AS YOU READ CHAPTER 12

- What aspects of a quasi-experiment make it different from other research designs?
- What is required to test causal relationships between variables?
- What is a pretest-posttest design? In what way is it a quasi-experiment?
- What is a time series design? In what way is it a quasi-experiment?

Consider a recent study that examined the claim that females are more social than males. The study, conducted by Benenson et al. (2009, Study 1), examined roommate satisfaction among 30 male and 30 female college students. All the students in the study reported having had one roommate at the time of the study. Half of the participants of each gender were having a current conflict with their roommate, and the other half for each gender reported planning to live with their current roommate for the rest of the current school year. All participants completed a questionnaire about their roommate. The authors reasoned that same-sex tolerance (e.g., being satisfied with a roommate who was the same gender as the participant) was related to the level of sociability of the participants. In other words, if females are more sociable, then they should show higher ratings of their roommate than males, indicating greater tolerance of same-sex, nonfamilial relationships. Contrary to the idea that females are more sociable and tolerant of same-sex friendships, results indicated that in both groups (conflict-with-roommate group and planning-to-continue-living-with-roommate group), more than twice as many males were satisfied with their roommate than females. From these results, the researchers concluded that males are more tolerant of same-sex friends than females are. However, the researchers could not conclude that the sex of the participants caused them to be more tolerant. This conclusion would have required that the researchers randomly assign participants to be male or female, and this is obviously not possible, as it would require the researcher choosing by chance who would be male and who would be female. Thus, the researchers are limited in the causal information they can gain from this study, because the

—— �֍ ——

Quasi-Experiment: a type of research design where a comparison is made, as in an experiment, but no random assignment of participants to groups occurs

—— ✥ ——

Random Assignment: participants are randomly assigned to levels of the independent variable in an experiment to control for individual differences as an extraneous variable

study is a **quasi-experiment** that does not contain a manipulated independent variable (see Chapters 4 and 11 for more discussion of independent variables and tests of causal relationships).

In other chapters of this text, many examples of quasi-experiments have been described, because this research design type allows for the comparison of groups that are typically of interest to psychologists. For example, gender, age, whether one smokes or not, handedness, and year in school are all quasi-independent variables that cannot be manipulated as true independent variables. Other variables, such as whether someone has experienced a divorce, an illness, or abuse, cannot ethically be manipulated. Thus, to investigate these variables, a researcher often conducts a quasi-experiment, where groups of participants can be compared on a behavior of interest, as in an experiment, but the quasi-independent variable is not manipulated, which leaves the study open to other possible explanations of the results. In other words, groups that have not been randomly assigned can be compared in a quasi-experiment, but one cannot gain strong causal information, because of the lack of **random assignment**.

A recent example of a quasi-experiment will illustrate some of the issues in this research design type. Benenson and Koulnazarian (2008) conducted a quasi-experiment to investigate at what age gender differences appear in help-seeking behaviors. Previous studies with adults and adolescents had shown that women tend to seek help from others more often than men. However, it is unclear how these gender differences develop. These researchers sought to determine if girls ask for help more often than boys at young ages (3 years and 6 years of age). In addition, children were grouped by socioeconomic status to examine differences between low and upper-middle socioeconomic status children. The children in the study were asked to complete a series of tasks (e.g., drawing objects), and the time they spent on the task before they asked for help was recorded. Overall, girls asked for help after a shorter time with the task than boys. In addition, younger children requested help faster than older children. Finally, children from the low socioeconomic status group requested help faster than the children from the upper-middle socioeconomic status group. Benenson and Koulnazarian concluded that gender differences in helping behavior may not be due to learned gender roles, because in children as young as 3 years old, girls requested help more quickly than boys. This study illustrates a basic quasi-experimental research design with three factors compared in the study: age, gender, and socioeconomic status. Each of these factors was used to group participants according to characteristics they had at the start of the study. None of these factors could be manipulated as independent variables (e.g., a researcher could not randomly assign participants to different age groups). Thus, the researchers cannot conclude that any of these factors *caused* the group differences found. It is possible that additional variables that vary with these factors (e.g., quality of education may differ with socioeconomic status, different parental attitudes may depend on socioeconomic status) contributed to the observed relationship between the factor and the help-seeking behavior measured. Figure 12.1 shows where in the research process the researcher must consider whether to implement a quasi-experiment.

Figure 12.1   Steps in the Research Process: Designing the Study

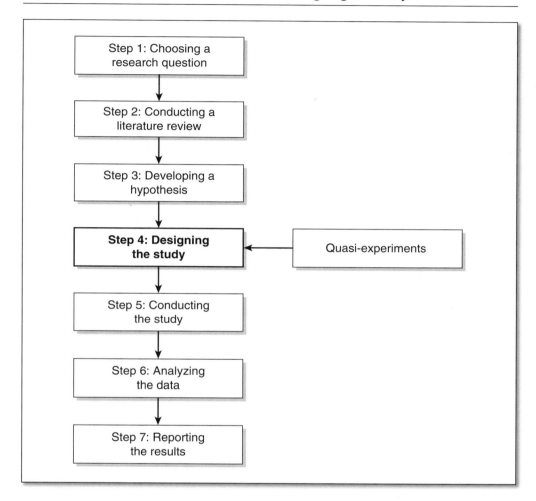

TYPES OF QUASI-EXPERIMENTS

The type of quasi-experiment illustrated by the preceding example is the simplest form of a quasi-experiment. It is in all other ways like an experiment, but the random assignment of participants to groups is lacking. In fact, Shadish et al. (2002) offer lack of random assignment as the definition of a quasi-experiment. While this definition holds for the designs that psychologists consider quasi-experiments, there are some specific types of quasi-experiments that are used in psychological research. In this chapter, we will consider two general types of quasi-experiments and the more specific forms each design type may take, depending on the goals of the researchers and the restrictions of the situation or behavior they wish to study.

Pretest-Posttest Designs

In the simplest type of **pretest-posttest design,** a behavior is measured twice: once before a treatment or condition is implemented (the pretest) and once after it has been implemented (the posttest). This design is a quasi-experiment because there is no random assignment of participants to the treatment. In this case, all the participants get the treatment. The researcher compares the scores from the pretest and the posttest, looking for a change based on the treatment or condition occurring between the two measurements. However, if a change occurs in this design, the researcher cannot automatically conclude that the treatment or condition caused the change because

Pretest-Posttest Design: a type of research design (often a quasi-experiment) where behavior is measured both before and after a treatment or condition is implemented

other factors (besides the treatment or condition) may have occurred as well between the two measurements. Consider a hypothetical study testing the effectiveness of a smoking-cessation program. It would be unethical to randomly assign some participants to smoke in order to conduct an experiment for this study because this would force participants to endure something harmful. Thus, a pretest-postest quasi-experiment would be a more appropriate design for testing the program's effectiveness. The study could be designed such that at pretest, participants report the number of cigarettes they smoked that week. They then take part in the program. After the program concludes, each participant again reports the number of cigarettes he or she smoked that week.

Suppose the number of cigarettes smoked goes down from pretest to posttest. Can the researcher conclude that the smoking-cessation program worked? Why not? What other possible explanations are there for the decline in smoking? There are several possible alternative explanations in this case. For example, suppose a study was reported in the media during the time between measurements that concluded that smoking has extremely harmful effects (i.e., a **history effect** biased the results—see Chapter 4 for more discussion of history effects as a source of bias). That may have caused the participants to be more motivated to quit, and they reduced the number of cigarettes smoked due to their new motivation. Another possibility is that a new law was passed to ban smoking in public places (another history effect). This is becoming more frequent as cities and states in the United States and cities and countries in Europe are passing such bans. The smoking rates may have

History Effect: events that occur during the course of a study to all or individual participants that can result in bias

declined because of the ban. There are many other possibilities for the results in this study that are plausible alternatives to the conclusion that the smoking-cessation program is the cause of the smoking decline.

Researchers can attempt to deal with some of the alternative explanations in pretest-posttest designs by including a control group. If participants are randomly assigned to the control group and the treatment group, the study becomes an experiment. However, in many situations random assignment to groups may not be possible. Without random assignment, the study is still a quasi-experiment, where it is difficult to rule out alternative explanations of the results. This design is a pretest-posttest design with **nonequivalent groups**, because group differences that might account for the results are not controlled by random assignment to groups. In this design, the researcher considers the difference between the pretest and posttest scores across the control and experimental groups. Was there a difference (larger or smaller) for the experimental group than the treatment group? If so, the treatment or condition received by the experimental group may

Nonequivalent Groups: groups compared in a study where participants are not randomly assigned

have caused this difference. However, group differences may also have caused this difference. Without random assignment to groups, it may be difficult to determine the cause. However, this design may be useful when random assignment is not possible.

Doherty and Hilberg (2007) conducted a pretest-posttest design with nonequivalent groups to examine the effect of an effective teaching standards model (e.g., discussion of topics being learned between students and teachers) on student achievement in primarily low-income elementary school students. Two elementary schools were compared: one school at which the standards for effective instruction developed by Tharp, Estrada, Dalton, and Yamauchi (2000) were being practiced and one school at which the standards were not being practiced. Standardized test scores for the children at the two schools were collected and compared at the beginning of the school year (pretest) and the end of the school year (posttest). The results showed that as teachers at the standards school used the standards to a greater extent in their teaching, language-arts scores showed a greater difference between the schools, with the "standards school" showing higher scores. The study involved students at two schools, where a difference in teaching technique existed between the schools and between individual instructors at the start of the study. In other words, children were not randomly assigned to teachers using the standards and teachers not using the standards. Thus, this study used a quasi-experimental design with a pretest-posttest method with nonequivalent groups.

One issue to consider for this type of study is that schools with low-scoring students are more likely to receive funding for standards studies such as the one described here. Thus, the standardized test scores that increased for students at the standards school may show **regression toward the mean** (see Chapter 4 for more discussion of this and other sources of bias relevant to quasi-experiments). In other words, a high score achieved at posttest may be an extreme score in some cases, and with additional testing, these students may score closer to their original mean (which is typically lower than the norm). Pretest-posttest designs are susceptible to bias due to regression toward the

Regression Toward the Mean: can occur when participants score higher or lower than their personal average—the next time they are tested, they are more likely to score near their personal average, making scores unreliable

mean because one extreme score (high or low) can skew the change in scores between the pretests and posttests. This source of bias should be considered when results from these types of studies are interpreted.

Shadish et al. (2002) recommend several variations to the pretest-posttest design with nonequivalent groups to allow researchers to rule out some possible alternative explanations of group differences. For example, one way to reduce the likelihood of extraneous effects on the pretest-posttest score difference is to include two pretests. If results show a similar pretest-posttest difference across the control and experimental groups, it will be unclear why this result occurred. The treatment may have caused the difference in the experimental group, whereas another factor (e.g., group characteristics that are different from the experimental group) caused the effect in the control group. Using two pretests will help the researcher understand these results. If both groups take Pretest 1 and Pretest 2 with a time delay between them, the researcher can compare the groups for baseline differences across the groups. Then Pretest 2 scores can be compared with Posttest scores (with the same time delay used as was used for the delay between Pretest 1 and Pretest 2) to see if the difference for each group is similar to the Pretest 1 and Pretest 2 score difference. This will clarify the control and experimental comparison.

Another suggestion by Shadish et al. (2002) is to allow both groups to be the experimental and control groups in alternating order. In other words, there are two posttests used: one after Group 1 has the treatment and Group 2 is the control, and one after Group 2 has the treatment and Group 1 is the control. This design will allow group differences to be controlled such that each group serves in each condition (experimental and control) once. Figure 12.2 illustrates this type of pretest-posttest design. However, not all designs allow this alternation of treatment and control across participant groups. In some cases, for example, the control condition cannot be given after the treatment without the treatment's affecting the behavior in the control condition. Consider a memory study where participants are asked to remember to look for an animal word to respond to while performing another task. The control condition involves performing the task without the instruction to look for the animal word. If participants first complete the task looking for the animal word, it may be difficult for them to stop looking for the animal word during the control condition that follows. Thus, this solution may not apply to all types of studies.

One major drawback to the pretest-posttest design is that the participants are tested twice on the same behavior. This can cause a source of bias known as **testing effects**. Testing effects occur when participants are tested multiple times and each subsequent test is affected by the previous tests. For example, participants may get better on the tests over time with practice. Alternatively, they may become fatigued or bored with the test after taking it once. Testing effects can occur in many types of designs (see Chapters 4, 9, and 11 for more discussion of testing effects in other contexts). In pretest-posttest designs, they can occur as the experience of the pretest changes how participants experience the posttest. One method of evaluating testing effects in pretest-posttest studies is the use of the **Solomon four-group design** (Shadish et al., 2002). In the Solomon four-group design, the pretest-posttest design with nonequivalent groups is used. However, two sets of each group type are included: one set that takes the pretest and posttest as illustrated in Figure 12.2 and one set that takes only the posttest to

Testing Effects: occur when participants are tested more than once in a study with early testing affecting later testing

Solomon Four-Group Design: pretest-posttest design with two sets of nonequivalent groups, one set that takes the pretest and posttest and one set that takes only the posttest

Figure 12.2   Illustration of Different Types of Pretest-Posttest Designs

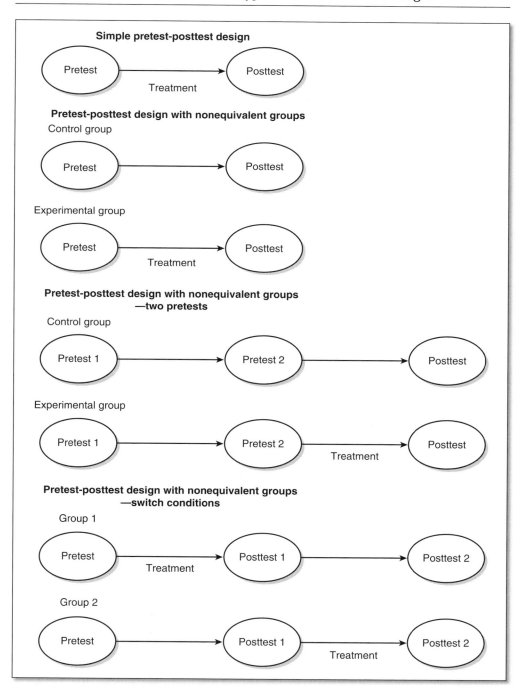

Figure 12.3 Solomon Four-Group Design

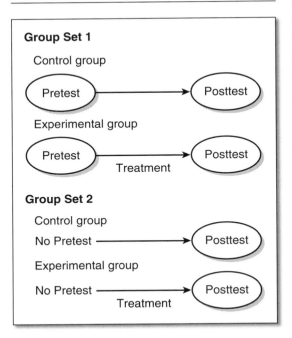

allow comparison of the two sets of groups. See Figure 12.3 for the full Solomon four-group design. Comparison across the group sets will indicate if testing effects occur. For example, comparing posttest scores for the groups that take the pretest and posttest and the groups that take only the posttest will allow the researcher to determine if testing effects have occurred in the posttest scores. If no testing effects have occurred, the scores should be similar for the two control groups and for the two experimental groups, as the only difference between each set is whether they have taken the pretest or not.

Time Series Designs

For some measures of behavior or attitudes, the measures may fluctuate a good deal from week to week or month to month. In these cases, a single pretest and a single posttest are unlikely to capture the true nature of the behavior. The pretest could occur at a time when scores happen to be particularly high or particularly low, which could bias the change in scores from pretest to posttest. **Time series designs** account for these fluctuations by measuring the behavior or attitude multiple times before the treatment and multiple times after the treatment over the same time period. Then the patterns of scores over time before and after the treatment are compared to determine if a difference has occurred. The patterns of scores are compared in a time series design, rather than two scores as in the pretest-posttest design. For example, a researcher may wish to determine if Americans were more depressed during the war in Iraq than before it. To study this question, the researchers may use a time series design, in which they recruit individuals from counseling centers who have been receiving counseling and have been taking a depression questionnaire each month during their treatment. With permission from the clients, the researchers can look at the pattern of depression for the year before the war started and for the year after the war started and compare the two patterns of scores. It is likely that over a year, a client's depression scores will fluctuate from month to month as holidays and seasons come and go. Thus, if there is no difference in scores before and after the war in Iraq, the two patterns of depression scores for the year (averaged across clients) should be similar.

Time Series Design: a research design where patterns of scores over time are compared from before a treatment is implemented and after a treatment is implemented

The time series design described above is called an **interrupted time series design** because the treatment is an independent event that the researchers have no control over. Events such as a war, passage of a new law, or other historical events are considered "treatments" in an interrupted time series design in that patterns of scores are compared before and after the event occurs. In many cases, the researchers are unable to predict the occurrence of the event. This limits them to measures that are collected periodically by other agencies. In other words, archival data are used as observations in the study (see Chapter 3 for a discussion of archival data observations). For example, specific agencies periodically collect information regarding the confidence people in different countries have in the economy (e.g., the Consumer Confidence Index; see www.conference-board.org/ for information about this measure). It is determined from responses to a survey the spending and savings activities of the people in a particular country.

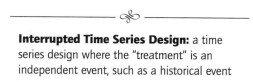

Interrupted Time Series Design: a time series design where the "treatment" is an independent event, such as a historical event

In weaker economic times in a country, the scores will be lower on this measure. Researchers can use this measure to determine if people's optimism about the economy is affected by various events, such as wars, laws, and other historical events, because the Consumer Confidence Index is continuously measured. Thus, patterns of scores can be compared before and after historical events to determine if a change has occurred. A time series design is appropriate for this measure because people's confidence in the economy tends to fluctuate naturally from month to month in different parts of the year.

A recent example of an interrupted time series design was conducted by Libby et al. (2007). These researchers conducted an investigation of antidepressant prescription rates in children before and after the U.S. Food and Drug Administration (FDA) issued a warning regarding the link between antidepressants and suicidal behavior in children. The warning was issued in October 2003. Thus, the researchers obtained archival data regarding antidepressant and alternative treatments of depression in children for each month for the 60 months before the FDA warning and for 24 months after the warning. The patterns of antidepressant prescriptions and alternative treatments were compared for the period before and the period after the warning. See Figure 12.4 for a graph of these patterns. The results indicated that in the 24 months following the warning, prescriptions for antidepressants to children with depression declined, whereas alternative treatment methods increased. In other words, Libby et al. found a relationship between the FDA warning and a change in the treatments prescribed for children with depression.

Similar designs with a researcher-implemented treatment are called **noninterrupted time series designs**. The behavior of interest is measured over time both before and after a treatment has been introduced. For example, suppose a researcher was interested in the effect of a new therapy on depression. The researcher may choose to conduct an interrupted time series design in this case because depressive symptoms may change throughout the year (e.g., be worse around holidays, get better when spring begins). Thus, in a noninterrupted time series design in this case, the

Noninterrupted Time Series Design: a time series design where the "treatment" is implemented by the researcher

participants' depression symptoms would be measured over a period of time before they began the new therapy (e.g., for 6 months or 1 year before). Then the new therapy would be given to the participants, and their depressive symptoms would be measured for the

Figure 12.4 Time Series Data for Treatment Rates of Children's Depression From Libby et al.'s (2007) Study

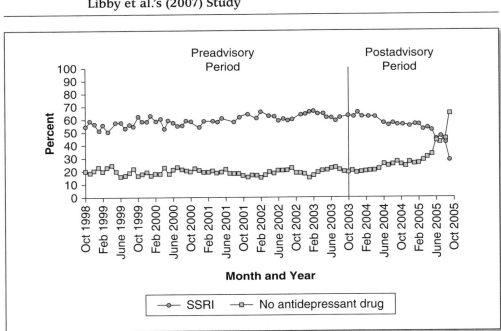

SOURCE: Reprinted with permission from the American Journal of Psychiatry, (Copyright 2007). American Psychiatric Association.

same period of time with the new therapy. As in the examples above, the pattern of depressive symptoms would be compared for the period before the new therapy and after the new therapy was implemented.

As with pretest-posttest designs, limitations of time series designs exist due to possible extraneous factors that may affect a score pattern change other than the treatment or event of interest. Thus researchers must be cautious in interpreting relationships found between the treatment or event and the results, as with all quasi-experiments. However, if a control group is included with random assignment of participants to the treatment or the control group, the study becomes an experiment, and more information regarding a causal relationship between the factors can be obtained. Random assignment of participants is much more likely in time series designs with a researcher-implemented treatment than an independent event examined in an interrupted time series design.

One final issue regarding time series designs should be considered. Due to the focus on patterns of scores over time, traditional data analysis techniques (such as those described in Chapter 14) are typically inadequate to testing hypotheses for these types of designs. Specialized statistical techniques are available, but they are too advanced for the scope of an introductory methods text and course.

CHAPTER SUMMARY

Reconsider the questions from the beginning of the chapter:

- What aspects of a quasi-experiment make it different from other research designs? A quasi-experiment can be similar in design to an experiment, but no true independent variable is manipulated in the study.
- What is required to test a causal relationship between variables? To test a causal relationship between variables, an independent variable must be manipulated such that the participants are assigned to levels of the independent variable by the researcher.
- What is a pretest-posttest design? In what way is it a quasi-experiment? A pretest-posttest design is a design in which the dependent variable is measured both before and after a treatment is implemented. It is a quasi-experiment because other factors may affect a change in scores besides the treatment (i.e., the third-variable problem). However, if a control group that does not receive the treatment is included with participants randomly assigned to the treatment or control group, the design becomes an experiment.
- What is a time series design? In what way is it a quasi-experiment? A time series design is similar to a pretest-posttest design in that the dependent variable is measured more than once. However, in a time series design, the dependent variable is measured many times over a period of time, which may or may not include a treatment. As with the pretest-posttest design, the pattern of scores examined in a time series design may be affected by factors other than the treatment.

THINKING ABOUT RESEARCH

A summary of a research study in psychology is given below. As you read the summary, think about the following questions:

1. In the most specific terms possible, describe the quasi-experiment design used in this study.
2. Can the researchers conclusively conclude that the changes they implemented caused the difference in the number of students enrolled in research experiences before and after the change? Why or why not?
3. Why do you think the researchers chose to consider the number of students enrolled in the experiences for several years before and after the changes (instead of just looking at the year before and the year after)?
4. Why is this study considered a quasi-experiment instead of an experiment? How could the design be changed to create an experiment?
5. What are some alternative explanations of the results reported by the researchers?

Study Reference

Wayment, H. A., & Dickson, K. L. (2008). Increasing student participation in undergraduate research benefits students, faculty, and department. *Teaching of Psychology, 35,* 194–197.

Purpose of the Study. The study was designed to evaluate changes made in a psychology department to increase undergraduates' participation in research experiences working with faculty members. Previous studies have shown that undergraduate research experiences are beneficial to students (Kardash, 2000; Landrum & Nelsen, 2002). However, many students choose not to participate in research experiences. Wayment and Dickson (2008) hoped to increase students' participation in research experiences through changes made in their department.

Method of the Study. In Spring 2006, five changes to the research experiences were made: (1) students who wished to participate in the research experience completed an application, (2) the opportunities for research experiences were advertised, (3) psychology majors completed a survey about the experiences as a means of informing them about the experiences, (4) students involved in research experiences were featured in the departmental newsletter, and (5) incentives were provided for faculty involved in the research experiences. The number of students enrolled in research experiences each year was recorded for the years before the changes were implemented (1996 to 2006) and then for 2 years after the change was implemented (2007 to 2008).

Results of the Study. Results showed that the number of students enrolled nearly tripled in the 2 years after the changes were implemented. See the figure for the pattern of results before and after the change.

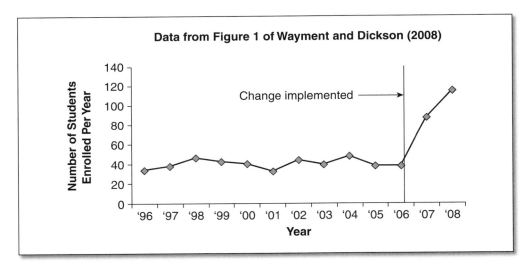

Conclusions of the Study. The researchers concluded that the changes that were implemented may have been effective in increasing the number of students who participate in undergraduate research experiences.

COMMON PITFALLS AND HOW TO AVOID THEM

Problem: Confusing experiments and quasi-experiments

Solution: Carefully consider the design of a study. Are groups compared without random assignment to the groups? If so, the study is likely a quasi-experiment.

Problem: Difference between pretest-posttest designs and within-subjects designs—this distinction can be confusing.

Solution: A within-subjects design is any design with an independent variable manipulated such that all participants received all levels of the variable. A pretest-posttest design specifically involves measurement of the dependent variable both before and after a treatment has been implemented. A special case of the pretest-posttest design may involve randomly assigned treatment and control groups in an experiment. In this type of design, the time of test (pre- and post-) may be considered a within-subjects independent variable. However, this is only the case if both treatment and control groups are included and participants are randomly assigned to the groups.

Problem: Confusing correlational studies and quasi-experiments

Solution: The goals of these two types of research design are very different. In correlational studies, two or more dependent variables are measured with the goal of testing the relationship between the variables. In a quasi-experiment, the goal is typically to compare groups that are not randomly assigned or to examine the change in the dependent variable after a treatment has been implemented. Thus, an examination of the goal of the study and the types of results that are reported for the study will help you distinguish these types of designs.

TEST YOURSELF

1. What aspects of a study allow tests of causal relationships?

2. Using a research question of interest to you, design a quasi-experiment that uses the pretest-posttest with nonequivalent groups design. Describe how your study would be conducted.

3. Describe a time series design that a researcher might conduct to investigate whether a change occurred in approval ratings of U.S. President George W. Bush before and after the U.S. government announced tax rebates in March 2008.

Answers: 1. Manipulation of an independent variable and control for extraneous variables that can be done with random assignment. 2. Answers will vary, but the design should include a pretest and posttest on the same behavior, nonrandomized experimental and control groups, and a treatment or condition implemented for the experimental group between the pretest and posttest measures. 3. Designs will vary, but the study should include surveys of approval ratings each month or so for a period of several months before March 2008 and several months after March 2008.

The Nuts and Bolts of Other Specialized Designs

CONSIDER THE FOLLOWING QUESTIONS AS YOU READ CHAPTER 13

- Why do developmental psychologists need specialized designs?
- What are the differences between longitudinal, cross-sectional, and cohort-sequential designs?
- What role do small-*n* designs play in psychological research?

For many of the designs discussed elsewhere in this text, some context was provided for which areas of psychology are most likely to employ those design types. In this chapter, we will consider two additional types of designs that were developed in specific areas of psychology to gain particular information about behavior. One set of specialized designs is used commonly by developmental psychologists to examine the differences in behavior across different-aged participants. The other type of design discussed in this chapter is the small-*n* design, one of the earliest designs employed by psychologists as they began to investigate basic processes involved in behavior. Small-*n* designs are now also commonly used in studies testing behavioral interventions. Each of these design types will be introduced in this chapter.

DEVELOPMENTAL DESIGNS

There are three main types of developmental designs (see Figure 13.1) that treat the factor of age in a different way: longitudinal designs, cross-sectional designs, and cohort-sequential designs. **Longitudinal designs** treat age as a **within-subjects variable** (see Chapter 11 for more discussion of within-subjects variables). In a longitudinal design, participants are tested at different ages in their lives. For example, a single sample of participants may be tested at age 5, at age 10, at age 15, and at age 20. In other words, each participant provides observations

243

Figure 13.1   Steps in the Research Process: Designing the Study

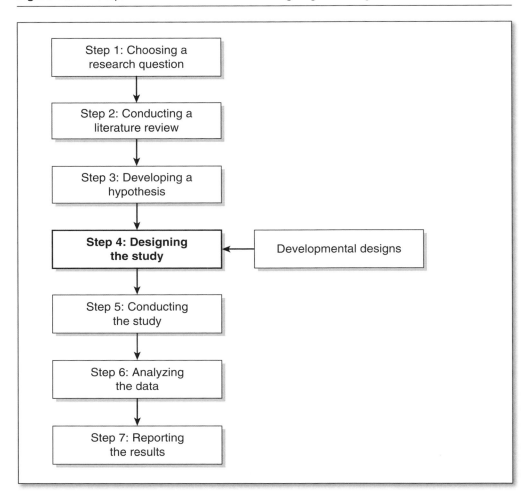

——————— ❧ ———————

Longitudinal Design: a developmental design where a single sample of participants is followed over time and tested at different ages

Within-Subjects Variable: each participant experiences all levels of the variable

at each of the ages tested in the study. Figure 13.2 illustrates the longitudinal design. This is how age is considered a within-subjects variable in the longitudinal design, although age is not an independent variable in this case because age cannot be manipulated.

Booth-LaForce and Oxford (2008) conducted a study that provides an example of a longitudinal design. Their study was designed to examine social withdrawal of children over time. Social withdrawal was measured by teacher reports of the students in the study each year while the students were in grades 1 through 6. By tracking social withdrawal over time, the researchers were

Figure 13.2   Longitudinal Design: Same Sample Is Tested at Different Ages

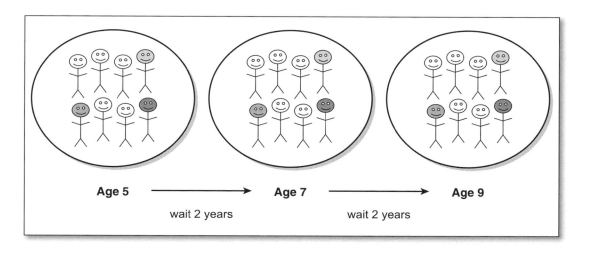

able to identify three groups of children: those not socially withdrawn, those who showed early social withdrawal and a decrease in social withdrawal over time, and those who did not show early withdrawal but showed increases in social withdrawal over time. The latter two groups each contained a small percentage of the sample. These researchers began recruiting the children for the study in 1991 at the time they were born but did not publish their study until 2008. Data collection in elementary schools took 6 years. This illustrates one of the disadvantages of the longitudinal design: It takes time to wait for the participants to age. Another disadvantage is that **attrition/mortality** (i.e., some participants do not complete the study) may occur over time as the study is conducted. Attrition can be a source of bias in the study if the participants who drop out are different from the participants who remain. Attrition can occur in longitudinal studies for various reasons. For example, participants may get tired of being in the study, or they may move and lose contact with the researchers. A third disadvantage is that testing effects may occur with multiple testings of the same participants. In other words, being tested on the measures early in the study can affect the later testings, as participants' scores may show effects of practice or fatigue.

Attrition/Mortality: occurs when participants choose not to complete a study

Testing Effects: occur when participants are tested more than once in a study with early testing affecting later testing

An alternative to treating age as a within-subjects variable, as in the longitudinal design, is to treat age as a between-subjects variable by testing different groups of participants of different ages with each participant tested only once for their age at the time of the study. Developmental designs that treat age as a **between-subjects variable**

— ✥ —

Between-Subjects Variable: each participant experiences only one level of the independent variable

Cross-Sectional Design: a developmental design where multiple samples of participants of different ages are tested once

(see Chapter 11 for more discussion of between-subjects variables) are called **cross-sectional designs**. These designs compare different age groups of participants, where each participant contributes data for only one age group. Figure 13.3 illustrates the cross-sectional design.

Zimmerman, Gerson, Monroe, and Kearney (2007, Experiment 1) provide an example of a cross-sectional design in their study that investigated the development of students' understanding of their own knowledge of a topic area and how well their perceived knowledge matched their actual knowledge in that area. Junior high school, high school, and college students were tested on their comprehension in several topic areas: psychology, biology, chemistry, and physics. Students also provided a measure of their perceived knowledge in each topic area. The difference between the students' perceived and actual knowledge was calculated for each topic area and age group. Zimmerman et al. found that the difference between perceived and actual knowledge differed by age group. Whereas junior and high school students were fairly accurate at judging their knowledge in the topic areas, the college students underestimated their knowledge in physics and chemistry. In addition, all age groups overestimated their knowledge in psychology. In other words, the college students knew more about physics and chemistry than they thought they did, and all students knew less about psychology than they thought they did. This study showed that the accuracy of perceived knowledge may decrease with age and depends on topic area.

Figure 13.3   Cross-Sectional Design: Different Samples Are Tested at Different Ages

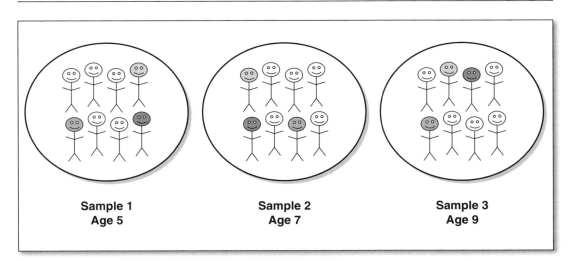

Sample 1
Age 5

Sample 2
Age 7

Sample 3
Age 9

As you might imagine, the cross-sectional design solves many of the problems that can occur with longitudinal designs. Each participant is tested only once, which reduces the chance of attrition. In addition, because the researcher collects data from all age groups at the same time, the study can be completed more quickly with a cross-sectional design. However, there are some drawbacks to the cross-sectional design that are more problematic than in longitudinal designs.

For example, if the age groups being tested contain participants from different generations, **generation effects** (also called **cohort effects**) might affect the results. These effects occur when the experiences of one generation (e.g., growing up with or without computers) are very different from those of another generation and affect the way the participants complete the task or measure

Generation/Cohort Effects: confound that may occur in cross-sectional designs due to different experiences that different generations have

in the study. For example, if younger and older adults are tested with a survey presented on a computer, it is possible that the older adults' may have more difficulty completing the survey because some lack experience with computers. In other words, the older participants may exhibit lower scores than the younger participants that are not due to the difference in age between the groups.

The third type of developmental design combines elements of the longitudinal and cross-sectional designs. In a **cohort-sequential design**, age is treated as both a between-subjects and within-subjects factor. Cohort-sequential designs begin with separate samples of different age groups, as in a cross-sectional design. Then these age groups are tested mul-

Cohort-Sequential Design: a developmental design where multiple samples of participants of different ages are followed over time and tested at different ages

tiple times as they develop to allow participants to be tested at multiple ages, as in a longitudinal design. Figure 13.4 illustrates the cohort-sequential design.

Chouinard and Roy (2008) conducted a cohort-sequential study to investigate the decline in motivation in math studies in high school students. A sample of 704 students in 7th grade and 625 students in 9th grade completed a scale that measured competency in math skills. All students were attending high schools in the Montreal, Ontario, Canada, area at the time of the study. Repeated administration of the competency scale occurred twice a year for 3 years. Thus, when the study was completed, the students who were first tested in 7th grade had completed 9th grade, and the students who were first tested in 9th grade had completed 11th grade.

Results showed that math motivation declined over the 3-year period for the students, confirming the researchers' prediction that math motivation declines during high school years. In addition, although boys scored higher than girls initially, they showed a faster decline in motivation scores than girls. Thus, the decline in motivation appeared to affect boys more than it affected girls.

Whereas a cohort-sequential study will take time to complete because researchers must wait for the participants to age (e.g., it took 3 years to collect the data in the study described above), it will allow researchers to compare ages quickly with the first testing of the different-aged samples. In addition, generation effects may be less problematic, because participants are also tested at multiple ages. Thus, in some cases, this design is preferable to either a longitudinal or a cross-sectional design.

Figure 13.4 Cohort-Sequential Design: Different Samples Are Tested at Multiple Times as They Age

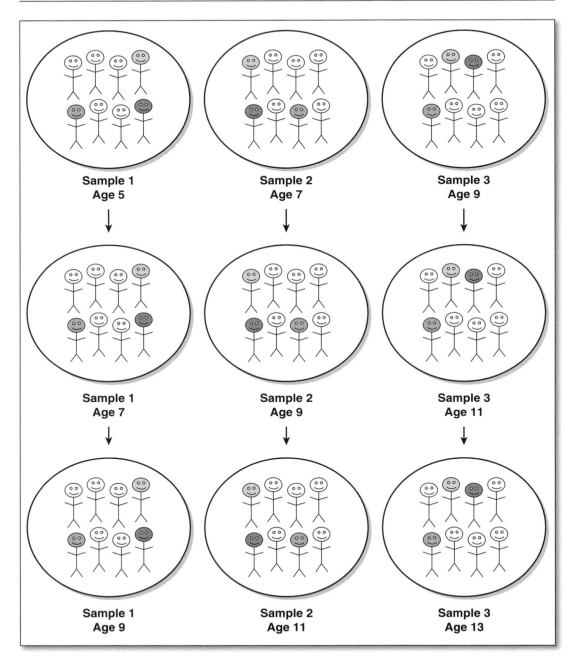

SMALL-*n* DESIGNS

Imagine a situation where a teacher identifies a child in a class who has behavioral problems. The child is disruptive in class during the lessons, and the teacher is frustrated. In an attempt to solve this problem, the teacher consults with a school psychologist, who conducts an experiment with a **small-*n* design** (see Figure 13.5) to determine if a treatment can be found that will change the disruptive student's behavior. The psychologist measures the student's disruptive behavior (e.g., number of times in a day the student talks in class without raising his or her hand) to determine the behavior rate that currently exists. This is called the **baseline measurement**. A treatment is then implemented (e.g., the student receives a sticker for each 15-minute period that he or she stays quiet during the lesson), and the disruptive behavior is measured again. The school psychologist finds that the disruptive behavior decreases with the treatment. However, to be sure that it was the treatment that caused the behavior to change (and not some other extraneous factor), the treatment is then ended, and disruptive behavior is measured again to take another baseline measurement. If the disruptive behavior returns without the treatment, then the psychologist can be fairly confident that the treatment is working. The psychologist may then recommend the teacher use this treatment to change the student's behavior or may try the treatment one more time to make sure the behavior is still affected by the treatment.

> **Small-*n* Design:** an experiment conducted with one or a few participants to better understand the behavior of those individuals
>
> **Baseline Measurement:** measurement of behavior without a treatment used as a comparison

The example described above illustrates a current use of a small-*n* design. These designs are sometimes called single-subject or single-case designs, but they often include more than one participant; thus, small *n* is a better descriptor of this design type. The goal of a small-*n* study is to understand an individual's behavior, either to better describe the behavior or in order to change that behavior. In a small-*n* design, this is accomplished through repeated measurement of behavior (Barlow & Hersen, 1984). The repeated measurement of behavior takes two forms: (1) **discrete trials designs**, where one or a few participants complete a large number of trials of a task to describe how performance on the task operates and (2) **baseline designs**, where the repeated measurement of the baseline behavior of one or a few participants is compared with their behavior during the implementation of a treatment.

> **Discrete Trials Design:** a small-*n* design that involves a large number of trials completed by one or a few individuals and conducted to describe basic behaviors
>
> **Baseline Design:** a small-*n* design that involves baseline measurements of behavior as compared with measures of behavior during the implementation of a treatment

The primary advantage of small-*n* designs comes from the large number of observations collected from one or a few participants. Using a large number of observations reduces the error in the data (seen in the low variability of the scores) and makes it easier for a researcher to detect an effect of an independent variable. Using a small number of participants also makes it easier for a researcher to control for extraneous factors that may

Figure 13.5   Steps in the Research Process: Designing the Study

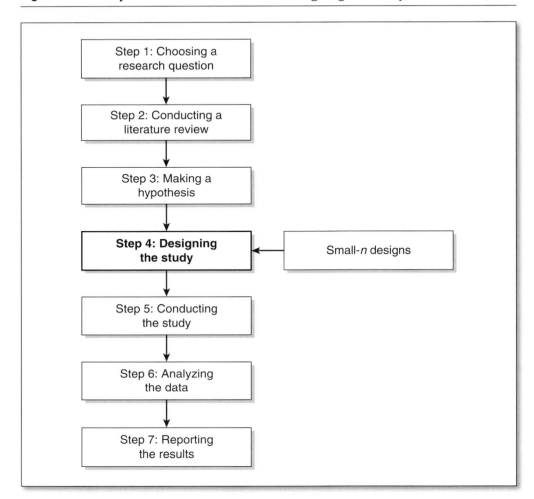

bias the data. This control increases the internal validity of the study. The main disadvantage to small-n designs is that the results cannot always be generalized to people outside the study. This is why they are typically used to study very basic behaviors (e.g., sensory processes, learning processes), where the behaviors being measured should be very similar from person to person, and for studies where the goal is to tailor a treatment to a specific person. In addition, small-n design cannot be used to measure many types of behavior. Due to the large number of observations collected, **carryover effects** can occur for tasks that may affect future performance over time. In other words, participants' experiences in the

---

Carryover Effects: occur when participants' experience in one condition affects their behavior in another condition of a study treatment condition can affect their later behavior in a second baseline condition that follows the treatment condition. Thus, researchers must consider these issues when choosing a small-n design.

Discrete Trials Designs

Some of the earliest studies in psychology used the discrete trials type of small-n design. Early psychologists, such as Weber, Fechner, Ebbinghaus, and Skinner were interested in describing basic behaviors such as sensory stimulation, memory, and conditioning (Barlow & Hersen, 1984). They accomplished this through repeated measurement of these behaviors over an enormous number of trials with a small number of participants. Ebbinghaus, for example, conducted his studies of basic memory processes using himself as his subject. He repeatedly memorized nonsense syllables (FAL, JIV, etc.) to perfection and then measured his memory for these syllables after a period of time had passed. From his work, researchers learned that most of the forgetting that occurs for information is rapid, tapering off with longer delays (Neath & Surprenant, 2003).

Discrete trials designs help researchers describe basic behavioral processes, such as the way that information is forgotten in memory. This can be done with just a few participants who complete a very large number of trials because this method will reduce the variability in the measurement of the behavior. Lower variability across trials (either within or across individual participants) increases the validity and reliability of the measurement of a behavior (see Chapters 6 and 7 for more discussion of the role of variability in the internal validity of a study). With the controls used in an experiment and the large amount of data collected under these conditions, discrete trials designs allow for good tests of causal relationships for behaviors where there are few individual differences. Thus discrete trials designs tend to achieve stable measures of behavior with high internal validity.

In current psychological research, discrete trials designs are typically used by researchers who study the basic processes of psychophysics and learning, also called the *experimental analysis of behavior* (Barlow & Hersen, 1984). For example, Magoon and Critchfield (2008) conducted a small-n design to better understand the consequences of positive and negative reinforcement with consistent (all positive or all negative reinforcement) or inconsistent (a mix of positive and negative reinforcement) schedules. They tested a general prediction supported by past studies that avoiding aversive events (negative reinforcement) has a stronger effect on behavior than positive reinforcement. These researchers reported data from three participants who completed approximately 45 hours of a task involving mouse clicks with different positive and negative reinforcement schedules. Different mouse clicks earned participants money (positive reinforcement) or kept participants from losing money (negative reinforcement), depending on the session and reinforcement schedule.

Participants completed trials in short sessions, several days a week for a number of weeks. Thus, each participant completed a large number of trials to collect stable measurements of his or her behavior in a series of reinforcement conditions. With this large number of measurements of the participants' behavior for the different reinforcement conditions, the researchers were able to provide a mathematical description of behavior. In other words, they described the data with a mathematical function based on the prediction that negative reinforcement should affect behavior more than positive reinforcement. This type of data analysis allows better understanding of the processes involved in the behavior and better prediction of a change in behavior as a function of one of the variables. Mathematical description of behavior is often a common goal of discrete trials designs, which is possible with the large number of measurements collected of basic behaviors. By analyzing the individual participant data in this manner, Magoon and Critchfield (2008) showed that the positive and negative reinforcement affected task behavior in a similar way, indicating that the hypothesis described earlier was not supported.

Baseline Designs

As described above, baseline designs involve experimental comparison of baseline behavior and behavior with a treatment. The goal is to determine if a treatment creates a desired change in the behavior of interest (often an undesirable behavior), a technique also called *behavior modification* (Barlow & Hersen, 1984). There are several ways that baseline designs can be conducted. In what is known as an **A-B-A design** or **reversal design** (Barlow & Hersen, 1984), the baseline measure of behavior (designated as Condition A) is first taken. Then the treatment (designated as Condition B) is implemented, and behavior is measured again, this time with the treatment. Finally, a baseline measure (A) is made again after the treatment has been stopped to determine if the baseline behavior appears once again after the treatment has been stopped. However, it is common in such designs for behavior to approach baseline levels but not fully achieve initial baseline levels after a treatment has been implemented (Barlow & Hersen, 1984). In other words, the effect of the treatment may carry over into the second baseline measure. A common variant of this procedure is the A-B-A-B design, where the treatment is then implemented a second time to determine if the behavior still changes with implementation of the treatment.

A-B-A/Reversal Design: a small-*n*, baseline design where the baseline behavior is measured, followed by implementation of a treatment, followed by another baseline measure after the treatment has ended

Tasky, Rudrud, Schulze, and Rapp (2008) conducted a study using a variant of the A-B-A design. They were interested in testing a treatment to improve task behavior for individuals who had suffered a brain injury. Three participants receiving inpatient rehabilitation after suffering brain trauma due to a car accident participated in the study. The goal of the study was to increase completion of tasks by the participants through a treatment that allowed the participants to choose which tasks they wished to complete during the session. Time on task was compared for the choice treatment and the baseline conditions, where tasks were assigned by the experimenter. An A-B-A-B design was used, with a modified baseline condition for the second baseline measurement. The second baseline was modified to assign tasks to the participants that they had chosen during the first treatment session. Figure 13.6 illustrates the results for each condition by participant. The graphs show that for each participant, the choice sessions increased time on task compared with the two baseline conditions. Thus, the researchers reported results supporting the idea that the treatment they tested was effective in improving the time all patients spent on the tasks they were given.

Figure 13.6   On-Task Results for the Participants in Tasky et al.'s (2008) Study

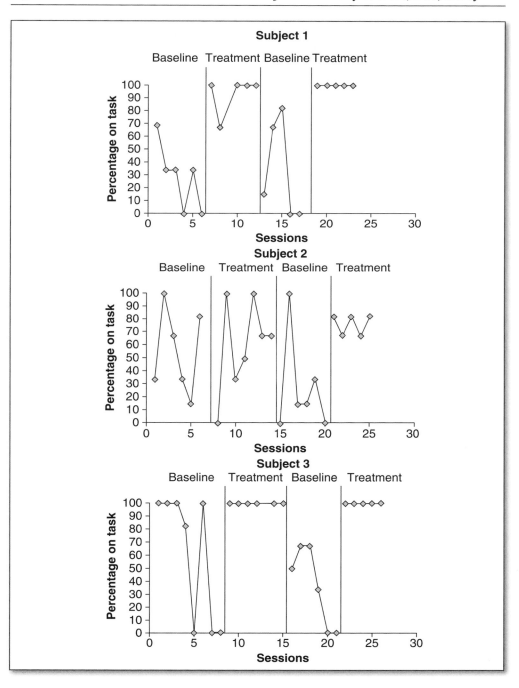

Data Analysis in Small-*n* Designs

Because there are no group means to present in small-*n* designs, data are often presented for the individual participants in the study (with no identifying information to protect their confidentiality). In fact, the graph seen in Figure 13.6 is a common method of reporting results from small-*n* designs, especially for baseline designs (Rosenthal & Rosnow, 2008). Inferential statistics are sometimes reported for discrete trials designs for within-subjects variables that are manipulated in these types of designs. It is common, though, for researchers to report mathematical descriptions of behavior in discrete trials designs, as in the example presented above by Magoon and Critchfield (2008).

CHAPTER SUMMARY

Reconsider the questions from the beginning of the chapter:

- Why do developmental psychologists need specialized designs? Developmental psychologists use specialized designs to allow them to examine different types of age effects in a study. Because age cannot be manipulated as a true independent variable, many of these designs are quasi-experiments that compare age across participant groups or within participant groups longitudinally.
- What are the differences between longitudinal, cross-sectional, and cohort-sequential designs? The primary difference in these designs is in how age is treated as a variable. In longitudinal designs, behavior is compared at different ages for a single group of participants over time. In a cross-sectional design, behavior is compared for different groups of participants of different ages. In cohort-sequential designs, different groups of participants of different ages (cohorts) are tested over time to see a change in behavior for each group as they age.
- What role do small-*n* designs play in psychological research? Small-*n* designs allow psychologists to test laws of behavior (often in mathematical form) and to test treatments that might be effective for a single participant or a small group of participants. These two goals are met in discrete trials and baseline designs, respectively.

THINKING ABOUT RESEARCH

A summary of a research study in psychology is given below. As you read the summary, think about the following questions:

1. What type of developmental design was used in this study? Explain your answer.
2. What are the advantages of the developmental design type used in this study? What are the disadvantages?
3. Was the study an experiment (see Chapter 11) or quasi-experiment (see Chapter 12)? How do you know?
4. What types of extraneous factors might affect the results in this study? Explain how each factor may have caused the results found by the researchers.

Study Reference

Levine, L. J., Burgess, S. L., & Laney, C. (2008). Effects of discrete emotions on young children's suggestibility. *Developmental Psychology, 44*, 681–694.

Purpose of the Study. Levine, Burgess, and Laney (2008) conducted a study to investigate the effect of children's emotions on their memory abilities and the likelihood that their memory accuracy would decline due to leading questions about their memories for a story. This knowledge may be useful in determining the conditions under which children's memories are less likely to be accurate, which is important in various applied situations, such as when children must testify in court about something they experienced.

Method of the Study. Four- and six-year-old children participated in the study. Each child was presented with three stories. A task at the end of each story was designed to elicit happiness, sadness, or anger. This manipulation of emotion was conducted by asking the children to help the character in the story in order to win a prize for themselves. Happiness was elicited by a successful winning of the prize with the correct response. Sadness was elicited by presenting no opportunity (after the instructions) to win the prize (i.e., no target was presented in the task). Anger was elicited by withholding the prize after a correct response from the child. The children were asked how they were feeling after the emotion manipulation occurred at the end of each story. Free recall of the events in the story then occurred. Suggestibility was then measured with leading questions about the story, with five out of the seven questions containing false information. This procedure was followed for all three stories.

Results of the Study. To check that the emotion manipulation actually elicited the appropriate emotions in the children, their emotional self-reports and coded facial expressions were compared for each emotional condition. A majority of the children showed the appropriate emotion for each condition. Thus, it was concluded that the children's emotions were effectively manipulated. For free recall, emotion condition did not affect memory abilities; however, 6-year-olds ($M = 10.97$) did recall more accurate pieces of information about the study than 4-year-olds ($M = 8.24$). For memory suggestibility, emotion condition did affect memory suggestibility. Children in the sadness and anger conditions responded incorrectly more often to the inaccurate leading questions than the children in the happiness condition. Figure 13.7 illustrates these results. In addition, 4-year-olds showed more suggestibility than 6-year-olds.

Conclusions of the Study. Levine et al. (2008) concluded that whereas free-recall abilities are not affected by emotion condition in children, suggestibility due to misleading questions is affected by emotion condition. Negative emotions, such as anger and sadness, lead to more inaccurate responses to false leading questions. In addition, younger children were more likely to be misled by the questions than the older children. Thus, emotional states and type of questioning should be considered when testing the memories of young children.

COMMON PITFALLS AND HOW TO AVOID THEM

Problem: Distinguishing experiments and quasi-experiments—developmental designs can be experiments or quasi-experiments.

Figure 13.7   Mean Number of Incorrect Responses by Emotion Condition

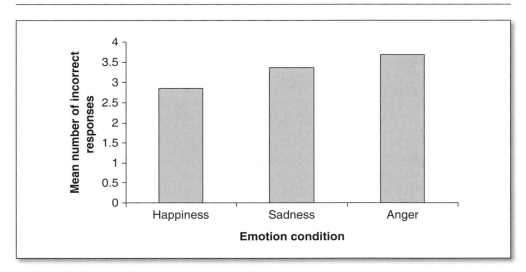

SOURCE: From Levine et al. (2008).

Solution: In a developmental design, age is included as a subject or quasi-experimental variable. Thus, if there is no manipulated variable, the design is a quasi-experiment. However, in some cases, researchers are interested in how the effects of a manipulated independent variable change for different ages. In these cases, the design is an experiment, because a true independent variable is included along with the age variable.

Problem: Assuming causal effects of age—it can be tempting to conclude that age effects on behavior are causal.

Solution: Remember that age cannot be manipulated as an independent variable. Thus, the third-variable problem (see Chapters 3, 10, and 11) will always be possible for effects of age on behavior. There are alternative explanations for a change in behavior with age.

TEST YOURSELF

Match the descriptions below with the correct design type:

(a) longitudinal, (b) cross-sectional, (c) cohort-sequential, (d) discrete trials small-*n* design, (e) baseline small-*n* design.

1. Two participants each complete 5,000 trials of a cognitive task to mathematically describe performance on the task.
2. Separate groups of 9-year-olds, 20-year-olds, and 50-year-olds complete a personality survey to determine if scores change with age.

3. Three-year-olds are recruited for a study that measures social skills as the participants age. Each participant is tested at age 3, 16, 25, and 35 to determine how social skills develop over time.

4. A school child who displays anxiety during math lessons participates in a study to test the effectiveness of an anxiety-reducing treatment. The anxious behaviors are measured before the treatment is implemented, while the treatment is being implemented, and then again without the treatment to compare anxious behaviors in the different conditions.

5. Participants born in the years 1960, 1980, and 2000 are tested initially on their vocabulary and spelling abilities. Then, each group is tested every 10 years to determine if the participants' initial abilities change as they age.

Answers: 1. d, 2. b, 3. a, 4. e, 5. c.

The Nuts and Bolts of Using Statistics

CONSIDER THE FOLLOWING QUESTIONS AS YOU READ CHAPTER 14

- Which statistical tests are best for different research designs?
- How do we choose an appropriate statistical test?
- How do we use SPSS to run statistical tests?
- What information is provided in an SPSS output?

Each time I teach statistics and research methods courses, one of the most difficult things for students to master is the skill of choosing an appropriate statistical test for a particular research design. There are many research designs to keep track of and several different common statistical tests used to understand data from these designs, so this process can sometimes seem confusing and overwhelming. However, the goal of this chapter is to simplify this process, to help you understand what kinds of tests are appropriate for different types of research designs and measurement scales, to help you choose an appropriate statistical test for a study, and to instruct you in using SPSS software to analyze data (Figure 14.1). In Chapter 7, the conceptual logic of inferential statistics was described generally for hypothesis tests. In this chapter, the discussion will focus on specific tests and how they are calculated. However, the current discussion will build on concepts covered in Chapter 7; thus, you should review Chapter 7 before reading this chapter.

Null Hypothesis: the hypothesis that an effect or relationship does not exist (or exists in the opposite direction of the alternative hypothesis) in the population

Critical Region: the most extreme portion of a distribution of statistical values for the null hypothesis, determined by the alpha level (typically 5%)

Scientific/Alternative Hypothesis: the hypothesis that an effect or relationship exists (or exists in a specific direction) in the population

Significant Test: the p value is less than or equal to alpha in an inferential test, and the null hypothesis can be rejected

Figure 14.1   Steps in the Research Process: Analyzing the Data

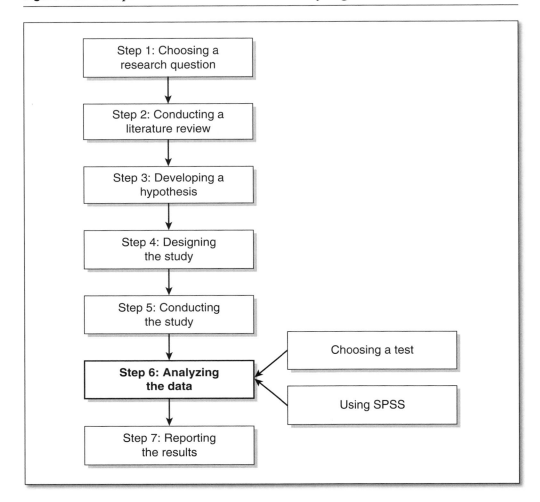

Recall from Chapter 7 that hypothesis tests are designed to look for evidence against the **null hypothesis** that predicts no difference between conditions or no relationship between variables, depending on what type of research question a study is designed to answer. This evidence comes in the form of extreme scores in the distribution of the statistic for scores obtained when the null hypothesis is true. When we conduct the statistical test based on the data from our study, our calculated statistic is compared with this distribution to determine whether our value is extreme or uncommon when the null hypothesis is true. If our calculated statistic falls in the most extreme portion of this distribution, called the **critical region**, we have enough evidence to reject the null hypothesis and accept the scientific/alternative hypothesis that there is a difference or relationship. In other words, our test is **significant** because we have rejected the null hypothesis. We will now turn our discussion to the specific statistics that are used for some of the research designs we have discussed, including how those statistics are calculated. The type of statistical test chosen depends on the type of hypothesis researchers make for a study. Different tests are used to test hypotheses regarding group differences than for hypotheses regarding relationships. See Chapter 7 for a discussion of how to state these types of hypotheses. Figure 14.2 provides a flow chart to help you choose the appropriate statistic for your study. This figure will be referenced as we discuss the different tests highlighted in the chart.

Figure 14.2   Statistical Test Decision Flow Chart

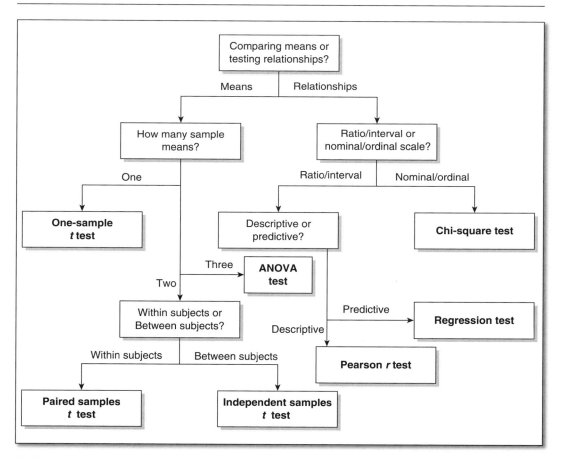

NOTE: Answer each question about the study design to arrive at a test (tests are listed in bold).

COMPARING GROUPS OR CONDITIONS

In experiments and quasi-experiments, hypotheses about effects are often tested by comparing groups (e.g., men and women) or conditions (e.g., visual presentation and auditory presentation). A significant difference between groups or conditions allows researchers to conclude that an effect exists in the population because they are able to reject the null hypothesis in a significant test. Sample mean differences can be caused by the effect, by sampling error, or both. Thus, statistical tests for effects are based on a ratio of the size of the difference in the sample means (that may contain both the treatment effect and sampling error) and sampling error to allow us to determine what part of the mean difference is due to the effect and which part is due to sampling error. The size of the statistic calculated is determined by the treatment effect because the sampling error in the denominator of the equation reduces the numerator of the equation according to how much error is in the data. In other words, a larger statistical value indicates a larger treatment effect because it represents the sample mean difference due just to the effect (i.e., sampling error has been removed in the ratio). Larger statistical values also lead to more **power** to detect effects with the test (see Chapter 7 for more discussion of power). Thus, reducing error can help increase power in a design. In equation form, the statistical value is expressed as follows:

---— ✄ ———---

Power: ability of a significance test to detect an effect or relationship when one exists (equal to 1—the probability of a Type II error)

$$\text{Statistic} = \frac{\text{Sample mean difference}}{\text{Sampling error}}.$$

As described above, the chance of obtaining this statistical value when the null hypothesis is true is then determined to look for evidence against the null hypothesis (i.e., a very low probability of obtaining this statistical value when the null hypothesis is true). The distribution of statistical values when the null hypothesis is true is used to determine the p value for the value calculated in the test. If the p value for the statistic is less than or equal to the alpha level, the null hypothesis is rejected, and the researcher concludes that there is an effect. If the p value is greater than the alpha level, the researcher cannot reject the null hypothesis and must conclude that there is no evidence of an effect. Remember, though, that you cannot conclude that there is no effect—the test will not provide evidence *for* the null hypothesis.

In inferential tests, sampling error is estimated from measures of variability in the sample. Variability of the sample indicates the amount of sampling error present because samples with high variability are less likely to be good representations of the population. The more the scores differ from one another, the less they will resemble the population mean. Thus, samples with high variability will have a larger margin of error in the population mean estimate (i.e., larger sampling error). This occurs because samples with high variability contain extreme scores that could affect the sample mean, giving a sample mean that is not very similar to the population mean. However, samples with low variability contain scores that are similar to one another and are more likely to represent the population mean.

Thus, if variability in a sample is high, there is likely to be more sampling error. This is why measures of variability are used for estimates of sampling error in inferential statistics. To view details of the calculations of the tests, see the Appendix.

Comparing Two Means With *t* Tests

The appropriate significance test to use to compare two means is a ***t* test**. There are three types of *t* tests used to compare means: the one-sample *t* test, the independent samples *t* test, and the repeated measures (or paired samples) *t* test (see Table 14.1 for a comparison of some of the commonly used inferential significance tests and the left portion of Figure 14.2 for the decisions leading to the use of the different *t* tests). A one-sample *t* test is often used when the population mean without a treatment is known and is being compared with a sample mean that represents the population with a treatment. Population means are known for certain types of variables, such as standardized tests that have been given to many samples in the past or were designed to have a specific population mean. IQ (Intelligent Quotient) tests, for example, have a population mean of 100. Thus, if a researcher wanted to determine if a treatment (e.g., a new drug) had an effect on IQ scores, he or she could collect IQ scores for a sample with that treatment

***t* test:** significance test used to compare means

TABLE 14.1	Some Common Inferential Statistics and Their Uses	
Statistical Test	**What It Tests**	**When to Use It**
One-sample *t* test	An effect	When the population mean without the treatment is known and is compared with a single sample
Independent samples *t* test	An effect	When two samples with different individuals are compared
Repeated measures/paired samples *t* test	An effect	When two related samples or two sets of scores from the same individual are compared
ANOVA	An effect	When more than two samples or sets of scores from the same individual are compared
Pearson *r* test	A relationship	When the relationship between two sets of scores is being tested
Regression	A relationship	When you want to predict an individual's score on one variable from the score on a second, related variable

and compare the sample mean with the known population mean of 100. The one-sample t test is designed for this situation. Another use of this test is when chance performance is the comparison value. Suppose participants complete an experiment where objects are presented subliminally during a task (e.g., Coke ads are flashed at very fast rates during movie ads). Participants are then given a recognition test for images of the ads, where two images are presented and participants must choose which one of the two was presented. If participants are able to process the subliminal ads, then their performance should be above chance (50%). If the ads were not processed and the participants are only guessing, then their performance should be similar to chance. Thus, the one-sample t test can be used to compare the mean recognition rate for the subliminal ads to the chance level of 50%.

The independent samples t test is used when two samples of different individuals are compared. Each sample represents the population for that group or condition. Thus, there are two sample means that are compared in the test. For example, if researchers are interested in differences in depression scores between men and women, they would collect a sample of men and a sample of women and compare the two sample means for depression scores. Each sample represents the population for that group. The independent samples t test will determine if the sample means are significantly different in this case.

If two related samples (e.g., each individual in one sample is matched with one individual in the other sample on some characteristic) or two sets of scores from the same individual (i.e., the individual provides scores in more than one condition) are compared, a repeated measures (also called a paired samples) t test is used. If two sample means are related from matched individuals or the same individual, the variability is likely to be lower, and an effect is more likely to be detected (i.e., the test will have more power) than if the samples are independent. In other words, these designs produce less error in the data than comparable between-subjects designs and, thus, have more power to detect effects that exist. In t tests, the standard deviation of the samples is used in the calculation of the sampling error for the denominator of the statistics equation.

Using SPSS to Conduct t Tests

When researchers conduct inferential statistics tests, they rarely conduct the tests with hand calculations (but see the Appendix for how to hand-calculate the tests so that you will understand how these tests are conducted). Instead, most researchers use a statistical software package, such as SPSS, to conduct the tests. The software package takes the raw data the researcher inputs, calculates descriptive statistics, and conducts significance tests that the researcher specifies. In other words, to use the software package to conduct inferential statistics tests, the researcher needs to know which tests are appropriate for the study, choose these tests in the software, and interpret the output that the software package generates for the tests. The output typically includes descriptive values (e.g., means, standard deviations), the value of the test statistic calculated (e.g., t, F, r) and the p value associated with the statistical value calculated. Researchers still need to compare the p value in the output to their chosen **alpha level** (usually .05) in order to determine if a test is significant, so that they are able to make a decision about the null hypothesis. In most cases, the software package will not indicate if a test is significant in the output for the test. Thus, even though the software package will complete the calculations, researchers still need to have a good working knowledge of statistics and how to use them in order to ensure that they use the software and interpret their data correctly.

_____ ✧ _____

Alpha Level: the probability level used by researchers to indicate the cutoff probability level (highest value) that will allow them to reject the null hypothesis

SPSS is a common software package used by psychologists to conduct statistical tests. Thus, we will focus on some of the basics of using this software. Different versions of SPSS may have a slightly different look, but the basic operations of typing in data and running the tests discussed in this chapter are very similar from version to version.

When you first open the SPSS program, you will see a window that allows you to choose to open saved data files or type in data into the Data Window. For the examples in this chapter, choose the "type in data" option to follow along. The Data Window will look like a large spreadsheet when it opens. There are tabs at the top that can be defined for different variables and cells for typing in data. Data can be typed in as numbers or strings of letters. The most important thing to remember about typing in data to the data window is that data from each individual participant (or matched set of participants) should be typed in across the rows. In other words, all the data from one participant or set of matched participants are contained in a single row. Thus, you will need to be familiar with your design before you type in your data. We will begin with a single group design that will compare the sample mean with a known population mean to use the one-sample _t_ test.

One-Sample _t_ Test

Example 1. Suppose that the example described above to determine if participants process and remember subliminal ads had been conducted with 10 participants. Percentage correct recognition scores for each participant were as given below:

Participant 1	56	Participant 6	65
Participant 2	60	Participant 7	70
Participant 3	49	Participant 8	44
Participant 4	35	Participant 9	58
Participant 5	51	Participant 10	47

The sample mean will be compared with the chance value of 50% that is expected if the participants are merely guessing in the recognition test. Looking at the chart in Figure 14.2, you can see that the one-sample _t_ test is appropriate for this example, because there is one sample mean to be compared with a known population mean.

To begin, type in the data above, one score per row, in the first column of the Data Window. Although different versions of SPSS differ in appearance, your Data Window should look similar to this:

	VAR0001
1	56.00
2	60.00
3	49.00
4	35.00
5	51.00
6	65.00
7	70.00
8	44.00
9	58.00
10	47.00

It is a good idea to label the column as the dependent variable, so choose the Variable View tab at the bottom of the Data Window. You will see a space to name the variable for each column in the data window. Simply type in a name for the variable in the first cell (e.g., "recog" for recognition scores). You can also include longer descriptions in the Label cell for that variable.

	Name	Type	Width	Decimals
1	recog	Numeric	8	2

To conduct the one-sample *t* test for these data, choose "Compare Means" from the "Analyze" menu at the top. The "Analyze" menu contains the options for the different tests and descriptive statistics a researcher may want to calculate for his or her design. Select the "One-sample *t*-test" option in the menu of tests. The window that opens will allow you to click the data column into the "Test Variable" position on the right to indicate that this column contains the dependent variable to be analyzed. You also need to indicate the known mean for comparison in the "Test Value" box. For the example above, the test value is 50 (for the chance value of 50%). When you click the "Ok" button, the analysis will begin automatically, and the output will appear in a separate Output Window. A view of the output window can be seen in Figure 14.3.

The output from the test contains several important values. The sample mean can be seen in the first box along with the standard deviation. These are the standard descriptive statistics included in the output for a *t* test. The *t* test values are included in the second box in the output. The *t* value (1.064 for Example 1), the **degrees of freedom** (abbreviated *df*, calculated from the sample size), and the *p* value listed in the Sig. column of the box. The default test is a two-tailed test in SPSS for *t* tests, but you can convert the value to a one-tailed test by dividing the *p* value in half if the means differ in the predicted

Degrees of Freedom: number of scores that can vary in the calculation of a statistic

Figure 14.3 Output Window From the One-Sample *t* Test in Example 1

t Test

One- Sample Statistics

	N	Mean	Std. Deviation	Std. Error Mean
Recognition Scores	10	53.5000	10.40566	3.29056

One- Sample Test

	Test Value = 50					
					95% Confidence Interval of the Difference	
	t	df	Sig. (2 – tailed)	Mean Difference	Lower	Upper
Recognition Scores	1.064	9	.315	3.50000	−3.9438	10.9438

direction (the one-tailed test has a critical region at one end of the *t* distribution that is twice the size of the critical region for a two-tailed test—thus, the one-tailed test has a *p* value that is half the *p* value for the two-tailed test). The *p* value in the output for Example 1 is .315. In Example 1, if there is an effect, we expect the mean recognition score to be higher than 50 %. In other words, a one-tailed test is warranted. Thus, we must divide the given *p* value in half to obtain a *p* = .1575 for this one-tailed *t* test. As this value is *not* equal to or lower than alpha of .05 (the standard alpha level used in psychological research), the null hypothesis cannot be rejected and must be retained. In other words, there is no evidence that participants in the example experiment remembered the subliminal ads because their performance was not better than what is expected by chance. If you need to report the outcome of this test in APA style, you might include a statement such as "The mean recognition score for subliminal ads (*M* = 53.50) was not significantly higher than the chance value of 50 %, *t*(9) = 1.06, *p* = .16, one-tailed." The statistical values (rounded here to two significant digits) are stated as support for a statement about the results of the study. If a two-tailed hypothesis had been made for this study, then the result would be reported as "not significantly different."

Independent Samples *t* Test

The other two *t* tests are conducted in a similar manner. As another example, suppose that in the study in Example 1, the researcher predicted a difference between men and women in how well subliminal ads are remembered. Thus, in Example 2

&

Between-Subjects Variable: each participant experiences only one level of the independent variable

Quasi-Independent/Subject Variable: variable that allows comparison of groups of participants without manipulation (i.e., no random assignment)
---

samples of each gender are compared. An examination of the chart in Figure 14.2 indicates that the independent samples *t* test is appropriate for this design. There are two sample means, and the design is considered **between-subjects**, because the samples are from different, unrelated participants. In this case, gender is a **quasi-independent** or **subject variable**, however, rather than a manipulated independent variable. The data for this study are given below.

Example 2. Independent Samples *t* Test

Men		Women	
Participant 1	56	Participant 11	70
Participant 2	60	Participant 12	68
Participant 3	49	Participant 13	41
Participant 4	35	Participant 14	50
Participant 5	51	Participant 15	32
Participant 6	65	Participant 16	72
Participant 7	70	Participant 17	41
Participant 8	44	Participant 18	61
Participant 9	58	Participant 19	39
Participant 10	47	Participant 20	55

The data for the men in the example are the same as data for the sample in Example 1. To add the data for the women to the SPSS Data Window, type them in the same column as the men in Rows 11 through 20. In Column 2, you will need to indicate which sample the data belong to. You can code Rows 1 through 10 in the second column with a "1" for men and Rows 11 through 20 with a "2" for women. In the Variable View, you can define these groups by indicating labels for each number in the Values column for this variable. Select the values cell for this variable and click on the gray box to open the definition window. You should also name this variable (e.g., gender).

To conduct the independent samples *t* test for these data, go back to the "Compare Means" tab in the "Analyze" menu and choose the "Independent-samples *t*-test" option. The test window will allow you to click over the recognition score column as the Test Variable and the gender codes as the Grouping Variable. You must then choose "Define Groups" to indicate that the values in this column range from 1 to 2. When you click "Ok," the test will automatically run, and the output will appear in the Output Window (see Figure 14.4). The

Figure 14.4 Output Window From the Independent-Samples *t* Test in Example 2

t Test

Group Statistics

Recognition Scores	gender	N	Mean	Std. Deviation	Std. Error Mean
	Men	10	53.5000	10.40566	3.29056
	Women	10	52.9000	14.44107	4.56667

Independent Samples Test

		Levene's Test for Equality of Variances		*t* test for Equality of Means					95% Confidence Interval of the Difference	
		F	Sig.	t	df	Sig.(2-tailed)	Mean Difference	Std.Error Difference	Lower	Upper
Recognition Scores	Equal variances assumed	2.217	.154	.107	18	.916	.6000	5.62870	−11.225	12.4255
	Equal variances not assumed			.107	16.361	.916	.60000	5.62870	−11.311	12.5109

first box in the output will provide descriptive statistics for each group. The second box will contain the test statistic and p value. For Example 2, the t value is .107 and the p value (see in the Sig. column) is .916. This is a two-tailed test (it is possible that either men or women could have higher recognition scores) so the p value given can be directly compared with alpha. Once again, the p value is not equal to or lower than alpha of .05, and the null hypothesis cannot be rejected. Thus, there is no evidence in these data that men and women differ in their memories for subliminal ads.

Notice that there are two rows of values for the t statistic for the independent samples test. The first row is labeled "Equal Variance Assumed," and the second row is labeled "Equal Variance Not Assumed." These statements refer to the **homogeneity of variances** that is an assumption of between subjects tests (t tests and ANOVAs). The assumption is that the variance of the scores in the population is equal across the groups. If this assumption is violated, the t test may be inaccurate. Thus, Levene's test for this assumption is provided in the output (left side of the second box). If this test is significant (comparing p to alpha), then the statistical values need to be adjusted, and the second row of values in this box should be used. The two rows in this box are given to allow for both possibilities.

Homogeneity of Variances: assumption of between-subjects t tests and ANOVAs that the variance in the scores in the population is equal across groups

Paired Samples t Test

To illustrate the paired samples t test, suppose that in Example 1 the researcher had been interested in comparing memory for two types of subliminal material: standard ads (e.g., Coke ads) and emotional ads (e.g., ads with a sexy model). Thus, in Example 3, one sample of participants is tested for their recognition of both standard ads and emotional ads. The chart in Figure 14.2 leads us to the paired samples t test for this example because the two sample means are from the same participants, making ad type a **within-subjects variable**. The data for Example 3 are given in the table below.

Within-Subjects Variable: each participant experiences all levels of the independent variable

Example 3. Paired Samples t Test

Participant No.	Standard Ads	Emotional Ads
1	56	71
2	60	59
3	49	66
4	35	78
5	51	49

Participant No.	Standard Ads	Emotional Ads
6	65	82
7	70	77
8	44	52
9	58	51
10	47	78

To set up the Data Window, you will need two columns of data, one for each condition. Remember that each row in the data window represents one participant; thus the pair of scores for an individual participant will appear in the same row. Define the variables according to the conditions (e.g., standard ads and emotional ads). To run the test, choose the "Paired-samples t test" in the "Compare Means" portion of the "Analyze" menu. To compare the two conditions, click the first one to add it as "Variable 1" and then the second condition as "Variable 2." Then, click the arrow to add them as a "Paired Variable." When you click "Ok," the test will run, and the output will appear in the Output Window.

The output will indicate descriptive statistics in the first box and the test statistic and p value in the third box (see Figure 14.5). For Example 3, the t value is −2.624 with a p value of .028. For this example, the p value is lower than alpha of .05. Thus, the null hypothesis (that there is no difference between the ad types) can be rejected and the alternative hypothesis (that there is a difference between the ad types) can be accepted. The means indicate which ad type was remembered better: In this case, the emotional ads ($M = 66.3$) were remembered better than the standard ads ($M = 53.5$), $t(9) = -2.62$, $p = .03$. The second box of the output provides a test of the relationship between the two sets of scores (see below for more information about tests for relationships).

Comparing More Than Two Means With ANOVA

When more than two means are being compared, such as with **multivalent variables** or **factorial designs** (see Chapters 4 and 11 for more discussion of these design types), the difference between the means becomes a bit more complicated to calculate (see Appendix for calculations). **Analysis of variance (ANOVA)** is used to test an effect when more than two groups or conditions are being considered. The average variance is used in the calculation of mean differences and sampling error, which is

Multivalent Variable: a variable that includes three or more levels—a design is considered multivalent if there is only one independent variable that contains three or more levels

Factorial Design: an experiment or quasi-experiment that includes more than one independent variable

Analysis of Variance (ANOVA): analysis of variance test used for designs with three or more sample means

Figure 14.5 Output Window From the Paired-Samples *t* Test in Example 3

t Test

Paired Samples Statistics

		Mean	N	Std. Deviation	Std. Error Mean
Pair 1	Standard Ads	53.5000	10	10.40566	3.29056
	Emotional Ads	66.3000	10	12.68464	4.01123

Paired Samples Correlations

		N	Correlation	Sig.
Pair1	Standard Ads and Emotional Ads	10	.118	.745

Paired Samples Test

		Paired Differences					t	df	Sig. (2-tailed)
					95% Confidence Interval of the Difference				
		Mean	Std. Deviation	Std. Error Mean	Lower	Upper			
Pair 1	Standard Ads and Emotional Ads	−12.800	15.42581	4.87807	−23.835	−1.7650	−2.624	9	.028

why the test is called *analysis of variance*. An *F* statistic is calculated for each effect tested based on the ratio of average variance between the condition means and the average variance within the conditions. The calculated *F* statistic is compared with the distribution of *F* values when the null hypothesis is true to determine the corresponding *p* value based on the critical region of the distribution set by the alpha level. In the chart in Figure 14.2, you can see that ANOVA is recommended for designs with three or more sample or condition means.

The comparison of means for each level of an independent (or quasi-independent) variable is called the **main effect**. Thus, an ANOVA will test main effects for each independent variable separately in the analysis. If a main effect is significant in an ANOVA, it indicates that there is a mean difference somewhere among the means tested. But the main effect does not tell you which means are different from one another. You must conduct additional tests, called **post hoc tests**, to determine which means are different. An interaction effect is also tested in an ANOVA for all combinations of independent variables. The **interaction effect** tests the effect of one independent variable at each level of the other variable. In other words, does the independent variable effect depend on the levels of another independent variable? The interaction effect is tested by comparing the difference in condition means across levels of one independent variable for each level of the other independent variable(s). Main effects and interactions have also been discussed in Chapter 11. In this chapter, we will focus on how to calculate main effects and interactions in an ANOVA using SPSS (but see the Appendix for hand calculations of these effects).

Main Effect: test of the differences between all means for each level of an independent variable in an ANOVA

Post Hoc Tests: additional significance tests conducted to determine which means are significantly different for a main effect

Interaction Effect: tests the effect of one independent variable at each level of another independent variable(s) in an ANOVA

Using SPSS to Conduct ANOVAs

Both the main effects and interaction effects for each combination of variables are run simultaneously in a single ANOVA for the entire design. However, the test options (and calculations—see the Appendix) differ for between-subjects and within-subjects variables. Thus, an example to test the main effect of each type of variable will be discussed along with an example of a factorial design.

Between-Subjects Design

Consider a study in which a researcher tests the effect of study modality on learning. Participants are randomly assigned to a modality condition: paper text, computer text, or computer with voice text. Participants are presented with text material on three different topics during a study phase. The material on each topic is presented in a manner consistent with the condition to which the participant was assigned. All participants then perform a word puzzle to distract them from the material for 10 minutes. After the puzzle task, all the participants complete a multiple-choice test for the material they studied. Percentage correct on the test is calculated for the participants in each condition. These data are presented in Example 4 on page 274.

Example 4. Between-Subjects ANOVA

Participant No.	Paper Text	Participant No.	Computer Text	Participant No.	Computer With Voice Text
1	74	11	88	21	72
2	62	12	90	22	86
3	59	13	54	23	93
4	78	14	79	24	91
5	65	15	85	25	80
6	90	16	78	26	79
7	45	17	92	27	84
8	51	18	74	28	75
9	67	19	89	29	78
10	71	20	77	30	92

To input the data into the Data Window in SPSS, you will enter the scores in one column, as with the data from Example 2, because both designs only contain between-subjects variables. The second column should be used to code the conditions with a different code number for each condition (e.g., "1" for paper text, "2" for computer text, and "3" for computer with voice text). Remember to name the variables and define the code values in the Variable View.

To run an ANOVA with a single between-subjects variable, you will also choose the "Compare Means" option in the "Analyze" menu. Then, select the "One-way ANOVA" test (one-way means one independent or subject variable). The variable definition window will appear. Click the Test Score column into the Dependent List window to define the dependent variable. Then click the text condition code column into the Factor window to define it as the independent variable. You must also choose the "Options" button and select "Descriptives" if you want to view descriptive statistics for the samples. The post hoc button will allow you to run post hoc tests along with the ANOVA. These tests will be useful if the text condition main effect is significant, indicating a difference between at least two of the text groups. Selecting the post hoc button will bring up a list of different post hoc tests. A comparison of these tests is beyond the scope of this text. However, the least significant difference (LSD), Bonferroni, and Tukey tests are common post hoc tests used in psychological studies (in order of conservativeness). Click "OK" to begin the ANOVA.

The output window will contain a box with descriptive statistics (if you choose that option), a box with the F statistic and p value, and a box with the post hoc tests (if you choose that option). The between-groups row of the statistics box in Figure 14.6 indicates a significant effect of text condition with $F = 7.036$ and a p value of .003. The test is significant,

Figure 14.6   Output Window From the Between-Subjects ANOVA in Example 4

Oneway

Descriptives

Test Score - Percentage Correct

	N	Mean	Std. Deviation	Std. Error	95% Confidence Interval for Mean Lower Bound	95% Confidence Interval for Mean Upper Bound
Paper text	10	66.2000	13.08774	4.13871	56.8376	75.5624
Computer text	10	80.6000	11.23684	3.55340	72.5616	88.6384
Computer with voice text	10	83.0000	7.37865	2.33333	77.7216	88.2784
Total	30	76.6000	12.89106	2.35357	71.7864	81.4136

Descriptives

Test Score - Percentage Correct

	Minimum	Maximum
Paper text	45.00	90.00
Computer text	54.00	92.00
Computer with voice text	72.00	93.00
Total	45.00	93.00

ANOVA

Test Score - Percentage Correct

	Sum ofSquares	df	Mean Square	F	Sig.
Between groups	1651.200	2	825.600	7.036	.003
Within groups	3168.000	27	117.333		
Total	4819.200	29			

(Continued)

Figure 14.6 (Continued)

Post Hoc Tests

Multiple Comparisons

Dependent Variable: Test Score - Percentage Correct

LSD

(I) Text Condition	(J) Text Condition	Mean Difference (I-J)	Std. Error	Sig.	95% Confidence Interval Lower Bound	Upper Bound
Paper text	Computer Text	−14.4000*	4.84424	.006	−24.3396	−4.4604
	Computer with VoiceText	−16.8000*	4.84424	.002	−26.7396	−6.8604
Computer text	Paper Text	14.40000*	4.84424	.006	4.4604	24.3396
	Computer with VoiceText	−2.40000	4.84424	.624	−12.3396	7.5396
Computer with voice text	Paper Text	16.80000*	4.84424	.002	6.8604	26.7396
	Computer Text	2.40000	4.84424	.624	−7.5396	12.3396

*The mean difference is significant at the .05 level.

because the *p* value is lower than alpha of .05. In other words, we can reject the null hypothesis that there is no difference between the condition means. This result might be reported as "The effect of text condition was significant, $F(2, 27) = 7.04, p = .003$." Although this test is significant, it does not tell us which conditions are different from each other.

The post hoc tests will indicate which pairs of means are significantly different from one another. Post hoc tests are different from normal sets of *t* tests because they adjust for an inflated alpha level. Each time a pairwise comparison is made, it becomes more likely that a **Type I error** is made. In other words, the likelihood of making a Type I error is higher for multiple *t* tests than for a single test. Thus, the post hoc tests keep alpha at .05 for each test by adjusting the alpha level for the set of tests based on the number of tests conducted. These tests are shown in the third box in

Type I Error: error made in a significance test when the researcher rejects the null hypothesis when it is actually true

Figure 14.6. The LSD test was chosen in this example. The box shows p values (in the Sig. column) lower than .05 for the paper text versus computer text and paper text versus computer with voice text tests but not for the computer text versus computer with voice text test. Thus, if we examine the means shown in the first box of Figure 14.6, we see that both of the computer conditions resulted in higher test scores than the paper text condition, but the two computer conditions did not differ from each other.

Within-Subjects Design

For within-subjects designs, two things will change in SPSS from the between-subjects example described above: (1) the data will appear in separate columns for each condition in the Data Window (remember that each participant or set of matched participants will have data in a single row), and (2) we will use the "Repeated Measures" test in the "General Linear Model" option of the "Analyze" menu.

For Example 5, consider an alteration to Example 4. Suppose the researcher in this study had asked each participant to study each one of the three topics in a different text condition (with different participants receiving different assignments of topic to text condition, a design feature called **counterbalancing** that is used to control bias—see Chapter 11 for more discussion of counterbalancing). Thus, Example 5 has the same data in each condition, but each set of scores comes from a single sample of participants instead of three separate samples. In other words, a within-subjects design was used. These data are presented in the table below.

Counterbalance: a control used in within-subjects experiments where equal numbers of participants are randomly assigned to different orders of the conditions

Example 5. Within-Subjects ANOVA

Participant No.	Paper Text	Computer Text	Computer With Voice Text
1	74	88	72
2	62	90	86
3	59	54	93
4	78	79	91
5	65	85	80
6	90	78	79
7	45	92	84
8	51	74	75
9	67	89	78
10	71	77	92

As indicated above, each of these conditions is listed in a different column in the Data Window in SPSS with the column labeled by condition. In addition, the within-subjects ANOVA is run by choosing the "Repeated Measures" test in the "General Linear Model" portion of the "Analyze" menu. This test is used to conduct an ANOVA for any design that contains a within-subjects variable. The first window that appears for this test is the within-subjects variable definition window. In the top space, name the variable (e.g., textcond) and then indicate the number of conditions for this variable (e.g., 3) by typing the number into the Number of Levels space and adding this variable to the list. Then, click "Define" to choose the columns for each level on the right side of the next window that appears. If your design also contained a between-subjects variable, you could define that variable here as well in the Between-Subjects factor box. To run post hoc tests for this design (in the case that the main effect of text condition is significant in the ANOVA), you must choose the "Options" button (the Post Hoc button is used only for between-subjects variables), click over the text condition variable into the Display Means for box and then check the Compare main effects box. You can then choose a post hoc test from the drop-down bar. You may also wish to choose the Display Descriptive Statistics option in this window. Click "Continue" and "Ok" to run the test.

The output (see Figure 14.7) will be more complex for the repeated measures test than for the other tests we have seen. However, the output will still contain the information needed to determine if the tests are significant. To evaluate the main effect of the text condition, look for the "Tests of Within-Subjects Effects" box. The first column of this box shows the F and p values. For Example 5, the $F = 6.245$ and $p = .009$. Thus, we can reject the null hypothesis that there is no difference in condition means, because the main effect of text condition is significant. The post hoc tests are shown in the box of the output labeled "Pairwise Comparisons." The conditions are indicated by code value with p values listed in the Sig. column. As in Example 4, the post hoc tests indicate that learning for the paper text condition is lower than both of the computer conditions, but the two computer conditions do not significantly differ from each other.

You will also see a box in the output for Mauchly's Test of Sphericity. **Sphericity** is an assumption of the repeated measures test. The assumption is that pairs of scores in the population have similar variability. If the sphericity test is significant in the repeated measures output, the F statistic needs to be adjusted in order to retain accuracy of the test. Thus, the "Tests of Within-Subjects Effects" box contains a few different corrections below the "Sphericity Assumed" row. The sphericity assumed values can be used if the sphericity test is not significant. However, if the sphericity test is significant, a correction should be used because violations of this assumption can increase the chance of a Type I error (Keppel & Wickens, 2004). A common correction used in psychological research is the Greenhouse-Geiser correction. A full discussion of the correction techniques is provided in Howell's (2009) statistics text.

Sphericity Assumption: assumption of the repeated measures (within-subjects) ANOVA that pairs of scores in the population have equal variance

Figure 14.7 Output From Output Window for the Within-Subjects ANOVA in Example 5

General Linear Model

Within-Subjects Factors

Measure: MEASURE_1

textcond	Dependent Variable
1	paper
2	comp
3	compvoice

Descriptive Statistics

	Mean	Std.Deviation	N
Paper text	66.2000	13.08774	10
Computer text	80.6000	11.23684	10
Computer with voice text	83.0000	7.37865	10

Multivariate Tests[a]

Effect		Value	F	Hypothesis df	Error df	Sig.
textcond	Pillai's Trace	.591	5.784[b]	2.000	8.000	.028
	Wilks' Lambda	.409	5.784[b]	2.000	8.000	.028
	Hotelling's Trace	1.446	5.784[b]	2.000	8.000	.028
	Roy's Largest Root	1.446	5.784[b]	2.000	8.000	.028

[a] Design: Intercept
  Within Subjects Design: textcond
[b] Exact statistic

(Continued)

Figure 14.7 (Continued)

Mauchly's Test of Sphericity[a]

Measure: MEASURE_1

Within-Subjects Effect	Mauchly's W	Approx.Chi-Square	df	Sig.
textcond	.975	.205	2	.902

Tests the null hypothesis that the error covariance matrix of the orthonormalized transformed dependent variables is proportional to an identity matrix.

Mauchly's Test of Sphericity[a]

Measure: MEASURE_1

Within-Subjects Effect	Epsilon[b]		
	Greenhouse-Geisser	Huynh-Feldt	Lower bound
textcond	.975	1.000	.500

Tests the null hypothesis that the error covariance matrix of the orthonormalized transformed dependent variables is proportional to an identity matrix.

a. Design: Intercept
   Within Subjects Design: textcond

b. May be used to adjust the degrees of freedom for the averaged tests of significance. Corrected tests are displayed in the Tests of Within-Subjects Effects table.

Tests of Within-Subjects Effects

Measure: MEASURE_1

Source		Type III Sum of Squares	df	Mean Square
textcond	Sphericity Assumed	1651.200	2	825.600
	Greenhouse-Geisser	1651.200	1.951	846.514
	Huynh-Feldt	1651.200	2.000	825.600
	Lower-bound	1651.200	1.000	1651.200
Error(textcond)	Sphericity Assumed	2379.467	18	132.193
	Greenhouse-Geisser	2379.467	17.555	135.541
	Huynh-Feldt	2379.467	18.000	132.193
	Lower-bound	2379.467	9.000	264.385

Tests of Within-Subjects Effects

Measure: MEASURE_1

Source		F	Sig.
textcond	Sphericity Assumed	6.245	.009
	Greenhouse-Geisser	6.245	.009
	Huynh-Feldt	6.245	.009
	Lower-bound	6.245	.034
Error(textcond)	Sphericity Assumed		
	Greenhouse-Geisser		
	Huynh-Feldt		
	Lower-bound		

Tests of Within-Subjects Contrasts

Measure: MEASURE_1

Source	textcond	Type III Sumof Squares	df	Mean Square	F	Sig.
textcond	Linear	1411.200	1	1411.200	12.168	.007
	Quadratic	240.000	1	240.000	1.617	.235
Error(textcond)	Linear	1043.800	9	115.978		
	Quadratic	1335.667	9	115.978		

Tests of Between-Subjects Effects

Measure: MEASURE_1

Transformed Variable: Average

Source	Type III Sumof Squares	df	Mean Square	F	Sig.
Intercept	176026.800	1	176026.800	2009.099	.000
Error	788.533	9	87.615		

(Continued)

Figure 14.7 (Continued)

Estimated Marginal Means
textcond

Estimates

Measure: MEASURE_1

textcond	Mean	Std. Error	95% Confidence Interval	
			Lower Bound	Upper Bound
1	66.200	4.139	56.838	75.562
2	80.600	3.553	72.562	88.638
3	83.000	2.333	77.722	88.278

Pairwise Comparisons

Measure: MEASURE_1

(I) textcond	(J) textcond	Mean Difference (I-J)	Std. Error	Sig.[a]	95% Confidence Interval for Difference[a]	
					Lower Bound	Upper Bound
1	2	−14.400*	5.512	.028	−26.869	−1.931
	3	−16.800*	4.816	.007	−27.695	−5.905
2	1	14.400*	5.512	.028	1.931	26.869
	3	−2.400	5.073	.647	−13.876	9.076
3	1	16.800*	4.816	.007	5.905	27.695
	2	2.400	5.073	.647	−9.076	13.876

Based on estimated marginal means

a. Adjustment for multiple comparisons: Least Significant Difference (equivalent to no adjustments).

*The mean difference is significant at the .05 level.

Multivariate Tests

	Value	F	Hypothesis df	Error df	Sig.
Pillai's trace	.591	5.784[a]	2.000	8.000	.028
Wilks' lambda	.409	5.784[a]	2.000	8.000	.028
Hotelling's trace	1.446	5.784[a]	2.000	8.000	.028
Roy's largest root	1.446	5.784[a]	2.000	8.000	.028

Each F tests the multivariate effect of textcond. These tests are based on the linearly independent pairwise comparisons among the estimated marginal means.

a. Exact statistic

Factorial ANOVA

To complete the discussion of ANOVA, we will now consider a simple factorial ANOVA with two independent variables, each with two levels (i.e., a 2 × 2 design). As in the previous two ANOVA examples, we will be interested in the main effects tested for each independent variable. In addition, an interaction effect will be considered. The example below is of a between-subjects design (i.e., both independent variables are manipulated between subjects); however, as described in the previous example, if any of the independent variables in a factorial design are manipulated within subjects, the repeated measures test should be used.

Example 6. Factorial ANOVA

Consider a study where memory is compared for different types of items. In this experiment, two factors are manipulated: the type of item one studies (either pictures or words) and the type of test one receives (recognition of items formatted as words or pictures). In this study, the researcher will consider if memory performance differs for studied pictures and words (i.e., the main effect of study format), differs for tested pictures and words (i.e., the main effect of test format), and whether format match (picture or word) across study and test is better than when the format mismatches (i.e., the interaction of these factors). Percentage correct recognition data are presented in the table below.

Participant No.	Picture Study Picture Test	Participant No.	Picture Study Word Test
1	92	11	68
2	88	12	50

(Continued)

(Continued)

Participant No.	Picture Study Picture Test	Participant No.	Picture Study Word Test
1	92	11	68
2	88	12	50
3	87	13	54
4	78	14	80
5	95	15	85
6	90	16	78
7	71	17	92
8	89	18	74
9	93	19	79
10	89	20	77
	Word Study Picture Test		**Word Study Word Test**
21	56	31	88
22	62	32	90
23	59	33	67
24	70	34	79
25	65	35	85
26	67	36	78
27	45	37	90
28	51	38	74
29	67	39	89
30	71	40	77

Recall from the examples above that the data should all be entered into one column in the Data Window in SPSS because each score is from a different participant. You will need two columns of codes, one for the study format and one for the test format. Remember to label the columns with the variable names and to insert value labels for the codes.

To run the two-way, between-subjects ANOVA, choose the "Univariate" test option in the "General Linear Model" portion of the "Analyze" menu. A definition window will appear where you can click over the dependent and independent (Fixed Factor box) variables. You will not need to select any post hoc tests for the main effects in this design because there are only two levels of each independent variable. An examination of the means will indicate which level resulted in higher recognition for any significant main effects. If you select "Descriptives" in the Options window, these means will appear in the output. Click "Ok" to begin the analysis.

The output will be similar to that for Example 4 above; however, three tests of interest will appear in the "Tests of Between-Subjects Effects" box (see Figure 14.8). The two main effects will be indicated in the rows with the variable labels ("study" and "test" for Example 6). The main effect of study format was significant, $F(1, 36) = 8.91, p = .005$; however, the main effect of test format was not significant, $F(1, 36) = 1.32, p = .257$. The means in the Descriptive Statistics box indicate that studied pictures ($M = 80.45$) were better remembered than studied words ($M = 71.50$), regardless of test format. This is a common finding in memory studies (Paivio, 2007). However, the interaction between study format and test format was also significant, $F(1, 36) = 31.96, p < .001$. Note that the p value in the output for the interaction is listed as .000. This value represents a value smaller than .0005 that has been rounded to three significant digits. In fact, p can never equal 0. The convention used in reporting such values is to indicate that the p was less than .001. The graph in Figure 14.9 illustrates this interaction. From the graph, one can see that the match in study and test format did affect recognition scores such that a match in format from study to test resulted in higher scores than the mismatch conditions.

Figure 14.8   Output From Output Window for the Factorial ANOVA in Example 6

Univariate Analysis of Variance

Between-Subjects Factors

		Value Label	N
Study format	1.00	Picture	20
	2.00	Word	20
Test format	1.00	Picture	20
	2.00	Word	20

(Continued)

Figure 14.8 (Continued)

Descriptive Statistics

Dependent Variable: Recognition Score

Study Format	Test Format	Mean	Std. Deviation	N
Picture	Picture	87.2000	7.29992	10
	Word	73.7000	13.08986	10
	Total	80.4500	12.42440	20
Word	Picture	61.3000	8.52513	10
	Word	81.7000	7.88881	10
	Total	71.5000	13.16894	20
Total	Picture	74.2500	15.36871	20
	Word	77.7000	11.29089	20
	Total	75.9750	13.42498	40

Tests of Between-Subjects Effects

Dependent Variable: Recognition Score

Source	Type III Sum of Squares	df	Mean Square	F	Sig.
Corrected model	3793.075[a]	3	1264.358	14.066	.000
Intercept	230888.025	1	230888.025	2568.673	.000
Study	801.025	1	801.025	8.912	.005
Test	119.025	1	119.025	1.324	.257
Study *Test	2873.025	1	2873.025	31.963	.000
Error	3235.900	36	89.886		
Total	327917.000	40			
Corrected Total	7028.975	39			

a. R Squared = .540 (Adjusted R Squared = .501)

Figure 14.9   Line Graph of the Interaction Between Study Format and Test Format in Example 6

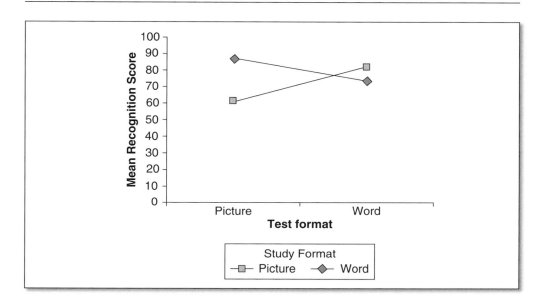

Looking for Relationships With Pearson *r* and Regression Tests

Different inferential statistics are used when one is testing hypotheses about relationships across distributions of scores. To simply determine if there is a relationship between two distributions, a **chi-square** or **Pearson *r* test** is conducted, depending on the type of scale used to measure the dependent variable (see Figure 14.2). The chi-square test is used for nominal and ordinal data, and the Pearson *r* test is used for interval and ratio data. Both tests will indicate if a significant relationship exists between variables in a data set.

Chi-Square Test: a significance test used to determine if a relationship exists between two variables measured on nominal or ordinal scales

Pearson *r* Test: a significance test used to determine if a linear relationship exists between two variables measured on interval or ratio scales

The Pearson *r* statistic tests linear relationships. The values of the statistic range from −1.0 to +1.0. A Pearson *r* of +1.0 represents a perfect positive relationship. A Pearson *r* of −1.0 represents a perfect negative relationship. A value of 0 indicates no relationship. The Pearson *r* statistic can be used as a descriptive statistic to simply describe the type and degree of relationship for the sample distributions. Values closer to +1.0 and −1.0 are stronger relationships. Values closer to 0 represent weaker relationships (see Figure 14.10). Pearson *r* can also be used as an inferential statistic to determine if a significant relationship exists between two variables. The test relies on the same principles as the comparison tests described above. The Pearson *r* value calculated from the sample distributions (based on overlap in scores

Figure 14.10 Possible Relationships Between Distributions With Corresponding Pearson *r* Values

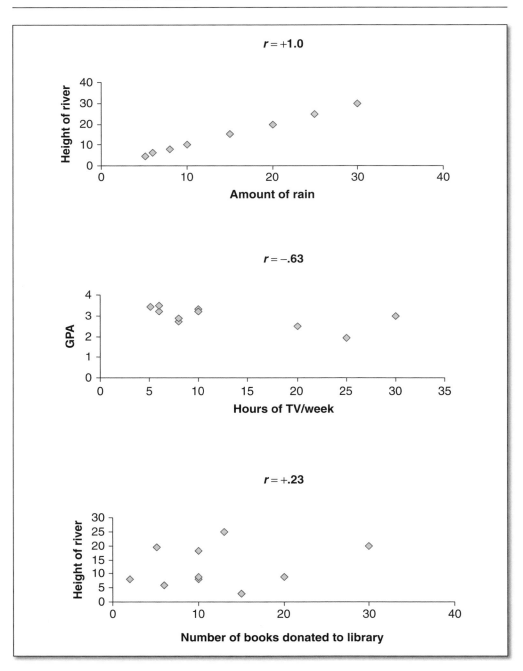

between the distributions with sampling error removed) is compared with the distribution of possible Pearson r values for samples of that size when there is no relationship in the population. If the sample Pearson r is an extreme score, in the most extreme 5% of the distribution, for example, there is evidence to reject the null hypothesis that there is no relationship (i.e., the test is significant) and accept the alternative hypothesis that there is a relationship (or a specific relationship if a one-tailed test is used).

Another way in which psychologists examine relationships between distributions is with regression. In a regression analysis, a researcher conducts a test to determine if a set of data can be described by a function. In **linear regression**, the test determines how well the data fit a straight line. If a function is found to fit the data well, the function can then be used to predict the score of

Linear Regression: a statistical technique that determines the best fit line to a set of data to allow prediction of the score on one variable from the score on another variable

one variable from the score of another variable. Thus, a regression analysis will provide information about how well the function describes the data and a function equation that can be used to make predictions of one variable from another variable. Figure 14.11 illustrates the equation fit to the data in a linear regression analysis. The r^2 value given in the graph indicates how well the line fits the data. Higher r^2 values indicate a better fit with a maximum r^2 value of 1.0 for a perfect fit (i.e., the data perfectly follow a straight line). In the case of linear regression with two variables, r^2 is simply the square of the Pearson r value.

Figure 14.11   Linear Regression Equation for Two Distributions

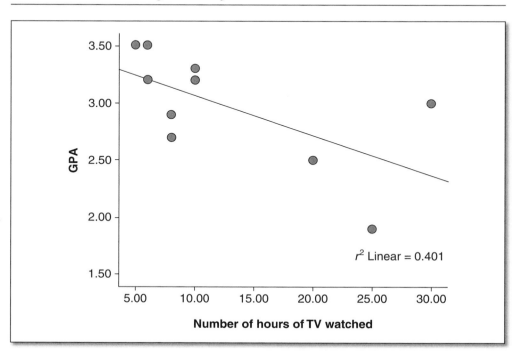

r^2 Linear = 0.401

Using SPSS to Conduct Chi-Square Analyses

Consider a study where older and younger participants are compared on their ability to remember to perform a task (e.g., mail a postcard) at some point in the future. The data in this study are on a nominal scale: the participant either remembers to mail the card (a response of "yes") or does not (a response of "no"). The data for the younger and older participants are presented in the table below.

Example 7. Chi-Square

Participant 1	Older	Yes	Participant 11	Younger	No
Participant 2	Older	Yes	Participant 12	Younger	No
Participant 3	Older	No	Participant 13	Younger	Yes
Participant 4	Older	Yes	Participant 14	Younger	Yes
Participant 5	Older	Yes	Participant 15	Younger	No
Participant 6	Older	No	Participant 16	Younger	No
Participant 7	Older	Yes	Participant 17	Younger	No
Participant 8	Older	Yes	Participant 18	Younger	Yes
Participant 9	Older	Yes	Participant 19	Younger	No
Participant 10	Older	Yes	Participant 20	Younger	Yes

The Data Window for this data set will contain two (or more) columns of the coded variables (e.g., "1" for yes response, "2" for no response in one column and "1" for older participants, "2" for younger participants in another column). To run the chi-square analysis, choose the "Crosstabs" option in the "Descriptive Statistics" portion of the "Analyze" menu. Click one variable into the Row box and the other variable into the Column box. Choose the statistics tab to click the chi-square test from the list. Click "Continue" and "Ok" to start the analysis.

The output from the chi-square is shown in Figure 14.12. The second box in the output shows the crosstabulation with the number of participants in each condition (Younger/yes, etc.). The values for the chi-square test are shown in the box labeled "Chi-square tests." The Pearson chi-square value of 3.333 is shown in the first row with its *p* value of .068. For this example, the relationship is not significant because the *p* value is greater than the alpha level of .05. In other words, the type of response ("yes" or "no") is not significantly related to the age group of the participants.

Figure 14.12   Output From Output Window for the Chi-Square Test in Example 7

Crosstabs
Case Processing Summary

	Cases					
	Valid		Missing		Total	
	N	Percentage	N	Percentage	N	Percentage
Age* Response	20	100.0%	0	.0%	20	100.0%

Age * Response Crosstabulation

Count

		Response		Total
		Yes	No	
Age	Older	8	2	10
	Younger	4	6	10
Total		12	8	20

Chi-square Tests

	Value	df	Asymp. Sig. (2-sided)	Exact Sig. (2-sided)	Exact Sig. (1-sided)
Pearson chi-square	3.333[a]	1	.068		
Continuity correction[b]	1.875	1	.171		
Likelihood ratio	3.452	1	.063		
Fisher's exact test				.170	.085
N of valid cases	20				

a. 2 cells (50.0%) have expected count less than 5. The minimum expected count is 4.00
b. Computed only for a 2x2 table

Using SPSS to Conduct a Pearson *r* Test

The Pearson *r* test can be used to test relationships when the variables are measured on interval or ratio scales. For example, suppose that in the study described in Example 7, the exact ages of the participants had been measured as well as the number of days that had passed before the participant remembered to perform the task of mailing the postcard. In this case, a Pearson *r* test can be used to determine if age is related to the number of days needed to remember the task. These data are given in the table below.

Example 8. Pearson *r* Test

Participant No.	Age	Number of Days	Participant No.	Age	Number of Days
1	81	1	11	21	3
2	77	0	12	18	10
3	69	0	13	19	8
4	73	2	14	24	7
5	89	0	15	20	5
6	67	1	16	21	8
7	65	1	17	22	7
8	70	0	18	18	6
9	78	2	19	19	7
10	75	0	20	20	9

The Data Window should contain two columns of data: the age and the number of days. To run the Pearson *r* test, choose the "Bivariate" test in the "Correlate" option in the "Analyze" menu. Click the two variables into the Variables box. The Pearson test box should be clicked. You can also choose to conduct a two-tailed test (either a positive or negative relationship is predicted) or a one-tailed test if the prediction is for a specific type (positive or negative) of relationship. Click "Ok" to run the test. The Correlations box in the output (see Figure 14.13) will indicate the Pearson *r* value (including the direction of relationship) in the first row and the *p* value in the second row. For Example 8, the variables are significantly related (negatively) with $r = -.90$ and $p < .001$. In other words, in this study as age increased, the number of days it took participants to remember to mail the card decreased.

Figure 14.13   Output From Output Window for the Pearson *r* Test in Example 8

Correlations

		Age	Days
Age	Pearson correlation	1	−.900*
	Sig. (2-tailed)		.00
	N	20	20
Days	Pearson correlation	−.900**	1
	Sig. (2-tailed)	.000	
	N	20	20

**Correlation is significant at the 0.01 level

Using SPSS to Conduct a Simple Linear Regression

An alternate method of analyzing the data in Example 8 is to conduct a simple linear regression analysis to examine the relationship between age and the number of days it took participants to mail the card. The simple linear regression will produce a linear function that allows researchers to predict one variable from another. In the case of this example, the researcher may wish to predict the number of days it would take participants to mail the card from their age.

Example 9. Simple Linear Regression

The simple linear regression for the data in Example 8 begins with the data set up in the Data Window the same way: Each variable is typed into a separate, labeled column in the Data Window. To conduct the analysis, choose the "Linear" option in the "Regression" portion of the "Analyze" menu. For this analysis, you must decide ahead of time which variable you are trying to predict (designated the dependent variable for the analysis) from the other (the predictor variable in this analysis). The dependent variable should be clicked into the Dependent box, and the predictor variable should be clicked into the Independent box. For Example 9, age is the predictor, and number of days is the dependent variable.

Figure 14.14 illustrates the output from the linear regression. The last box contains the output information needed to determine the regression equation and whether age significantly predicts number of days. The *t* test in the bottom row provides the significance test. In this case, the test is significant, $t(18) = -8.78$, $p < .001$. Thus, age significantly predicts number of days to mail the card. The prediction can be made from the following equation:

$$\text{Number of days} = -0.11 \text{ Age} + 9.21.$$

Figure 14.14   Output From Output Window for the Simple Linear Regression Test in Example 9

Regression

Variables Entered/Removed[a]

Model	Variables Entered	Variables Removed	Method
1	age[b]	.	Enter

a. Dependent Variable: days
b. All requested variables entered

Model Summary

Model	R	R^2	Adjusted R^2	Std. Error of the Estimate
1	.900[a]	.811	.800	1.59066

a. Predictors: (Constant), age

ANOVA[a]

Model		Sum of Squares	df	Mean Square	F	Sig.
1	Regression	195.006	1	195.006	77.071	.000[b]
	Residual	45.544	18	2.530		
	Total	240.550	19			

a. Dependent Variable: days
b. Predictors: (Constant), age

Coefficients[a]

Model		Unstandardized Coefficients		Standardized Coefficients	t	Sig.
		B	Std. Error	Beta		
1	(Constant)	9.209	.707		13.035	.000
	Age	−.113	.013	−.900	−8.779	.000

a. Dependent Variable: days

The slope of the regression line is −0.11, and it is given in the Age row of the Coefficients box. The intercept of the equation is 9.21, and it is given in the Constant row of the box. Thus, for a participant of 50 years of age, the predicted number of days to mail the card is as follows:

$$\text{Number of days} = -0.11(50) + 9.21 = 3.71.$$

CHAPTER SUMMARY

Reconsider the questions from the beginning of the chapter:

- Which statistical tests are best for different research designs? As described in this chapter, different designs and measurement scales call for different types of statistical tests. The chart in Figure 14.2 can help you decide which test is appropriate for different designs and measurement scales.
- How do we choose an appropriate statistical test? As seen in Figure 14.2, a test is chosen based on (1) whether you are comparing means or looking for relationships, (2) what type of measurement scale was used to collect the data, and (3) the design of the study (the number of independent variables, the number of levels of the independent variables, etc.)
- How do we use SPSS to run statistical tests? SPSS is a software package that allows researchers to compute descriptive and inferential statistics. Different inferential statistics require different types of tests to be run within the SPSS program. Descriptions of several of these tests are included in this chapter.
- What information is provided in an SPSS output? SPSS output differs a bit from test to test, but the output for all tests described in this chapter include sample means and standard deviations, the statistical value (t, F, r, etc.), and the p value that corresponds to the statistic calculated.

THINKING ABOUT RESEARCH

A summary of a research study in psychology is given below. As you read the summary, think about the following questions:

1. Is the goal of this study to test an effect or a relationship? Given your answer and the design of the study, what is the appropriate statistical test for this study (see Figure 14.2)?
2. The description of the results indicates three significant differences and one nonsignificant difference. How should the p values compare with alpha for the significant differences? What is the lowest p value that could have been obtained for the nonsignificant difference (assume $\alpha = .05$)?
3. Suppose the same participants had participated in both the synchronous and control groups (i.e., they had done the walk twice with different groups in different conditions). How does that change the design of the study? What is the correct statistical test for the changed design?
4. Suppose that in reality, shared activities do not affect cooperation, trust, or connectedness. In this case, what type of error have the researchers made in this study?

Study Reference

Wiltermuth, S. S., & Heath, C. (2009). Synchrony and cooperation. *Psychological Science, 20,* 1–5.

Purpose of the Study. The researchers were interested in the effects of joint activities (e.g., synchronous marching in the military) on the subsequent behavior of group members. They asked several research questions regarding this effect: (1) Do joint activities result in similar coordinated behavior across group members? (2) Do joint activities result in a feeling of connectedness with group members? (3) Do joint activities result in trust among group members? (4) Do joint activities result in feelings of happiness among group members?

Method of the Study. Thirty individuals participated in the study. They followed an experimenter in groups of three on a walk around campus. Walks took place in one of two conditions: the synchronous condition and the control condition. For the synchronous condition, groups walked together in step. For the control condition, groups walked normally. The participants were then asked to complete an exercise with their group that was presented as a separate and unrelated experiment. In the exercise, group members had to choose numbers between 1 and 7, such that higher numbers and smaller differences between numbers chosen by group members earned the group members higher amounts of money. Group members could not communicate during the game. Thus, group members who cooperated with each other were more likely to choose higher numbers. After the exercise, participants completed a survey asking them to rate how connected they felt with group members during the walk, how much they trusted other group members after the walk, and how happy they felt on a 1 to 7 scale.

Results of the Study. The synchronous and control groups were compared on the measures. Synchronous groups chose higher numbers ($M = 5.40$) in the first round of the exercise than the control groups ($M = 3.60$), indicating that group members coordinated more in the synchronous groups. Synchronous groups also indicated that they felt more connected ($M = 4.50$) than the control groups ($M = 2.90$) and that they trusted their group members more ($M = 5.60$) than the control groups ($M = 4.10$). However, no difference in happiness was found between the two group types ($M = 4.70$ for synchronous groups, $M = 4.80$ for control groups).

Conclusions of the Study. Wiltermuth and Heath (2009) concluded from their results that shared activities among group members lead to greater cooperation across group members, greater trust among group members, and a greater feeling of connectedness among group members. However, their hypothesis that shared activities lead to greater happiness of group members was not supported by the results of this study.

COMMON PITFALLS AND HOW TO AVOID THEM

Problem: Confusing independent and related samples tests—a common error made by students learning to conduct statistical tests is choosing the wrong type of *t* test for a study's design or entering data into the SPSS Data Window incorrectly for the design.

Solution: Remember that independent samples tests are for studies with groups made up of different, unrelated participants, and scores are entered into a single column in the Data Window with a second column for the group codes. Related samples tests are for studies with participants receiving all the conditions or groups of participants who are matched in some way. For related samples tests, scores for different conditions go in separate columns; no group codes are needed.

Problem: Confusing levels and conditions—with a factorial design, the difference between levels and conditions can be confusing.

Solution: Remember that levels are specific to an independent variable and conditions represent the combinations of levels of different variables in a factorial design. Thus, means for each level that are compared in main effects tests are different from the means for conditions that are considered in an interaction effect.

TEST YOURSELF

Reconsider the studies described in the Test Yourself section of Chapter 7 (assume $\alpha = .05$ for all tests).

1. Suppose you conducted a study to test the hypothesis that social pressure affects memory accuracy. You set up a study where participants view a video of a person robbing a convenience store. Then, half of the participants watch a video of other "participants" discussing the crime. In reality, the "participants" in the video are part of the experiment, and some of the details of the crime that are discussed are inaccurate. The actual participants are told that they should consider other people's perspectives on the crime because it is difficult for any one person to accurately remember all the details. The other half of the participants do not view the video discussion of the crime but are also told that it is difficult for any one person to accurately remember all the details of the crime. Thirty minutes after viewing the original crime video, all participants are given a recognition memory test about details of the crime. For this study, answer the following questions:

   (a) Using the chart in Figure 14.2 and what you know about the design of this study, what is the correct statistical test that should be used to analyze the data?

   (b) What is the null hypothesis that will be tested in the statistical test you described in (a)?

   (c) Suppose that 10 participants participated in each group in the study. For the recognition accuracy data provided below, use SPSS to conduct the correct statistical test to analyze these data.

   - *Video Discussion Group:* 67, 80, 69, 72, 75, 79, 66, 71, 69, 79
   - *No Video Discussion Group:* 78, 65, 79, 84, 88, 79, 89, 90, 85, 87

   (d) From the SPSS output you obtained, what can be concluded about the null hypothesis you stated in (b) above?

2. Suppose you conducted a study to determine if some people have the ability to predict which of two cards a poker player has been dealt for a poker hand. The study involves a single sample of people who claim to be "better than average poker players." In the study, all participants are asked to view a poker player being given a card from the dealer. They are asked to judge from the player's reaction whether the card is a card dealt to the player that will "complete a four of a kind hand" or "not complete a four of a kind hand." They complete 100 judgment trials, and their overall percentage accuracy is calculated. In other words, across all trials, the participants have a 50%

chance of being correct if they have no ability to interpret the player's "poker face" (i.e., they are guessing). If they are able to interpret the player's poker face, the participants should perform better than chance (50%) in correctly choosing which type of card the player has been dealt.

(a) Using the chart in Figure 14.2 and what you know about the design of this study, what is the correct statistical test that should be used to analyze the data?

(b) What is the null hypothesis that will be tested in the statistical test you described in (a)?

(c) Suppose that 10 participants participated in the study. For the accuracy data provided below, use SPSS to conduct the correct statistical test to analyze these data.

- *Sample Accuracy Data:* 50, 44, 51, 45, 52, 53, 52, 50, 56, 51

(d) From the SPSS output you obtained, what can be concluded about the null hypothesis you stated in (b) above?

Now, consider a new study.

3. A social psychologist is interested in how ad types affect desire to purchase different types of products. She asks 20 participants to participate in an experiment where video ads are shown to the participants for either a new car model or a new energy drink. The video ads either highlight that the product promotes a feeling of youthfulness (i.e., young, active people are featured in the ad) or a feeling of attractiveness (i.e., attractive people are featured in the ad). Participants are randomly assigned to view one of the four videos. After viewing the video, each participant is asked to rate his or her desire to purchase the product on a 1 to 7 scale, where higher numbers indicate more desire to buy.

(a) What are the independent variables in this experiment? Describe the levels for each independent variable.

(b) Based on this design, what is the appropriate statistical test for analysis of the data? What effects will be tested in this analysis?

(c) For data listed below, conduct the statistical test you described in (b) above. Which effects are significant?

- *Youthfulness Car Ad:* 5, 4, 5, 6, 3
- *Youthfulness Energy Drink Ad:* 7, 6, 7, 7, 6
- *Attractiveness Car Ad:* 3, 4, 3, 4, 5
- *Attractiveness Energy Drink Ad:* 5, 6, 6, 5, 6

(d) From the outcome of the tests, what can be concluded about the effects of ad type and product type on desire to buy a product?

Answers: 1a. The design contains two groups of unmatched participants. Thus, the appropriate test is an independent samples *t* test to compare the means for the video discussion and no video discussion groups. 1b. The null hypothesis tested in the analysis will be that there is no mean difference between video discussion and no video discussion groups in the population. 1c. SPSS output indicates that the video discussion group had mean recognition accuracy of 72.7% (*SD* = 5.23), and the no video discussion group had a mean recognition accuracy of 82.4%

($SD = 7.52$). The test indicated that the no video discussion group had a significantly higher mean recognition score than the video discussion group, $t(18) = -3.35$, $p = .004$. 1d. Because the p value of .004 is less than alpha (.05), we can conclude that the null hypothesis is false and that there is a difference between video and no video groups in the population. 2a. The design contains a single sample of participants. The sample mean will be compared with a known population mean when the participants have no poker ability (50% guessing accuracy). Thus, the appropriate test is a one-sample t test to compare the sample mean with the population mean of 50%. 2b. The null hypothesis tested in the analysis will be that there is no difference between the population mean of participants claiming to have poker abilities and the population mean of 50%. 2c. SPSS output indicates that the sample mean was 50.4% ($SD = 3.57$). The test indicated that the sample mean did not significantly differ from 50%, $t(9) = 0.36$, $p = .73$. 2d. Because the p value of .73 is greater than alpha (.05), we do not have evidence against the null hypothesis and must retain it. 3a. There are two independent variables in this experiment: ad type (youthfulness, attractiveness) and product type (car, energy drink). 3b. This is a factorial design, and an ANOVA should be used to analyze the data. The main effect of each independent variable (ad type and product type) will be tested to compare means for the levels (youthfulness vs. attractiveness and car vs. energy drink) of that variable on its own, and an interaction effect between the two variables will also be tested to determine if the effect of one independent variable depends on the level of the other variable. 3c. Based on the p values reported in the output, the main effects of ad type, $F(1, 16) = 6.23$, $p = .02$, and product type, $F(1, 16) = 27.77$, $p < .001$, are both significant. However, the interaction between ad type and product type were not significant, $F(1, 16) = 0.08$, $p = .785$. 3d. We can conclude that youthfulness ads ($M = 5.60$, $SD = 1.35$) result in higher desire-to-buy ratings than attractiveness ads ($M = 4.70$, $SD = 1.16$). We can also conclude that energy drink ads ($M = 6.10$, $SD = 0.74$) result in higher desire-to-buy ratings than car ads ($M = 4.20$, $SD = 1.03$).

Appendix

Statistical Calculations

Calculation formulas and examples are provided below for descriptive and inferential statistics discussed in Chapters 7 and 14.

DESCRIPTIVE STATISTICS

These examples use the data set (X values): 4, 3, 5, 3, 2, 4, 5, 3, 2, 1.

Statistic	Formula/Definition	Calculations
Mean (M)	$M = \dfrac{\Sigma X}{n}$	$M = \dfrac{(4+3+5+3+2+4+5+3+2+1)}{10} = \dfrac{32}{10} = 3.2$
Median	Middle score or average of middle scores	Order scores from lowest to highest: 1, 2, 2, 3, 3, 3, 4, 4, 5, 5 Average middle scores: (3 + 3)/2 = 3
Mode	Most common score or scores	3
Range	Difference between highest and lowest scores	Range = (5 − 1) = 4
Variance	$\text{Variance} = \dfrac{\sum (X - M)^2}{n-1}$	$\text{Variance} =$ $\dfrac{\begin{array}{l}[(4-3.2)^2 + (3-3.2)^2 + (5-3.2)^2 + (3-3.2)^2 + \\ (4-3.2)^2 + (5-3.2)^2 + (3-3.2)^2 + (2-3.2)^2 + (1-3.2)^2]\end{array}}{(10-1)} = 1.73$
Standard deviation (SD)	$SD = \sqrt{\dfrac{\sum (X-M)^2}{n-1}}$	$SD = \sqrt{\dfrac{\begin{array}{l}[(4-3.2)^2 + (3-3.2)^2 + (5-3.2)^2 + (3-3.2)^2 + \\ (2-3.2)^2 + (4-3.2)^2 + (5-3.2)^2 + (3-3.2)^2 + \\ (2-3.2)^2 + (1-3.2)^2]\end{array}}{(10-1)}} = 1.32$

NOTE: Σ = sum all values after this symbol, n = number of scores.

INFERENTIAL STATISTICS

Test	Example
One-sample t test	Sample values (X values): 4, 3, 5, 3, 2, 4, 5, 3, 2, 1 Population mean (μ) = 3.0, n is the number of scores in the sample $$t = \frac{(M - \mu)}{SD/\sqrt{n}} = \frac{(3.2 - 3.0)}{1.32/\sqrt{10}} = \frac{.2}{.42} = .48$$ This calculated t value is then compared with the appropriate t critical value (based on alpha and df of [$n-1$]) to determine significance. See www.psychology.ilstu.edu/psy138/resources/tables.html
Independent samples t test	Sample 1 values (X_1 values): 4, 3, 5, 3, 2, 4, 5, 3, 2, 1 Sample 2 values (X_2 values): 2, 3, 2, 3, 2, 2, 4, 3, 2, 2 $$t = \frac{(M_1 - M_2)}{\sqrt{s_p^2/n_1 + s_p^2/n_2}}$$ s_p^2 (pooled variance)—based on variance of each sample and n for each sample $$s_p^2 = \frac{(n_1 - 1)(SD_1^2) + (n_2 - 1)(SD_2^2)}{(n_1 - 1) + (n_2 - 1)}$$ $SD_1^2 = 1.73$ (from descriptive statistics section above) $$M_2 = \frac{2 + 3 + 2 + 3 + 2 + 2 + 4 + 3 + 2 + 2}{10} = 2.5$$ $$SD_2^2 = \frac{\begin{array}{c}[(2 - 2.5)^2 + (3 - 2.5)^2 + (2 - 2.5)^2 + (3 - 2.5)^2 + \\ (2 - 2.5)^2 + (2 - 2.5)^2 + (4 - 2.5)^2 + (3 - 2.5)^2 + \\ (2 - 2.5)^2 + (2 - 2.5)^2]\end{array}}{(10 - 1)} = .5$$ $$s_p^2 = \frac{(10 - 1)(1.73) + (10 - 1)(.5)}{(10 - 1) + (10 - 1)} = \frac{15.57 + 4.5}{18} = 1.12$$ $$t = \frac{(3.2 - 2.5)}{\sqrt{1.12/10 + 1.12/10}} = \frac{.7}{.47} = 1.43$$ This calculated t value is then compared with the appropriate t critical value (based on alpha and df of [$n_1 + n_2 - 2$]) to determine significance. See www.psychology.ilstu.edu/psy138/resources/tables.html

Test	Example
Related/Paired samples *t* test	Condition 1 values: 4, 3, 5, 3, 2, 4, 5, 3, 2, 1
	Condition 2 values from same or matched subjects: 2, 3, 2, 3, 2, 2, 4, 3, 2, 2
	t is calculated in this test based on difference scores for each participant or across matched pairs. Thus, difference scores are first calculated by subtracting the score in Condition 2 from the score for Condition 1 for each participant (e.g., 4 − 2 for Participant 1).
	Difference scores (*D* values): 2, 0, 3, 0, 0, 2, 1, 0, 0, 1
	Mean of *D* scores $(M_D) = \dfrac{(2+0+3+0+0+2+1+0+0-1)}{10} = .7$
	$SD \text{ of } D \ (SD_D) = \sqrt{\dfrac{\sum (D - M_D)^2}{n - 1}} =$
	$\sqrt{\dfrac{\begin{array}{l}[(2-.7)2+(0-.7)2+(3-.7)2+(0-.7)2+ \\ (0-.7)2+(2-.7)2+(1-.7)2+0-.7)2+ \\ (0-.7)2+(-1-.7)2]\end{array}}{10-1}} =$
	$\sqrt{\dfrac{14.1}{9}} = 1.25$
	$t = \dfrac{M_D}{SD_D / \sqrt{n}} = \dfrac{.7}{1.25 / \sqrt{10}} = .\dfrac{7}{.4} = 1.75$
	This calculated *t* value is then compared with the appropriate *t* critical value (based on alpha and *df* of [*n* − 1]) to determine significance. See www.psychology.ilstu.edu/psy138/resources/tables.html
One-way, between-subjects ANOVA	Sample 1 (X_1 values): 10, 15, 20, 13 (M_1 = 14.50)
	Sample 2 (X_2 values): 15, 25, 30, 25 (M_2 = 23.75)
	Sample 3 (X_3 values): 20, 17, 25, 20 (M_3 = 20.50)
	Overall mean for all samples (M_T) = 19.58
	$F = \dfrac{SS_A / a - 1}{SS_{\text{error}} / a(n - 1)}$

(Continued)

(Continued)

Test	Example
	$SS_A = n \sum (M_A - M_T)^2$ Sum of squared deviations for Factor A term (SS_A): n = number of scores per sample, M_A indicates each sample mean $SS_A = 4[(14.5 - 19.58)^2 + (23.75 - 19.58)^2 + (20.5 - 19.58)^2]$ $\quad = 4[25.81 + 17.89 + .85] = 4(44.55) = 178.20$ $a - 1 = 3 - 1 = 2$ a = number of groups in Factor A (df for Factor A term) $SS_{error} = \Sigma(X - M_A)^2$ Sum of squared deviations for error term (SS_{error}): X is an individual score, M_A is the sample mean for that score $SS_{error} = [(10 - 14.5)^2 + (15 - 14.5)^2 + (20 - 14.5)^2 + (13 - 14.5)^2 +$ $(15 - 23.75)2 + (25 - 23.75)2 + (30 - 23.75)2 + (25 - 23.75)2 +$ $(20 - 20.5)2 + (17 - 20.5)2 + (25 - 20.5)2 + (20 - 20.5)2]$ $\quad = [20.25 + .25 + 30.25 + 2.25 + 76.56 + 1.56 + 39.06 + 1.56 +$ $.25 + 12.25 + 20.25 + .25] = 204.74$ $a(n - 1) = 3(4 - 1) = 9$ (df for error term) $F = \dfrac{178.2/2}{204.74/9} = \dfrac{89.1}{22.75} = 3.92$ This calculated F value is then compared with the appropriate F critical value (based on alpha and df values) to determine significance. See www.psychology.ilstu.edu/psy138/resources/tables.html
Factorial, between-subjects ANOVA	Samples for two factors (A and B), each with two levels (1 and 2) Sample $A1$, $B1$ ($X_{A1, B1}$ values): 67, 80, 75, 77, 78 ($M_{A1, B1}$ = 75.40) Sample $A2$, $B1$ ($X_{A2, B1}$ values): 65, 59, 70, 62, 60 ($M_{A2, B1}$ = 63.20) Sample $A1$, $B2$ ($X_{A1, B2}$ values): 59, 60, 67, 52, 60 ($M_{A1, B2}$ = 59.60) Sample $A2$, $B2$ ($X_{A2, B2}$ values): 87, 90, 82, 86, 85 ($M_{A2, B2}$ = 86.00)

Test	Example
	Overall means for Factor A: $M_{A1} = 67.50$, $M_{A2} = 74.6$

Overall means for Factor A: $M_{A1} = 67.50$, $M_{A2} = 74.6$

Overall means for Factor B: $M_{B1} = 69.30$, $M_{B2} = 72.80$

Overall mean for all scores: $M_T = 71.05$

$a = 2$ (number of levels for Factor A)

$b = 2$ (number of levels for Factor B)

$n = 5$ (number of scores per group)

Three effects tested: Main effect of Factor A (F_A), Main effect of Factor B (F_B), and Interaction of A and B ($F_{A\times B}$)

$$F_A = \frac{SS_A/(a-1)}{SS_{\text{error}}/ab(n-1)}$$

$(a-1)$ is df for Factor A term, $ab(n-1)$ is df for error term

$$F_B = \frac{SS_B/(b-1)}{SS_{\text{error}}/ab(n-1)}$$

$(b-1)$ is df for Factor B term

$$F_{A\times B} = \frac{SS_{A\times B}/(a-1)(b-1)}{SS_{\text{error}}/ab(n-1)}$$

$(a-1)(b-1)$ is df for interaction $A \times B$ term

$$SS_A = 5(2)\sum[(67.5-71.05)^2 + (74.6-71.05)^2] = 252$$

$$
\begin{aligned}
SS_{S/AB} = \sum \big[&(67-75.4)^2 + (80-75.4)^2 + (75-75.4)^2 + (77-75.4)^2 + \\
&(78-75.4)^2 + (65-63.2)^2 + (59-63.2)^2 + (70-63.2)^2 + \\
&(62-63.2)^2 + (60-63.2)^2 + (50-59.6)^2 + (60-59.6)^2 + \\
&(67-59.6)^2 + (52-59.6)^2 + (60-59.6)^2 + (87-86)^2 + \\
&(90-86)^2 + (82-86)^2 + (86-86)^2 + (85-86)^2 \big] \\
= \;&327.2
\end{aligned}
$$

$$F_A = \frac{252/(2-1)}{327.2/[2(2)(5-1)]} = \frac{252}{20.45} = 12.33$$

$$SS_B = 5(2)\sum[(69.3-71.05)^2 + (72.8-71.05)^2] = 61.25$$

$$F_B = \frac{61.25/2-1}{327.2/[2(2)(5-1)]} = \frac{61.25}{20.45} = 3.00$$

(Continued)

(Continued)

Test	Example
	$SS_{A \times B} = n \sum (M_{AB} - M_A - M_B + M_T)^2$, where M_{AB} is the AB condition mean, M_A is the mean for that level of Factor A, and M_B is the mean for that level of Factor B $SS_{A \times B} = 5 \sum [(75.4 - 67.5 - 69.3 + 71.05)^2 + (86 - 74.6 - 72.8 + 71.05)^2]$ $= 1862.45$ $F_{A \times B} = \dfrac{1862.45/[(2-1)(2-1)]}{327.2/[2(2)(5-1)]} = \dfrac{1862.45}{20.45} = 91.07$ Each of these calculated F values is then compared with the appropriate F critical value (based on alpha and df values) to determine significance. See www.psychology.ilstu.edu/psy138/resources/tables.html
Pearson r correlation	Measure 1 values (X values): 4, 3, 5, 3, 2, 4, 5, 3, 2, 1 ($M_X = 3.2$ from above) Measure 2 values (Y values): 2, 3, 2, 3, 2, 2, 4, 3, 2, 2 ($M_Y = 2.5$ from above) $r = \dfrac{\sum [(X - M_X)(Y - M_Y)]}{\sqrt{\sum [(X - M_X)^2 \Sigma (Y - M_Y)^2]}} =$ $\dfrac{\begin{array}{l}[(4-3.2)(2-2.5) + (3-3.2)(3-2.5) + (5-3.2)(2-2.5)+ \\ (3-3.2)(3-2.5) + (2-3.2)(2-2.5) + (4-3.2)(2-2.5)+ \\ (5-3.2)(4-2.5) + (3-3.2)(3-2.5) + (2-3.2)(2-2.5)+ \\ (1-3.2)(2-2.5)]\end{array}}{\sqrt{\begin{array}{l}[(4-3.2)^2 + (3-3.2)^2 + (5-3.2)^2 + (3-3.2)^2 + (2-3.2)^2+ \\ (4-3.2)^2 + (5-3.2)^2 + (3-3.2)^2 + (2-3.2)^2 + (1-3.2)^2] \\ [(2-2.5)^2 + (3-2.5)^2 + (2-2.5)^2 + (3-2.5)^2 + (2-2.5)^2+ \\ (2-2.5)^2 + (4-2.5)^2 + (3-2.5)^2 + (2-2.5)^2 + (2-2.5)^2]\end{array}}} =$ $\dfrac{[-.4 + -.1 + -.9 + -.1 + .6 + -.4 + 2.7 + -.1 + .6 + 1.1]}{\sqrt{\begin{array}{l}[0.64 + 0.04 + 3.24 + 0.04 + 1.44 + 0.64 + 3.24 + 0.04 + 1.44 + 4.84] \\ [0.25 + 0.25 + 0.25 + 0.25 + 0.25 + 0.25 + 2.25 + 0.25 + 0.25 + 0.25]\end{array}}} =$ $\dfrac{3}{\sqrt{[15.6][4.5]}} = \dfrac{3}{8.38} = .36$ This calculated r value is then compared with the appropriate r critical value (based on alpha and df of $[n - 2]$) to determine significance. See www.psychology.ilstu.edu/psy138/resources/tables.html.

Test	Example
Linear regression	Predictor variable values (X values): 4, 3, 5, 3, 2, 4, 5, 3, 2, 1 ($M_X = 3.2$ from above)
	Outcome variable values (Y values): 2, 3, 2, 3, 2, 2, 4, 3, 2, 2 ($M_Y = 2.5$ from above)
	$\hat{Y} = bX + a$: regression line to predict Y value ($\hat{Y}$) from the value of X, must calculate b (slope of the line) and a (the intercept of the line—the value of Y when $X = 0$)
	$$b = \frac{\sum (X - M_X)(Y - M_Y)}{\sum (X - M_X)^2}$$ the numerator of this
	equation is equivalent to the numerator of the Pearson r calculation done above (3.00); the denominator is the sum of squared deviations for the predictor variable X (SS_X)
	$$SS_X = [(4 - 3.2)^2 + (3 - 3.2)^2 + (5 - 3.2)^2 + (3 - 3.2)^2$$ $$+ (2 - 3.2)^2 + (4 - 3.2)^2 + (5 - 3.2)^2 + (3 - 3.2)^2$$ $$+ (2 - 3.2)^2 + (1 - 3.2)^2] = 15.6$$
	$b = \dfrac{3}{15.6} = .19$. This is the slope of the "best fit" line
	$a = M_Y - b(M_X) = 2.5 - .19(3.2) = 1.89$. This is the intercept for the "best fit" line
	Thus, the regression equation is $\hat{Y} = .19X + 1.89$
	This equation can be used to predict a value of the outcome variable Y from the predictor variable X.
Pearson chi-square test	Frequency data from Example in Chapter 14:

	Older	Younger	Total
Yes	8	4	12
No	2	6	8
Total	10	10	

(Continued)

(Continued)

Test	Example
	The first step is to calculate expected frequencies for each combination of factors above if there is no relationship between these factors: $$f_e = \frac{f_{column}(f_{row})}{n}$$ Expected older (yes): $f_e = \dfrac{10(12)}{20} = 6$ Expected older (no): $f_e = \dfrac{10(8)}{20} = 4$ Expected younger (yes): $f_e = \dfrac{10(12)}{20} = 6$ Expected younger (no): $f_e = \dfrac{10(8)}{20} = 4$ Expected frequencies: |	Older	Younger
---	---	---
Yes	6	6
No	4	4	 The chi-square statistic is calculated from the difference between the observed and expected frequencies: $$\chi^2 = \sum \frac{(f_{observed} - f_{expected})^2}{f_{expected}} = \frac{(8-6)^2}{6} + \frac{(4-6)^2}{6} + \frac{(2-4)^2}{4} + \frac{(6-4)^2}{4}$$ $$= .67 + .67 + 1 + 1 = 3.34$$ This calculated χ^2 value is then compared with the appropriate χ^2 critical value (based on alpha and *df* of number of columns × number of rows) to determine significance. See www.psychology.ilstu.edu/psy138/resources/tables.html.

Glossary

A-B-A/Reversal Design: a small-*n* baseline design where the baseline behavior is measured, followed by implementation of a treatment, followed by another baseline measure after the treatment has ended

Abstract: a summary of an article that appears at the beginning of the article and in searchable databases of journal articles

Alpha Level: the probability level used by researchers to indicate the cutoff probability level (highest value) that will allow them to reject the null hypothesis

Amount Variable: variables that include levels with a different amount of the treatment changing from level to level

Analysis of Variance (ANOVA): analysis of variance test used for designs with three or more sample means

Applied Research: research conducted with the goal of solving everyday problems

Archival Data: a data collection technique that involves analysis of preexisting data

Attrition/Mortality: occurs when participants choose not to complete a study

Authority: relying on a knowledgeable person or group as a means of knowing about the world

Bar Graph: a graph of the means for different conditions in a study where the bar height represents the size of the mean

Baseline Design: a small-*n* design that involves baseline measurements of behavior as compared with measures of behavior during the implementation of a treatment

Baseline Measurement: measurement of behavior without a treatment used as a comparison

Basic Research: research conducted with the goal of understanding fundamental processes of phenomena

Between-Subjects Variable: each participant experiences only one level of the independent variable

Bivalent Independent Variable: an independent variable with two levels—a design is considered bivalent if it contains only one bivalent independent variable

Carryover Effects: occur when participants' experience in one condition affects their behavior in another condition of a study

Case Study: a research design that involves intensive study of particular individuals and their behaviors

Causal Hypothesis: a prediction about the results of a study that includes the causes of a behavior

Causal Research Question: a research question that asks what causes specific behaviors to occur

Central Tendency: representation of a typical score in a distribution

Chi-Square Test: a significance test used to determine if a relationship exists between two variables measured on nominal or ordinal scales

Closed-Ended Response Scale: participants respond to survey questions according to the response options provided by the researcher

Cluster Sample: sample chosen randomly from clusters identified in the population

Coercion: forcing participants to participate in research without their consent

Cohort-Sequential Design: a developmental design where multiple samples of participants of different ages are followed over time and tested at different ages

Confederate: a person who is part of a research study, but acts as though he or she is not, to deceive the participant about the study's purpose

Confidentiality: it is the researcher's responsibility to protect the participants' identity and right to privacy (including participant responses) during and after the research study

Confounding Variable: an extraneous factor present in a study that may affect the results

Consent Form: a form provided to the participants at the beginning of a research study to obtain their consent for the study and explain the study's purpose and risks and the participants' rights as participants

Construct Validity: indicates that a survey measures the behavior it is designed to measure

Content Analysis: an archival data collection technique that involves analysis of the content of an individual's spoken or written record

Control Group: the group of participants in an experiment who do not experience the treatment level of the independent variable

Convenience/Purposive Sample: sample chosen such that the probability of an individual being chosen cannot be determined

Counterbalance: a control used in within-subjects experiments where equal numbers of participants are randomly assigned to different orders of the conditions

Correlational Study: a type of research design that examines the relationships between multiple dependent variables, without manipulating any of the variables

Coverage Error: a sampling error that occurs when the sample chosen to complete a survey does not provide a good representation of the population

Criterion-Related Validity: determining the validity of the scores of a survey by examining the relationship between the survey scores and other established measures of the behavior of interest

Critical Region: the most extreme portion of a distribution of statistical values for the null hypothesis determined by the alpha level (typically 5%)

Cronbach's Alpha (α): method of testing scores' internal consistency that indicates the average correlation between scores on all pairs of items on a survey

Cross-Sectional Design: a developmental design in which multiple samples of participants of different ages are tested once

Data-Driven Hypothesis: hypothesis for a study that is based on the results of previous, related studies

Debriefing: discussing the purpose and benefits of a research study with subjects, often done at the end of the study

Deception: misleading participants about the purpose or procedures of a research study

Deduction: using logical reasoning and current knowledge as a means of knowing about the world

Deductive Reasoning: using general information to make a specific prediction

Degrees of Freedom: number of scores that can vary in the calculation of a statistic

Demand Characteristics: a source of bias that can occur in a study due to participants' changing their behavior based on their perception of the study and its purpose

Dependent/Response Variable: a variable that is measured or observed from an individual

Descriptive Hypothesis: a prediction about the results of a study that describes the behavior or the relationship between behaviors

Descriptive Research Question: a research question that asks about the presence of behavior, how frequently it is exhibited, or whether there is a relationship between different behaviors

Descriptive Statistics: measures that help us summarize data sets

Determinism: the assumption that phenomena have identifiable causes

Discrete Trials Design: a small-*n* design that involves a large number of trials completed by one or a few individuals and conducted to describe basic behaviors

Discussion: section of an APA-style article that compares the results of a study to the predictions and the results of previous studies

Distribution: a set of scores

Distribution of Sample Means: the distribution of all possible sample means for all possible samples from a population

Double-Blind Design: procedure used to control for experimenter bias by keeping the knowledge of the group assignments from both the participants and the researchers who interact with the participants

Empiricism: gaining knowledge through systematic observation of the world

Experiment: a type of research design that involves manipulation of an independent variable, allowing control of extraneous variables that could affect the results

Experimental Group: the group of participants in an experiment who experience the treatment level of the independent variable

Experimenter Bias: a source of bias in a study created when a researcher treats groups differently (often unknowingly) based on knowledge of the hypothesis

External Validity: the degree to which the results of a study apply to individuals and realistic behaviors outside the study

Face Validity: on the surface, a study or scale appears to be intuitively valid

Factorial Design: an experiment or quasi-experiment that includes more than one independent variable

Field Experiment: an experiment conducted in the participants' natural environment

Frequency Distribution: a graph of a distribution showing the frequency of each response in the distribution

Generation/Cohort Effects: confounding that may occur in cross-sectional designs due to different experiences that different generations have

Haphazard/Volunteer Sample: sample chosen from the population such that available individuals are chosen

Hawthorne Effect: a source of bias that can occur in a study due to participants' changing their behavior because they are aware that they are being observed

History Effect: events that occur during the course of a study to all or individual participants that can result in bias

Homogeneity of Variances: assumption of between-subjects t tests and ANOVAs that the variance in the scores in the population is equal across groups

Hypothesis: prediction regarding the results of a research study

Independent Variable: a variable in an experiment that is manipulated by the researcher such that the levels of the variable change across or within subjects in the experiment

Inductive Reasoning: using specific information to make a more general prediction

Inferential Statistics: a set of statistical procedures used by researchers to test hypotheses about populations

Informed Consent: obtaining consent from participants for participation in research after the participants have been informed about the purpose, procedure, and risks of the research

Institutional Animal Care and Use Committee (IACUC): committee of knowledgeable individuals that oversees the ethics of research with nonhuman animal subjects at an institution

Institutional Review Board (IRB): a committee of knowledgeable individuals who oversee the ethics of research with human participants conducted at an institution

Interaction Effect: tests the effect of one independent variable at each level of another independent variable(s) in an ANOVA

Internal Consistency: a form of reliability that tests relationships between scores on different items of a survey

Internal Validity: the degree to which a study provides causal information about behavior

Internet Sample: sample chosen from the population by recruiting on the Internet

Interrater Reliability: a measure of the degree to which different observers rate behaviors in similar ways

Interrupted Time Series Design: a time series design where the "treatment" is an independent event, such as a historical event

Interval Scale: a scale of data measurement that involves numerical responses that are equally spaced, but scores are not ratios of each other

Interviews: a data collection technique that involves direct questioning of individuals about their behaviors and attitudes

Introduction: a section of an APA-style article that introduces the topic of the study, reviews relevant background studies, and presents predictions for the data

Intuition: relying on common sense as a means of knowing about the world

Latin Square: partial counterbalancing technique where the number of orders of conditions used is equal to the number of conditions in the study

Levels of the Independent Variable: different situations or conditions that participants experience in an experiment because of the manipulation of the independent variable

Likert Scale: a scale of responses that measures a participant's agreement or disagreement with different types of statements, often with a rating from 1 to 5 or 1 to 7

Line Graph: a graph of the means for different conditions in a study where each mean is graphed as a point and the points are connected in a line to show differences between mean scores

Linear Regression: a statistical technique that determines the best fit line to a set of data to allow prediction of one variable from the other

Literature Review: a process of searching for and reviewing previous studies related to a study being developed to add to the knowledge in an area and make appropriate predictions about the data

Longitudinal Design: a developmental design where a single sample of participants is followed over time and tested at different ages

Main Effect: test of the differences between all means for each level of an independent variable in an ANOVA

Matched Design: a between-subjects experiment that involves sets of participants matched on a specific characteristic with each member of the set randomly assigned to a different level of the independent variable

Maturation: natural changes that occur to the participants during the course of a study that can result in bias

Mean: the calculated average of the scores in a distribution

Median: the middle score in a distribution, such that half of the scores are above and half are below that value

Method: section of an APA-style article that describes the participants, design, stimuli, apparatus, and procedure used in the study

Mode: the most common score in a distribution

Multivalent Variable: an independent variable that includes three or more levels—a design is considered multivalent if there is only one independent variable that contains three or more levels

Naturalistic Observation: a data collection technique involving noninvasive observation of individuals in their natural environments

Negative Relationship: a relationship between variables characterized by an increase in one variable that occurs with a decrease in the other variable

Nominal Scale: a scale of data measurement that involves nonordered categorical responses

Nonequivalent Groups: groups compared in a study where participants are not randomly assigned

Noninterrupted Time Series Design: a time series design where the "treatment" is implemented by the researcher

Nonresponse Error: a sampling error that occurs when individuals chosen for the sample do not respond to the survey, biasing the sample

Nonverbal Scale: survey response scale that involves pictorial response categories for participants with low verbal skills (e.g., children)

Null Hypothesis: the hypothesis that an effect or relationship does not exist (or exists in the opposite direction of the alternative hypothesis) in the population

Nuremberg Code: set of ethical guidelines developed for research with human participants based on information gained during the Nuremberg trials after World War II

Observation: relying on what one observes as a means of knowing about the world

One-Tailed Hypothesis: only one direction of an effect or relationship is predicted in the alternative hypothesis of the test

Open-Ended Response Scale: participants respond to survey questions in any manner they feel is appropriate for the question

Operational Definition: the definition of an abstract concept used by a researcher to measure or manipulate the concept in a research study

Order Effects: occur when the order in which the participants experience conditions in an experiment affects the results of the study

Ordinal Scale: a scale of data measurement that involves ordered categorical responses

Outcome Variable: the dependent variable in a correlational study that is being predicted by the predictor variable

Outliers: extreme high or low scores in a distribution

p Value: probability value associated with an inferential test that indicates the likelihood of obtaining the data in a study when the null hypothesis is true

Parsimony: the assumption that the simplest explanation of a phenomenon is most likely to be correct

Pearson r Test: a significance test used to determine if a linear relationship exists between two variables measured on interval or ratio scales

Peer Review: a process that takes place prior to publication of an article in many journals where experts make suggestions for improving an article and make a recommendation about whether an article should be published in the journal

Placebo: a sugar pill given to the control group in a drug study to allow all groups to believe that they are receiving a treatment

Plagiarism: claiming another's work or ideas as one's own

Population: a group of individuals a researcher seeks to learn about from a research study

Positive Relationship: a relationship between variables characterized by coupled increases in the two variables

Post Hoc Tests: additional significance tests conducted to determine which means are significantly different for a main effect

Power: ability of a significance test to detect an effect or relationship when one exists (equal to 1—the probability of a Type II error)

Predictive Research Question: a research question that asks if one behavior can be predicted from another behavior to allow predictions of future behavior

Predictor Variable: the dependent variable in a correlational study that is used to predict the score on another variable

Presence/Absence Variable: a variable that involves a manipulation with a level that involves the treatment and a level that does not involve the treatment

Pretest-Posttest Design: a type of research design (often a quasi-experiment) where behavior is measured both before and after a treatment or condition is implemented

Probability Sample: sample chosen such that individuals are chosen with a specific probability

Psychometrics: area of psychological research that involves the development, validation, and refinement of surveys and tests to measure psychological constructs

Qualitative Data: nonnumerical participant responses

Quantitative Data: numerical data

Quasi-Experiment: a type of research design where a comparison is made, as in an experiment, but no random assignment of subjects to groups occurs

Quasi-Independent/Subject Variable: variable that allows comparison of groups of participants without manipulation (i.e., no random assignment)

Quota Sample: sample chosen from the population such that available individuals are chosen with equivalent proportions of individuals for a specific characteristic in the population and sample

Random Assignment: participants are randomly assigned to levels of the independent variable in an experiment to control for individual differences as an extraneous variable

Range: the difference between the highest and lowest scores in a distribution

Ratio Scale: a scale of data measurement that involves numerical responses, where scores are ratios of each other

Reaction Time: measurement of the length of time to complete a task

Regression Toward the Mean: can occur when participants score higher or lower than their personal average—the next time they are tested, they are more likely to score near their personal average, making scores unreliable

Reliability: the degree to which the results of a study can be replicated under similar conditions

Response Rate: the percentage of people out of the total number available who respond to a survey

Results: section of an APA-style article that presents a summary of the results and the statistical tests of the predictions

Risk-Benefit Analysis: weighing the risks against the benefits of a research study to ensure that the benefits outweigh the risks

Sample: the group of individuals chosen from the population to represent it in a research study

Sampling Error: the difference between the observations in a population and in the sample that represents that population in a study

Scatterplot: a graph showing the relationship between two dependent variables for a group of individuals

Scientific/Alternative Hypothesis: the hypothesis that an effect or relationship exists (or exists in a specific direction) in the population

Significant Test: the *p* value is less than or equal to alpha in an inferential test, and the null hypothesis can be rejected

Simple Effects Tests: statistical tests conducted to characterize an interaction effect when one is found in an ANOVA

Simple Random Sample: sample chosen randomly from the population such that each individual has an equal chance of being selected

Single-Blind Design: procedure used to hide the group assignment from the participants in a study to prevent their beliefs about the effectiveness of a treatment from affecting the results

Small-n Design: an experiment conducted with one or a few participants to better understand the behavior of those individuals

Social Desirability Bias: bias created in survey responses from respondents' desire to be viewed more favorably by others, typically resulting in overreporting of "positive" behaviors and underreporting of "negative" behaviors

Solomon Four-Group Design: pretest-posttest design with two sets of nonequivalent groups, in which one set takes the pretest and posttest and one set takes only the posttest

Sphericity Assumption: assumption of the repeated measures (within-subjects) ANOVA that pairs of scores in the population have equal variance

Split-Half Reliability: method of testing scores' internal consistency that indicates if the scores are similar on different sets of questions on a survey that address similar topics

Standard Deviation: a measure representing the average difference between the scores and the mean of a distribution

Stratified Random Sample: sample chosen from the population such that the proportion of individuals with a particular characteristic is equivalent in the population and the sample

Survey Research: a research study that uses the survey observational technique to measure behavior

Systematic Observation: data collection technique in which control is exerted over the conditions under which the behavior is observed

t Test: significance test used to compare means

Testability: the assumption that explanations of behavior can be tested and falsified through observation

Testing Effects: occur when participants are tested more than once in a study, with early testing affecting later testing

Test-Retest Reliability: indicates that the scores on a survey will be similar when participants complete the survey more than once

Theory: an explanation of behavior that can be tested through research studies

Theory-Driven Hypothesis: hypothesis for a study that is based on a theory about the behavior of interest

Third-Variable Problem: the presence of extraneous factors in a study that affect the dependent variable and can decrease the internal validity of the study

Time Series Design: a research design in which patterns of scores over time are compared from before a treatment is implemented and after a treatment is implemented

Two-Tailed Hypothesis: both directions of an effect or relationship are considered in the alternative hypothesis of the test

Type I Error: error made in a significance test when the researcher rejects the null hypothesis that is actually true

Type II Error: error made in a significance test when the researcher fails to reject the null hypothesis that is actually false

Type Variable: a variable that involves a manipulation of types of a treatment

Variability: the spread of scores in a distribution

Variable: an attribute that can vary across individuals

Variance: the standard deviation of a distribution squared

Within-Subjects Variable: each participant experiences all levels of the variable

References

Abramson, P. R. (1984). *Sarah: A sexual biography*. Albany: State University of New York Press.

Adair, J. G. (1984). The Hawthorne effect: A reconsideration of the methodological artifact. *Journal of Applied Psychology, 69,* 334–345.

Ahern, A. L., & Hetherington, M. M. (2006). The thin ideal and body image: An experimental study of implicit attitudes. *Psychology of Addictive Behaviors, 20,* 338–342.

American Psychological Association. (2001). *Publication manual of the American Psychological Association* (5th ed.). Washington, DC: Author.

American Psychological Association. (2002). *Ethical principles of psychologists and code of conduct.* Retrieved June 15, 2008, from www.apa.org/ethics/code2002.pdf

American Psychological Association. (2003). *1999 Doctorate Employment Survey.* Retrieved January 11, 2008, from http://research.apa.org/des99report.html#patterms

American Psychological Association. (n.d.). *Research with animals in psychology.* Retrieved June 15, 2008, from www.apa.org/science/animal2.html

Anderson, B., & Harvey, T. (1996). Alterations in cortical thickness and neuronal density in the frontal cortex of Albert Einstein. *Neuroscience Letters, 21,* 161–164.

Ashe, S. E. (1955). Opinions and social pressure. *Scientific American, 193,* 31–35.

Baker, J. C., Hanley, G. P., & Mathews, R. M. (2006). Staff-administered functional analysis and treatment of aggression by an elder with dementia. *Journal of Applied Behavior Analysis, 39,* 469–474.

Ban, S. W., Lee, M., & Yang, H. S. (2004). A face detection using biologically motivated bottom-up saliency map model and top-down perception model. *Neurocomputing: An International Journal, 56,* 475–480.

Barlow, D. H., & Hersen, M. (1984). *Single case experimental designs: Strategies for studying behavior change.* New York: Pergamon Press.

Barnett, R. C., Marshall, N. L., & Singer, J. D. (1992). Job experiences over time, multiple roles, and women's mental health: A longitudinal study. *Journal of Personality and Social Psychology, 62,* 634–644.

Bartecchi, C., Aldever, R. N., Nevin-Woods, C., Thomas, W. M., Estacio, R. M., Bartelson, B. B., et al. (2006). Reduction in the incidence of acute myocardial infarction associated with a citywide smoking ordinance. *Circulation, 114,* 1490–1496.

Beck, A. T., & Steer, R. A. (1993). *Beck Anxiety Inventory Manual.* San Antonio, TX: Psychological Corporation.

Beck, A. T., Steer, R. A., & Brown, G. K. (1996). *Manual for the Beck Depression Inventory-II.* San Antonio, TX: Psychological Corporation.

Benenson, J. F., & Koulnazarian, M. (2008). Sex differences in help-seeking appear in early childhood. *British Journal of Developmental Psychology, 26,* 163–169.

Benenson, J. F., Markovits, H., Fitzgerald, C., Geoffroy, D., Flemming, J., Kahlenberg, S. M., et al. (2009). Males' greater tolerance of same-sex peers. *Psychological Science, 20,* 184–190.

Bhattacharya, S. (2006, January 10). Hwang faked all research on human stem cells. *New Scientist, 10.* Retrieved June 15, 2008, from www.newscientist.com/article.ns?id=dn8557

Birnbaum, M. H. (2001). *Introduction to behavioral research on the Internet*. Upper Saddle River, NJ: Prentice Hall.

Boezeman, E. J., & Ellemers, N. (2008). Volunteer recruitment: The role of organizational support and anticipated respect in non-volunteer's attraction to charitable volunteer organizations. *Journal of Applied Psychology, 93,* 1013–1026.

Boger, K. D., Tompson, M. C., Briggs-Gowan, M. J., Pavlis, L. E., & Carter, A. S. (2008). Parental expressed emotion toward children: Prediction from early family functioning. *Journal of Family Psychology, 22,* 784–788.

Bohbot, V. D., & Corkin, S. (2007). Posterior parahippocampal place learning in H.M. *Hippocampus, 17,* 863–872.

Booth-LaForce, C., & Oxford, M. L. (2008). Trajectories of social withdrawal from grades 1 to 6: Prediction from early parenting, attachment, and temperament. *Developmental Psychology, 44,* 1298–1313.

Bramel, D., & Friend, R. (1981). Hawthorne, the myth of the docile worker, and class bias in psychology. *American Psychologist, 36,* 867–868.

Brandt, A. (2000). Racism and research: The case of the Tuskegee syphilis experiment. In S. M. Reverby (Ed.), *Tuskegee's truths: Rethinking the Tuskegee syphilis study* (pp. 15–33). Chapel Hill: University of North Carolina Press.

Brody, J. E. (1996). Good habits outweigh genes as key to a healthy old age. *New York Times*. Retrieved June 3, 2009, from www.nytimes.com/1996/02/28/us/good-habits-outweigh-genes-as-key-to-a-healthy-old-age.html?scp=1&sq=alzheimers%20cognitive&st=cse

Broyles, L. M., Tate, J. A., & Happ, M. B. (2008). Videorecording in clinical research. *Nursing Research, 57,* 59–63.

Burger, J. M. (2009). Replicating Milgram: Would people still obey today? *American Psychologist, 64,* 1–11.

Campbell, W. K., Bosson, J. K., Goheen, T. W., Lakey, C. E., & Kernis, M. H. (2007). Do narcissists dislike themselves "deep down inside"? *Psychological Science, 18,* 227–229.

Cheung, F. M., Leung, K., Fan, R., Song, W., Zhang, J., & Zhang, J. (1996). Development of the Chinese Personality Assessment Inventory (CPAI). *Journal of Cross-Cultural Psychology, 27,* 181–199.

Chiang, H. (2008). Communicative spontaneity of children with autism: A preliminary analysis. *Autism, 12,* 9–21.

Chouinard, R., & Roy, N. (2008). Changes in high school students' competence beliefs, utility value, and achievement goals in mathematics. *British Journal of Educational Psychology, 78,* 31–50.

Coane, J. H., & McBride, D. M. (2006). An investigation of false memory in perceptual implicit tasks. *Acta Psychologica, 123,* 240–260.

Cohen, J. (1988). *Statistical power analysis for the behavioral sciences* (2nd ed.). Hillsdale, NJ: Lawrence Erlbaum.

Cohen, J. (1990). Things I have learned (so far). *American Psychologist, 45,* 1304–1312.

Cohen, J. (1994). The earth is round ($p < .05$). *American Psychologist, 49,* 997–1003.

Compton, M. T., Goulding, S. M., & Walker, E. F. (2007). Cannabis use, first-episode psychosis, and schizotypy: A summary and synthesis of recent literature. *Current Psychiatry Review, 3,* 161–171.

Corneille, O., Monin, B., & Pleyers, G. (2005). Is positivity a cue or a response option? Warm glow vs evaluative matching in the familiarity for attractive and not-so-attractive face. *Journal of Experimental Social Psychology, 41,* 431–437.

Coyle, T. R., & Pillow, D. R. (2008). SAT and ACT predict college GPA after removing g. *Intelligence, 36,* 719–729.

Creasey, G., & Ladd, A. (2005). Negative mood regulation expectancies and conflict behaviors in late adolescent college student romantic relationships: The moderating role of generalized attachment representations. *Journal of Research on Adolescence, 14,* 235–255.

Crowne, D. P., & Marlowe, D. (1960). A new scale of social desirability independent of psychopathology. *Journal of Consulting Psychology, 24,* 349–354.

DeSouza, E., & Fansler, A. G. (2003). Contrapower sexual harassment: A survey of students and faculty members. *Sex Roles, 48,* 519–542.

Dillman, D. A. (2000). *Mail and Internet surveys: The tailored design method.* New York: Wiley.

Doherty, R. W., & Hilberg, R. S. (2007). Standards for effective pedagogy, classroom organization, English proficiency, student achievement. *Journal of Educational Research, 101,* 24–34.

Egan, L. C., Santos, L. R., & Bloom, P. (2007). The origins of cognitive dissonance: Evidence from children and monkeys. *Psychological Science, 18,* 978–983.

Ehinger, K. A., & Brockmole, J. R. (2008). The role of color in visual search in real-world scenes: Evidence from contextual cuing. *Perception and Psychophysics, 70,* 1366–1378.

Fowers, B. J., & Olson, D. H. (1993). ENRICH Marital Satisfaction Scale: A brief research clinical tool. *Journal of Family Psychology, 7,* 176–185.

Fromkin, V., Krashen, S., Curtiss, S., Rigler, D., & Rigler, M. (1974). The development of language in Genie: A case of language acquisition beyond the "critical period." *Brain and Language, 1,* 81–107.

Gardner, H. (1999). *Intelligence reframed: Multiple intelligences for the 21st century.* New York: Basic Books.

Geraerts, E., Bernstein, D. M., Merekelbach, H., Linders, C., Raymaekers, L., & Loftus, E. F. (2008). Lasting false beliefs and their behavioral consequences. *Psychological Science, 19,* 749–753.

Gino, F., & Schweitzer, M. E. (2008). Blinded by anger or feeling the love: How emotions influence advice taking. *Journal of Applied Psychology, 93,* 1165–1173.

Goleman, D. (1995). *Emotional intelligence.* New York: Bantam Books.

Grant, D. A. (1948). The Latin Square principle in the design and analysis of psychological experiments. *Psychological Bulletin, 45,* 427–442.

Green, S. B., & Salkind, N. J. (2007). *Using SPSS for Windows and Macintosh: Analyzing and understanding data* (5th ed.). Upper Saddle River, NJ: Pearson/Prentice Hall.

Green, S. M., Hadjistavropoulos, T., & Sharpe, D. (2008). Client personality characteristics predict satisfaction with cognitive behavior therapy. *Journal of Clinical Psychology, 64,* 40–51.

Greenwald, A. G. (1975). Consequences of prejudice against the null hypothesis. *Psychological Bulletin, 82,* 1–20.

Greenwald, A. G., McGhee, D. E., & Schwartz, J. L. K. (1998). Measuring individual differences in implicit cognition: The implicit association test. *Journal of Personality and Social Psychology, 74,* 1464–1480.

Heidenreich, B. A. (1993). Investigations into the effects of repeated amphetamine administration and crus cerebri lesions on the electrophysiology of midbrain dopamine neurons in the rat. *Dissertation Abstracts International, 53,* 4522.

Hilts, P. J. (1996). *Memory's ghost: The nature of memory and the strange tale of Mr. M.* New York: Touchstone.

Hite, S. (1987). *Women and love: A cultural revolution in progress.* New York: St. Martin's Press.

Howell, D. C. (2009). *Statistical methods for psychology.* Belmont, CA: Wadsworth.

Hund, A. M., & Plumert, J. M. (2003). Does information about what things are influence children's memory for where things are? *Developmental Psychology, 39,* 939–948.

Hwang, W. S., Rho, S. I., Lee, B. C., Kang, S. K., Kwon, D. K., Kim, S., et al. (2005). Patient-specific embryonic stem cells derived from human SCNT blastocysts. *Science, 308,* 1777–1783.

Hwang, W. S., Ryu, Y. J., Park, J. H., Park, E. S., Lee, E. G., Koo, J. M., et al. (2004). Evidence of a pluripotent human embryonic stem cell line derived from a cloned blastocyst. *Science, 303,* 1669–1674.

Kahn, J. H., & Hessling, R. M. (2001). Measuring the tendency to conceal versus disclose psychological distress. *Journal of Social and Clinical Psychology, 20,* 41–65.

Kardash, C. M. (2000). Evaluation of undergraduate research experience: Perceptions of undergraduate interns and their faculty mentors. *Journal of Educational Research, 92,* 191–201.

Keller, M. C., Fredrickson, B. L., Ybarra, O., Côté, S., Johnson, K., Mikels, J., et al. (2005). A warm heart and a clear head: The contingent effects of weather on mood and cognition. *Psychological Science, 16,* 724–731.

Keppel, G., & Wickens, T. D. (2004). *Design and analysis: A researcher's handbook.* Upper Saddle River, NJ: Pearson.

Krantz, J. H., & Dalal, R. (2000). Validity of Web-based psychological research. In M. H. Birnbaum (Ed.), *Psychological experiments on the Internet* (pp. 35–60). San Diego, CA: Academic Press.

Lakin, J. L., Chartrand, T. L., & Arkin, R. M. (2008). I am too just like you: Nonconscious mimicry as an automatic behavioral response to social exclusion. *Psychological Science, 19,* 816–822.

Landrum, R. E., & Nelson, L. R. (2002). The undergraduate research assistantship: An analysis of the benefits. *Teaching of Psychology, 29,* 15–19.

Landsberger, H. (1955). Interaction process analysis of professional behavior: A study of labor mediators in twelve labor-management disputes. *American Sociological Review, 20,* 566–575.

Lee, L., Frederick, S., & Ariely, D. (2006). Try it, you'll like it: The influence of expectation, consumption, and revelation on preferences for beer. *Psychological Science, 17,* 1054–1058.

Lester, D. (2006). Understanding suicide through studies of diaries: The case of Cesare Pavese. *Archives of Suicide Research, 10,* 295–302.

Levine, L. J., Burgess, S. L., & Laney, C. (2008). Effects of discrete emotions on young children's suggestibility. *Developmental Psychology, 44,* 681–694.

Libby, A. M., Brent, D. A., Morrato, E. H., Orton, H. D., Allen, R., & Valuck, R. J. (2007). Decline in treatment of pediatric depression after FDA advisory on risk of suicidality with SSRIs. *American Journal of Psychiatry, 164,* 884–891.

Lipman, P. D., & Caplan, L. J. (1992). Adult age differences in memory for routes: Effects of instruction and spatial diagram. *Psychology and Aging, 7,* 435–442.

Loftus, E. (1993). Psychologists in the eyewitness world. *American Psychologist, 48,* 550–552.

Loftus, E. F. (2005). Planting misinformation in the human mind: A 30-year investigation of the malleability of memory. *Learning and Memory, 12,* 361–366.

Loftus, G. R. (1993). A picture is worth a thousand *p* values: On the irrelevance of hypothesis testing in the microcomputer age. *Behavior Research Methods, Instruments, & Computers, 25,* 250–256.

Lui, M., & Rosenfeld J. P. (2008). Detection of deception about multiple, concealed, mock crime items, based on a spatial-temporal analysis of ERP amplitude and scalp distribution. *Psychophysiology, 45,* 721–730.

Luo, S., Chen, H., Yue, G., Zhang, G., Zhaoyang, R., & Xu, D. (2008). Predicting marital satisfaction from self, partner, and couple characteristics: Is it me, you, or us? *Journal of Personality, 76,* 1231–1265.

Lyness, K. S., & Judiesch, M. K. (2008). Can a manager have a life and a career? International and multisource perspectives on work-life balance and career advancement potential. *Journal of Applied Psychology, 93,* 789–805.

Magen, E., Dweck, C. S., & Gross, J. J. (2008). The hidden zero effect: Representing a single choice as an extended sequence reduces impulsive choice. *Psychological Science, 19,* 648–649.

Magoon, M. A., & Critchfield, T. S. (2008). Concurrent schedules of positive and negative reinforcement: Differential-impact and differential-outcomes hypotheses. *Journal of the Experimental Analysis of Behavior, 90,* 1–22.

Matsukura, M., Luck, S. J., & Vecera, S. P. (2007). Attention effects during visual short-term memory maintenance: Protection or prioritization? *Perception & Psychophysics, 69,* 1422–1434.

McBride, D. M., Coane, J. H., & Raulerson, B. (2006). An investigation of false memory in perceptual implicit tasks. *Acta Psychologica, 123,* 240–260.

McNally, R. J. (2003). Recovering memories of trauma: A view from the laboratory. *Current Directions in Psychological Science, 12,* 32–35.

Messick, S. (1995). Validity of psychological assessment: Validation of inferences from persons' responses and performances as scientific inquiry into score meaning. *American Psychologist, 50,* 741–749.

Middlemist, D. R., Knowles, E. S., & Matter, C. F. (1976). Personal space invasions in the lavatory: Suggestive evidence for arousal. *Journal of Personality and Social Psychology, 33,* 541–546.

Mihai, A., Damsa, C., Allen, M., Baleydier, B., Lazignac, C., & Heinz, A. (2006). Viewing videotape of themselves while experiencing delirium tremens could reduce the relapse rate in alcohol-dependent patients. *Addiction, 102,* 226–231.

Milgram, S. (1963). Behavioral study of obedience. *Journal of Abnormal and Social Psychology, 67,* 371–378.

Mook, D. G. (1983). The state of the art and the fate of the earth. *Journal of the Experimental Analysis of Behavior, 40,* 343–350.

Moore, D. S., & Johnson, S. P. (2008). Mental rotation in human infants: A sex difference. *Psychological Science, 19,* 1063–1066.

Moore, D. W. (2004). *Sweet dreams go with a good night's sleep.* Retrieved January 11, 2008, www.gallup.com/poll/14380/Sweet-Dreams-Good-Nights-Sleep.aspx

Morales, L. (2008). *Most Americans consider smoking very harmful.* Retrieved August 5, 2008, from www.gallup.com/poll/109129/Most-Americans-Consider-Smoking-Very-Harmful.aspx

Morin, C. M., Belanger, L., & Fortier-Brochu, E. (2006). Sleep, insomnia, and psychopathology. *Canadian Psychology/Pschologie Canadienne, 47,* 245–262.

Morphy, H., Dunn, K. M., Lewis, M., Boardman, H. F., & Croft, P. R. (2007). Epidemiology of insomnia: A longitudinal study in a UK population. *Sleep: Journal of Sleep and Sleep Disorders Research, 30,* 274–280.

Mueller, C. M., & Dweck, C. S. (1998). Praise for intelligence can undermine children's motivation and performance. *Journal of Personality and Social Psychology, 75,* 33–52.

Nairne, J. S. (2006). *Psychology.* Belmont, CA: Thompson Wadsworth.

National Commission for the Protection of Human Subjects of Biomedical and Behavioral Research. (1979). *Belmont report.* Washington, DC: U.S. Department of Health and Human Services.

Nauta, M. M. (2007). Assessing college students' satisfaction with their academic majors. *Journal of Career Assessment, 15,* 446–462.

Neath, I., & Surprenant, A. (2003). *Human memory.* Belmont, CA: Wadsworth.

Nuseir, K., Heidenreich, B. A., & Proudfit, H. K. (1999). The antinociception produced by microinjection of a cholinergic agonist in the ventromedial medulla is mediated by noradrenergic neurons in the A7 catecholamine cell group. *Brain Research, 822,* 1–7.

Oakes, W. (1972). External validity and the use of real people as subjects. *American Psychologist, 27,* 959–962.

O'Hanlon, C. G., & Roberson, D. (2006). Learning in context: Linguistic and attentional constraints on children's color term learning. *Journal of Experimental Child Psychology, 94,* 275–300.

Olson, K. R., Banaji, M. R., Dweck, C. S., & Spelke, E. S. (2006). Children's biased evaluations of lucky versus unlucky people and their social groups. *Psychological Science, 17,* 845–846.

Olzmann, J. A. (2007). Pathogenic mechanisms of DJ-1 in Parkinson's disease. *Dissertation Abstracts International: Section B: The Sciences and Engineering, 68,* 2857.

Pal, S., & Saksvik, P. O. (2008). Work-family conflict and psychosocial work environment stressors as predictors of job stress in a cross-cultural study. *International Journal of Stress Management, 15,* 22–42.

Patterson, C. L., Uhlin, B., & Anderson, T. (2008). Clients' pretreatment counseling expectations as predictors of the working alliance. *Journal of Counseling Psychology, 55*, 528–534.

Platt, J. R. (1964). Strong inference. *Science, 146,* 347–353.

Reiniger, H. (Producer). (2001). *Discovering psychology* (updated ed.) [Television series]. Burlington, VT: Annenberg.

Retrospection: Social sciences' problematic interfaces with the social order. (2008). *PsycCRITIQUES, 53.* Retrieved June 9, 2009, from http://psych.hanover.edu/research/exponnet.html

Roediger, H. L., III, & McDermott, K. B. (1993). Implicit memory in normal human subjects. In F. Boller & J. Grafman (Eds.), *Handbook of neuropsychology* (Vol. 8, pp. 63–131). Amsterdam: Elsevier.

Rosenthal, R., & Rosnow, R. L. (2008). *Essentials of behavioral research: Methods and data analysis* (3rd ed.). New York: McGraw-Hill.

Rosnow, R. L., Rosenthal, R., McConochie, R. M., & Arms, R. L. (1969). Volunteer effects on experimental outcomes. *Educational and Psychological Measurement, 29,* 825–846.

Sackett, P. R., Kuncel, N. R., Arneson, J. J., Cooper, S. R., & Waters, S. D. (2009). Does socioeconomic status explain the relationship between admissions tests and post-secondary academic performance? *Psychological Bulletin, 135,* 1–22.

Schnall, S., Benton, J., & Harvey, S. (2008). With a clean conscience: Cleanliness reduces the severity of moral judgments. *Psychological Science, 19,* 1219–1222.

Schnall, S., Haidt, J., Clore, G .L., & Jordan, A. H. (2008). Disgust as embodied moral judgment. *Personality and Social Psychology Bulletin, 34,* 1096–1109.

Schuler, H. (1982). *Ethical problems in psychological research.* New York: Academic Press.

Sears, D. O. (1986). College sophomores in the laboratory: Influence of a narrow data base on social psychology's view of human nature. *Journal of Personality and Social Psychology, 51,* 515–530.

Shadish, W. R., Cook, T. D., & Campbell, D. T. (2002). *Experimental and quasi-experimental designs for generalized causal inference.* Boston: Houghton Mifflin.

Sharratt, M. (1996). *Galileo: Decisive innovator.* London: Cambridge University Press.

Smith, S. M., & Moynan, S. C. (2008). Forgetting and recovering the unforgettable. *Psychological Science, 19,* 462–468.

Sue, S. (1999). Science, ethnicity, and bias: Where have we gone wrong? *American Psychologist, 54,* 1070–1077.

Szekely, C. A., Breitner, J. C. S., & Zandi, P. P. (2007). Prevention of Alzheimer's disease. *International Review of Psychiatry, 19,* 693–706.

Tasky, K. K., Rudrud, E. H., Schulze, K. A., & Rapp, J. T. (2008). Using choice to increase on-task behaviors in individuals with traumatic brain injury. *Journal of Applied Behavior Analysis, 41,* 261–265.

Tharp, R. G., Estrada, P., Dalton, S. S., & Yamauchi, L. A. (2000). *Teaching transformed: Achieving excellence, fairness, inclusion, and harmony.* Boulder, CO: Westview Press.

Tversky, A., & Kahneman, D. (1981). The framing of decisions and the psychology of choice. *Science, 211,* 453–458.

U.S. Department of Agriculture. (2007). *Animal Welfare Act.* Retrieved June 15, 2008, from www .aphis.usda.gov/animal_welfare/downloads/awa/awa.pdf

U.S. Department of Health and Human Services. (2005). *Code of federal regulations.* Retrieved June 15, 2008, from www.hhs.gov/ohrp/humansubjects/guidance/45cfr46.htm

Van Bavel, J. J., Packer, D. J., & Cunningham, W. A. (2008). The neural substrates of in-group bias: A functional magnetic resonance imaging investigation. *Psychological Science, 19,* 1131–1139.

Vogt, W. P. (2005). *Dictionary of statistics and methodology* (3rd ed.). Thousand Oaks, CA: Sage.

Vohs, K. D., & Schooler, J. W. (2008). The value of believing in free will: Encouraging a belief in determinism increases cheating. *Psychological Science, 19,* 49–54.

Wagman, J. B., & Taylor, K. R. (2005). Perceiving affordances for aperture crossing for the person-plus-object system. *Ecological Psychology, 17,* 105–130.

Wallis, C. (1987, October 12). Back off, buddy. *Time, 130,* 68.

Wayment, H. A., & Dickson, K. L. (2008). Increasing student participation in undergraduate research benefits students, faculty, and department. *Teaching of Psychology, 35,* 194–197.

Wilson, R. S., Scherr, P. A., Schneider, J. A., Tang, Y., & Bennett, D. A. (2007). Relation of cognitive activity to risk of developing Alzheimer disease. *Neurology, 69,* 1911–1920.

Wiltermuth, S. S., & Heath, C. (2009). Synchrony and cooperation. *Psychological Science, 20,* 1–5.

Witelson, S., Kigar, D. L., & Harvey, T. (1999). The exceptional brain of Albert Einstein. *Lancet, 353,* 2149–2153.

Wynn, K. (1992). Addition and subtraction by human infants. *Nature, 358,* 749–750.

Xin, Z. (2001). *Values and behaviors in Chinese college students.* Unpublished doctoral dissertation.

Zimbardo, P. G. (1973). On the ethics of intervention in human psychological research: With special reference to the Stanford prison experiment. *Cognitions, 2,* 243–256.

Zimbardo, P. G. (1974). On "Obedience to authority." *American Psychologist, 29,* 566–567.

Zimmerman, C., Gerson, S., Monroe, A., & Kearney, A. M. (2007). Physics is harder than psychology (or is it?): Developmental differences in calibration of domain-specific texts. In D. S. McNamara & J. G. Trafton (Eds.), *Proceedings of the twenty-ninth annual Cognitive Science Society* (pp. 1683–1688). Austin, TX: Cognitive Science Society.

Index

About the Author

Dawn M. McBride is an associate professor of psychology at Illinois State University, where she has taught research methods for the past 11 years. Her research interests include automatic forms of memory, false memory, prospective memory, and forgetting. In addition to research methods, she teaches courses in introductory psychology, human memory, and a graduate course in experimental design. She is a recipient of the Illinois State University Teaching Initiative Award. Her out-of-work interests include spending time with her family, traveling, watching Philadelphia (her place of birth) sports teams, and reading British murder mysteries. She earned her PhD in cognitive psychology from the University of California, Irvine, and her BA from the University of California, Los Angeles.

Supporting researchers for more than 40 years

Research methods have always been at the core of SAGE's publishing program. Founder Sara Miller McCune published SAGE's first methods book, *Public Policy Evaluation*, in 1970. Soon after, she launched the *Quantitative Applications in the Social Sciences* series—affectionately known as the "little green books."

Always at the forefront of developing and supporting new approaches in methods, SAGE published early groundbreaking texts and journals in the fields of qualitative methods and evaluation.

Today, more than 40 years and two million little green books later, SAGE continues to push the boundaries with a growing list of more than 1,200 research methods books, journals, and reference works across the social, behavioral, and health sciences. Its imprints—Pine Forge Press, home of innovative textbooks in sociology, and Corwin, publisher of PreK–12 resources for teachers and administrators—broaden SAGE's range of offerings in methods. SAGE further extended its impact in 2008 when it acquired CQ Press and its best-selling and highly respected political science research methods list.

From qualitative, quantitative, and mixed methods to evaluation, SAGE is the essential resource for academics and practitioners looking for the latest methods by leading scholars.

For more information, visit **www.sagepub.com**.